Peter Ackroyd

THE HISTORY OF ENGLAND

VOLUME V

DOMINION

MACMILLAN

First published 2018 by Macmillan
an imprint of Pan Macmillan
20 New Wharf Road, London N1 9RR
Associated companies throughout the world
www.panmacmillan.com

ISBN 978-0-2307-0643-9

1 3 5 7 9 8 6 4 2

A CIP catalogue record for this book is available from the British Library.

Typeset by Palimpsest Book Production Ltd, Falkirk, Stirlingshire
Printed and bound by CPI Group (UK) Ltd, Croydon, CR0 4YY

Visit **www.panmacmillan.com** to read more about all our books
and to buy them. You will also find features, author interviews and
news of any author events, and you can sign up for e-newsletters
so that you're always first to hear about our new releases.

DOMINION

Contents

List of illustrations

1

Malign spirits

At the end of *Vanity Fair* (1848) William Makepeace Thackeray closes his novel of the mid-nineteenth century with a relevant homily: 'Ah! Vanitas Vanitatum! Which of us is happy in this world? Which of us has his desire? or, having it, is satisfied? – Come, children, let us shut up the box and the puppets, for our play is played out.'

Now the time has come to open the box once more, to dust down the puppets and set them on their feet. These are not the characters of the novel, however, but the characters of the Victorian world who surround it, animate it and give it its characteristic flavour of cunning, greed and good spirits.

The previous volume of this sequence ended with a universal peace and the removal of Napoleon Bonaparte from the stage, but the pleasures of peace were never more fleeting. More than twenty years had passed since the First Coalition of 1793 in which the demands of the army and the navy, the requirements of the men and the importunities of the allies had kept the farmers, the industrialists and the merchants busily engaged in the serious business of making money. For corn and cotton, for wheat and weapons, the demand had seemed limitless. But it was not so. The *Annual Register* of 1815 noted that the signs of 'national glory' had been altogether removed by the evidence of 'general depression'.

Yet Wellington was still the national hero, and Britain the victor in a race that confirmed its new power in the world. Somehow or other it had acquired seventeen new colonies, with an attendant prestige and influence that would last at least fifty years. But it was no good cheering the departing pipers when they had nowhere to go; the most fortunate veterans found employment in their previous trades, but for many disbanded men only a life of penury and vagrancy beckoned. Some put their military training to good use, however, in organizing Luddite marches and directing the rioters who were soon enraged by hunger and want of work.

The post-war depression lasted for some six years, and with little understanding of the arcane principles of economics the populace had to find something, or someone, to blame. It was deemed to be the fault of the government, therefore, or rather of the laxity and profligacy of those who directed it. There was a call for 'cheap government', but nobody really knew how to manage the feat. The fear and loathing that the governing class incurred did not dissipate and had much to do with further riots and calls for political and electoral reform.

There were still many who lived in an earlier time. There were gentlemen who drank a couple of bottles of port before bed, even though drunkenness was growing quite out of fashion. The court and high society were venerated by some in a world where commercial wealth and the merchant were creeping forward. The richer neighbours of the London suburbs still kept a cortège of footmen and of carriages driven by coachmen in wigs. The counting houses and mercantile businesses of the City were conducted with exquisite anonymity, using only a brass plate under the bell-handle for advertisement. The streets in the vicinity were just wide enough for two brewers' drays to pass without colliding. Every man, and woman, knew his, or her, place according to rank, wealth and age.

Yet by the second and third decades of the nineteenth century a new air of earnestness and energy was visible to observers. This was the era in which the characters of Charles Dickens's novels belong – Martin Chuzzlewit, Nicholas Nickleby, Philip Pirrip known as Pip, and of course Dickens himself, of quick step and bright eye, who would think nothing of walking 30 miles each day. The characters of the fictional world display moral vigour in a manner entirely consonant with a new age. As the *Daily News* wrote on the day after Dickens's death, 'in his pictures of contemporary life posterity will read, more clearly than in contemporary records, the characters of nineteenth century life'. We can see clearly among other essayists and novelists, too, the broad outlines of the nineteenth century, in its brooding melancholy and in its ribald humour, in its poetry of loss and in its fearfulness, in its capacity for outrage or pity and its tendency towards irony and diffidence, in its embrace of the material world as well as its yearning (at least among the serious middle classes) towards spirituality and transcendence. But we cannot get too close to our forebears. Their world is not ours. If a twenty-first-century person were to find himself or herself enmired in a tavern or lodging house of the period he would no doubt be sick – sick with the smells, sick with the food, sick with the breath of others and the general atmosphere all around.

The word of these early years was 'pluck', meaning the courage and ability to take on all challenges. It was also known as 'mettle' and 'bottom', a deep inhalation of breath before the ardour of the Victorian era. They were obliged, in the words of one cleric, 'to rush through the rapids'. They differed from their predecessors and their successors with their implicit faith in the human will; whatever their various religions might have been, this was the founding principle. They were determined to get to the other side with all the energy they could muster. The cult of independence came with it, immortalized at a later date in the 'self-help' preached by Samuel Smiles. It became part of the battle of life, as the phrase was, filled with manifest duty and diligence. Work was the greatest of all disciplines. The qualities needed were determination, hardness, energy, persistency, thoroughness and inflexibility. These were the cardinal virtues of the coming Victorian era.

This was a young society bolstered by the astonishing increase in the birth-rate; a population of 12 million in 1811 had reached 14 million by 1821 and 21 million by 1851; approximately half were under twenty and living in urban or semi-urban conditions. It is impossible fully to explain this significant rise in numbers, unless it be the organic response of a country on the edge of a giant transition, but the decline in infant mortality must have played a part. Where a modern household will tend to comprise three or four members, that of the early nineteenth century contained six or seven; very large families were also common. The religious census of 1851 reported that 7 million people attended a place of religious worship on Sunday, approximately half of them Anglican. Yet the same survey estimated that 5.5 million people did not care to attend a church or chapel at all. England was at a poise or balance which, from the religious point of view, could only go downwards.

The youthfulness may help to account for the vivacity that was everywhere apparent. The creed of earnestness survived for almost a hundred years, at which point it was parodied by Oscar Wilde. Yet the new dance of the day was the waltz, introduced in 1813 and at first considered 'riotous and indecent' because of the close proximity of the partners; it swirled and whirled its way through the ballrooms of England, with the barely repressed energy that marked the era.

The victors of 1815 picked over the bones of the world at the congress in Vienna. Europe now consisted of four great powers – Russia, Austria, Prussia and Great Britain – of which three were autocracies and the last scarcely a democracy. A few men held up the globe. One of them, Lord Castlereagh, foreign minister in Whitehall, was intent upon preserving that shibboleth of ages, the balance of power. The might of England itself was not in doubt, and he told the Commons that 'there was a general disposition to impute to us an overbearing pride, an unwarrantable arrogance and haughty direction in political matters' which he was not inclined to deny. It was also said of Castlereagh that he was like a top 'which spins best when it is most whipped'.

The prime minister, Lord Liverpool, had shifted from ministerial place to place but had already been the chief minister since the assassination of Spencer Perceval in 1812. He was a Tory of a kind familiar in the period; he disliked reform or change except of the most gradual kind, and was most concerned to sustain the apparent or nominal harmony of existing society. It was said that, on the first day of Creation, he would have implored God to stop the confusion immediately. He may have dreamed, as did many of his colleagues, of Catholic emancipation and free trade, but these were problems for another day. His job was to keep his supremacy warm. Liverpool made no great impact on his contemporaries, but he did not seem to care. Disraeli called him the 'Arch Mediocrity', and that might be considered to be his greatest achievement. The usual truisms about chief ministers were applied to him; he was honest and he was tactful. He was diplomatic, cautious and reliable, all of them tickets to oblivion, and sat quite comfortably in the Lords where it was relatively easy to acquire a reputation for wisdom. In 1827 he retired, from ill health, after fifteen years as chief minister, but no sooner had he left than he was forgotten.

Before he is completely embalmed with platitudes, a little spark of interest may be kindled. Liverpool was prone to weep at moments of stress, overwhelmed by what were called 'the weaks'. He was considered to be too 'spoony' for his own good, a word translated by another generation as 'wet'. He could not observe the *Morning Post* without trembling, and a wife of one of his colleagues, Charles Arbuthnot, described 'a deliberately cold manner' and a 'most querulous, unstable temper'. So much for the tactful and equable appearance, which may be merely a mask for deep uncertainty and dismay. The early decades of the nineteenth century are sometimes presented as those of Regency flightiness before the little hand of Victoria firmly grasped the sceptre. But a contemporary, Sydney Smith, reported these years to be characterized by 'the old-fashioned, orthodox, hand-shaking, bowel-disturbing passion of fear'. Liverpool's predecessor, Spencer Perceval, had been assassinated, not without public rejoicing. Nothing about the period was secure, with reports of rioting, rumours of conspiracy and revolution, threats of famine and another European war.

Lord Liverpool was a Tory at a time when the party label meant very little. Without any real discipline the two major formations of Whig and Tory were little more than disparate factions under a succession of temporary leaders. In 1828 the duke of Clarence said that the names 'meant something a hundred years ago, but are mere nonsense nowadays'. The Whigs had fallen from power in 1784 when they ceased to represent comfortable authority and had become an oligarchic faction opposed to the king. The Tories under William Pitt had taken over power and were reluctant to return it. William Hazlitt compared them to two rival stagecoaches that splashed mud over each other while travelling along the same road.

The Tories complained of the Whigs' negative attitude to the royal prerogative and their appetite for reforms such as Catholic emancipation; the Whigs in turn believed that the Tories were deaf to popular demands and too indulgent to executive power. There was not much else to separate them. Macaulay tried to dignify their respective positions as 'the guardian of liberty and the other of order', testifying to his genius in bringing regularity to the world in words. Lord Melbourne, a future Whig chief minister, said simply that the Whigs were 'all cousins'. It was this lurking unease at a family affair that suborned their position. Byron said it in Canto XI of *Don Juan* (1823):

> Nought's permanent among the human race,
> Except the Whigs *not* getting into place.

Policy was formed behind the arras or, as it was known, on the back stairs. Cabinets were often convened without any purpose or agenda, and the ministers would look at one another with a blank surmise. No cabinet minutes were kept, and only the prime minister was allowed to make notes, which were not always reliable. If it was not government by department, since departments were still ramshackle affairs, it was government by private committee. There were no party headquarters until the 1830s. The party leaders of the day were highly reluctant to pronounce on public policy. It could be compromising. The poll books of the unreformed electorate were equally bewildering and haphazard, and votes were influenced by one local grandee or one predominant issue.

Liverpool had many nicknames, among them 'Old Mouldy' and 'the Grand Figitatis'. In his defence, he had much to fidget about. The post-war decline and depression aroused an already resentful nation dazed after years of war. The agricultural interest was at odds with the government, since an influx of cheap foreign corn led to a steep decline in prices. But if corn were raised artificially to a much higher price, popular unrest might ensue. What to do? The farmers feared, and many of the people hoped, that the progress of free trade was inexorable. Lower prices and profits threw many out of employment, however, and their number was increased by the influx of veterans from the war. It happened every time, but no one ever seemed to be prepared for it. Work was scarce and wages were low; the only commodity in abundance was unemployment. The threat of violence was never very far.

Riots had begun in 1815, particularly in North Devon, and in succeeding months they filled the country. They were joined by those agitating for industrial reform, and in particular for the relief of child labour. There was a belief abroad that practical and positive change was at least possible. Hence came the stirrings of political reform. And what was to be done with those many millions of people who had been amassed as part of the newly acquired empire? What of the Irish, for example, who had been part of the Union since 1800? One minister, William Huskisson, observed that all parties were 'dissatisfied and uneasy'.

In 1815 no one had seen a train on land or a steamboat on water; horse-drawn cabs and omnibuses did not appear on the London streets until thirteen years later. Everybody, except those who were some-bodies, walked everywhere. The stagecoach would have been too expensive to use on a daily basis. So the massive crowds made their way forward as best they could. Soon after dawn, among the pedestrians foot-sore and weary, the clerks and office boys were already jostling their way into the City, streaming in from the outlying areas. Apprentices were sweeping their shops and watering the pavements outside, the children and servants were already crowding the bakers' shops. If you were fortunate you might, in the vicinity of Scotland Yard, see the coal-heavers dancing. Even in the early hours, sex was still the only pleasure of the poor. Alleys and bushes were used as public lavatories as well as for other more intimate purposes, and sexual intercourse with prostitutes was not uncommon for a couple of pennies.

A contemporary Londoner, Henry Chorley, noted that especially in the morning 'people did their best, or their worst, to show their love of music, and express their gaiety, or possibly their vacancy of mind, by shouting in the streets the songs of the day'. Popular tunes were whistled in the streets or in taprooms or ground out by barrel-organs. Prints were sold in the street, characteristically placed inside upturned umbrellas, and the more enterprising print shops would continually change their displays. Already at work were the coster girls, the oyster-sellers, the baked-potato men and the chestnut vendors. A little later on, just before noon, came the negro serenaders and the glee-singers. The observant walker would know the weavers' houses of Spitalfields, the carriage makers of Long Acre, the watch-makers of Clerkenwell and the old-clothes stalls of Rosemary Lane. Dog fights, cock fights, public hangings, pleasure gardens and pillories all added to the general air of excitement and display.

The nights became brighter. London at night had been only partly illuminated by oil and candle. But then the twin agencies of gas and steam became visible. Gas introduced into the streets a 'brilliancy' which outshone all others. The agitators and advanced political speculators had been right all along. This was an age of progress, after all. The country was in the process of slowly losing its eighteenth-century character. But the bellies of the poor were still empty. Not for the suffering were the taverns and the chop-houses. Even the penny potatoes were out of reach.

In March 1815, a Corn Law was enacted which prohibited the import of foreign corn until the domestic product reached 80 shil-lings a bushel, and as a result the price soared too high. With no remedy proposed, the poor and the disaffected fell to riot. The members of parliament complained that they were being tossed to and fro like shuttlecocks between battledores. There was in truth little understanding of economic theory, even though in 1807 John Ruskin's father noted that 'the one science, the first and greatest of sciences to all men . . . is the science of political economy'. The farmers themselves might as well have been engaged in high calculus; they relied upon observation and experience, common sense and *Old Moore's Almanack*.

The recession gathered pace and Robert Southey remarked in the *British Review* that it was mournful 'to contemplate the effects of extreme poverty in the midst of a civilised and flourishing state'. The Corn Law riots in London were ineffective, but Luddism returned to Nottingham. There were riots from Newcastle upon Tyne to Norfolk, in Suffolk and Cambridgeshire. In 1816 gangs of the unemployed surged through Staffordshire and Worcestershire, and it was reported that large numbers of people 'had been parading the streets and assembling in groups, using the most threatening language'. The *Liverpool Mercury* marked the end of the year 'with sorrow in our habitations and with famine in our streets, and with more than a fourth part of the population of the country subsisting on alms'. This was the period when the anger of the public press mounted ever higher with prints such as the *Black Dwarf* and *Cobbett's Weekly Political Register*. They were supported and circulated by radical societies, none more effectively than the network of Hampden clubs which began in London and soon migrated to the north-east. A penny a week subscription was not considered too dear for spreading the word among spinners, weavers, artisans and labourers about state bribery and corruption. There were fears, however, that radicalism might have in its hands an instrument for a mass movement. It was in this period that 'radical' was first coined for any group of supposed malign spirits who, according to the vicar of Harrow, encompassed 'the rejection of Scripture' and 'a contempt for all the institutions of your country'. The home secretary called them 'the enemy', and for some time any dissident or opposition force was automatically known as 'radical'.

A larger dilemma had also been identified. In his *Observations on the Effect of the Manufacturing System* (1815) Robert Owen noted that 'the manufacturing system has already so far extended its influence over the English Empire as to effect an essential change in the general character of the mass of the people'. They were becoming specialized machines designed only to accumulate profit for their employers. Machines themselves served to promote and maintain the division of labour, where each worker had a relatively simple and specialized role. Machinery guaranteed uniformity of work as well as uniformity of product, and acted as a check against inattention or idleness. Machinery promoted a rational and regulated system of labour. It had happened silently and almost invisibly. Now the economists and some of the more advanced agriculturalists were eager to understand what was happening, and were ready to open the book of a new world. Among the first audiences at the new technical lectures on finance were Robert Peel and George Canning, two Tories on the rise.

The monarch was in name George III, but he was now gibbering and deluded. The royal master was the Regent, the Prince of Wales, who was described by the duke of Wellington as 'the worst man I ever fell in with in my whole life, the most selfish, the most false, the most ill-natured, the most entirely without one redeeming quality'. It was in this period of hunger and riot that the Prince Regent began to build the Brighton Pavilion. He was forever blowing bubbles of stone.

2

The Thing

Cant was the moral cloud which covered the nineteenth century. It was part of the age of respectability. Byron wrote in 1821 that 'the truth is, the grand *primum mobile* of England is Cant; Cant political, Cant poetical, Cant religious, Cant moral, but always Cant, multiplied through all the varieties of life'. He threatened to convert Don Juan into a Methodist as an example, but there were already many Dissenters as well as Anglicans who turned to God for the sake of propriety. Cant was the mirror of self-interest disguised as benevolence, of greed posturing as piety, of a 'national interest' that took into account the fortunes of only a few favoured families. Cant encompassed the politician who smiled while remaining a villain; cant was the language of the moral reformer who closed public houses on Sunday; the political vocabulary of the nation, often praised for its classical structure and its resonant periods, was mainly cant. Historians have often been amazed by the prolixity and ardour of the members of the nineteenth-century parliament; but the words were cant. Most people, at least those with any self-awareness, were conscious that their professed beliefs and virtues were hot air, but they conspired with others to maintain the fraud. Never has a period been so concerned to give the right impression.

Cant was for example the basis of the Quadruple Alliance in the autumn of 1815. It had been preceded by a Holy Alliance between Russia, Austria and Prussia. When holiness is credited with the business of nations, it is best to be wary. The foreign policies of the nations were now supposed to be directed by love and charity, but in truth the sovereigns were afraid of each other as well as of their own people. Castlereagh described the Holy Alliance as a 'piece of sublime mysticism and nonsense' invented by a monarch whose mind was 'not entirely sound', but he did nothing to stop the Prince Regent from privately giving it his approval. Some love and charity might become useful, however, since the 'Quadruple Alliance' was designed with the express intention of consolidating the unity of monarchs and casting out the dynasty of the Bonapartes. So the 'Concert of Europe', as it became known, with Castlereagh its principal conductor, began with a peal of trumpets.

The great temple of cant in Westminster opened its doors in the early days of 1816, and its followers flocked into the Commons and the Lords. Castlereagh controlled the Commons and Lord Liverpool the other house. Why was the army not entirely disbanded? Why did the Prince Regent wear the uniform of a field marshal when opening parliament? What was the significance of the Royal Military Asylum? Of the real ills of the nation nothing much was said. 'I am concerned to think that the prevailing distress is so severely felt in your county', the home secretary, Viscount Sidmouth, told one member, 'but I see no reason for believing that it would or could be alleviated by any proceedings at a public meeting, or by parliament itself.' When some shearmen asked to be sent to North America, Liverpool replied that 'machinery could not be stopped in the woollen trade'.

Income, or property tax, had been announced as a wartime contingency to be abolished when hostilities ceased. But in this parliament of 1816 the government withdrew the promise and, to general anger and consternation, wished to continue the imposition of a shilling on the pound. It became, as always, a shouting match, and the government lost the vote. Income tax was repealed. But, like the vampires of the ages, it was asleep and not dead. Castlereagh wrote to his brother, Charles, that 'you will see how little what you call a strong government can effect against the tide of the day in this country'. Castlereagh, as leader of the House of Commons, was already reviled by many as one of the authors of domestic oppression. Shelley had a rhyme about him in *The Mask of Anarchy* (1819):

> I met Murder on the way –
> He had a mask like Castlereagh –
> Very smooth he looked, yet grim;
> Seven blood-hounds followed him . . .

He was by no means as bad as he was portrayed, but it is easy to disparage virtue as vice concealed. So tranquillity can be mistaken for lack of feeling, and amiability for lack of principle. He was in fact as anxious and as restless as it was possible to be, a state of mind that would eventually lead him to a razor and a quick death. At this juncture his administration was left with a revenue of £9 million to face an expenditure of £30 million. It was forced to resort, in part, to indirect taxes on a variety of products. In one cartoon the chancellor of the Exchequer, Nicholas Vansittart, appears in a tub and asks the laundress: 'How are you off for soap?' But in a subsequent vote of confidence the Tories narrowly avoided defeat; their natural supporters hung on for fear of something worse.

Soap was the least of the problems. All the disappointments of the time erupted in a flood of casual riot and mayhem. From April to the end of May the price of bread, in particular, became the principal grievance of the people. The farmers, the shopkeepers, the butchers, the bakers, were attacked and their premises vandalized. It was one indication for the new century that the ancient violence of the population had never been quelled. The recent war was all but forgotten. Now the cry was for 'bread or blood', by which was meant country gentlemen's blood, aristocratic blood and monopolists' blood. English blood, in other words. The price of bread steadily rose.

In their alarm the gentlemen and large farmers flocked to the cause of the Tories. A few months before they had been denounced as a cabal of self-seeking rulers intent upon subverting the nation's liberties. They were now the official face of law and order that were being grievously threatened. The Whigs had wished to denounce them as traitors to the nation; now they had become its guardians. The Tories seemed always best able to profit from general discontent.

William Cobbett, who can better be described as a radical rather than Whig or Tory, had a pen capable of expressing the general discontent. In one sense he wanted to return to an older England without paper money and national debt, the stock jobbers and the factory towns. He pledged his faith in a quiet and more decent nation based upon the traditions of an equal society untainted by money. He believed, as many did not, that general electoral reform was the key to quieten unrest. He was largely supported by weavers and other artisans who were being destroyed by industrialism. But he could not change a society with such allies alone.

He was rough-spoken, dogmatic and intensely satirical, but he got to the heart of the matter. 'Who will pretend that the country can, without the risk of some great and terrible convulsion, go on, even for twelve months longer, unless there be a *great change of some sort* in the mode of managing the public affairs.' He feared that 'the Thing was biting so very sharply'. For him 'the Thing', otherwise known as Old Corruption, was the mass of venality and bribery which sucked out the lifeblood of the nation. His argument, if not his language, was already being extended further than he could have envisaged. Two years before, in 1814, *The Times* began to be printed by steam power. A new player had entered the scene. Despite the best efforts of the administration to limit or control the circulation of radical newspapers, the appetite for news in a disturbed and uncertain period could not be effectively controlled. Between 1800 and 1830 sales of the public prints had doubled. In 1816 Cobbett began to publish his *Political Register* as a pamphlet at the price of twopence. It circulated among the industrious classes, but was disparaged by their nominal superiors as 'Tuppenny Trash'. On 12 October of that year he called for a 'Reformed Parliament, elected by the people themselves'.

Cobbett was well aware of the enemies he faced, and described them to his mother as 'wicked and hard-headed wretches who are stimulating indigence to madness and crime'. He had seen the same noble families, the same faces and the same cousins; he had heard 'hear hear' brayed from the same voices. He was sick to the soul with it. Were any people 'so debased, so absolutely slaves as the poor creatures who, in the *"enlightened"* North, are *compelled* to work fourteen hours in a day, in a heat of *eighty-four degrees*, and who are liable to punishment for *looking out at a window of a factory*'. He had seen the vagrants in the road, he had seen wanderers, going they knew not whither, in search of work. He had seen the cottages falling apart from wind and rain. And he asked: what will be the end of it?

The parish poor houses, before the workhouses took hold, were receptacles for 'the vile, the dissolute and the depraved' together with a scattering of the infirm and the imbecile. The plight of the poor in early Victorian England has been described so often that it might seem almost superfluous. Cobbett wrote with a fine ear for mixed metaphor that they were 'as thin as herrings, dragging their feet after them, pale as a ceiling, and sneaking about like a beggar'. If a third of the population are in poverty throughout the nineteenth century, it is only by a trick of style or an aptitude for hypocrisy that it can be called prosperous. Yet so it was called. Their lives did not materially differ from generation to generation. A woman in 1894, after a century of change, asked how she kept a family of five children on 17 shillings a week, replied: 'I am afraid I cannot tell you very much, because I worked too hard to think about how we lived.' The labouring poor were in turn surrounded by a superfluity of people. Among them we might see the spirit of the Reverend Thomas Robert Malthus arguing that the redundant poor were a grievous burden in the competition between the rise of population and the means of subsistence. The unemployed and the unemployable were the enemy.

Cobbett was rivalled in eloquence and power, if not in acumen and intelligence, by Henry Hunt, another orator in the popular cause. In the middle of November 1816 he addressed a large assembly on Spa Fields in Islington; one of his supporters carried a pike with the cap of liberty aloft. It did not need a sage to realize that the spirit of French revolt was abroad. Two weeks later a similar demonstration created more trouble, when a blood-stained loaf was paraded towards the City. The protesters were swiftly cleared from the Royal Exchange by troops, since the authorities were not inclined to treat it as an amateur jape. A few years before, in the previous century, the cry of reform was hardly ever raised. Now it was on the lips of link-boys and chair-men. An inner circle of men plotted violent revolution, while a large number were content to attend tavern meetings, smoke their pipes and drink confusion to their enemies.

They were too apathetic for individual action but were happy enough
be part of a crowd at a meeting or to lend their voice to the
cacophony.

The opposition party of Whigs was in singular disarray, having
no coherent proposals of its own. In any case the Whigs had no
appetite for the kind of reform for which the radicals were agitating.
To their opponents they were nothing but aristocrats and country
gentlemen, for the moment a junior branch of 'the Thing'. Outrage
was, in any case, good politics for all sides. The Tory ministers in
turn did what they could to provoke treason and rebellion with spies
and agents provocateurs, and at the end of 1816 Cobbett wrote in
the *Political Register* that 'they sigh for a Plot. Oh how they sigh!
They are working and slaving and fretting and stewing; they are
sweating all over: they are absolutely pining and dying for a plot!'

Then came the next-best thing. At the end of January 1817
the Prince Regent was driving in his carriage after the opening
of parliament when something – a stone, a bullet, a falling piece of
masonry – cracked his window. No one cared at all about the Regent,
dead or alive, but it suited everyone's habits to pretend to believe
so. The Regent himself seemed happy with the attention, and boasted
about his sanguine response to the outrage. It seems that he was
not a man to be frightened by riff-raff. Castlereagh came into the
Commons with a much more serious demeanour. He gave an impression of glacial self-confidence.

A series of hastily arranged committees now provided evidence
to parliament that secret societies and a furtive rebel militia were
intent upon storming the Bank of England and the Tower. As a
result the law of habeas corpus, whereby prisoners could not be kept
without charge, was abolished; it was a singular blow against British
liberties. A series of repressive measures known as the Coercion
Acts or Gagging Acts was also passed, and all meetings were banned
on the grounds of sedition. Lectures of medicine and surgery were
thereby forbidden and the Cambridge Union was closed down. The
domestic furore helped to conceal the dire state of the economy,
which was close to collapse. A Whig activist, George Tierney, told
his colleagues that the ministers were 'at the wits' end' and that 'all
the lower followers of the government were desperate'. National
bankruptcy might in truth be as bad as revolution.

The furore created by the prosecution of the radicals in February 1817 set off another series of domestic fires. 'All that we want', the Norwich Union Society said, 'is the constitution of our country in its original purity, whereby the people may be fairly, fully and annually represented in Parliament, the House of Commons cleared of that numerous swarm of Placemen and Pensioners who fatten upon the vitals of an half famished and oppressed people.' In military conflict, this would be known as a 'forlorn hope'. Parliament, before the salutary burning of 1834, was dark, badly lit and badly ventilated. The washing of bodies and the cleaning of clothes were not considered to be a priority. The members put their legs on the backs of the adjacent benches, or were half-sprawled on the floor, coming and going out at will, groaning, laughing, exchanging jokes, bellowing, yawning, talking nonsense, interrupting for the fun of it – all the more flagrant because social and political revolution was on everyone's lips.

The multiple petitions of the Hampden clubs to the Prince Regent for the amelioration of the severe economic conditions had met with no response. So the weavers and spinners of Manchester embarked on a grand pilgrimage towards London in order to submit their own petition to him; among their demands, propagated in many other quarters, were universal suffrage and annual parliaments.

They were known as the 'blanketeers' because they wore shawls and blankets to keep them warm. But they never stood a chance. They were turned back before they reached Derbyshire and dispersed, not without much anguish. But they could not have come through. Cobbett himself had travelled to the United States to avoid prosecution. Their collapse in the face of the yeomanry provoked another rebel 'conspiracy' in Ardwick, a district of Manchester. There was talk of 'a general insurrection' and a 'general rising'. Whigs and Tories were whipping themselves into an hysteria. Conspiracies and revolts could now be found under every bush and behind every hedge, but subsequent court hearings were abandoned when it transpired that the only evidence came from informers. It could have happened. It might have happened. In other countries it did happen. And yet the English poor, and the majority of the middle classes, proved remarkably quiescent. They never rose. Castlereagh was on at least one occasion recognized by the London mob. 'Who is the man who comes here in powder?' was the cry raised at the sight of his powdered wig. He was forced to run for safety, but the atmosphere of London was not that of Paris. He was not strung up from a lamp-post in Piccadilly.

The furore caused by the prosecutions of radicals quickly died down when it became obvious that juries were not likely to prosecute supposed malefactors who were in effect really malcontents. The leaders of the Spa Fields meetings were released without charge. The radicals were left with the impression that they had not spoken the right words to fire a nation, that something had gone unexpressed. The authorities did nothing further, and the interest in radical propaganda diminished.

The events of the next few months had a similar air of being half-finished, half-done. A good harvest of 1817 and better prospects for trade helped to change the sullen mood. Lord Exmouth noted that 'the panic among the farmers is wearing off; and, above all that hitherto marketable article, discontent, is everywhere disappearing'. As agriculture improved, so did trade increase. It was believed that the time was right for habeas corpus to be restored, and the breach in liberty mended. The state had been shaken but was stabilized. In 1818 a grant of £1 million was made for the construction of one hundred new churches, which can legitimately be taken as a vote of thanks; the administration was becoming more religious by the day.

Confidence and self-assertion may also have helped to lengthen the whiskers. Where in the Napoleonic Wars the military of England tended to be clean-shaven, little by little the hair grew back. Moustaches had crept in by 1820 but they in turn were replaced by large whiskers, which had conquered the light cavalry and the heavy dragoons by the 1860s. All the men grew their hair long, and it was quite common for a man to wind a long lock around his cap. The fashions in facial hair are persistent. The men who came back from the Crimean campaign were always bearded, and within a decade the male civilians had followed the pattern.

Whether God was swayed by one hundred churches built in His honour is an open question. In the summer of 1818, in more favourable conditions of trade, the Tories decided to go to the country, which meant that body of freeholders whose land brought in 40 shillings a year. The qualification was open to manipulation though, and since there was no register of electors, the claims and counter-claims always threatened to destroy the process. That is why general elections were held over two or three weeks. They consisted of fairs, drunken sprees, settlings of old scores, battles of fists and were a cause of endless parades, marches and taproom sessions. It was believed by those who supported the system that *concordia discors*, creating harmony out of conflict, was the fruit of the ancient British constitution – which never in fact existed. One Tory politician, Sir Robert Inglish, stated that it grew and flourished as a tree and 'there is, so far as I know, no evidence that our House was ever selected upon any principle of representation of population, or upon any fixed principle of representation whatever . . . It has adapted itself, almost like another work of nature, to our growth.'

As it was the Whigs gained thirty-three seats, which made no tangible difference to the diverse and divided House of Commons which met at the beginning of 1819. One member noted that the government 'is so completely paralysed that they dare do nothing'. The Prince Regent was becoming afflicted with paranoia and hardly went out; his cumbrous size made it difficult, in any case, for him to cut a gracious figure. The Whigs themselves were timid of public attention for fear of the horrid day when they might be asked to form an administration. The early pages of George Eliot's *Felix Holt: The Radical* (1866), set in 1832, contain a representative scene between mother and son:

'But I shall not be a Tory candidate.'
Mrs Transome felt something like an electric shock.
'What then?' she said, almost sharply. 'You will not call yourself a Whig?'
'God forbid! I'm a Radical!'
Mrs Transome's limbs tottered, she sank into a chair.

In this session of parliament many fine words were spoken about the state of the nation's finances and proposals were made for cutting expenditure and even for raising taxes. It was clear to almost everyone that economic reform was inevitable. One select committee was ordered to consider the problems of currency, and another those of public finance. The administration had finally summoned up the courage to fight what Castlereagh had once called 'the ignorant impatience of taxation'.

One government measure is worth mentioning, if only as a harbinger of greater reforms. In 1819 a Factory Act, or more accurately a Cotton Factory Act, was passed after four years of agitation. It forbade the employment of children under nine in the cotton factories and restricted the rest of child labour to twelve hours a day. This seems almost a cruel joke in the face of the general suffering, and only two convictions were obtained under its code, but at the time it was violently opposed for 'singling out' cotton. The humanitarian sense, roused by slavery and foreign barbarism, did not yet reach out to the working population of the country. Yet the Factory Act did mean that for the first time the administration had turned its face against unchecked laissez-faire in the workings of the economy. It also meant that the government now had the opportunity, and power, to overrule the wishes of parents. It took a century or more to complete the work.

One man may step forward as a begetter, if not the only begetter, of necessary change. Robert Owen was the son of a shopkeeper who became, at an early age, the manager of a cotton mill in Manchester. When he opened his own factory in New Lanark, in Scotland, he paid attention to his employees as well as his profits. His contention was that circumstances form character, and he set about to undertake the education and recreation of the children in his charge. He opened the first infants' school in Britain and arranged a 'support fund' for the sick and aged. His influence and example had a direct effect upon subsequent factory legislation and earned him the title of the first great industrial reformer.

In the spring and early summer of 1819 there were demonstrations and mass meetings in Glasgow, Manchester, Leeds and elsewhere in favour of a wider franchise. Parliament, noting the distance between the malcontents and Westminster, chose to ignore them. There had been calls for reform before and nothing had ever happened. Why test the water now? But the circumstances had changed. News came that millworkers were forming armed bands. A royal proclamation was issued, denouncing the combative language of the people. A great public meeting in Manchester was announced for 16 August. For the Tories, the fear of revolution once more emerged. On the appointed day Henry Hunt, now popularly known as 'Orator' Hunt, made his way through the gathering and mounted the platform. No sooner had he started to speak than a group of yeomanry was seen advancing towards him. The crowd bayed and booed, but the yeomen drew their swords and struck out. The hussars joined them in the general furore, which resulted in eleven deaths and some hundreds of demonstrators wounded. The place was St Peter's Field, and the bloody event became known as Peterloo.

It was a breaking point. The size of the crowds, and the nature of the events, shocked many of those who did not believe that an autocratic regime should work its will in England. But now 'the Thing' had bowed, taken off its hat, and showed its face. When 'Orator' Hunt made his way to London, before his trial, he was greeted by some 300,000 people. The figure is perhaps questionable, as all estimates of size are, but there is some testimony from John Keats, who told his brother George that 'the whole distance from the Angel at Islington to the Crown and Anchor was lined with multitudes'. The Crown and Anchor is close to what is now Euston station. There was also a less obvious consequence of the divisions in the nation. In October 1819 it was remarked that 'the most alarming sign of the times is that separation of the upper and middle classes of the community from the lower, which is now daily and visibly increasing'.

Something would have to be done, even though no one was quite sure what 'doing' should entail. Taxes were as always the chief complaint. As Sydney Smith put it in the *Edinburgh Review* of January 1820, 'taxes upon every article which enters into the mouth, or covers the back, or is placed under the foot'.

The immediate remedy was not a remedy at all, but a series of bills named the Six Acts. Public meetings of more than fifty people were forbidden, unauthorized military training was prohibited, and the right of the authorities to enter private houses without warrant was confirmed. The measures did not include the suspension of habeas corpus, as before, but they inaugurated one of the most extensive investigations of radicalism in nineteenth-century history. They did not accomplish very much in the end, but the Six Acts were universally derided and condemned. Cobbett declared: 'I was not born under Six-Acts.' When the Prince Regent returned from a holiday in Cowes he was 'hissed at by an immense mob' outside his front door and Lady Hertford, his mistress, was almost tipped out of her chair before being rescued by the Bow Street Runners.

The home secretary, Viscount Sidmouth, had convinced himself that a conspiracy was waiting around the corner. Many of those in authority in fact feared for their necks in some general insurrection, and in 1820 their anxieties were partly reinforced by a small plot that became known as the Cato Street Conspiracy. Cato Street was a narrow thoroughfare close to Paddington. Secreted in the loft of an unprepossessing building a few conspirators, animated by enthusiasm rather than good sense, planned to seize London and to kill as many members of the cabinet as possible. Sidmouth knew all about it in advance and simply allowed it to go on as a salutary warning to any other political adventurer. The principal conspirators were hanged and their heads cut off. It was the last act of repression for some years, largely because there was no more reason for it. The country had been cowed, or persuaded, or bribed, into quietude.

It seems sometimes that the government had a secret pact with its enemies, but that would be a conspiracy theory to outmanoeuvre any conspiracy which had emerged since the Napoleonic War. More mundane considerations might have been at work. Alcohol may have played a part in the general feeling of overexcitement and perturbation that had afflicted everyone in public life for as long as anyone could remember. Sidmouth was known to drink twenty glasses of wine at dinner before attending parliament. This was not considered to be excessive. He was one of many ministers of the crown who suffered from gout. It may have had its current meaning, as an inflammation of the arteries in the foot, but it could also be associated with depression and with the excessive consumption of alcohol. One can hazard the conjecture that Sidmouth's bibulousness represented an average quantity at Westminster, and that there were occasions when the proceedings resembled a barroom brawl.

Farce and tragedy had already turned to pantomime on the accession of the Prince Regent as George IV at the end of January 1820. His father, mad and blind, and bearded like a prophet, had been suspended somewhere between the living and the dead. He spoke to the dead as if they were still alive, and of the living as if they had been interred. His death on 29 January 1820 made nothing happen except to elevate his son to the throne. A new member of the strange family had come into the world in the preceding year. Alexandrina Victoria was better known by her second name. She was the daughter of Prince Edward, fourth son of George III, and Princess Victoria of Saxe-Coburg-Saalfeld. Her mother's family were all Germans, and she took pride in that fact; she married a German, and German was often the language of her court at Windsor and elsewhere.

George IV was already known to be fat, lazy and profligate. He had not endeared himself to many of his subjects by sending a message of congratulations to the magistrates of Manchester after Peterloo. It was said that he could at least have waited for an inquiry. But he did not dominate the farce. That starring role was reserved for his wife, Queen Caroline, who on the elevation of her husband was determined to claim all her rights as queen of Great Britain. Never was there a less likely queen; she, like her husband, was fat and profligate. She had entertained a string of lovers and now, in an aura of ill winds propagated by her lack of hygiene, set sail for her country.

They had married in unfortunate circumstances some twenty-five years before in St James's Chapel, where the Prince could hardly stand upright. The shock of seeing, and smelling, his betrothed was too much for him and Lord Melbourne commented that 'the prince was like a man doing a thing in desperation; it was like Macheath going to execution; and he was quite drunk'. Time was no healer. Princess Caroline created much scandal on her forced separation from her husband. She used Europe as her playground or payground and on one occasion in the Middle East rode into Jerusalem on an ass. She went to a ball with half a pumpkin on her head. On her return to England as presumed queen, the new king attempted every means of removing her, including a trial for adultery, prompting many remarks of a sarcastic ad hominem nature. But she survived the ordeal. Henry Brougham cross-examined the witnesses against her, to hear the reply 'Non mi recordo' time and again. It became a catchphrase of the moment, like the verse of an Italian song. The bill against her was abandoned. The trial was the only subject of conversation. 'Have you heard anything new about the queen?' was the question.

The extraordinary aspect of this ill-starred affair was the popularity she earned among the English populace. She was cheered and applauded wherever she went. She was for a while the queen of all hearts. She had been misused by the administration and mistreated by the king. Was that not also the condition of the country? Whether she knew it or not, she was a radical figurehead, embodying all the wrongs of the king's unhappy and abused people. The women of London joined the city's radicals in organizing large meetings and rallies in her cause. It seemed that the administration might be overturned by the plight of one woman. Sarah Lyttelton, a member of the royal court and wife of an MP, wrote that the king 'is so unpopular, his private character so despised, and everything he does so injudicious as well as unprincipled that one can hardly wish him well out of it, except for the fear of a revolution'.

But then, in a matter of weeks, all pity and sympathy for Caroline disappeared. A verse became popular:

> Most gracious queen, we thee implore
> To go away and sin no more,
> But if that effort be too great,
> To go away at any rate.

When she accepted an annuity of £50,000 from the administration, she lost her audience. When she turned up at the doors of Westminster Abbey, in the summer of 1821, unsuccessfully trying one door after another in order to take part in the coronation ceremony of her estranged husband, she was mocked with cries of 'Shame!' and 'Off!'. She was more or less abandoned, and died a few weeks later unmourned. Her fall from popular grace was in part due to the fickleness and forgetfulness of crowds who were eagerly waiting for the next scandal or sensation. The lesson was not lost on the more astute politicians who came to the conclusion that no popularity, or unpopularity, lasts for very long.

There were other ministers who sensed another change in the prevailing atmosphere. Robert Peel, a junior minister with a future before him, wrote to ask a friend in March 1820 'whether he did not think that the tone of England was more Whig — to use an odious but intelligible phrase — than the policy of the government' and whether there was now a belief that the mode of government had to be changed. He was more accurate than he could have guessed, and within two years he had been propelled into Lord Liverpool's Tory ministry in order to alleviate the strictures of the Criminal Code. It was for this and other reasons that the 1820s seemed relatively quiet after the excitement of previous years and before the reform meetings of the 1830s.

One Whig measure was introduced, or alluded to, by Lord Liverpool in May 1820 to a deputation of City merchants. The advantages of free trade were calling to him. He knew that certain people believed that Britain had prospered under a protective system, but he was certain that the nation flourished in spite of it. In his slow, indirect and infinitely cautious way he did not put forward proposals of his own. Instead he set up parliamentary committees to examine the numerous and complex questions involved in what was by any standards a reversal of policy; as a result, goods might be imported into England in foreign ships. Foreign goods might be transported from any free port. Three hundred obsolete statutes on the laws of commercial navigation were repealed. The *Annual Register* described the measures as 'vast beyond all question . . . this being the first instance in which practical statesmen have professed to act under the more literal principles of political economy'. So the process had begun.

By 1825 a Chair of Political Economy was established at Oxford. Memoirs and letters are full of the subject. Viscount Sidmouth wrote in the spring of 1826: 'we hear nothing on all sides, at dinners, parties, in church, and at the theatre, but discussions on political economy and the distresses of the times'. Rarely has an academic discipline attracted so much attention with animated discussion on labour and profit, paper and bullion. An interesting connection can be discerned between theatricals and radical politics. The whole point and excitement of the Georgian theatre lay in its wilful blending of the real and the imaginary, which drew 'dreamers of illimitable dreams', including those nineteenth-century radicals who were as eager to change the conditions of their time as they were forthright in their optimism and their belief in progress. In the 'low' theatres, too, the emphasis was on the change and uncertainty of life where poverty, disease and unemployment were part of the drama.

The world beyond the seas was, as always, a cauldron of infinite troubles. In 1820 four revolutions broke out in Europe; Spain, Portugal, Naples and Piedmont were bubbling. Some of the nations of the Quadruple Alliance, pledged from the beginning to the support of monarchy, were ready to intervene. Castlereagh, the British foreign secretary, was not. He wanted nothing to do with it, especially since the doctrine of non-intervention had become a matter of state policy. He told one colleague that 'he was sick of the concern, and that if he could well get out of it would never get into it again'. England would play no part in continental broils. This stance might lead to a loss of influence upon the stage of the world, but anything was better than to become involved in affairs of which human foresight could not conceive the end.

In a message directed to Austria's foreign minister, Prince Metternich, Castlereagh advised that 'he must take us for better or worse as we are, and if the Continental Powers cannot afford to travel at our pace, they need not expect us to adopt theirs. It does not belong to our system.' He deplored 'dashing'. A significant Cabinet State Paper of 5 May 1820 declared: 'this country cannot and will not act upon abstract and speculative principles of precaution'. In the early summer of the following year he declared in the Commons that 'for certain states to erect themselves into a tribunal to judge of the internal affairs of others was to arrogate to themselves a power which could only be assumed in defiance of the law of nations and the principles of common sense'. He had all the pragmatism and practicality which the English applaud. The last thing the Foreign Office needed was an ideologue.

Trade was also climbing ever upwards and at the opening of parliament in 1820 the king felt able to say that 'in many of the manufacturing districts the distresses . . . have greatly abated'. Even the French chargé d'affaires noted 'the tranquillity which obtains in London and generally throughout England'. The king could go forward with a light heart, except that there was nothing else light about him. The thick and luxurious coronation robe added great weight to an already large frame, and during the ceremony he was constantly on the verge of fainting before being revived by sal volatile. Yet he still put on a good show. He may have been uncouth and sometimes ridiculous but he knew when he was on parade. In the month after the ceremony he travelled to Ireland, where he appeared 'dead DRUNK', according to an observer. This was the moment his wife chose to expire from drink and disappointment, and Castlereagh reported that George 'bears his good fortune with great propriety'. 'This', he said on his arrival at Dublin, 'is one of the happiest days of my life.'

3

Eternity work

Nothing in these days was left untouched by religious controversy. Religion was the air that the 'respectable' breathed. The religion of the day was in itself neither hot nor cold. Some parts were boiling while others were lukewarm. There was a Low Church of Evangelicals and Dissenters, and there was a High Church that moved towards Catholic ritual. There was also a Broad Church, Whig in its theology, that embraced a nationally based religion. Out of these great movements of faith came sects and groups that put their faith in general providence or special providence, in atonement or in hellfire. Calvinists, Methodists, Quakers, Arminians, Presbyterians, Congregationalists and Baptists were all part of an informal 'Evangelical Alliance' that looked for points of contact with the Anglicans. There was among them a general and discernible movement towards piety and righteousness. But that was only to be expected. Eight out of nine of a Cambridge crew, having won the Oxford and Cambridge boat race on the Thames, went on to the East End for their missionary work. Among the Anglicans of the 'Established Church' there was not so much enthusiasm. They worshipped that which was customary and respectable, and perhaps looked with more horror on a poor man than an evil man. As Samuel Butler wrote of a rural congregation in *The Way of All Flesh* (1903), set in 1834: they were 'tolerators, if not lovers, of all that was familiar, haters of all that was unfamiliar; they would have been equally horrified at hearing the Christian religion doubted, and at seeing it practised'. They were decent, undiscerning people.

A report by the census-takers of 1851 remarked that 'working men, it is contended, cannot enter our religious structures without having impressed upon their notice some memento of their inferiority. The existence of pews, and the position of the free seats, are, it is said, sufficient to deter them from our churches.' As for the indigent poor and those close to absolute poverty, no one really expected them to attend church or chapel. They would probably have been ejected if they attempted to do so. One costermonger admitted to Henry Mayhew, the social inquirer, that 'the costers somehow mix up being religious with being respectable, and so they have a queer sort of feeling about it. It's a mystery to them.'

What really interested observers was the fact that many of the 'respectable' classes had no faith at all. They were armoured with scepticism against the arguments of priests and preachers. Many of them did not know what to believe – if anything. The French historian Hippolyte Taine remarked that the average Englishman or Englishwoman believed in God, the Trinity and Hell, 'although without fervour'. And that was the key. It was not a secular nation. It was an indifferent one. Hellfire preachers were regarded as a novelty and a spectator sport, even though they had many spirited followers. Ecstasies and faintings, so popular in the eighteenth century, were no longer the English style. The only source of communal passion now came in the form of hymns. The deathly hush of the English Sunday, denounced by Dickens among others, was a clear sign that the Church bred no passion and no enthusiasm. There was no sense of a popular faith which could still be found, for example, in Russia or America. There was instead an irritable dissatisfaction with the tenets of established faith; in particular the belief in hell was under siege. It became possible to be less dogmatic and less specific, with certain doctrines silently dropped. There still remained regional differences, however, that had been maintained since the seventeenth century; Anglicanism lay in the south-east of the country, for example, and Primitive Methodism in the south-west and north-west.

Lord Liverpool himself was of a 'methodistical' temper, and in

1812 had been instrumental in passing an act for the further toleration of Dissenters. William Cobbett, in his *Rural Rides* (1830), described them as 'a bawling, canting crew' and 'roving fanatics', but they had already become a large part of the congregation of England, from the Quakers to the Countess of Huntingdon's Connexion, all of whom held themselves apart from the Church of England. They in turn were prohibited from attending Oxford or Cambridge universities and were obliged to be married in chapels or buried in graveyards under the auspices of Anglican clergymen.

The largest religious group, after the orthodox, was that alliance between Evangelicals and utilitarians which did much to shape the temper of the age. The passion for moral reform was deep within both of them, with the belief in reason and the faith in renewal as the twin paths to enlightenment. To study and to labour, to preach and to denounce idleness and luxury; these were the twin elements of secular belief and religious faith which changed the nature of English sensibility. The Evangelicals practised the strictest interpretation of Scripture, a good companion to the 'felicific calculus' of the utilitarians who sought the greatest good for the greatest number. They shared pragmatism and dogmatism in equal measure, and were the moral agents for social as well as religious reform. 'It is', according to one of their number 'eternity work'. But they were also zealous to redeem the time. A deluge of pamphlets and periodicals, concerned with self-improvement and practical morality, was aimed at anyone who could read.

Providence, progress and civilization were parts of God's law. The Evangelicals preached individual regeneration, and the utilitarians promoted the doctrine of self-help. Their first success was the introduction of the treadmill into the regime of prisons, and by the 1830s their convictions had become public policy. Not all they preached was dour; the Evangelicals campaigned vigorously against the slave trade while the utilitarians attacked the Corn Laws and other obstacles to free trade. They demanded reform, and their joined forces helped to dissolve the politics of the 1820s. They drew in people who were on the brink of industrial change. George Eliot wrote that 'the real drama of Evangelicalism – and it has abundance of fine drama for anyone who has genius enough to discern and reproduce it – lies among the middle and lower classes'. These were the classes who changed Britain utterly.

Charles Babbage, a Londoner born in Walworth in 1791, was one of the greatest inventors and analysts of the nineteenth century who fully fashioned what he called the 'difference engine' and the 'analytical engine', which are the direct predecessors of the digital computer. They were elaborate affairs of punched cards and dials which few people ever understood or now understand. Curiously enough, given his reputation as a reactionary force, the duke of Wellington seemed implicitly to realize the potential of the machines.

From the age of seventeen Babbage became obsessed with algebra; what made these figures live? He was so confident of his abilities with numbers that he dreamed of creating them in a mathematical process. He recollected that: 'The first idea which I remember of the possibility of calculating tables occurred either in the year 1820 or 1821 . . . I expressed to my friend the wish that we could calculate by steam . . .' This was in part a metaphor, since in a different account he recalled: 'I am thinking that all these tables [pointing to the logarithms] might be calculated by machinery.' Steam, engines and machinery were all part of the cloud of knowing. After he sketched some designs he fell ill with a nervous complaint. He had envisaged an engine for making mathematical tables which presaged a new world of machine tools and engineering techniques. It was so far ahead of other calculating tools that for his contemporaries it was equivalent to putting a television set in the hands of monkeys.

It was called the 'difference engine' because it computed tables of numbers by the method of finite differences. But then within a short time he began work on what became known as the 'analytical engine', which was essentially an automatic calculator. It worked like a cotton mill; the materials, the numbers, were kept in a storehouse apart from the mechanism until they were processed in the mill. Each part was designed to carry out its function, such as addition and multiplication, while being connected with every other part. He described it as an engine 'eating its own tail'. He wrote that 'the whole of arithmetic now appeared within the grasp of mechanism'. These reflections might have come from another world, and were ignored until the middle of the twentieth century. They have been described as 'one of the great intellectual achievements in the history of mankind'. Few people in England showed the slightest interest.

The engine was out of its time. Its technology was too advanced to be understood adequately. It was the most ingenious and complex machine ever built, but it had leaped across a historical period which had yet to be assimilated. We cannot be sure how many other devices or inventions have fallen through the cracks of time. A replica of the 'analytical engine mill' is exhibited in the Science Museum of London and still resembles some strange god hauled from an unknown cave. Somehow it still remains out of time. There is also another survivor. Half the brain of Charles Babbage is preserved in the Hunterian Museum, with the other half in the Science Museum.

The fact that the name of Babbage is still not as well known as the poets and novelists of the period is testimony to the fact that the Victorian intelligentsia did not take kindly to applied science. One who persisted through the sheer weight of his genius was Jeremy Bentham. He may properly be described as the 'pan-progenitor' (to adapt one of his neologisms) of utilitarians and the felicific calculus. Although he began his work and his investigations in the eighteenth century, he is best seen in the context of the succeeding century. He was another great London visionary, born in Spitalfields in 1748, a practical genius who may be placed beside Babbage himself. Bentham was not widely known in his own life-time, despite the plaudits that have been heaped on him ever since. He and Babbage can still be hailed as prophets without honour.

Bentham propounded in all his work for reform the simple belief in 'the greatest happiness of the greatest number', a radical maxim that propelled him through the thorny ways of legal reform, prison reform and Poor Law reform. If he had been a Christian, he might have taken as his motto Luke 3:5 – the crooked ways will be made straight, and the rough ways smooth. He was in part responsible for the working of the Reform Act of 1832, which led the way to adult male suffrage, and propounded the notion that 'every law is an evil, for every law is an infraction of liberty'. The pursuit of rational solutions by means of rational methods was the greatest problem of the age. It was the music of the machine, of competition and progress. To be or not to be was no longer the question. That had become, does it work?

Bentham also helped to establish the Mechanics' Institutes, which became one of the self-proclaimed glories of the Victorian Age. They were a venue not only for mechanics but for clerks or apprentices or shopkeepers who had been stirred by glimpses of the world of knowledge before and, so far, beyond them. The Institutes in fact became the venue of the middle classes, always aspiring, rather than the manual labourers for whom they were originally intended. Nevertheless, many of the most interesting biographies and fictions of the period are concerned with the arduous and sometimes painful exercise of self-education in the face of difficulties. There were some who got up before dawn to study by candlelight, those who read by the light of a tavern fire, those who would walk thirteen miles for a bookshop, even those who paid a penny to read the newspaper in the local alehouse.

The nineteenth century was not necessarily an ally to religion, therefore, as later pages will show. The growing regard for science as a mode of knowledge was not helpful for those who fostered religious truth, and the increasing indifference to religion itself was one of the first signs of what would become a more secular society. The Christian faith became more fractured and uncertain. The drama of evolution superseded that of redemption, and it became clear that the scientific model offered more insights into the practical business of life than any pamphlet by the Society for Promoting Christian Knowledge.

Charles Darwin's *On the Origin of Species by Means of Natural Selection, or the Preservation of Favoured Races in the Struggle for Life* (1859) is as quintessentially Victorian as the Great Exhibition or the Albert Hall. Its thesis is based upon the twin imperatives of struggle and competition, and in the consequent race of life the 'northern forms were enabled to beat the less powerful southern forms'. There is nothing here of atonement, redemption or grace. It is a dark world indeed, dominated by the necessity of labour and the appetite for power, in which combat and slaughter are the principal components. To see Victorian civilization from the vantage point of Charles Darwin is to see it more clearly. He had also adopted Malthus's doctrine that populations grow faster than their means of subsistence, and are thus doomed to extinction. This also is a key to Victorian melancholy, which was perhaps as influential as Victorian optimism.

It is of no surprise that the study of the gospels was losing ground to the investigation of stratigraphic geology. It is perhaps no more wonderful that the domain of science remained largely in the hands of Nonconformists rather than Anglicans. Geology had become the most popular of the sciences, and its adherents felt free to speculate upon the spans of millions of years. But the most significant aspect of geology in the nineteenth century lay in the fact that these adherents were amateurs drawn to the study through sheer intellectual curiosity. It was a topic for curates. The most prominent of the amateurs, however, was Mary Anning of Lyme Regis, born in 1799. Her father was a cabinetmaker but he soon began to neglect his occupation for the sake of fossil hunting. Lyme was the perfect location. The crumbling of the region's cliffs had already begun in earnest and the fossils embedded therein were ripe for plucking. From an early age Mary Anning accompanied her father on fossil expeditions and it can only be assumed that his advice and her experience gave her an otherwise preternatural skill in recognizing and identifying the remains of previously unknown species. She was, according to a childhood friend, 'a spirited young person of independent character who did not much care for undue politeness or pretence'. This bravura was generally laid to the fact that at the age of fifteen months she survived a great lightning strike which killed three people; she had been a sickly infant, as were so many of the babies of Lyme, but from that time forward she was spirited and adventurous.

Her pursuit survived her father's death, which may even have quickened her search for what were known variously as Cupid's wings, ladies' fingers and devil's toenails. Some of these she sold to visitors near the coach stop at the Blue Cups Inn in Lyme. It was not unusual for her to charge half a crown for an ammonite laid on a cloth with others on a table. Her first great success, however, came in the summer of 1811 when her younger brother, Joseph, came across the outlines of a strangely shaped head. It was embedded in a geological formation known as the Blue Lias, consisting of limestone and shale. He had no time to dig out the rest of the fossil, and the task fell to Mary. It took her a year of painstaking digging and excavating what seemed to some to be a large crocodile. But as she pieced it together, bone by bone, she eventually reconstructed a creature more than 17 feet long. It was to be called ichthyosaurus. From that time forward she became a geological celebrity. John Murray, a fellow enthusiast, noted: 'I once gladly availed myself of a geological excursion and was not a little surprised at her geological tact and acumen. A single glance at the edge of a fossil peeping from the Blue Lias revealed to her the nature of the fossil and its name and character were instantly announced.'

It was believed astonishing that 'this poor ignorant girl' could talk with professors and other eminent geologists on their own terms and with equal knowledge. Yet she was not mentioned in lectures and she was not invited to colloquia. She was only a female. She wrote to a friend, Anna Maria Pinney, that 'the world has used me so unkindly, I fear it has made me suspicious of all mankind. I hope you will pardon me, although I do not deserve it. How I envy you your daily visits to the museum!' Pinney herself wrote of her that 'men of learning have sucked her brains and made a great deal by publishing works of which she furnished the contents while she derived none of the advantages'.

In pursuit of the light of the early decades of the nineteenth century, therefore, the student could look in vain at John Henry Newman's tracts or Charles Spurgeon's gospel missions in Southwark. He or she might look instead at Humphry Davy and the beginning of electrochemistry, at John Dalton and the atomic hypothesis, Michael Faraday or Thomas Young. Religion was not of course altogether neglected. Books such as Henry Brougham's *Discourse on the Objects, Advantages and Pleasures of Science* (1826), published by the Society for the Diffusion of Intellect, were seen as an advantageous branch of natural theology. Charles Lyell in *Principles of Geology* (1830–33) declared that 'we discover everywhere the clear proofs of a Creative Intelligence, and of His foresight, wisdom and power'. Shorn of Darwin's savage vision, this was better than a sermon in St Paul's Cathedral.

4

A queasy world

Struggle was not very far from the surface of life. In August 1822 Castlereagh cut his throat with a penknife. The unending and weary oppression of work and watchfulness had taken its toll. He had been speaking and behaving oddly for some days; when a household servant tried to cheer him, he put his hand to his forehead and murmured: 'I am quite worn out here. Quite worn out.' He asked for an audience with the king, to whom he confided that he was homosexual and that he was ready to flee the country before exposure as such; he behaved oddly enough for the king to warn Lord Liverpool of his condition. He believed, in what was perhaps the final stage of a nervous breakdown, that he had been observed in a male brothel three years before and that he was still being blackmailed. This may or may not have been true, and there is some anecdotal evidence to support it, but it is significant that his mind gave way at a time when London itself was gripped by a homosexual scandal involving the bishop of Clogher in County Tyrone, who had been caught with a soldier. To avoid what he considered to be an overwhelming public and private scandal, Castlereagh put the knife to his throat.

By the end of 1820 it was already clear that, in men and measures, the cabinet would change or would surely fall. With Castlereagh gone, Liverpool's administration had suffered a severe blow. It was also clear that Castlereagh's greatest opponent, George Canning, would have to take his place. Canning had been ready to depart for India as governor general, but he could not resist the allure of high office at home. There was no one to match his popularity or his oratory; only he had the vitality and political intelligence to take on the Foreign Office while at the same time becoming leader of the House of Commons. Nevertheless, he had made many enemies as a result of his pro-Catholic stance. It was said that Castlereagh never gave a speech without making a friend, while Canning never opened his mouth without losing one. Wilberforce said that the lash of his sarcasm 'would have fetched the hide off a rhinoceros'. He was always plotting and scheming. Apparently he would not 'take his tea without a stratagem', but in fact his policy was essentially that of Castlereagh conducted with more elan and publicity. He was a different kind of politician, much to the dismay of those of the old school. He dwelled in the open. It was to his disadvantage that he was the son of an actress, but he needed no fine inheritance to make his way. As soon as he entered the cabinet it was said that he began to look and behave as if he were prime minister. Wellington said that Canning's temper was enough to blow him up. He was, as one contemporary put it, 'perpetually doing & undoing'. A distinction is often drawn between 'Whig Tories' or 'ultra-Tories'. But the phrases mean very little, and it is better to speak of those who supported Canning and those who detested him. Lord Liverpool, apparently more reticent and disengaged than ever, kept the balance.

Lord Liverpool had in fact accepted reinforcements for his administration from a group of disenchanted Whigs under the leadership of Lord Grenville, who had migrated in search of offices and emoluments. The marquess of Buckingham, for example, received a dukedom, while one of his acolytes gained a seat in the cabinet. Everybody won. Liverpool's government had been further revived by the steady rise of Robert Peel. Peel had become chief secretary for Ireland at the age of twenty-four, and by all accounts acquitted himself well. He did everything well, in fact, and in 1822 he first joined the cabinet as home secretary, to be joined there by William Huskisson at the Board of Trade. The change of men had an instinctive, if not immediate, effect upon the administration. It seemed stronger and more robust, filled with the energy of new ambitions. Some observers disagreed that 'Old Corruption' could change. 'To be sure', Cobbett wrote, 'when one dies, or cuts his throat (as in the case of *Castlereagh*), another *one* comes; but, it is the *same body*.'

Anyone with eyes to see, or ears to hear, knew what was going on. The poetry of Shelley and Byron, together with the prose of William Hazlitt, helped to encourage a mood of sharp or sullen cynicism against the nefarious powers of authority. Robert Southey attacked them as 'men of diseased hearts and depraved imaginations, who, forming a system of opinions to suit their own unhappy course of conduct, have rebelled against the holiest ordinances of human society . . .' It is hard not to sense the strength of feeling against the nobility and the 'booby squires' who might have been Whig or Tory for all the writers cared. In this period there were no fewer than nineteen Sunday newspapers. Seditious pamphlets and broadsheets against the administration found a lucrative market, and the new king was abused as roundly as Liverpool or Canning. For the legislators it was in many respects similar to living on the very rim of a volcano. Canning relished this uncomfortable position and, unlike his predecessor, played to the gallery whenever the occasion demanded it.

Opinion, such as it existed, was essentially a phenomenon of the middle classes that were now discovering their own strength. It was not a question of policy as such – although an issue like income tax could raise the slumbering beast – it was obeisance to an accepted code of duty, thrift and industry, any infraction of which had the direst consequences. The voting public were all middle class now.

It has been said that the newly refreshed cabinet was in every respect more 'Whig' than its predecessor. Peel began to liberalize the criminal code and brushed away the litter of fussy and outmoded legislation, abolishing the death penalty for a hundred different crimes. In the process he fashioned a revolution in nineteenth-century criminal justice. He changed the laws on transportation, abolished judges' perquisites in favour of salaries, and simplified the criminal law. In all those measures he earned Canning's approbation. The Metropolitan Police force came a little later.

William Huskisson, at the Board of Trade, had turned his

attention to free trade. It was the catchphrase of the time, although its effects on prices or on the labour market were not properly understood. He followed earlier measures by reducing the tariff on imported goods and by allowing foreign vessels into English ports. It was a long time coming. More than one hundred years before, in *Windsor Forest* (1713), Alexander Pope had prophesied that:

> The time shall come, when, free as seas or wind
> Unbounded Thames shall flow for all mankind . . .

Huskisson also ventured to touch on the price of corn as a preliminary measure to the abolition of the Corn Laws in 1832. He could not hope to please both farmer and consumer, and there were so many special interests involved (including the wealth of the landowning gentry and the possibility of starvation among the poorer classes) that he had to move slowly. He set up a sliding scale where the duty on imported corn varied with its price in the domestic market. It was assumed, by those who did not understand it, to be a form of compromise. And in that muddled state it passed.

Just as Huskisson further opened up the protected economy of the nation, so Canning defied conventional diplomatic wisdom by recognizing the emergent South American nations. But Canning was always fated to be the lightning conductor of the storm of change. When he had taken on the Foreign Office after Castlereagh's death he was confronted by another Congress of the 'Holy League' determined to extirpate popular liberties. But Canning was never a member of what was known as 'the Vienna Club', the old boys who had carved up Europe between themselves. He would have nothing to do with it, and he registered his displeasure by warning that if France or Spain should dare to invade Portugal, Britain's old ally, Canning would undoubtedly intervene. The duke of Wellington, who acted as Britain's representative at the Congress, had declared: 'we stand alone, and we do so by choice'. It was not in Britain's interests to alter the internal administration of other nations, but it was her choice to recognize and to nurture de facto governments that had sprung up from popular demand. It need hardly be said that the motivating principles were those of trade and finance.

When the Spanish began to surrender their South American colonies to the French, the English merchants, furious that trade could be snatched from them, found a strong ally in their government. British merchant ships acted as an unofficial war fleet to maintain supplies and communications between the various rebel territories. Simón Bolívar had an army of six thousand British volunteers to prove his part as 'the Liberator' for a string of countries from Venezuela to Ecuador. Canning was the single most important politician to lead the charge, or at least the insurrection. Towards the end of the conflict Britain recognized Colombia, Mexico, Brazil and Argentina as independent states; Venezuela and Honduras then joined the magic circle, thus guaranteeing that the South American continent would never again be enslaved by the Spanish empire. Native Amerindians, however, were to endure many decades of forced labour at the hands of Spanish settlers.

Most of the cabinet were opposed to supporting rebels against the lawful authorities; the monarchs and monarchists of Europe were horrified at the prospect of a string of new republics across the ocean. Plots against Canning were engineered in the capitals of Europe, with the active or tacit approval of some members of the cabinet, but they came to nothing. He said later that there was a conspiracy 'to change the policy of this government by changing *me*'. Canning had the inestimable advantage of the Americans on his side. In the Monroe Doctrine of December 1823 the Americans had announced that 'the American continents, by the free and independent condition which they have assumed and maintain, are henceforth not to be considered as subjects for any future colonization by any European powers'. Canning put it more succinctly in the Commons: 'Contemplating Spain as our ancestors had known her, I resolved that if France had Spain, it should not be Spain with the Indies. I called the New World into existence to redress the balance of the Old.' George IV was violently opposed to any independence for previously subject nations; the agitators for liberty were no less than traitors to their own imperial monarch, Ferdinand VII. Such matters touched too close to home. He refused to read out Canning's report at the beginning of parliament, complaining that his gout made it impossible for him to walk and that he had lost his false teeth. Yet he could do nothing to restrain the policy and wish of George Canning. The last links of royal power were beginning to rust.

The question of Catholic emancipation had also divided the cabinet, with Peel opposed and Canning in favour. 'There is little feeling, I think,' Peel wrote, 'in this country, upon the question. People are tired of it, and tired of the trouble of opposing it, or thinking about it.' This was undoubtedly true of those whose religion was comfortably placed. The Roman Catholic Relief Act of 1791 had dismantled many of the hurdles by allowing freedom of worship and liberating Catholics from the Oath of Supremacy. But in the hypothesized 'age of improvement' it was not enough. And then there was the little question of Catholic Ireland, which was not to be wished away. The Union of 1800 had abolished the Irish parliament but had left nothing in its place except a wholly inadequate civil service and bungling English administrators. The Anglo-Irish aristocracy was in large part venal and impotent while the Catholic peasantry had been brutalized and impoverished by English rule. To allow the vote to Roman Catholics in England and in Ireland was a measure of natural justice that was ever more necessary in the nineteenth century. Canning pushed and pulled at it with all his tenacity and taste for the spotlight. How was it possible to assist Simón Bolívar in his wish and desire for independence while at the same time denying Daniel O'Connell a similar courtesy?

A Catholic Association was established by O'Connell in the early months of 1823 after Irish hopes had been raised by the Whigs and dashed by the monarchy, even as the condition of the Irish themselves steadily grew more unruly and impatient. Most of them lived off what little land they possessed while being harassed by rack-rent landlords and obliged to pay one-tenth of their produce in tithes to a Protestant Church. When the more militant Catholics turned against their oppressors they were bullied and beaten by the Protestant 'Peep-o-Day Boys' and the 'Ribbonmen'; they in turn relied upon 'the Defenders'. In 1825 the Association was suppressed, but it reinvented itself as a group for educational purposes. It fooled nobody, but it was more difficult to prosecute. It was O'Connell who brought the priests and laity together in combination.

Combination had once been equivalent to conspiracy, but it had become a word of much wider import. The Combination Act of 1799, prohibiting the formation of trade unions, had been passed as part of the reaction to the Jacobin scare of that time. Yet in the

1820s combinations sprang up among groups as disparate as tailors, shipwrights, sawyers and coopers. They regulated wages, limited the number of apprentices and refused to work with those that had not joined them. A parliamentary committee discovered that some of these groups had been in informal existence for almost a century, but only in the 1820s were they given a name and an identity. The Stockport Cotton Jenny Spinners Union Society was formed in 1824, at the same time as other 'union societies' emerged in the familiar trades. They were known as 'trade unions' because they represented those in an historic trade; they had nothing to do with the working classes of the factories and mills.

One of the leading figures of this nascent union movement was Francis Place, conventionally known as 'the radical tailor of Charing Cross'. He was one of those city radicals who have as long a history as the city itself; wherever there are large groups of men and women there will be common discontent and shared grievances. He had organized a strike among the makers of leather breeches, then an indispensable part of the working costume, but his failure in that effort did not dissuade him from helping to organize other radical associations. His chief aim, however, was to abolish the legislation which forbade the forming of trade unions. With the help of allies in parliament, a Combination Act was passed in 1825 which defined the rights of trade unions in a very narrow sense as meeting to bargain over wages and conditions – anything else might be construed as criminal. The act allowed workers 'to enter any combination to obtain an advance or to fix the rate of wages, or to lessen or alter the hours or duration of the time of working, or to decrease the quantity of work . . .' The *Sheffield Mercury* of 8 October 1825 reported that the mechanics of the kingdom, in combination, were ready to act in accordance with these narrow limitations. The act was passed during a period of prosperity but, when that prosperity faltered and began to fade, the new trade unions were ill equipped to deal with the slump.

The Catholic Association continued to thrive in Ireland under Daniel O'Connell's leadership. The Roman Catholic Church supported it, and used its money for membership fees, and O'Connell himself became one of the heroes of Whig reform. Ireland was no less a candidate for victimhood than Sicily or Greece, and it became natural to talk of 'the poor Irish' as a race rather than as a special class. George IV did not help matters. He wrote to Robert Peel that 'the king is apprehensive that a notion is gone abroad that the king himself is not unfavourable to the Catholic claims . . . he will no longer consent to Catholic Emancipation being left as an open question in his Cabinet'. The letter was of course shown to Wellington, among others, who wrote: 'If we cannot get rid of the Catholic Association, we must look to civil war in Ireland.'

There had always been talk of civil war, and the temperature was raised when in 1825 a reform politician, Sir Francis Burdett, introduced an Emancipation Bill. It passed through the Commons by the end of April 1825; Peel and Lord Liverpool threatened to resign if the bill passed its final hurdles. Liverpool declared that 'my particular rejection of the Roman Catholic religion is that it penetrates into every domestic scene, and inculcates a system of tyranny never known elsewhere . . .' The old and familiar cry of 'No Popery!' was once more heard through the land. The Lords rejected the bill, but it was widely apparent that in terms of natural justice and national peace the Catholics would eventually succeed.

But then came the financial crash of 1825, the popping of yet another bubble of greed and overconfidence. By the middle of 1826 the once overworked mills were forced to close down, and their workers were put on short time. It seemed natural, even inevitable, for the economy to prosper for a few years and then go into decline. But nobody fully understood the lesson. A see-saw economy, as it has sometimes been called, was the image of this financial age. The major panic, the eye of the storm, lasted for ten days when many of the major institutions shut their doors against the blast.

The financial crisis coincided with the Catholic crisis, hitting landlords, farmers, artisans and social reformers alike. 'As to ministers,' one MP had observed, 'they had fully proved their inability to govern. Never was the community so universally impressed with the conviction of the incapacity of their responsible ministers as at the present moment; so general was the feeling that all ranks of men looked to their removal as their only hope.'

The general situation was exacerbated by a chronic shortage of corn after a bad harvest. Very few people held land of their own, and the paucity of corn led to general and genuine distress. Many businesses were forced to close, and it was widely rumoured by the Evangelical population that the hand of God had been raised against the nation in a fit of justified wrath. Edward Irving had begun his visionary ministry two years before, and many now said that his denunciations and prophecies were nothing less than revealed truth. Was the second advent about to occur? Talk of apocalypse, divine punishment and the wrath to come was commonplace. John Martin painted *The Destruction of Pompeii and Herculaneum* in 1822, and Edward Bulwer-Lytton's novel *The Last Days of Pompeii* was published in 1834.

Parliament was more prosaic and practical. Half a million quarters of bonded corn were released from the warehouses, much to the chagrin of the landowners and farmers. Canning announced the measure to a plainly dissatisfied House of Commons. 'I never saw', one observer, Thomas Creevey, noticed, 'anything like the fury of both Whig and Tory landholders at Canning's speech, but the Tories much the most violent of the two.' It was considered to represent nothing less than the destruction of the Corn Laws. It was believed that the liberty of the market in corn had other malign consequences, since the attack upon landowners and farmers was one step closer to a general reform which would 'bring the overthrow of the existing social and political system of our country'. To destroy the Corn Laws would undermine the inherited system. According to the reformers, however, to support the Corn Laws would extinguish freedom for ever. The language was meant to be, and was taken to be, serious. Some even blamed the scarcity of corn on the effects of free trade and innovation. Canning had an answer. 'Those who resist indiscriminately all improvement as innovation', he said, 'may find themselves compelled at last to submit to innovations, although they are not improvements.'

But even in their anger, and in the face of famine, the landowners did not attempt to thwart popular demand or tempt the wrath of God. The skies were searched for signs. The anger of the Almighty was further divined when a rag, tag and bobtail English army, intent upon annexation of the prosperous Ashanti region in West Africa, was defeated by the Ashanti themselves on the banks of the Adoomansoo, and all its officers beheaded. News from a region so remote, and so difficult to pronounce, only served to emphasize God's power.

An election was held in June 1826 but it blew neither hot nor cold, with perhaps the faintest breeze for the Protestant cause. Lord Liverpool held on for a while, progressively enfeebled.

In an episode that might claim symbolic significance the duke of York, an arch-Tory and heir to the throne, died of dropsy at the beginning of January 1827, and was buried during an interminable service in St George's Chapel at Windsor. It was attended by the duke of Wellington, the bishop of Lincoln, the duke of Montrose, George Canning and other dignitaries, but the bitter cold and the plain stone floor of the freezing chapel affected some of those who had come to the funeral. The bishop died, while both Wellington and Canning fell seriously ill. The old guard were being cut down by a cold scythe.

Lord Liverpool, in the face of all this discontent, finally made up his mind and died. He suffered a fatal seizure, six weeks after he had seen the duke of York lowered into the grave, but lingered for eighteen months before his surcease. His death let loose the dogs of party war, unmuzzled at last after a decade or more of false harmony, vicious rumour and whispered insult. Canning was the natural successor, but on his appointment as first minister six of his cabinet colleagues resigned. He was obliged to bring in some Whig colleagues, but it was rumoured that he was half a Whig himself. Palmerston, then secretary at war, took his side in the dispute against what he called 'the stupid old Tory Party'. 'On the Catholic question,' he wrote, 'on the principles of commerce; on the corn laws . . . on colonial slavery . . . on all these questions and everything like them the government finds support from the Whigs and resistance from their self-denominated friends.' Did Canning not espouse the cause of the Catholics in marked contrast to Robert Peel, one of those ministers who had resigned? There were some who jeered that Peel and his friends were now officially 'his Majesty's opposition'. Only Liverpool had been able to keep order among them, which was perhaps his largest claim to competence. Had he secretly agreed with Peel or with Canning? No one ever knew. He was reserved, taciturn and enigmatical. The under-secretary at the Home Office decided that 'Liverpool had fewer personal friends and less quality for conciliating men's affections than perhaps any Minister that ever lived.'

But he lived in a queasy and uneasy world. Lord Holland wrote, at the end of 1826: 'Political parties are no more. Whig and Tory, Foxite and Pittite, Minister and Opposition, have ceased to be distinctions, but the divisions of classes and great interests are arrayed against each other – grower and consumer, lands and funds, Irish and English, Catholic and Protestant.' The duke of Wellington observed that government in this period was 'impractical'.

5

The door of change

So George Canning stepped forward to become the first prime minister with the open support of those Whigs whom he had invited into office. He was distrusted by many, but it seems unlikely that a conspiracy or a cabal was waiting to undo him. The people who refused to serve with him, citing his support for the Catholics, did so openly enough. He began governing with some success, managing to formulate and pass a budget. Foreign affairs were still his first and last concern; he was obliged to negotiate with Greece, Turkey, Spain and Portugal over their various grievances. 'I am quite knocked up', he told a fellow minister. But the foreign secretary of the time, Lord Dudley, saw more of him than most others. He wrote that 'never did I hear from him an unkind, peevish or even impatient word. He was quicker than lightning, and even to the very last gay and playful . . .' This does not contradict William Hazlitt's more censorious judgement of a man who liked to play 'the game of politics' involved in 'dilemmas in casuistry' and 'pretexts in diplomacy'. He was still always the cleverest boy at Eton, full of gimmicks and easy eloquence. Hazlitt added that 'truth, liberty, justice, humanity, war or peace, civilisation or barbarism, are things of little consequence, except for him to make speeches upon them'. He had enough fluency and engaging fancy to give some evidence for that claim.

Nature, rather than his protean sensibility, brought him down. He told the king that he felt 'ill all over' and on 8 August 1827, after one hundred days in office, he died so peacefully that no one around him noticed. He was one of those nineteenth-century statesmen who worked themselves to death in an almost literal manner. Without a proper civil service, without a proper party, he had no one except his friends and immediate family to support him. Wine did the rest. His foreign enemies rejoiced because, like Oliver Cromwell, his domestic reputation was 'but a shadow of the glory he had abroad', where he was known as the terror of tyrants.

He had of course left important business behind him, and in his last hours his mind was wandering over Portugal without anyone understanding what he meant. The hopes of the more liberal Tories crashed with him. It seemed to many that the Catholic cause, in particular, had been lost.

Canning's successor is perhaps the least known of all British prime ministers. Viscount Goderich was known as 'Goody Goderich' and the 'Blubberer' for his apparent weakness against any challenge. It is said that he burst into tears when he handed his resignation to the king. He could no more manage the balance of Whigs and Tories than he could have followed Charles Blondin on a tightrope across Niagara. He lasted just six months and holds the remarkable record for a prime minister of never having appeared in parliament. He had only one thin skin, and shrank from any attention.

There is no evidence that Goderich or his ministers shared Canning's fascination with foreign affairs, and it was only coincidence that during Goderich's short ministry the British navy achieved a remarkable victory. Admiral Codrington, in an effort to aid the Greek war for independence from the Ottoman empire, sent a Turkish squadron to the bottom of Navarino Bay. In this action he was allied with the French and Russian navies, but the concerted action did not win instant independence for Greece. It was nevertheless the harbinger of that country's secession from the Ottoman empire. Metternich said that the action 'began a new era' in European affairs. New eras come and go but the duke of Wellington, in particular, wished to maintain the Ottoman empire as a counterweight to Russia.

Whether Goderich approved of the undertaking at Navarino is

of no consequence. He did not last long enough to make his opinion important. Huskisson had said of the new prime minister that 'his health has been suffering, his spirits are worn out, and his fitness for business and power of deciding upon any questions that come before him are very much impaired'. He was said to be as firm as a bulrush. And so with great relief he resigned. He had neither appetite nor aptitude for the high post, and therefore tired of it quickly and completely.

The king, perhaps rueing his appointment, now chose quite a different leader in the redoubtable duke of Wellington. There must be a truism somewhere that good soldiers do not always make good politicians. Wellington never paid heed to public opinion. What he knew best was the battlefield. What was Portugal to him but the site of so many victories? After the first cabinet of the new administration he is reported to have said: 'An extraordinary affair. I gave them their orders and they wanted to stay and discuss them.' Wellington had Peel beside him, as home secretary and leader of the Commons, but he could not keep the cabinet intact. After that first cabinet one of the ministers noted that they exhibited 'the courtesy of men who had just fought a duel'. The lord chancellor said that 'we should have no cabinets after dinner. We all drink too much and are not civil to each other.' They met, and disputed, and disagreed. They could concur on nothing. Wellington was deeply dismayed that, having accepted the post as first minister, he could no longer be commander-in-chief of the armed forces; such a dual post would have smacked of military tyranny. The king already regretted his appointment as prime minister and accused him of want of flexibility. There was a phrase. Either King Arthur must go to the devil, or King George will return to Hanover. Wellington's first name was Arthur.

Peel himself was scathing about some of his more conservative colleagues: 'Supported by very warm friends, no doubt, but these warm friends being prosperous country gentlemen, foxhunters &c &c most excellent men who will attend one night, but who will not leave their favourite pursuits to sit up till two or three o'clock fighting questions of detail . . .'

Peel knew, better than anyone else at Westminster, that detail is at the heart of policy. The administration was at best a shaky coalition of disparate interests, comprising his own supporters, the erstwhile supporters of Canning, and the king himself. 'I must work for myself and by myself,' Wellington told a colleague, 'and please God however I may suffer I shall succeed in establishing in the country a strong government, and then I may retire with honour.' The best of intentions, however, may be thwarted.

There had been some fortunate episodes, one of the most important being the success of the Whigs in managing to repeal the Test and Corporation acts in the spring of 1828. These acts had been devised to exclude Protestant Dissenters from a share in the administration. If they took Protestant communion on certain days of the year, they might take office under the crown. These obligations were lifted, and public offices became open to Dissenters who now enjoyed equality with the members of the Established Church. It was another step in the movement towards social liberation. It had the additional effect, considered only in passing, that the previously indissoluble bonds of Church and State had been broken. It was widely believed that Catholic emancipation was sure to follow. We may have a presentiment of the dying words of Arthur from Tennyson's 'The Passing of Arthur' in *Idylls of the King*: 'The old order changeth, yielding place to new . . .'

The repeal of the Sacramental Test Act, as it was known, had been proposed by one of the more prominent Whigs of the age. Lord John Russell came from an old and distinguished Whig family. Russell was an exiguous and apparently frail man who had reserves of strength and will that astonished his opponents. He was rather small and prim, with a reedy old-fashioned voice that he bequeathed to later members of his family. His household at Pembroke Lodge has been described as 'timid, shrinking, that of a snail withdrawing into its shell full of high principle and religious feeling'. He was high-minded and thin-skinned. Victoria would consider him 'impulsive', 'imprudent' and 'vain'. Compared to what she said of other political leaders, this was almost praise. One foreigner noted, however, 'his apparent coldness and indifference to what was said by others'. A frigid intellect was another aspect of the Whig aristocracy. He had the natural flair and hauteur of a solidly based Whig family, but had quick wits and keen spirits that navigated him through the parliamentary turmoil.

In the same spring of 1828 the supporters of Canning, motivated by pique or perhaps by a misunderstanding, left Wellington's cabinet in a body. It was in fact a rather eminent body. Viscount Melbourne, Viscount Palmerston and Lord Dudley Ward went out together and, according to David Cecil:

> the three went to see Huskisson and then, leaving their cabriolets to follow slowly behind them, strolled back through the balmy silence of the spring night for a final consultation. Ward walked between the two others. 'Well,' he began, 'now that we are by ourselves in the street, and no one but the sentry to hear, let me know right and left what is next to be done – in or out?'
>
> 'Out,' said Palmerston and William [Melbourne] echoed him . . . Poor Ward made a last try. 'There is something in attaching oneself to so great a man as the Duke.' 'For my part,' retorted William unmoved, 'I do not happen to think he is so great a man. But that is a matter of opinion.'

Next day they were all three out.

Much to the delight of the Tories, gone were Huskisson, Palmerston and other notable parliamentarians. Wellington had let them go with so little remonstrance it became clear that he had not really wanted them with him in the first place. They had been chosen because they had acted as Canning's worry beads, but they were not indispensable. With Wellington and Peel solely in charge, a Tory Paradise opened its gates.

In June 1828, a by-election in County Clare was won by Daniel O'Connell. He was a reformer, not a revolutionary, but supported any likely measure for the liberation of oppressed peoples. He opposed any act of violent intimidation or agitation in Ireland, however, believing that liberty by means of parliament was stronger and safer than liberation by armed struggle. But there were three faces to O'Connell: the one he presented to his close allies, the one he eventually demonstrated to the House of Commons, and the one he showed to his people. That was his skill and strength as a leader. To his people he was a man of his native soil, a man of Ireland with the eloquence of a barroom orator. In parliament he was passionate and at times almost incoherent. To his friends he was urbane and even languid. He was a master of mood and of tempo.

It had occurred to him, as to others, that although Catholics might not sit in Westminster there was nothing to prohibit them from standing for election, so he stood in the by-election for County Clare. He won the day. He could not take his place at Westminster because he was a Catholic and would not take the oath of allegiance. What was to be done? If he were refused a place on the benches it might create the conditions for a rebellion and even civil war in Ireland. If he did take his place it might prompt a similar situation in England, where the king clung – like a limpet or, perhaps, like a drowning man – to the Coronation Oath. It would need a palace revolution to move him. When you mix in the hive of zealous reformers, and the ever tempestuous Protestant mob roaming the streets of London, the dilemma was all too clear. There could be no general election since the Catholics, now following O'Connell's example, would elect a phalanx of Roman Catholic MPs who could not be permitted to take their seats. If the Catholic Association had now proved stronger than the traditional landed interests, what was the point of the Protestant Constitution itself, which growled and pawed the ground but could do nothing?

Wellington and the king talked for hours, the king often in tears of grief and anger. Wellington was now convinced that Catholic emancipation was the only viable and practical course. The king grew more and more agitated until madness threatened him as it had his father. Lady Holland, the Whig hostess, heard from reliable sources that he talked for hours on the dreaded topic 'and worked himself up into a fury whenever the subject was mentioned'. He threatened to retire to Hanover and never return to England. He boasted or pretended that he had fought at Waterloo. Wellington now believed that he had truly gone mad. But Wellington and Peel both knew that the game was up, and that the Irish could no longer be barred from Westminster. Hands were wrung. More tears were shed. Kisses were given and returned, at least on the king's side. Eventually, on 4 March 1829, the king wrote to Wellington:

My dear Friend, as I find the country would be left without an administration, I have decided to yield my opinion to that which is considered by the Cabinet to be for the immediate interests of the country. Under these circumstances you have my consent to proceed as you propose with the measure. God knows what pain it causes me to write these words. GR.

It had to be done. It was done. The king could only be a diminished figure in the administration of the country.

Peel introduced the Catholic Relief Bill in March 1829. Everyone knew it was coming: Peel knew that the Catholic hour was at hand, Wellington knew it too. Perhaps no force on earth could now have stopped it. Daniel O'Connell's erstwhile opponent in County Clare, Vesey Fitzgerald, sounded the alarm. 'I believe their success inevitable – that no power under heaven can arrest its progress. There may be rebellion, you may put to death thousands, you may suppress it, but it will only put off the day of compromise . . .' It passed its third reading by the end of the month and in April passed the Lords by a majority of two. 'Arthur [Wellington] is King of England,' the king complained. 'O'Connell is King of Ireland and I suppose I am Dean of Windsor.' The king seems to have persuaded himself that he had most of the country behind him. Others thought that 'public opinion' would be a force for liberal change but, in reality, it had no steady or certain voice.

On 13 April the bill received the royal assent, and Catholic Emancipation became law. The members of that once proscribed religion could now hold any public office in the United Kingdom with the exception of the Lord Chancellorship of England and the Lord Lieutenancy of Ireland. Not all ran smoothly. The removal of Catholic disabilities would be balanced by a sharp rise in the Irish county franchise of minor landholders; the threshold was raised from a 40 shilling to a £10 freehold. Two hundred thousand electors lost their right to vote. The Catholic Association, once the cradle of Daniel O'Connell, was no more. But no Jesuits were allowed to instruct novices, in the hope that the black brigade would wither away.

It could be argued, however, that after 300 years the Anglican ascendancy had now come to an end. With the role of the sacred steadily being marginalized, the clergy of the Church of England took the role of the occupational professionals, imbibing the secular habits and manners of lawyers and others. The number of graduate clerics increased, and Church authority was transferred to a Privy Council Judicial Committee.

In the process the Tory party, the original anti-Catholic combination, had been reduced, with 173 members of the Commons and one hundred of the Lords fighting to the last stage. There was more to come. The door of change had been opened, and through it could be glimpsed the vista of electoral reform and the repeal of the Corn Laws. Peel and Wellington were widely regarded as traitors to their cause. The dowager duchess of Richmond, believing that Wellington had 'ratted' on the Protestant cause, filled her drawing room with stuffed rats bearing the names of the ministers of the crown. But Wellington was more blasé; he did not care about the Catholics 'one pin' as long as they were gentlemen. Stirred as if by a trumpet, six Catholic peers entered the House of Lords for the first time. But it was not a question of party, Whig or Tory; they added their voices to the mixed response of various individuals to various matters of public concern. Charles Greville, the political diarist, remarked that 'if Government have no opponents, they can have no great body of supporters on whom they can depend'. It was said, just to complicate matters, that the Wellington administration was 'a Tory government with Whig opinions'.

This indeterminacy of opinion was one of the reasons why Robert Peel was able to push through so many legislative acts as home secretary. In 1829 he engineered his Metropolitan Police Improvement Bill, which at another time would have been highly controversial. Three hundred and fifty men had once been expected to supervise a city of more than a million people. 'Think of the state of Brentford and Deptford, with no sort of police at night!' Peel told Wellington. 'I really think I need trouble you with no further proof of the necessity of putting an end to such a state of things.' So he organized a highly efficient force of 2,000 men, arranged in a number of divisions, under the supervision of two magistrates or 'police commissioners'. By the autumn of 1829 the 'Peelers' or 'bobbies', named after their creator, were on their beat with iron-framed top hats and truncheons. They were not necessarily popular, suspected of spying on the poorer sort in order to defend the property of the rich. When a man was accused of murdering a policeman in a riot, he was acquitted by the jury with a verdict of 'justifiable homicide'. There had been so much furore and frenzy in the year that Peel took the opportunity of sketching the outline of a quite new society.

The idea of a police force was met with horror as an assault upon individual liberty. Could not a sword or a pistol do the job? The hue and cry, as well as the ever vigilant mob, were always available in an unhappy incident. That was surely enough? 'What! Is this England?' Cobbett asked of the new police. 'Is this the land of *manly hearts*? Is this the country that laughed at the French for their submissions?' Yet all the authoritarian agencies of the day, whether they were utilitarians or Evangelicals, were not to be stopped. Too much unrest in the country provoked the need for further security.

The problems of the Catholics were eclipsed by the crisis of corn. All the people – tradesmen, manufacturers, farmers, labourers – were still enduring the hard conditions and 'distressful times' first manifest in 1826. The member of parliament for Kent stated that all the farmers in his county were insolvent. The silk weavers of Somerset were obliged to live on half a crown a week, hardly enough for salt and potatoes. In March riots erupted in London and were matched in Manchester, Ashton-under-Lyne and elsewhere. The Riot Act was read in Stockport. It was a matter for Peel to decide at what point the studied neutrality of the government should degenerate into armed intervention. In 1830 the Manchester Political Union and the Metropolitan Political Union were established to promote social and political reform. Strikes, reform meetings and political activism by various trades also maintained their pressure for the next two years. At the close of the year, Thomas Attwood established the Birmingham Political Union and held what was the largest-ever indoor meeting. It was no wonder that the propertied classes were beginning to feel in a state of siege.

6

False hope

By 1830 the strikes had reached a climax, many of them directed against the 'knobsticks' or scabs who insisted on working. One union newspaper, the *Union Pilot and Co-operative Intelligencer*, proclaimed in the spring of that year that 'the improvements of machinery will soon enable them *to do without you*'. A plethora of unions grew up – the Grand National Union, the Potters' Union, the Grand National Consolidated and the Operative Builders' Union. 'The history of these Unions', Friedrich Engels wrote, 'is a long series of defeats of the working men interrupted by a few victories.' By which he meant that the laws of economics, or perhaps the laws of capitalism, were irrefragable.

Spectators of the struggle for Catholic liberation noticed one or two matters that pertained to coming disorder. They observed that just two or three cabinet ministers could persuade or cajole the monarch to agree to proposals which he profoundly deplored. They observed that the same two or three members of the cabinet, if powerful enough, could sway the Commons and the Lords with arguments as well as threats and bribes. They observed also that the country as a whole did not particularly care about the constitutional measures which so exercised their leaders. Perhaps the giants and bugbears of conventional political discourse did not exist after all. The people may have been frightened of their own shadows.

Not a dog barked when the Catholics and Dissenters were granted their civil liberties. The country was not the one that nursed the anti-Catholic Gordon riots fifty years before.

It has been suggested that the 'middle classes' were too concerned with their social and financial well-being to care much for the religious controversies of the period. Catholics and Dissenters, after all, could both aspire to being gentlemen. An anonymous article appeared in the *Quarterly Review* of January 1830, and gave a name to the rise of the middle classes. It confirmed that they were:

> decidedly and conscientiously attached to what is called the Tory, and which might with more propriety be called the Conservative party; a party which we believe to compose by far the largest, wealthiest, and most intelligent and respectable portion of the proportion of this country and without whose support any administration that can be formed will be found deficient both in character and stability.

The word 'Conservative' was swiftly taken up. By the singular mysteries of numerology or chronology it was in this same year that the Whigs, once fissiparous, began to congregate together and to form a coherent platform of party policies.

The rural poor were less fortunate. The only reform they wanted (apart from the rapid extermination of farmers and landowners) was the number of coins in their patched and worn trousers. They came to a large extent from the stock of unemployed agricultural labourers who had haunted the English countryside since the end of the Napoleonic War. Many of the others were factory workers thrown out of employment by the gyrations of the manufacturing system. By 1830, just as the rudimentary workers' associations were taking shape, so the agricultural labourers organized themselves into the fictional body of 'Captain Swing', the name they used to sign their letters. In the summer of the year the threshing machines of East Kent were attacked; by October one hundred had been destroyed, together with the paraphernalia of rural tyranny epitomized by the tithe barns and the old workhouses. The rick-burners had fire in their hands. They were protesting against tithes and enclosures, game laws and poor laws, and all the other constituents of rural misery and impoverishment. More than a thousand violent incidents occurred within a year.

The Swing Riots were not a national or coordinated movement; they emerged from a hundred local grievances which all found their centre in the need for basic subsistence. Francis Jeffrey, a Scottish advocate and editor, wrote: 'The real battle is not between Whigs and Tories, Liberals and illiberals, and such gentleman-like denominations, but between property and no-property, between Swing and the law.' Another Whig notable, Earl Grey, wrote in February 1830: 'all respect for station and authority entirely lost – the character of all public men held up to derision . . .'

King George IV himself was now in a parlous condition, 'scratching himself to pieces'. His reaction to Catholic emancipation, his hysterical antics, his copious tears, his prostrations, his temper and his shameless mimicking of his closest ministers did not endear him to Wellington and his cabinet colleagues. His last days were marked by volatile moods, sometimes lethargic and sometimes voluble, sustained by laudanum, cherry brandy and other cordials. This was the moment when the king began his slow but inexorable journey to the grave with the unspoken wish of his people that it might be concluded sooner rather than later. 'My boy, this is death!' he announced to a courtier, as if he had been expecting a long-awaited visitor. And so it was. Nobody mourned him. No one cared.

His successor was William IV, the 'Sailor King' of manifestly good intention but awkward manners. 'Look at that idiot,' George IV used to say of him. 'They will remember me, if he is ever in my place.' But of course they did not. The new king's head was shaped rather like a pineapple, but there was a great deal of pith inside. He was called 'the Sailor King' because he had been for a while Lord High Admiral, and there were intimations that he was something of a Whig. 'There is a strong impression abroad', Charles Greville wrote in his notable diary, 'that the King is cracked, and I dare say there is some truth in it. He gets so very cholerick and is so indecent in his wrath.' This had been said of almost every sovereign since the first William, and might be said to be an occupational hazard.

Yet the fourth William had a benign, and almost raffish, demeanour. He was described by one contemporary as 'a little, old, red-nosed, weather-beaten, jolly-looking person, with an ungraceful air and carriage'. He walked down the street alone, and attracted large crowds. When he rode out on his horse he often offered Londoners 'lifts'. Melbourne remarked that 'he hasn't the feelings of a gentleman; he knows what they are, but he hasn't them'.

The death of the king rendered an election necessary, but the only question seemed to be whether William would favour Wellington and his Conservatives or turn his attention to Earl Grey and the Whigs. The campaign was begun on 23 July but was interrupted and enlivened by news of another Paris revolution. It is a matter of conjecture how many Englishmen were aware of events across the Channel, but there was no doubt some connection with the fervours of 'Captain Swing' and the events of July in Paris when the regime of Charles X gave way to the constitutional monarchy of Louis Philippe. The bourgeoisie threw out the aristocrats with little bloodshed, but many in England trembled for their own country's constitutional balance.

In the event, the election of 1830 settled nothing, but it brought forward all those issues of agricultural reform and electoral change that had dominated the last ministry. The Swing Riots had been enough to cause something close to panic among the landowning class. They wanted peace at almost any price, and the demand for political reform became ever more pressing.

Yet the Tories were in no position to guarantee it. They were already in an advanced state of decay, having been breaking up for some years over such measures as the Corn Laws and Catholic Emancipation. There were ultra-Tories, liberal Tories and Tory Tories with any number of splits and sects. This is of course characteristic of all political parties, but excessive good fortune or excessive misfortune can emphasize schisms and increase divisions. In a debate after the beginning of the new parliament, Earl Grey made a speech in which he urged the necessity of 'reforming Parliament'. The duke of Wellington rose to reply and, in a speech which totally misread the mood of the country, he remarked that he had no intention of introducing reform and that 'I will at once declare that . . . as long as I hold any station in the government of the country, I shall always feel it my duty to resist such measures when proposed by others.' His speech was greeted with some protest.

When the duke sat down he asked a colleague what was going on. 'I have not said too much, have I?' 'You'll hear of it,' Lord Aberdeen replied.

The stocks fell on the following morning, and by the evening one member after another rose to remonstrate with Wellington. The Dictator had disowned Reform. It was as simple as that. It was soon feared that the 'radicals' – whoever they might be in the present circumstances – were bent on creating discord in the streets of London. The fear of instability mounted with rumours of a civil rebellion to topple the administration and monarchy in the recent French manner. Placards were circulated. 'To arms! To arms! Liberty or death!' The authors might be accused of plagiarism as well as insurrection. But the populace had more common sense than the incendiaries, and the crowds on the streets of the city remained in good humour. The day ended without a rifle shot. A few half-hearted attempts at riot in Buckinghamshire, Hampshire, Wiltshire and Berkshire were quickly dissipated by the lords lieutenant of the various counties.

The duke of Wellington reflected on the period some years later. 'I induced', he wrote, 'the magistrates to put themselves on horse-back, each at the head of his own servants and retainers, grooms, huntsmen, game-keepers, armed with horse-whips, pistols, fowling pieces, and what they could get, and to attack in concert, if necessary, or singly, these mobs, disperse them, destroy them, and take and put in confinement those who could not escape.' The defence of the realm was conducted still in almost medieval fashion.

But for Wellington the blunder of his speech proved his downfall. It was compounded by what seemed an act of cowardice. The king was supposed to attend a city banquet on Lord Mayor's Day. The administration refused to allow it. They were not afraid of an attempt upon the king but upon the duke. The Commons was in a familiar state of uproar at the pusillanimity of the cabinet. The presence of the new police also provoked hostility as a French-inspired innovation against personal liberty. Wellington could no longer command the majority in his own party, let alone in the Commons. After a vote against his ministry he tendered his resignation to the new king, and William IV called for Earl Grey to lead a new Whig administration. The Wellington ministry itself had lasted for approximately three years, full of misery and misunderstanding, and now it fell unregretted. So the duke was succeeded by an earl, a confirmed Whig who is now better known as a tea than a man. Grey was an imperturbably aristocratic figure with an elevated forehead suitable for lofty thoughts. He loved 'the people' in the abstract but, as was said, he loved them at a distance. His perorations in parliament were as measured and stately as his demeanour. He had the look and manner of an elder statesman almost as soon as he joined parliament at the age of twenty-three.

Grey's Whig cabinet was the most aristocratic gathering since the eighteenth century. Only three commoners found a place in a company of thirteen. Lord Palmerston, as an Irish peer, also sat in the House of Commons, but he can hardly be described as a commoner. Democracy was not even an issue. Yet every second thought was of reform. Grey was 'deeply dejected' at the prospect of becoming first minister, according to a colleague, and was complaining constantly. Not the least of his problems was the dilemma set by reform. He had often in the past signalled his favourable interests in the subject, but he could hardly be described as a democrat. His purpose was to maintain the aristocracy and buttress its power with remedial measures. He believed that proper reform would 'find real capacity in the high Aristocracy . . . I admit that I should select the aristocrat, for that class is a guarantee for the safety of the state and the throne.' He was restoring the old identity of the Whigs as aristocrats who directed and supervised the cause of reform. Disraeli later, and quite justifiably, described the orthodox Whig as 'a democratic aristocrat', even if it was a term which he professed not to understand. The cabinet itself was a broad coalition of conflicting interests. One Tory, the duke of Richmond, was a member. The new ministers replaced a Tory party that had been pre-eminent for the larger part of sixty years. There used to be a saying that everybody loves a lord.

A committee was established to consider reform as the burning question of the day. It was believed by Grey and his colleagues that it was necessary to effect 'such a permanent settlement of this great and important question, as will no longer render its agitation subservient to the designs of the factious and discontented – but by its wise and comprehensive provisions inspire all classes of the community with a conviction that their rights and privileges are at length duly secured and consolidated . . .' There was no appeal to the people. There was no talk of liberty and equality, let alone of fraternity. These were not matters that concerned the members of the committee. Their overriding ambition was to preserve the unity and harmony of the country, and in particular to preserve the property rights of the landed gentry. The key word was 'finality', which could only mean that the Whigs retained power indefinitely. By also including the more respectable freeholders in its provisions, the committee hoped to bring forward some conciliation between the landowners and the middle class so that both might reign unimpeded in their own domain. In January 1831 Grey wrote to a colleague: 'I am going tomorrow to Brighton to propose our plea of reform. It is a strong and effectual measure. If the King agrees to it, I think we shall be supported by public opinion. If he does not – what is to come next?' His fears seemed to be illusory. The king approved of the reform project in all its details.

Or so he said. He did not wish to defy or contradict his new first minister. He had some sense of what was known as 'the spirit of the times'. Even as the social and economic condition of the country had changed significantly, the political system had remained immobile. Descriptions of it included paralysis and putrescence. Cornwall returned forty-four members while Leeds, Birmingham and Manchester returned none. In the borough of Old Sarum two members were elected by seven voters, but in fact the votes were attached to empty fields, as the landowner controlled the franchise. The list of absurdities was immense. The reformers had every justification on their side except the crucial one. Whatever the oddities and failures of the system, it worked. It maintained what the king described to Palmerston, now the new foreign secretary, as the 'tranquillity of States and the Peace and Prosperity of the country'. The consequences of change might be frightful. The great figures of former parliaments would no longer be introduced into the system but would be replaced by ranks and ranks of mediocrities controlled by the electors. The landed interest would be subdued by a new urban or mercantile class with no traditional ties to the country. This would be only the beginning of a national transformation; England would become London, ruled by mobs and demonstrations.

The debate on the Reform Bill, therefore, took place in a state of great excitement. On the night of 1 March 1831, the leader of the House of Commons, Lord John Russell, began to read out the details of his proposal. Many of those present had anticipated that some twenty or thirty constituencies would be dissolved or changed. Russell, however, had determined that fifty-six 'rotten boroughs', each with two members, should be abolished. Thirty other constituencies were to lose one of their members, while 143 seats were to be transferred to the counties and the new towns. The uproar was immense, wholly commensurate with the most radical change in the electoral system yet attempted. A total of 102 seats, at the very least, would no longer exist. Others, yet to be determined, would take their place.

The Tories erupted into hysterical laughter at the enormity of the plan. It just did not seem possible. 'Such a scene as the division of last Tuesday I never saw, and never expect to see again . . . It was like seeing', Lord Macaulay wrote to an acquaintance, 'Caesar stabbed in the Senate House, or seeing Oliver take the mace from the table.' He explained how the Commons waited in intense excitement for the final tally of votes as 'Charles Wood, who stood near the door, jumped upon a bench and cried out "They are only three hundred and one." We set up a shout that you might have heard to Charing Cross, waving our hats, stamping against the floor, and clapping our hands.' He described the demeanour of those who had opposed Reform. 'And the jaw of Peel fell; and the face of Twiss was as the face of a damned soul; and Herries looked like Judas taking his necktie off for the last operation.' The news soon passed from club to club in Westminster and beyond, where the calls went around of 'We've beat 'em' and 'The game's up' and 'They're done for'.

The bill had passed by one vote, however, which was the next-worst thing to defeat. Grey was now determined to dissolve parliament, no doubt in expectation of a larger majority in favour of Reform. But the opposition was determined to avoid what was considered to be an unhappy fate and spoke eloquently against any move to dissolve. The king considered this to be a design against his prerogative, and he rode down to Westminster with the fixed decision to dissolve. It was done.

The subsequent election of 1831 was known as the 'Dry Election', since for the first time the voters did not need to be bribed to cast their vote. Dickens's account of the Eatanswill election in *The Pickwick Papers* (set in 1827 but published in 1836) was a poignant reminder of the bribery and drunkenness that habitually took place. The men were kept continually drunk and locked in the public house until it was time to vote. Grey dissolved parliament and precipitated a general election with a popular cry of 'The Bill, the whole Bill, and nothing but the Bill'. It was irresistible to all those except the constitutionally timid. It was, perhaps, the closest event to a referendum that England had ever known. London itself was decked with 'illuminations' for the event, a euphemism for mayhem and blackmail on the streets. Those who did not put a lighted candle in a prominent position had their windows smashed. You could follow the trail of the mob by the litter of broken glass.

A meeting of the National Reform Association in the Crown Tavern on Museum Street declared that 'the evils inseparable from misgovernment, having at length pressed upon the people with a severity too great to be any longer quiescently endured, their first efforts have been directed to put an end to a system, the workings of which have entailed upon them such accumulated ills . . .' The duke of Wellington believed the revolution had begun and saw nothing ahead but civil war and bloodshed. This had by now become a truism, with about as much reality as a bad dream. But it persisted. In the event the ministry of Earl Grey was returned with a much increased majority of 136. The Whigs themselves were surprised by the extent of support for Reform, and were even alarmed by the depth of popular feeling which they had aroused.

The debate on the second Reform Bill began in the summer, as the Thames continued its slow and noisome passage through the vicinity of Westminster. It seemed that at the time of heat everything was in decay. Everything stank of corruption. The second Reform Bill was passed in June 1831 and was carried with a majority of 136. Determined efforts to stall it were successful as proponents of the bill began to suffer from the burden of argument and division. Russell's strength began to fail, and he was forced to relinquish his position to Viscount Althorp, whose natural robustness also gave way under the strain. It did not reach the Lords until September. At the beginning of October it was rejected by the peers with a majority of forty-one. Then came the reckoning. The *Chronicle* and the *Sun* appeared in mourning black, but the *Chronicle* announced that 'the triumph of the wicked does not last for ever'. Parts of Nottingham Castle were burned down, and a meeting in Birmingham of 150,000 people pledged that no taxes would be paid until Reform was introduced. Francis Place, the radical reformer, made a speech in which he declared that 'no reality we can create will be sufficient for our purposes. We must work on Earl Grey's imagination. We must pretend to be frightened ourselves.'

Widespread violence followed in Bristol and for the first time since the seventeenth century some country houses were fortified with cannon. The magistrates warned that no rioter or demonstrator could be killed for fear of a conviction for murder. No one wanted to be responsible for another Peterloo. The bishops were hooted in the street, and were afraid to go about their diocesan business. Cobbett reported that 'every man you met seemed to be convulsed with rage . . . a cry for a republic seemed pretty nearly general'. Thomas Attwood's 'Political Union' in Birmingham was followed by similar societies, to the extent than an amalgamated National Political Union was established in London with the purpose of extending the suffrage to the lower middle classes and the working people. This was considered to be a threat to law and order, and the authorities attempted, largely in vain, to forestall their effect.

Disruption in the body politic was compounded by physical disease. In the autumn of 1831 cholera began to work its way through the city. John Hogg, a physician, described how 'the disease generally began by relaxation of the bowels without pain, the evacuations being colourless'. This was followed by spasmodic pains in the bowels and diarrhoea; the condition of the invalid rapidly worsened with 'excessive torture and prostration of strength'. Death was heralded when the body turned blue or livid, and the vital powers failed with 'occasional evacuation of a chocolate-like fluid'. Fortunately death came within thirty-six hours. The epidemic increased in intensity. A placard was posted in Lambeth in the summer of 1832 asking:

has DEATH (in a rage) been invited by the Commissioners of Common Sewers to take up his abode in Lambeth . . . In this pest-house of the metropolis, and disgrace to the nation, the main thoroughfares are still without common sewers . . . unless something be speedily done to allay the growing discontent of the people, retributive justice in her salutary vengeance will commence her operations with the lamp-iron and the halter.

In the midst of death and disease, the political fire still burned. Despite the incendiary language, one comfort was available to the administration; people who are sick, or demoralized, do not start a revolution. Instead the victims often decided to take what was known as 'the cold water cure' by jumping off Waterloo Bridge.

The first and second Reform bills had fallen on the hurdle of the Lords, but a third attempt was made at the end of 1831 and the beginning of the following year. The Lords, fearful of social disorder and of threats to their privileges, passed it on 14 April 1832. Yet, astonishingly enough, three weeks later they passed a hostile amendment and the bill was lost once again. It was not wise to play the game of hazard with the populace. The duke of Wellington was once more asked to form a government with the express intention of introducing more moderate Reform. The country was now against him, with the promise of a run against the Bank of England with the slogan 'to stop the Duke, go for gold'. But he had already stopped. In these unprecedented circumstances he could not form a government.

The king sweated in his chamber. No possible combination or contortion including Wellington would ever work. The only possible remedy was to pack the Lords with so many compliant peers that Reform would be passed. The king wept and struggled, wept and prayed, but he knew that the end had come. So he wrote a note. 'His Majesty authorises Earl Grey, if any obstacle should rise during the further progress of the Bill, to submit to him a creation of Peers to such extent as shall be necessary to enable him to carry the Bill.' It was enough. The threat was sufficient. The existing peers were more concerned with their status than with the voting rights of their inferiors. Most of them now prepared to absent themselves from the Reform vote and thus avoid the creation of new peers. How many might there be? Forty? Fifty? It was unthinkable. It could not happen. On 4 June 1832, the Reform Bill passed its third reading.

It was once believed that the new situation injected a popular vitality into the electoral process, and that the middle class had been able to surmount the interests of the upper classes. The evidence suggests otherwise. The old firm was still in place. All previous forms of corruption were still practised, although perhaps not so blatantly. 'Pocket boroughs', controlled by one grandee or family, were still to be found. Sudbury and St Albans were still open to the highest bidder. Peers and landowners continued to exercise unusual and unmerited electoral influence. Gang warfare between the parties was taken for granted. Without the secret ballot that was introduced later in the century, the constituents could be 'worked' and bribed by any number of means.

There was no sea-change in the voting system, with an extra 217,000 voters to add to the existing 435,000. There was a slow decline in the number of sons of peers and baronets in the Commons, but the landed interest lost only one hundred representatives in the course of thirty-five years. Some radicals were elected in the first reformed parliament, but only a sprinkling among the usual array of vested interests. John Stuart Mill wrote to a friend in 1833 that 'our Gironde is a rope of sand . . . there are no leaders, and without leaders there can never be organisation. There is no man or men of commanding talent among the radicals.' The Gironde had been a group of twelve French Republicans. But this was no revolution. In *Considerations on Representative Government* (1861) Mill concluded that it did nothing to change the nature of representation or to make room for any minorities within the general population. It was in effect a plausibly efficient way of maintaining the existing social system while gratifying the pretensions of some urban dwellers and radical enthusiasts. The proposals had nothing to do with manhood suffrage or annual parliaments, which had once been the indispensable demands of the radicals. Grey presented it as a reassertion of ancient, which is to say invented, rights. The crown, the landed interest, the middle classes and the people were meant to fit together like a political Rubik's cube.

Nevertheless, it was accepted by some for want of anything better and by others in expectation of further innovation. It transpired that the landed interest could join now with the upper middle class and the more prosperous urban interests. It dismayed the Tories, perhaps, but it was well suited to the Whigs who could envisage a vast combination of interests to keep them in power. Reform had nothing to say, however, to the working class or to the lower middle class. They stayed where they were. If they were not £10 householders (occupying but not necessarily owning a house with a rental value of £10 a year) they were disqualified from voting. The proletariat, to use an anachronistic word, was not part of the system. Reform had nothing to do with democracy. Democracy was as incomprehensible as it was undesirable. The principal motive of Reform was expediency rather than principle; it abolished certain abuses, but other anomalies and inconsistencies were left in place. The aristocrats may have suffered a little (although even this is doubtful) but the radicals and reformers really gained very little. What Grey wished for was a crumb to the hungry, and the quelling of the possibility of insurrection. He foresaw, or said he foresaw, no need for any further improvements.

Yet this bill might act as a spur to greater change. John Bright, a leading radical, said that 'it was not a good Bill, but it was a great Bill when it passed'. The fact that it was passed at all, in other words, was a measure of its greatness. No such measure had been introduced or accepted in any other English parliament, and it wholly discounted Edmund Burke's theory that the electoral system could only be altered by organic and instinctive means. There was nothing organic or instinctive about the Reform Bill of 1832. It was devised by men with a mission to preserve their caste and to consolidate the stability of the state.

Other aspects of governance were revealed in the process. It had become clear that in any confrontation between the people and the Lords, the Lords must yield. The affluent middle class had played a part, too, which in itself marked an important change in the administration of England. Grey himself was entitled to feel some elation at his eventual triumph; if it had come to the making of peers, the king would have been forced to comply with a measure he profoundly detested. There was no contest.

One MP, Alexander Baring, warned that 'in a reformed parliament, when the day of battle came, the country squires would not be able to stand against the active, pushing, intelligent people who would be sent from the manufacturing districts'. And could it be said that he was entirely wrong? There was indeed some apprehension about the proceedings of the first Reformed parliament in English history, with the fear that it might prove to be ungovernable. One cabinet minister prophesied that if the government 'lose the control in the first session over the reformed House, the Meteor will be hurried into space, and Chaos is at Hand'. By the end of 1833 Grey's son was describing the ministry as 'utterly without unity of purpose and the sport of every wind that blows'. It was supposed that nobody could govern successfully or effectively. When the duke of Wellington had been asked what he thought of the new reformed parliament he replied: 'I have never seen so many bad hats in my life.'

Yet the real effects of the Reform Bill were more significant than sartorial matters. The middle-class interest, now estimated to be approximately 20 per cent of the population, had grown in responsibility and influence; petitions were now flooding into the royal closet on matters concerning the slave trade and the corn trade. The power of the political unions and the labour combinations gave material advantage to the proponents of factory reform and trade union reform. The importance of political parties themselves was greatly enhanced by the influx of newly enfranchised voters and, from the 1830s, central party organizations and partisan clubs became part of the landscape of politics.

The redistribution of the 'pocket boroughs', and the subsequent dearth of independent members, therefore meant that party ties had grown stronger and more obvious. The two parties were left in charge of the field. As a result, reform had become the keyword of the political vocabulary. The Whigs wanted reform to preserve aristocratic privileges by making concessions to the middle classes. The Tories wanted reform to protect the poor in the old paternalist fashion with, for example, the concept of 'just price'; the Tories attacked the new Poor Law, also, as an affront to the traditional authority of the landed gentry.

What infuriated many observers was that everything had

changed and nothing had changed. That in fact seems to be the nature of English life. It was a revolution which had not changed the nature of governance. William Cobbett, as so often, put it most memorably. 'Those happy days of political humbug are gone forever. The gentlemen opposite are opposite only as to mere local position. They sit on the opposite side of the house: that's all. In every other respect they are like the parson and the clerk; or perhaps rather more like rooks and jackdaws; one caw and the other chatter, but both have the same object in view: both are in pursuit of the same sort of diet.' One outsider clambering to get in, Benjamin Disraeli, asked in 1835: 'What do they [the radicals] mean by their favourite phrase, THE PEOPLE'S HOUSE . . . ? . . . these Commons form a class in the State, privileged, irresponsible. And hereditary, like the Peers.'

The Lords had submitted but no lasting power had yet been secured over them. The Commons had won its victory, but it was still not supreme within the commonwealth. Many unanswered questions hovered over the relative status of the king and parliament. Whenever you came close to any question, however, you found muddle, ambiguity, inconsistency, deviousness and false hope.

7

The inspector

The Reform parliament, as it became known, was dissolved on 3 December 1832. In the ensuing election Grey achieved a large majority over his opponents in the new parliament which assembled on 29 January 1833. The Whigs were crowned with the laurels of Reform and comprised 441 members compared to 175 Tories under the leadership of Wellington and Peel. Peel was generally considered to be 'the coming man'.

The new administration under Grey included some radicals heartened by the support for Reform. Three measures were crucial to their new stance as reformers opposed to the implacable Tories: the Factory Act of 1833, the Act for the abolition of slavery throughout the empire of 1833, and the New Poor Law of 1834, were the principal fruits of their activity. Their ambitions had a Benthamite cast, since Bentham and Bentham's laws were congenial to younger and more liberal Whigs.

The Factory Act had its origin fourteen years earlier when Robert Peel had suggested a ten-year-old limit and a ten-hour day for the infants who worked in the cotton factories. He was following in the steps of his father, a rich textile manufacturer intent upon improving the conditions of his employees. The proposals disappeared into the hot air of the Commons, from which they emerged weak and practically unenforceable. However, they were revived by the troubled conditions of 1830 when Richard Oastler, a reformer, described in a letter to the *Leeds Mercury* the conditions of 'thousands of our fellow-creatures and fellow-subjects, both male and female, the miserable inhabitants of a Yorkshire town, Parliament are this very moment existing in a state of slavery, more horrid than are the victims of that hellish system "colonial" slavery'. The county of Yorkshire was now represented in parliament by the giant of anti-slavery principles, Henry Brougham, who had been fighting the system for almost twenty years.

Oastler's description caused a great stir. But the 'factory system' was still only imperfectly understood, and one commentator noted in 1842 that 'the factory system is a modern creation; history throws no light on its nature, for it has scarcely begun to recognise its existence . . . an innovating power of such immense force could never have been anticipated'. If the characters of Rabelais – Gargantua and Pantagruel – had suddenly come into existence they could not have caused more consternation than the new dispensation of affairs. Everything seemed too large, too complex, too diverse, to comprehend. To think on a national scale about armies and defences was not a new thing but to take a perspective on sanitation, education, housing and work had never before been attempted.

At the end of 1831 John Cam Hobhouse introduced a Ten Hours Bill to limit the employment of factory children, as a result of which a committee was established to investigate the conditions of what were already called 'the white slaves'. An act came into force on 1 March 1834, which forbade the employment of children under nine, maintained a forty-eight-hour week for children between the ages of nine and thirteen, and a daily maximum of twelve hours for those between thirteen and eighteen years. It was widely flouted or ignored, and many complained that such government measures were in deliberate opposition to the principles of free trade and fidelity to contract. Yet a stand had been made. For the first time the administration took responsibility for the plight of children under eighteen. It was the first hesitant and flawed step towards a national system of education, although no one could have anticipated such an outcome.

As a result of the new legislation, independent inspectors of the cotton factories were introduced to ensure that government legislation was obeyed; it was part of the increase in bureaucratic control that led to inspectors of prisons, of housing, of building regulations, of paving and of street lighting. By the 1840s it was generally agreed that local issues should be governed by a central authority with its own bands of supervisors. The role of inspectors in every public service – sanitation and education among them – was one of the most significant aspects of the Victorian social system which was slowly transformed from the promptings of private initiative to the structures of state intervention. The 'Society For This' and the 'Society For That' gave way to the blue book and the Home Office.

One recent study of the influence of Evangelical belief on social and political matters in the first half of the nineteenth century has been Boyd Hilton's *The Age of Atonement*, its title an apt indication of the prevailing mood among the Christian devotees who, like all citizens of a newly revised world, looked back with horror and outrage at those who came before them.

The children of the mines provoked shame, if nothing else, in the middle-class households of the country. The death of children became one of the central motifs of the age. 'Is Little Nell dead?' asked those who had waited for the ship bearing *The Old Curiosity Shop* to the port of New York in 1841. The son of the assassinated prime minister, Spencer Perceval, touched upon the raw sensibility of the age when he stood up in the Commons and declared: 'I stand here to warn you of the righteous judgment of God, which is coming on you, and which is now near at hand.' Colleagues tried to drag him down to his seat and *Hansard* reported that 'indescribable confusion prevailed'. It was in this atmosphere that the act for the abolition of slavery passed in the summer of 1833.

It had been the favoured reform of Evangelicals, and particularly of those reformers who came to be known as the Clapham Sect. Twenty-six years before, the slave trade had been abolished, and now slavery itself was banned within the bounds of empire. The original request had come from the Society of Friends, and their missionary or propagandizing qualities animated the political, humanitarian and philanthropic movements of the age. There was another factor. The slave trade had been conducted along the ocean and coastal routes, but England's maritime supremacy was supposed to carry with it the force of law. All slaves under the age of six were to be freed unconditionally, therefore, while those above that age were to become apprentices with limited hours of labour and guaranteed wages. How quickly and completely these conditions were met on the other side of the world is another matter, but the slave owners were given £20 million in compensation.

Yet the free men of England themselves were not necessarily at liberty, bound by the iron shackles of poverty as tightly as any regimen of slaves. By 1830 one-fifth of the nation's revenues were devoted to poor relief, against a scene of rick-burning, lawless wandering and the breaking of machines. With the dissolution of the old society, in which poverty was part of the hierarchical order of things, comfortable notions of the necessity of the labouring poor, and the holiness of poverty, were quite out of date. In 1832 the Royal Commission on the Poor Laws had completed its work and had come to the conclusion that no previous scheme of poor relief served its purpose.

So a new system of poor relief was introduced at this time, with the purpose of distinguishing between those who would not work and those who could not work. The old Poor Law was maintained by the people of the local parish, who best knew the circumstances of those who claimed relief; it had been operating since the beginning of the seventeenth century but was now regarded by the new breed of bureaucrats as outmoded and outworn. The New Poor Law was proposed in 1834 as a model of organization and efficiency. It was the Benthamite way. The old parishes were grouped into 'unions' which, under the supervision of three Poor Law commissioners in Whitehall, controlled the novel institution of 'workhouses' as instruments of containment and control. The new policy of central determination and local administration became the key contribution of the nineteenth century to social policy.

The Whitehall commissioners became known as 'the three bashaws [pashas] of Somerset House', 'the Three-Headed Devil King' or 'The Three'. The instruments of their power were the local boards of guardians who ensured that only the sick or the properly indigent were permitted to enter the workhouse. Outdoor relief to able-bodied men was prohibited. Poverty was not enough; after all, the adult male could work himself out of poverty. Workhouses themselves were so constituted as to repel any but those in dire need; families were split up, the necessities of life were severely rationed and the inmates were obliged to take up repetitive, useless and wearisome tasks. One supporter of the system, the Reverend H. H. Milman, wrote that 'the workhouses should be a place of hardship, of coarse fare, of degradation and humility; it should be administered with strictness – with severity; it should be as repulsive as is consistent with humanity'.

The introduction of this harsh regimen does in part explain the origin of Chartism as a mass movement of protest. The workhouses were hated by the people, and particularly by the poor; they were the agents of oppression and were known as 'Bastilles'. To be obliged to enter a workhouse was, in effect, to go into a prison. The workhouse was also the child of the reformed parliament; no previous parliament could have created anything so uniform or so bureaucratic. It needed the Whigs, the reformers, the dogmatists and the Benthamites to bring it to fruition. It should also be remembered that the New Poor Law was proposed and passed by the Whigs rather than the Tories. Many Tories supported it, of course, but there was a band of radical Tories who denounced it as the enemy of the people. The suspicion of such institutions soon ran very deep, and accounts in part for the reluctance of parents to send their children into the new schools, which were often built in the dreary grey stone of the workhouse. Disraeli knew it as the new 'Brutalitarianism'. This image of dour severity and no less harsh sanctimony endured for many decades as an example of what came to be known as 'Victorianism'. It sprang out of high ambition and solid principle but, as soon as the light shone upon it, it became oppressive and disheartening.

In this period Princess Victoria began a number of 'journeys' through England in order to acquaint herself with the country of which she would one day be mistress. In one of the first entries in her diary she wrote that 'we just passed through a town where all coal mines are and you see the fire glimmer at a distance in the engines in many places. The men, women, children, country and houses are all black . . .' Her slight insouciance at the sight of her suffering subjects would be a token of the reign. As a young woman, too, she was possessed of a fierce temper during which she would lash out at those around her. King William was fond of his niece, but had nothing but contempt for the princess's mother, the duchess of Kent, whom he suspected of manipulation and betrayal. Victoria did not have a happy childhood, therefore, alternately bullied and overprotected. She grew up in a glasshouse, while those around her were more interested in benefits for themselves than advantage for the girl. But she had a shrewd eye for insubordination. Even when small she was every inch a queen and preferred companions who played an obeisant role. 'I may call you Jane,' she told one childhood acquaintance, 'but you must not call me Victoria.' She may have been a prisoner in all but name, but she was a spoiled prisoner; all her life she remained headstrong, capricious and demanding.

She was an exacting correspondent, and it has been calculated that if her letters were placed from end to end they would encompass 700 volumes. This is a Victorian tendency taken to extremes. Fortunately for everyone concerned, the old king died a month after Victoria had come of age, thus avoiding a regency in which the new queen would have had to defer to the duchess of Kent and her advisers.

8

Steam and speed

The first steamboat crossed the Channel in 1816. If the wind was not strong the crossing took between three or four hours. A paddle-steamer soon rode out from Newhaven to Dieppe, while other steamers chugged away in the vicinity of Hamburg and Gothenburg. The first railway route was a ramshackle effort, its rails stretching only a couple of miles to the local colliery, and it is now generally agreed that the railway age really began in 1815. That is when steam rose to a new height. Many people are aware of James Watt's inspiration from a boiling tea kettle, but few have seen the engraving of *Allegory on the Significance of Steam Power*. Watt sits dreaming in a corner while a circle of steam surrounds a vision of factories, chimneys and mills as a foretaste of the new England.

Steam came slowly. An engraving of 1809, *Richard Trevithick's Railway Circus*, shows the inventor and engineer guiding his steam locomotive in a circle in front of a throng of spectators just as if he were parading a tame elephant at a circus. The entertainment was called 'Catch Me Who Can'. But its central significance was missed.

The railway represented, in the phrase of the period, 'the annihilation of time and space'. The landscape itself seems to have changed. It had long since lost its natural woodland but now its heaths, wastes and village commons were in this period 'enclosed' within small patches and areas, partly to make way for the new railway lines. For foreign travellers the English countryside presented a garden-like system of hedges and fences. Yet it was not necessarily picturesque. The northern factory towns, soon to be linked by the railway, were grim enough to compete with the broken-down slums of London where the air was foul and the water poisonous. In some of the rural districts, cottages were still made of mud and road scrapings, while huts of turf still contained the peasant and the pig equally. This is as much part of early nineteenth-century England as the Corn Laws and George IV. The trains would soon run at a speed whereby a blackened city slum might flash past after a colliery and not be distinguished from it.

The building of the railways was the largest human endeavour to take place in so short a time. The Stockton–Darlington Railway, under the supervision of George and Robert Stephenson, was opened in 1825, and the Manchester–Liverpool Line five years later. The Stockton–Darlington's main line from Shildon to Stockton covered 22 miles, the longest for any locomotive. But the line was also used as a public thoroughfare shared with steam goods trains, horse-wagons and a rail stagecoach. The beginnings of any great enterprise are mixed and uncertain. The steam engine was by now well enough known, however, as were the metal rails that carried it on its short journeys. But nobody had any idea what a railway carriage should look like. The first of them were simply carriages designed for roads that were then placed on railway wheels, with a boot for articles and a rack on the roof for luggage. The carriages had a length of about 20 feet, a width of 6 feet and a body height of 6 or 7 feet; they were like *Alice in Wonderland* carriages, had *Alice* then been written.

The explosion had begun. Between the end of 1844 and the beginning of 1849 more than 3,000 miles of track had been laid, as opposed to 172 miles of new roads and streets; in this period the number of train journeys rose from 33 million to 60 million. It is not at all wonderful that the salient aspects of this period were universally attributed to 'SPEED'. The canals were finished, the turnpike was an anachronism and the roads were neglected. The traps, the gigs, the flys, the chariots, the phaetons, the wagonettes, the dog-carts and the Whitechapels were soon things of the past. But what was the point of speed? William Cobbett met a countrywoman who had never in her life gone beyond the boundaries of her parish. He admired her and complained that 'the *facilities* which now exist of *moving human bodies from place to place* are amongst the *curses* of the country, the destroyers of industry, of morals and, of course, of happiness'. Meanwhile the great dock system of London was being given its final shape with the East and West India, London, Commercial and Surrey Docks completed by 1816.

The great novelty of speed was the most surprising aspect of life. One contemporary, W. R. Greg, remarked upon a life 'without leisure and without pause – a life of *haste* . . . we have no time to reflect where we have been and whither we intend to go'. This has no doubt been the complaint of many generations in which change is pre-eminent. When Thomas de Quincey's 'The English Mail Coach' was published, with all its intimations of speed and doom, it had already been overtaken by the rushing train. In the year before that essay's publication, Charles Dickens chronicled the apotheosis of the railway in *Dombey and Son* (1848) as the lines stretched out from London towards the unknown future. The headmaster of Rugby school, Thomas Arnold, stated in 1832 that 'we have been living . . . the life of three hundred years in thirty'. In the early years of the twenty-first century, the idea of change has been incorporated and is part of the human nervous system. In the days of the railway it administered an electric shock. In 1833 Bulwer-Lytton observed that 'every age may be called an age of transition . . . the passing-on, as it were, from one state to another never ceases; but in our age the transition is *visible*'. This was also the year in which the term 'scientist' was coined.

It had become what Carlyle called a 'Mechanical Age' of which the characteristics soon became evident. It encouraged uniformity and anonymity. It encouraged decorum and restraint. It was an age of quickness of action and reaction, quick at meals, quick at work, quick at dressing. Look deep into the Thames and you might see a tunnel already four years in the making, attended by diving bells. Look up and you could see the hydrogen balloons in the sky. Soon there would be no more exhausted horses and drunken post-boys, no more cries of 'All right!' as the coaches left the yards of the inns. Everything was moving forward.

Ralph Waldo Emerson, in *English Traits* (1856), observed that 'mines, forges, mills, breweries, railroads, steam-pump, steam-plough, have operated to give a mechanical regularity to all the habit and action of men'. The steam engine became the metaphor of the age, and there were many discussions on the notional benefits of men operating like machines. Well, that would be progress.

Nevertheless, this was an age when it was not considered either just or fashionable to decry progress, especially when by the end of the 1840s the presence of electricity became known to a large audience. Its significance as an agent of material advance and increased production was quickly understood. The idea of an electrical culture which could be co-opted into an industrial machine culture was infinitely promising. The voltaic pile invented at the beginning of the nineteenth century, and the discovery in 1820 that an electric current created a magnetic field, afforded new means of controlling and changing the natural world. The Victorians were the progenitors of science, the spectators of science, the demonstrators of science and the elucidators of science. Its practitioners were viewed as both shamans and showmen since electricity, in particular, had become the key component of an age which elicited wonder and surprise. In the National Gallery of Practical Science, a flea could be magnified to the size of a very large elephant, and an electrical eel was seen to stun its prey. (The death of the eel attracted much newspaper comment.) Faraday's 'Christmas lectures' were inaugurated in 1825. He was the seer who announced in November 1845 that light, heat and electricity were 'merely modifications of one great universal principle'.

If the world could be viewed as an electrical scheme, then the scientist became its natural interpreter and, perhaps, its exploiter. Nineteenth-century texts are filled with references to energy and power. The fashion for mesmerism, for example, was based upon the belief that the powers of the human body could be conducted and controlled by means of an invisible electrical fluid creating an 'animal magnetism' that bound one person with another; electricity was described by the English physicist James Joule as 'this surprisingly animated elemental fire'.

In this period, theories of heat, light velocity and electricity were intimately related to the dynamic nature of energy. All was of a piece. These theories were in turn connected to the suppositions about power and dominance that governed social and sexual relations. The concept of political and social 'system' would emerge in the 1840s but already discussion centred on 'the dynamics of systems', on 'fields of force' and on 'magnetic centres'. It is appropriate that the specifically English contribution to the science of the period lay primarily in physics and in the analysis of energy; it was a world spinning around electricity, magnetism, electromagnetism and thermodynamics. Specialist research societies, such as the London Electrical Society, emerged with a new breed of professional or specialized scientists. One very rewarding experiment lay in the application of electricity to a recently hanged corpse, where 'every muscle in his countenance was simultaneously thrown into fearful action; rage, horror, despair, anguish and ghastly smiles. At this point several of the spectators were forced to leave the apartment from terror or sickness, and one gentleman fainted.'

This is close to the territory of Mary Shelley's *Frankenstein; or The Modern Prometheus* (1818), in which the human being becomes in part a machine to be galvanized into life. It was one of the emblems of the nineteenth century, based upon the vision of factory workers being as mechanical as the machinery they attended and reduced in status to nothing more than 'galvanized corpses'. Machinery was the agent of control and regulation, of order and of discipline.

In 1836 insects began to appear on a continually electrified stone, eliciting the deduction that electricity had in fact created them. The experimenter, Andrew Crosse, reported that 'on the twenty eighth day these insects moved their legs, and in the course of a few days more detached themselves from the stone and moved over the surface at pleasure, although in general they appeared adverse to motion, more particularly when first born'. This is as ghastly as the account of the revivified corpse, and elicited equivalent responses of horror. The local farmers, believing that the electrical insects had blighted their crops, performed an exorcism in the vicinity. Leaving aside the possibility that the whole exercise was an elaborate hoax, it is assumed that the creatures were cheese mites or dust mites that had contaminated the equipment. The experiment was not replicated.

So if electricity was a living force then perhaps its machines could live? 'No classes of beings', Samuel Butler wrote in *Erewhon* (1872), 'have in any time past made so rapid a forward movement. Should not that moment be jealously watched, and checked while we can still check it? And is it not necessary for this end to destroy the more advanced of the machines which are in use at present, though it is admitted that they are in themselves harmless?' The threat was real. 'The delicacy of the machine's construction' will aid the advance of machine language as intricate as our own 'daily giving them greater skill and supplying more of that self-regulating, self-acting power which will be better than any intellect . . . surely if a machine is able to reproduce another machine systematically, we may say that it has a reproductive system'. And so the argument continued, accurately conveying the concerns of a much later period.

This is best understood in the context of the theology of the nineteenth-century world, the great burning lamp to which all paid their obeisance. The temples of this new deity were the Victorian exhibition halls, among them the Adelaide Gallery in the Lowther Arcade and the Polytechnic Institution in Cavendish Square. Here could be found a steam gun, a ferro-electric globe and an oxyhydrogen microscope. A 70-foot canal had been constructed to demonstrate the abilities of a paddle-driven steamboat. The collection was highly eclectic, including 'weapons taken from the natives of Owhyhee, who were engaged in the murder of Captain Cook'. It suggests that even as late as the 1840s the elements of scientific progress were classified as wonders or marvels rather than the discoveries of men. They had no epistemological status of their own. The objects of the exhibition could also be seen as consumer items, similar to those in the new shopping arcades that were becoming part of the commercial world; the engines and machines that had previously been left for the workshop and the factory were steadily taking their place in a more familiar and acquisitive environment.

By 1830, industrialization had increased with more facility and progress than in any other country. England's exports, too, were greater than elsewhere; the nation was producing 80 per cent of Europe's coal and 50 per cent of Europe's iron. All the steam engines in the world came from England, and in 1832 Nathan Rothschild argued that England was 'the Bank for the whole world. All the transactions in India, in China, in Germany, in the whole world, are guided here and settled in this country.' Yet in a sense the projections are spurious. They represent the account book of London and the nation. They know nothing of its life. Alton Locke, in Charles Kingsley's novel of the same name, recollected London in this flourishing period. 'I am a Cockney among Cockneys . . . my earliest recollections are of a suburban street; of its jumble of little shops and little terraces, each exhibiting some fresh variety of capricious ugliness.' God had made him a Cockney for a purpose, 'that I might learn to feel for the wretches who sit stifled in reeking garrets and workrooms, drinking in disease with every breath, bound in their prison-house of brick and iron, with their own funeral pall hanging over them, in that canopy of fog and poisonous smoke, from their cradle to their grave. I have drunk of the cup of which they drink.' Did anyone ever tell them that their city, without form or colour or life, was the 'Bank for the whole world'?

Even if it was a bank for the world, it was not necessarily a welcome one. The whole purport of British foreign policy, under a succession of ministers, was to remain disentangled from the affairs of Europe as much as shame and danger would allow. In the spring of 1831 Austrian troops advanced into Modena and Parma in order to suppress rebellion and to counter French claims of suzerainty. The consequences were obvious enough, and the general conflagration would turn northern Italy into a battlefield. The war between the two sides lasted for almost two years. Viscount Palmerston, as foreign secretary of the time, made the English policy plain. 'It will be impossible for England to take part with Austria in a war entered into for the purpose of putting down freedom and maintaining despotism; neither can we side with France in a contest the result of which may be to extend her territories: we shall therefore keep out of the contest as long as we can.' What of the people who witnessed the Austrians marching through their territories? 'If we could by negotiation obtain for them a little share of constitutional liberty, so much the better; but we are all interested in maintaining peace . . .' It is one of the defining moments of English foreign policy. Peace meant trade. Peace meant industrialization. Peace meant low taxes and prosperity. Peace was paramount.

There had been a jolt. In September 1830, a trial run of the steam engine known as the *Rocket* was advertised; its boiler was painted sunflower yellow, and its chimney was white. This was the springtime of the machine. William Huskisson, the member of parliament for Liverpool, had agreed to be present on 15 September to witness the railway journey from that city to Manchester. It was already being acclaimed as the sensation of the hour. One prominent engineer of the period, Nicholas Wood, wrote that the projected railway seemed, by a common unanimity of opinion, to 'be deemed as *the* experiment which would decide the fate of railways. The eyes of the whole scientific world were upon that great undertaking.'

The journey began smoothly enough at Liverpool and a stop was made at Parkside to take in water; the invited guests were told not to leave their carriages. Nevertheless, Huskisson leapt from his carriage to the ground between the tracks. He went over to greet the duke of Wellington, travelling in another carriage, when he was suddenly aware of the fact that the Rocket was bearing down on him on the parallel set of rails. A door was opened and hands were outstretched to help him; but he could not haul himself into the carriage; he fell onto the track and his legs were mangled by the locomotive. Huskisson died a few hours later. The death of a young and already well-known politician was in itself a considerable shock to the newspaper-reading public, but to die in such a gruesome and unprecedented manner provoked a sensation. It seems that Huskisson had never seen a train before, and was under the impression that like a horse or a stagecoach it could move out of the way.

It was also cause for sensation that one of the locomotives transported the ailing body of Mr Huskisson some 15 miles in twenty-five minutes, when it was generally believed that the railway could manage only 8 or 10 miles an hour. The actual and unprecedented speed struck observers and commentators with astonishment. So, paradoxically, the first fatal railway accident confirmed the supremacy of the train and conveyed to the public the power and possibility of the new form of transport. Suddenly it seemed that the island had shrunk in size. The elasticity of time itself was exemplified by the fact that one member of Lord Liverpool's cabinet was robbed by a highwayman and another killed by a train.

In 1830, too, the actress Fanny Kemble had been permitted to travel on one of the new locomotives by its progenitors, the

Stephensons, and reported that 'you can't imagine how strange it seemed to be journeying on thus without any visible cause of progress other than the magical machine, with its flying white breath and rhythmical unvarying pace . . . I felt as if no fairy tale was ever so wonderful as what I saw . . .' The instinctive analogy of complex machinery with magic and fairy tale is one of the more interesting characteristics of the first half of the nineteenth century. George Stephenson himself said, many years later, that 'as I look back at these stupendous undertakings, it seems that we had realised in our generation the fabled powers of the magician's wand'. It was the only language of wonder then available. Fanny Kemble herself was an insatiable seeker after sensation, and can be said to have thrown caution to the winds; but the great majority of railway passengers were, at that time, nervous travellers. The speed, the noise and the sheer novelty of being driven by a locomotive along metal lines were causes of anxiety if not of outright fear.

The Railway Regulation Act of 1844, passed long after Huskisson's accident had been forgotten, was designed to consolidate the minimum standards for what had already become a means of mass transport. The first railway 'boom' was already taking place. Some investors had been made nervous by the publication of such pamphlets as *Railroad Impositions Detected*, which claimed that the Manchester and Liverpool railway had not made 1 per cent profit. Cautious investment and gradual success changed the views of speculators, however, with the signal intervention of the London to Birmingham line that opened in the autumn of 1838. In 1844, 800 miles of route were authorized by parliament; in the following year almost 3,000 miles were so approved. 'The press supported the mania,' as one writer of 1851 put it, 'the government sanctioned it: the people paid for it. Railways were at once a fashion, and a frenzy. England was mapped out for the iron roads.' Within fifty years sea was linked to sea, river to river as well as ports, towns, cities, markets and mines. The recent past was already slipping from view. The old inns and ancient country taverns became one of the prime objects of the camera to evoke what was being seen as 'old England'. They were becoming part of the antiquarian tradition which had always been popular among the English. They were picturesque and made a pretty photograph.

It has been calculated that the most popular subject among Victorian photographers was the ruin; it could summon up sweet passages of silent thought which, as it were, sealed off the sights and sounds of the modern day. The poet Sadakichi Hartmann remarked on the daguerreotype that 'it lies in its case among old papers, letters and curios. A frail casement of wood with black embossed paper. We cannot resist the temptation to open and glance at it . . . The image of some gentleman with a stock or some lady in a bonnet and puffed sleeves appears like a ghost-like vision.' This might be the equivalent of reading a book of history such as this one, as the first railway engines pass through our field of vision.

A new system of communication had also been developed in this period, and its practicality was first adduced in 1827 when a telegraphic message was transmitted from Holyhead to Liverpool in approximately five minutes. Ten years later a telegraphic system was installed along the Great Western Line, and a cable between England and France successfully laid in 1851. At a time when, it was said, a householder sent a letter to his local fire company to warn that his house was on fire, the immediacy of the telegraph altered all perceptions of time and space. When a young man, Charles Bright, was knighted in 1858 for laying the first transatlantic cable, *The Times* described it as 'the greatest discovery since that of Columbus' and 'a vast enlargement . . . given to the sphere of human activity'. Dickens concurred that it was 'of all our modern wonders the most wonderful'. Such superlative praise was not then out of place. To transmit a message across hundreds of miles of space was considered tantamount to an increase in the rate of human evolution.

9

The pig is killed

By the beginning of 1834 the administration of Earl Grey was under duress. Throughout the previous year he had been contemplating resignation. 'I go like a boy to school, and with very little expectation of finding myself equal to the discharge of any duties.' His private doubts were compounded by the fissiparous state of his party in the Commons, where senior ministers clashed over the details of policy. Robert Peel did not want the Whig ministry to fall, however, until his party was ready to take over the administration. The problem was that some 150 nominal Whigs might also be classified as reformers or radicals; their politics were not clearly known and they were in effect unpredictable. One of them was a prizefighter, and another had fought a duel with his tutor, but the radical 'wing', if it can be so called, also included such old reformers as William Cobbett. It was in the interests of the Tories, therefore, to assist the government in moments of embarrassment or likely defeat; they had no more wish than the moderate Whigs for a radical coup.

The strain of maintaining this precarious position, as well as various crises in foreign policy, were the reasons for Grey's reluctance to continue. His son complained that Grey 'has no longer the energy to control a set of men each of whom is in this manner pursuing his separate interests ... and the Government is consequently utterly without unity of purpose, and the sport of every wind that blows'. A windswept government is an unlikely refuge. Grey confessed often enough that he was worn out but that his colleagues would not let him go.

The impression is of ministers talking themselves to death. They could deal with specific measures but they could not bring themselves to discuss the principles of their actions. It would be too foolhardy. The problems of Ireland were characteristic of this, where some advised reform and reconciliation while others recommended more severe actions. The results were half-measures and contradictory signals of intent. The Coercion Act of 1833, for example, was one of the first issued by the Reform administration. It was supposed to enforce the powers of the government of Ireland against radical activity, by creating something very like martial law. Yet at the same time the administration attempted to placate the Catholics and to propose a bill for reform of the Church of Ireland. Some bishoprics were to be removed and the more fervent Protestant clergymen to be excluded from the more pious Catholic parishes. Something was given, and something taken away.

This was part of the 'Irish Question', although it was not at all clear what the question was. Disraeli wondered whether it meant the pope or potatoes. It might more tentatively be ascribed to Church tithes, or 'the cess'. Some ministers wished them to be appropriated for the sake of the state, while others insisted that they should remain in the control of the Irish Church. When the cabinet split on that question, four ministers resigned. Ireland was an open wound which no English government could heal. Various proposals were made to Daniel O'Connell in order to acquire the support of the Irish members, but Grey and others were not inclined to agree with any bargain or compromise. When O'Connell decided that he had been duped he rose in the Commons and declared in strong and colourful language that he had been betrayed. 'There,' Lord Althorp whispered to John Russell, 'now the pig's killed.' Althorp had been one of those who misled O'Connell, and he now resigned. So hopeless were the disagreements in the administration, so uncertain were its principles on the matter of Ireland, that Grey also resigned a few days later. 'My political life is at an end,' he said, with something like relief. Ireland had done for him.

Melbourne put the matter best. 'What all the wise promised has not happened, and what all the damn fools said would happen has come to pass.' Did it mean that the entire ministry would go down, with Grey playing the role of the captain on the deck? When asked the question he replied: 'In theory, yes, but, in fact, no.' The king himself favoured a form of coalition, which might mean Wellington and Peel together with the more suitable Whigs. It was not going to happen. Wellington politely refused on the grounds that it would be almost impossible to unite men 'who appear not to concur in any one principle or policy'. Even the king conceded the point. Reluctantly he chose to ask Melbourne, as the only Whig who would 'do', largely on the grounds that he was considered to be no threat to anyone. Melbourne professed detachment on the matter. His private secretary, Thomas Young, said that 'he thought it was a damned bore', but what else could he do? It was perhaps his duty to obey his sovereign or, perhaps, inwardly, in the secret sessions of his heart, he realized the opportunity. Young had told him, at the time: 'Why damn it such a position never was occupied by any Greek or Roman and, if it only lasts two months, it is worthwhile to have been Prime Minister of England.' 'By God that's true,' Melbourne replied. 'I'll go.' Classical allusions always had an effect on the more aristocratic of the politicians eager to invoke honour and nobility under any circumstances.

Melbourne never betrayed his feelings in any matter, and would always speak inconsequentially to maintain his reserve. He was reluctantly chosen by the king 'after cautioning him against the admission of persons with visionary, fanatical or republican principles'. The advice was not necessary. Melbourne would no more favour a fanatic or a visionary than a Roman monk or Egyptian conjuror. One of his first measures was to abandon the Coercion Bill and propose something milder. This was much to the discomfort of the king, however, who had thought the original bill to be too pacific.

The problems associated with Catholicism were not reserved to Ireland alone. There had in England always been an element in favour of Anglo-Catholicism, a High Church movement that wished to retain the ritual and ceremony of the Roman Church. It was an attempt to exorcize the spirit and nature of the Reformation and bring the English Church back into the purview of the old faith. It was of course utterly resented by the majority of Protestants who saw it as a threat to the modest and domestic demeanour of Anglicanism. But there were many now within the Established Church who were creeping towards the cross of the Roman benediction.

In the autumn of 1833 a pamphlet was issued that became the first of ninety, entitled *Tracts for the Times*, that conveyed the essential spiritual position of High Anglicanism; those who supported these doctrines in turn became known as Tractarians and, since many were based at Oxford University, were collectively called the Oxford Movement. One of their adherents, Dean Church, described the tracts as 'brief stern appeals to conscience and to reason, sparing of words, utterly without rhetoric, intense in purpose'. They had been preceded by a sermon in the summer of the year 1833 at St Mary the Virgin, Oxford, on the theme of 'national apostasy'; the sermon was delivered by John Keble, who was then renowned for *The Christian Year* (1827), a series of poems for Christian festivals. He, too, wished to revitalize the established faith with a strong attachment to the Church fathers and a reaffirmation of the beauty of holiness.

The first tract had been composed by John Henry Newman, whose sense of spiritual purpose and simplicity of sentiment were at the centre of the new movement. His austerity and purity were emblematic of the high sense of resolve among the Tractarians who affirmed the Apostolic Succession against the Latitudinarianism inherited from the eighteenth century and the complacent pieties of the orthodox Anglican communion. Newman and his colleagues were like apostles in the desert of nineteenth-century convention. 'I am but one of yourselves,' he wrote in the first sentences, 'a presbyter, and therefore I conceal my name, lest I should take too much on myself by speaking in my own person. Yet speak I must, for the times are very evil, yet no one speaks against them.' They were utterly opposed to liberalism and the tendency to soften the moral authority of dogma. They were part of the spiritual earnestness of the nineteenth century and can be seen as complementary to the Evangelical revival embodied in Wilberforce and the Clapham Sect. All of them reflected the godliness of English faith.

They reminded many Christians of the limits of established

piety, and as a result provoked a controversy that haunted the nine-teenth century. They were called Romanists or worse. Some of them were expelled from their colleges and excluded from the pulpit. From a lay perspective they might have been considered as enemies of the crown because of their allegiance to the pope. They in fact posed no threat at all. They were thoroughly loyal and, with their ingrained obeisance to authority, were perhaps more dependable than free-thinkers or Dissenters. They were in no sense related to the Catholic Association of O'Connell.

This was indeed a time of associations, fraternities and clubs for kindred spirits. But when did an association become a trained band, and when did a fraternity become a guild or even a union? In 1834, partly under the guidance of Robert Owen, the Grand National Consolidated Trade Union was established. It had been preceded by a Grand General Union of all the Operative Spinners of the United Kingdom and by a National Association for the Protection of Labour. These organizations were largely concerned with the preservation of the living standards of their members, but the Grand National Consolidated Trade Union had larger ambi-tions. It wanted to take aim against the Reform Act of 1832, which had left five out of six working men without a vote. Under the stimulus of Owen the Grand Union proposed to organize every trade or industry so that the working people could take control of the economic machinery of the country. It was perhaps an inspiring idea and drew some half a million supporters. But like many utopian projects it fell at that moment when reality breaks through. A myriad of strikes flared up without taking fire, and the workers were systematically ground down by the actions of politicians and magistrates. The employers had already fought back with something known as 'the presentation of the document', in which each man seeking work signed a promise to renounce the trade unions and all their works.

This is the context for the Tolpuddle Martyrs, six farm labourers from Dorset who were sentenced to seven years' labour in Aus-tralia. Their offence had been to swear certain 'secret oaths' to bind them together when in fact they were following standard union practice in such matters. Melbourne and his colleagues upheld the judgement, thus earning the contumely of most of the working population and many of their political allies. A great demonstration was organized in London for what was called 'the day of the trades', but it seemed to lead precisely nowhere. Melbourne had in fact an instinctive sympathy with discipline and punishment ever since his days at school. He told his sovereign that flogging always had an 'amazing effect' upon him; it delighted him so much that he practised it on his serving maids.

Melbourne's first attempt at government lasted only four months. His cabinet was buffeted by resignations, and he himself was aware of a most uncertain political future. 'There exists a general uneasiness about something,' Wellington wrote in October to the king's brother, the duke of Cumberland, 'nobody knows what, and dissatisfaction with everything.' Melbourne himself gave at least the appearance of calm or even ennui. Everyone had been astounded by his rise to the premiership. He seemed lackadaisical, preferring not to do anything remotely radical. When the Hollands, a family of Whig grandees, visited Melbourne in his new state they 'found him extended on an ottoman *sans* shirt, sans neckcloth, in a great wrapping gown and in a profound slumber'. One of his favourite phrases was 'It's all the same to me'. He was well known for judgements of a similar nature. 'I generally find', he said, 'that nothing that is asserted is ever true, especially if it is on the very best authority.' His knowledge of history was profound, if in his case ineffective, but he was castigated when he admitted that he had not read Wordsworth's *The Excursion*. This was a period when even the grandest politicians had a working knowledge of the best of contemporary literature. 'I've bought the book,' he said. 'It's amazing when you leave a book on the table how much you know what is in it, without reading it.' We may summarize his politics with a short note: 'When in doubt, do nothing.'

But then there was a purge, at least of a symbolic kind. In the early evening of 16 October 1834, a red glow illuminated the sky. It soon became clear to the surprise and delight of eager observers that the Houses of Parliament were burning down. It was for some the most memorable event they would ever witness, as the great seat of empire subsided in flames. Many people immediately considered it to be a conspiracy. Could it have been Catholics or, worse, the Irish? Could it have been the French or the Russians? Could it have been radicals or trade unionists? Others believed it to have issued from the hand of God as a punishment for the passing of the Reform Act two years before. For others, it was simply a welcome relief. The old parliament had been cramped and constricted with all the damp and noisome smells of an ancient establishment; its tortuous corridors were an image of the delays and divagations of law-making. Its immediate neighbourhood shared the contagion. The cardinal-archbishop of Westminster, Cardinal Wiseman, described 'the labyrinth of lanes and courts and alleys and slums, nests of ignorance, vice, depravity and crime'. Slum was a new word, but everyone knew instinctively what it meant.

Much of this was erased by the fire that spread so widely and so furiously that at midnight the light was that of noon. 'It was a perfect fairy scene', one observer recalled, testifying once more to the realm of magic and wonder that lay just beneath the nineteenth-century psyche. When parts of the building tumbled down, sometimes in the midst of the crowds, some applauded as if it were an exhibition. The artist Benjamin Haydon wrote that 'the feeling among the people was extraordinary – jokes and radicalism universal'. In moments of enthusiasm the real feelings of nineteenth-century Londoners emerged. 'There's a flare-up for the House o' Lords', 'A judgement on the Poor Law bill', 'There go the Hacts [Acts]'. At first light on Friday morning the devastation was clear. The Painted Chamber and the Commons Library were destroyed. The frontage of the Commons and the arcade in front of the House of Lords had gone; the facade had collapsed, the walls were in ruins and the roofs caved in.

While the smoke still rose over Westminster, the king had told Melbourne what everybody knew or guessed – that the Whig ministry, beset by resignations and departures, was in no position to maintain the government of the country; the strength of the administration in the Commons was so weak that the sovereign felt obliged to call for Wellington to take over the post of first minister. The duke demurred, however, and recommended Robert Peel, who was considered by all parties to be the most resourceful of all claimants. The fact that Peel was a Tory rather than Whig seemed to matter not at all. It did cause some controversy, however, that the king had effectively ousted his government without any recourse to parliament or the public. No monarch would ever dare the experiment again.

The Tories had waited for this moment with Robert Peel at their head. Whig or Tory, he was the natural successor in principle as well as in policy. Peel was at that moment in Italy, however, and Wellington acted as his caretaker. The duke took over the conduct of the country just as if he were filling a vacancy in the army command. He occupied all the offices of state from the middle of November to the beginning of December. He was called the dictator, not the caretaker, but he had none of Cromwell's piercing ambition. He simply wanted regularity and efficiency. It was a time of much speculation, and in his novel *Coningsby* (1844) Disraeli recalled the winter of 1834: 'What hopes, what fears and what bets! . . . Everybody who had been in office, and everybody who wished to be in office; everybody who had ever had anything, and everybody who ever expected to have anything, were alike visible.'

When Peel arrived in haste from Rome he came back to a country which was ready for a general election. He sensed the mood. Melbourne had concluded of the Reform Act that 'if it was not absolutely necessary, it was the foolishest thing ever done'. Yet for Peel it was a decisive step which had created a new electorate. It was his task to engage this new electorate in a programme of limited reform. He had a strong if not subtle mind and, as he said, approached problems of politics as if they were problems of mathematics.

The circumstances of the country were ready for his attention. The responsibilities of ministers had increased considerably over the past two decades and had nurtured a group of parliamentary managers as well as experts on foreign, economic and imperial affairs. There was need of a first minister who could grasp the political complexities of his office as well as the political requirements of the time. The extension of parliamentary business engaged public attention, and there was rarely a period in which newspapers and periodicals commanded a larger audience. Their attentiveness and detailed reporting would encourage a new kind of minister. Peel might be one of the first.

Peel dissolved parliament in the closing week of 1834 with perhaps some hope that he might increase the strength of his party and perhaps even by some miracle of electoral politics acquire the mastery. He delivered what would now be called a manifesto in the guise of a letter to his constituents at Tamworth, thus reinforcing a new interest in what can be called public opinion; he promised a thorough reform of Church and State, and declared that the Reform Bill was a 'final and irrevocable settlement of a great constitutional question'. In this 'Tamworth Manifesto', Peel maintained that he was addressing 'that great and intelligent class of society' in order to present them with 'that frank exposition of general principles and views which appears to be anxiously expected'. He was in other words talking to those people who had been the beneficiaries of the Reform Act, and promising action on their behalf. In the event he gained the large number of ninety-eight seats, but it was still not enough to claim a majority. He had the additional disadvantage of facing a union of opposing parties. In a parliamentary agreement known as the Lichfield House compact, the Whigs, the radicals and the Irish agreed to work together for Peel's downfall. When the new parliament met on 18 February he knew that he was still on borrowed time. This was not a good omen for a new prime minister. But Peel might hang on, if only because the alternative was a government led once more by Melbourne.

He suffered six defeats in as many weeks and by the spring of 1835 it was clear to the king and the first minister that they were driving down a road that had 'No Thoroughfare' at its head. The final curtain closed when Peel was defeated in an act concerning Irish tithes. It is one of the many paradoxes of these difficult years that Ireland brought down more than one English government. Yet the hundred days or so in which he held office did wonders for Peel's public reputation as a strong and purposeful politician. He had in the process helped to form a Conservative party freed from instinctive reaction and from the image of the rock-hard duke standing guard over its traditional values. *The Times* described his resignation as 'a grievous national calamity', and blamed the 'excess of party zeal' that had brought him down. There were complaints that the parties in opposition had made a compact without any shared principles except that of destroying the prime minister.

Peel had become a commanding figure; terse, reticent, with no appetite for small measures. He revealed himself to be of strong administrative mind. He was perhaps a politician without ideals, but what were ideals good for? That is why the Tamworth Manifesto was worthy of what Disraeli called 'a party without principles', a taunt that would later be thrown back at Disraeli himself. Daniel O'Connell remarked of Peel that 'his smile was like a silver plate on a coffin', but this coldness or hauteur was in part the product of shyness. He was genuinely a withdrawn person. Disraeli, in a later pen-portrait, remarked that 'he was very shy, but forced early in life into eminent positions, he had formed an artificial manner, haughtily stiff or exuberantly bland, of which, generally speaking, he could not divest himself'. He was from the beginning, as Lord Rosebery said, always 'the same able, conscientious, laborious, sensitive being'. He was rich enough, but he was not a lord and suffered under his questionable status. He retained his Lancashire accent throughout his life. He was above all a man of practical measures, never so much at home as in the House of Commons. He was often compared to a beacon over the rocks, a pilot in a storm-tossed sea and a light upon the horizon. Other clichés might suggest themselves. He had difficulties with individual members – sometimes he would close his eyes, sometimes look away – but if you presented him with a knotty problem he would almost certainly untie it. He also had an enormous sensitivity to pain, and once fainted when his finger was caught in a door.

So after his first foray into government he stepped down, as the *Annual Register* suggested, 'not merely as the first but without a rival', while his Whig opponents, dazed by the harsh treatment which the king had previously given them, lacked strength and purpose. Melbourne and Russell, their principal men, had not much to comfort them in Peel's brief ascendancy except the prospect of office. There was very little choice for William but to reinstate Melbourne as first minister, a humiliation for the sovereign who had effectively dismissed him a few months before. It had been demonstrated that parliament and people had more power than the monarch.

The old parliament was now little more than a blackened shell after the great fire, and the new members assembled in a badly singed but still serviceable House of Lords, while the lords themselves were accommodated in the Painted Chamber that had largely escaped the flames. Melbourne guided the Lords while Russell was the dominant figure in the Commons. All the liberals, the moderates, the ultra-radicals, the radicals and the philosophic radicals huddled together in the service of Melbourne. As a result of the Lichfield House compact, the Whigs also depended upon the support of Daniel O'Connell's Irish MPs to command a majority. They were the key. The parliamentary radicals, under whatever name, were of no account in comparison; they soon dwindled into sects or less than sects. Their weakness allowed Russell to oppose further changes to the Reform Act, which the radicals ardently wished for, and why he became known as 'Finality Jack'.

The Tories had also been variously named, but the high Tories or ultra-Tories and the liberal Tories could all be enlisted under the banner of the Conservative party. It had its own club, the Carlton, its own associations and its own agents. There was, however, a crucial difference which eventually cost Peel dear. He hoped and believed that he was capable of constructing a modern Tory party ready for the challenges of the 1830s; but in fact the majority of the party were farmers, landlords and tenants whose chief preoccupation was the price of corn and the value of the agricultural interest. The preoccupations of Peel and of the Tory party did not necessarily cohere.

The second ministry of Melbourne was dominated by the prospect of a Municipal Corporations Act that had been under discussion by a select committee of parliament. A royal commission reported: 'there prevails amongst the great majority of the incorporated towns a general and, in our opinion, a just dissatisfaction with the municipal institutions; a distrust of the self-elected municipal councils . . . a distrust of the municipal magistracy; a discontent under the burdens of local taxation'. It could not be a more comprehensively damaging report. The towns and counties were in the power of a group of self-selected oligarchs; the mayor and the councils collected the revenues for their own purposes, to enrich themselves or to maintain the power of their families in the localities. The act which came into law in 1835 as a result of these deliberations destroyed the power of civic guilds and all those self-interested parties of tradesmen and craftsmen who controlled the wealth of the town.

Instead the municipal franchise was to be given to all permanent ratepayers or householders, who were to choose their representatives for a three-year period. Mayors and aldermen were to be guided by elected town councils. It was the municipal version of the Reform Act. It passed through Melbourne's hands, as first minister of the day, but it is doubtful whether he had much to do with it. Although the act applied only to the larger towns it had broken the cold spell of inanition that had settled over the country boroughs for many generations. It could be said, in fact, that the new breed of town councillors were more effective than members of parliament in such matters as public health and sanitation. Nonconformists and Dissenters were sometimes a majority on the town council, leading perhaps to more enlightened policies. 'It marshals all the middle class in all the towns of England,' one observer wrote, 'and gives them monstrous power too.'

That power was clear enough to Melbourne, who stirred himself to promote the interests of Dissenters. In 1836 his administration created a civil register of births, marriages and death, thus breaking an Anglican monopoly, as well as enacting a Dissenters' Marriage Bill which allowed civil marriage for the first time. In the same year London University received its charter, allowing the entrance of Dissenters who were still barred from the ancient universities. It would be agreeable to ascribe good intentions to Melbourne, but the truth is that he wished to keep the Dissenters on his parliamentary side. They were some of his strongest supporters.

In the same session, the stamp duty on newspapers was lowered from fourpence to a penny. The *Morning Chronicle*, for example, quickly became a paper of some stature and was described by John Stuart Mill as 'the organ of opinion in advance of any which had before found regular advocacy in the newspaper press', by which he meant that it was the first newspaper to introduce Benthamite theory into press discussion.

Melbourne's Tory opponents were joined in spirit by the king and even by some members of the Whig party. It might seem that he stood on an eminence surrounded by swirling waters, but time and tide were working for him. The Irish and the radicals did not wish to lose him, for fear that the Tories would take his place. Peel had set a course of moderation, until such time as he could depend on a solid victory in an election. That time was still to come. Essentially Melbourne's administration was kept in office with Peel's indirect support. They were both men of conservative temper who could work together without seeming so to do. Yet Melbourne was not altogether in command of his destiny. He was working in the shadow of the king's deep displeasure; William IV had never wanted him back.

Melbourne himself, however, was the very best leader for such a situation; he exuded bonhomie and had no principles to preserve at any cost. He was therefore infinitely malleable and flexible. A government measure might be adopted by the Commons only to be thrown out by the Lords; a period of discussion and compromise would follow, at the end of which a quite different measure would be proposed. Melbourne did not object to such a state of affairs, as long as he had his cabinet with him. 'I will support you as long as you are in the right,' one member told him. 'That is no use at all,' he replied. 'What I want is men who will support me when I am wrong.' He was not in any sense a reformer. Delay, postponement and ambiguity were his stock-in-trade. Even when his Municipal Corporation Act was thrown out for the first time by the Lords he did not seem to care. 'What does it matter?' he asked. 'We have got on tolerably well with the councils for five hundred years.' The measure did eventually pass the Lords and become law. 'We must see how it works,' Melbourne stated. This was the distance he always maintained in the affairs of the world. In any case he left most of the detail to the ministrations of Russell, who had the ambition and the appetite for government and was thus doomed to disappointment.

Melbourne also had an indispensable ally in the cabinet with Viscount Palmerston as foreign secretary, who soon enough would strengthen this alliance with his marriage to Emily Lamb, Melbourne's sister. Palmerston had held his post, apart from the brief Peel episode, since 1830; before that he had been a lord at the Admiralty and secretary at war. So he was used to the diplomatic game, which he fought with cunning and bravado. Like Melbourne he had no particular policy that could be associated with him, unless it were the pragmatic one of keeping Britain one step ahead of her enemies. He worked well and wisely, even though he was cordially hated by those who worked for him; this was because he made sure that they laboured hard and conscientiously.

When the country's vital interests were at stake, he could be both formidable and resolute. He intervened in Belgium, in Portugal, in Spain and in Syria. In all cases Palmerston believed that Britain's reputation was at risk and so, like a policeman of the Western world, it was the foreign minister who ensured that it was respected as well as feared. He was in one sense the only light in Melbourne's ailing ministry. He seemed to speak his mind. He explained, for example, that 'these half-civilised governments, such as those of China, Portugal, South America, all require a dressing down every eight or ten years to keep them in order . . . their minds are too shallow to receive an impression that will last longer than some such period and warning is of little use. They care little for words and they must not only see the stick but actually feel it on their shoulders before they yield.' He tapped a vein of xenophobia and self-assertion that at a slightly later date would be called jingoism.

The jingoes were soon to be found in the Stock Exchange, in the army and the navy, in the streets of fashion where the 'swells' gathered, among clerks and dockers and shopkeepers. It was believed that Palmerston had divined the national spirit. He called Austria 'an old woman' and 'a European China'. He could bully and he could bluster. He was sometimes called 'Lord Pumicestone' for his ability to rub his allies in the wrong way. He was more generally known as the more kindly 'Pam' or the more mysterious 'The Mongoose', perhaps because of his ability to scotch foreign snakes. Bulwer-Lytton remarked that 'generally when Lord Palmerston talks of diplomacy, he also talks of ships of war'. He sent weapons directly from Woolwich arsenal to the rebels in Sicily because of his distaste for the actions of King Ferdinand of Naples. He was no lover of rulers, hereditary or otherwise. Louis Philippe called him '*l'ennemi de ma maison*' and at a later date Victoria constantly complained that he was taking vital decisions without consulting her or her husband. To this he merely shrugged his shoulders. He always mastered the facts, and he always knew that he was right. He treated the world as if it were a great game, improvising or giving way wherever required.

Palmerston was the proponent of what was called 'restless

meddling activity', admonishing sovereigns, threatening prime ministers and generally stirring the large cauldron of international politics. Melbourne claimed to the queen that 'his principle and his practice, too, is that nothing fails, except weakness and timidity, and this doctrine is generally right'. A case in point concerned North Africa, when Mehemet Ali, the pasha of Egypt, decided to rebel against his nominal superior, the sultan of Turkey. This was not to Palmerston's liking, since the decline or disintegration of the Ottoman empire, ruled by the sultan, might give Russia or France the opportunity to gain the spoils of Egypt. France in particular was seen as a major threat, with the unspoken rivalry between the two nations ever present. Palmerston did what he liked to do, by conducting negotiations and making deals without his colleagues being able to play any role.

France soon faced a quadrilateral alliance between England, Russia, Austria and Prussia. It might be called the Northern alliance. But the prospect of war with France unnerved the English cabinet. When Palmerston proposed to make a treaty with the three nations, two members of the cabinet threatened to resign. At this Melbourne was seriously alarmed. Any split, or hint of a split, would be bound to damage him. 'For God's sake,' he said, 'let nobody resign or we'll have everybody resigning.' Palmerston was unmoved and professed complete disinterest in French threats. He merely said that they were bluffing. He persevered. Melbourne grew ill under the strain. The streak of nervous hysteria, fully exposed at times of crisis, was one of the most important characteristics of the Victorian sensibility. A few years later, Melbourne would write to Russell of the Queen that 'it might make her seriously ill if she were to be kept in a state of agitation and excitement'. Arthur Young, the writer and social observer, was ostensibly speaking of the electric telegraph, but he had made a more general point when he referred to a 'universal circulation of intelligence, which in England transmits the least vibration of feeling or alarm, with electric sensitivity, from one end of the Kingdom to another'.

It might be described as the apocalyptic imagination. It was widely reported, on the basis of some obscure or invented texts, that London would be swallowed by a conflagration on 17 March 1842. *The Times* of that day reported: 'the frantic cries, the incessant appeals to heaven for deliverance, the heart-rending supplications for assistance, heard on every side during the day, sufficiently evidenced the power with which this popular delusion had seized the mind of these superstitious people'. The wharves were crowded with people waiting for a steamboat to take them from the city, and the trains departing from London were crowded; others sought refuge in the fields. But nothing happened.

Palmerston was right all along. He confronted the French king, Louis Philippe, with the prospect of conflict. The king backed down, and soon enough Mehemet Ali's military bluff was called. This bloodless victory over the French was a cause of immense rejoicing in England, and it was perhaps the only foreign triumph that the Melbourne government could claim.

Palmerston proceeded with an ad hoc policy but it was none the worse for that. He was perfectly clear-sighted about the direction of national affairs and, on the rare occasions when he propounded something like a philosophy, he was invariably practical in his analysis. There was always talk of the Ottoman empire being 'in decline' or 'in decay', for example, but Palmerston remarked that 'half the wrong conclusions at which mankind arrive are reached by an abuse of metaphors, and by mistaking general resemblance or imaginary similarity for real identity. Thus people compare an ancient monarchy with an old building, an old tree or an old man . . .' But there was no such similarity.

He once said that 'it is a narrow policy to suppose that this country or that is to be marked out as the eternal ally or the perpetual enemy of England. We have no eternal allies and no perpetual enemies. Our interests are eternal; and those interests it is our duty to follow.' He might also have said that he had no eternal party affinity, since he was always at arm's length from his nominal leader. He preferred his own path. He stumbled on occasions, as we shall see, but always got up, brushed himself down, and continued on his way.

10

Young hopefulness

Agricultural and industrial unrest had continued through the 1830s. There had been fluctuations in prices, profits and rents that affected everyone. The seven fat years of corn, followed by the seven lean years, of Pharaoh's dream in Genesis 41 might have been the symbol of the time. Nobody understood the reason for these changes, apart from the dictates of the seasonal cycle, and were quite unable to deal with the expanded demand or the sudden depression. Social unrest and riot had been exacerbated by the New Poor Law and by higher taxes, while events such as the Tolpuddle agitation did not bode well for the Melbourne administration.

In 1836 a group of London and Yorkshire radicals, including social reformers such as William Lovett and Francis Place, determined to establish the London Working Men's Association. In May 1837, at a grand meeting in the British Coffee House on Cockspur Street, the Association issued its demands, which became known as the Six Points. These were for annual parliaments, universal male suffrage (female suffrage was believed to be a step too far), equal electoral districts, the removal of the property qualification for members of parliament so that young reformers might have a chance to attain the prize, secret ballots to deter bribery and bullying, and the payment of members of parliament once they had been brought there. This was to be of assistance to the working-class member who had no other source of funds. The points at issue soon became known as The Charter and its adherents as Chartists.

The People's Charter gave voice to the poor and the hungry who had not before been helped by the Reform Acts already passed. The miseries imposed by the New Poor Law also sharpened the injuries they sustained. The administration had bribed some of the middle classes, but they had turned their faces against all the rest.

In the autumn of the year the Irish activist Feargus O'Connor began the publication in Leeds of the *Northern Star*, which echoed all the remonstrances and denunciations of the Chartist orators where the workhouses became Bastilles and their dietary servings 'hell broth'. Even at the price of four and a half pence it had the largest circulation of any newspaper outside London with its mixture of economic, social and political news from the vantage point of the oppressed.

Thomas Attwood, whose Birmingham Political Union had been disbanded, now joined the new great hope of the Chartists in provoking public reform. It would be wrong to dismiss these first Chartists as dreamers or insurgents out of their time. They were quite aware of the power of Irish nationalism, for example, and of colonial insurgents who might assist them in their own battles against the English authorities. In practical fact, however, the motives of the Chartists were unclear; their supporters came from so wide a field, and their aspirations, whether rural or urban, were so diverse that any form of organized leadership was almost bound to fail. It was a mass movement but its size did not help to define it, and its class consciousness was based upon mass rallies and meetings that seemed merely to inflame both speakers and audiences. It was a new type of organization, too, since it included the paraphernalia of speeches and mass meetings with the assistance of pamphlets, posters and newspapers. Never had a militant organization been so well organized.

A distinction was drawn between 'moral force' Chartists and 'physical force' Chartists. It sounds like a clear alternative, but the boundary remained confused. The hand-loom weavers, one of those groups of workers who were most savagely hit by economic change, were generally for 'physical force'. The muddle was further compounded by the association between some Chartists and some

Methodists who met on the same premises and sang the same hymns. The movement remained at the front of popular consciousness for the next three years. It was always connected with the fear of violence among the authorities but, in fact, very little occurred in these years of anxiety.

The radicals in parliament were becoming more and more frustrated by the delays and hesitations over every piece of legislation by the Whigs. One radical MP, John Arthur 'Tear 'em' Roebuck, complained that one day the mood was Whig and on the next day the reverse. 'The Whigs, have ever been an exclusive and aristocratic faction, though at times employing democratic principles and phrases as weapons of offence against their opponents . . . When out of office they are demagogues; in power they become exclusive oligarchs.' They were aristocratic in principle, and democratic in pretence. They came forward with large promises and mean performances. Their talk had been vague, and their measures largely ineffective and useless.

Yet Melbourne, the object of this anger, had one immense advantage. He knew that the king was dying and that his successor, a young girl of eighteen, did not have William's prejudices. She did not share the same history. The closing days succeeded quickly. Throughout May and June 1837 King William deteriorated, and on 20 June he was dead from a heart attack. William died in the early morning, and Melbourne hardly waited for first light before informing Victoria of her new place in the world. The administration was in truth immeasurably strengthened by the death of the old man and the consecration of a new young sovereign. And why should the world mourn the old man's passing? It is true that he passed the Reform Act and, if he were remembered for it, it was probably enough. Yet in the seven years of his reign he had also passed Municipal Reform, the abolition of slavery and the New Poor Law. Or perhaps it should be said that he let them pass. 'He was odd,' Queen Victoria wrote in her journal. 'Very odd, and singular, but his intentions were often ill-interpreted.'

The king had died at just the right moment, a month after Victoria had come of age. Thus the young queen was disencumbered of all the courtiers, attendants, relatives and politicians who would have taken advantage of the regency to influence her. The young woman enjoyed to the full her newly discovered freedom. 'Since it has pleased Providence to put me in this station,' she wrote, 'I shall do my utmost to fulfill my duty towards my country. I am very young and perhaps in many, though not in all things, inexperienced, but I am sure that very few have more real good will and more real desire to do what is fit and right than I have.'

She found an unexpected companion in Viscount Melbourne, who took on the role of paterfamilias to the young queen. His wit and imperturbable calm helped her to understand the political world around her, and his advice was practical rather than idealistic. It might have been said that he treated her like a daughter and she treated him like a father, except for that hedge of divinity which stands around the queen. He did teach her, however, some of that cool self-possession which she evinced all her life. He informed her that he did not go to church in case he should hear something 'extraordinary' from the pulpit. He advised her against reading Charles Dickens, since the novelist might provoke depressing thoughts. This was not perhaps the best advice for the conditions of the time. The Fleet Prison in *The Pickwick Papers* (1836) and Jacob's Island in *Oliver Twist* (1838) were far worse than even the novelist could bear to describe. The health of the metropolis did not in fact materially improve until 1870, the year of Dickens's death.

The subsequent general election, on the death of the old monarch, brought back the Whigs with Melbourne, but Peel and the Tories were not far behind. Among the members led by Peel were William Ewart Gladstone, who had entered parliament five years before, and one new member, Benjamin Disraeli, but of course the new queen stood close by the side of Melbourne. She was capricious, she possessed a bad temper, but she liked what she called 'mirth' and dancing. Melbourne enjoyed the company of his new sovereign to the extent that he began to ignore parliamentary business. He had never enjoyed the rigmarole, but now he had happier reasons to let it slide. The queen had his full attention. She had had enough of those people who wished to take advantage of her; Melbourne had no such ambition. 'She is the honestest person I have ever known,' he once said. 'The only difficulty is to make her see that you cannot always go straightforward, that you must go round about sometimes.' He was alluding to her direct nature that would normally brook no obstacles. 'When he is with her,' Princess de Lieven, the wife of the Russian ambassador, stated, 'he looks loving, contented, and a little pleased with himself . . . dreamy and gay, all mixed together.'

On 5 November 1837, Victoria opened her first parliament. The Tories had high hopes for a new session but the large number of single-minded Irish members could not help but dampen their expectations. It was business as usual with the added complication of the Chartists around the corner. So this is perhaps the best occasion to introduce that amorphous group of men and women who have been given the title of 'early Victorians'. They were the loud, brusque, colourfully dressed progenitors of the more serious and industrious mid-Victorians; the latter, unlike their animated predecessors, would no more wear a blue cravat and velvet trousers than a flat cap and workmen's boots. We see the early Victorians in the pages of Dickens, whose portraits of railway magnates, crossing sweepers, charity boys, spinsters, schoolmasters, retired nautical folk, private detectives, coffee-shop managers, second-hand clothes merchants, copying clerks and ladies' maids comprise a wide world of which they could not see the horizons.

To speak in the broadest possible terms, and with ample possibility of contradiction, this was a world of boisterous energy and novelty, of excitement and of enthusiasm, of speed and sensation, of vigour and of bravado. Successive social reform movements were often led by the same core of fervent supporters. The artisans, tradesmen and shopkeepers, who seem so often to be the backbone of the emerging society, were independent in thought and in religion, individualist and non-deferential. This was the electorate of the Reform Acts. George Eliot, in 1872, looked back upon those times when reforms were begun 'with a young hopefulness of immediate good which has been much checked in our days'. In *The Last Days of Pompeii* (1834) Bulwer-Lytton interjected that 'we moderns have fire, and passion and energy – we never sleep, we imitate the colours of painting, its life and its actions'. The writers of the time were voluminous – the three-volume novels must stretch to the crack of doom – but they were not necessarily verbose. Ruskin,

Carlyle, Scott and Dickens could not be usefully abbreviated. It is a mark, perhaps, of innovation that the leading writers of the day looked upon the eighteenth century with something like contempt. Dickens himself added some false shelves in his library with the book-backs emblazoned with the 'Wisdom of our Ancestors' that included volumes on 'Ignorance' and 'Superstition'.

Yet there is never light without shadow. There is another aspect of the 1830s which is infinitely more revealing. The great year of the Charter was 1838, in which the authorities anticipated attendant meetings, speeches, demonstrations, petitions and riots; one Chartist, writing at the end of the century in a memoir entitled *Memoirs of a Social Atom* (1903), recalled that: 'people who have not shared in the hopes of the Chartists, who have no personal knowledge of the deep and intense feelings which animated them, can have little conception of the difference between our own times and those of fifty or sixty years ago. The whole governing classes – Whigs even more than Tories – were not only disliked, they were positively hated by the working population.' There was real political antagonism in the various movements and societies, and in 1838 many mass meetings of working people were held by torchlight to protest their fate. At Bolton and at Stockport, at Ashton and at Leigh, many thousands gathered and 'formed into processions traversing the principal streets, making the heavens echo with the thunder of their cheers . . . the banners containing the more formidable devices viewed by the red light of the glaring torches, presented a scene of awful grandeur'. It was as if the towns themselves were on fire.

The unions held aloof, as did the more radical Whigs. The leaders of the Corn Law agitation, which was even then growing fiercer, were not part of the movement. Chartists were about politics and not economics. This was in large part a working-class demonstration of power. It had its roots in the centuries of popular agitation that had marked the history of England from Wat Tyler to John Ball and Jack Cade, as well as the Radical Associations, Political Unions and Democratic Associations of more recent years. The administration looked on in mounting horror at the size and spread of the protests; but one observer was more astute than most. 'The Tories', Charles Cavendish Fulke Greville wrote in his diary of June 1837, 'prognosticate all sorts of dismal consequences none of which of course will come to pass. *Nothing* will happen because in this country *nothing* ever does.'

That was not strictly true. Something did happen in the autumn of 1838. An Anti-Corn Law League was established in Manchester with the sole aim of the 'total and immediate abolition of the Corn Laws'. The League was properly based in the city where the cotton industry had declared the modern triumph of the machine and the vital issue of free trade in British commerce. Free trade was the central imperative. Was the farmer allowed to buy cheap and sell dear, as the market demanded, or should there be restrictions and tariffs on imported grain to keep the prices and profits of English farmers high? The Conservatives, ostensibly the party of the land-owners and estate managers, were naturally in favour of maintaining the Laws; their opponents, from Whigs to radicals, were intent upon removing them so that corn could be cheaper.

There were many Dissenting ministers who were ready to declare that the Corn Laws 'were against the Law of God, anti-scriptural and anti-religious'. The League launched a campaign, organized largely by Richard Cobden and John Bright, that was in effect a religious movement based upon the success of the anti-slavery cause where religion and politics also could not easily be distinguished. Free trade was itself something of a religious nostrum that encompassed cheaper food, more exports, larger employment and greater prosperity. Since nation would stretch out to nation, it would encourage peace as well as plenty. John Bright declared that this was a movement 'of the commercial and industrial classes against the lords and great proprietors of the soil'. Bright was a Quaker who declared that 'in working out our political problems, we should take for our foundation that which recommends itself to our conscience as just and moral'. The balance of trade was firmly in England's favour, and free trade was deemed to be for 'world bettering'. So material advances were intimately linked to moral improvement, fulfilling one of the great nineteenth-century prin-ciples. Palmerston wrote that 'Commerce is the best pioneer of civilisation.'

The Anti-Corn Law League therefore mounted its national campaign with journals and pamphlets, speeches and meetings and demonstrations, denouncing 'a bread-taxing oligarchy, a handful of swindlers, rapacious harpies, labour-plunderers, monsters of impiety, putrid and sensual banditti . . .' In turn the farmers called those in favour of the repeal of the Corn Law 'brutes, drudges, clodpates, bullfrogs, chawbacons and clodpoles'. The situation became ever more agitated throughout 1838 as the price of bread steadily rose. It rose from 55 shillings a quarter in January to 72 shillings in September and 74 shillings in December. In January of the following year, it was almost 80 shillings. Melbourne heard the mutterings of those who demanded free trade, but he chose to ignore them. 'I doubt whether property or the institutions of the country can stand it', he said. It may be that he was not ready to endure the wearisome disputes and crises that had accompanied the Reform Act. 'I am listless and ill and unable to do anything, or think,' he said, 'which does not suit the time.'

It was Peel, the Conservative, who eventually led the charge for repeal. He was a practical administrator rather than a political philosopher, and it had already occurred to him that the price of wheat was far too high to be tolerated, with the situation made infinitely worse by the poor harvests of Ireland. In Ireland the dead were heaped up daily, while the newspapers revealed that men, women and children were dying of hunger in Scotland and England. Peel was a politician who, once convinced of the principle of a measure, never left it. He was not to be swayed by the vast preponderance of the Conservative party who wished to retain the Corn Laws. It was for them an article of faith, whereas for Peel it was one of reason and justice. The perilous situation in Ireland, where bad wheat had driven out the good after a series of harvests, was also one which could not be ignored. And if he could not rely on his Conservative party, he could still find allies enough elsewhere.

The Chartists had been no less eager than the Leaguers. At the beginning of February 1839, a General Convention of the Industrious Classes met in London to accept the Charter and to draw up a petition which would be sent around the country. It was essentially a national convention of the Chartists with one member representing a number of areas and, as its name implies, it encouraged reform rather than revolution. It had nothing to do with the movement of the trade unions; as one bricklayer put it, 'trade unions are for botching up the old system; Chartists are for a new one.

Trade unions are for making the best of a bad bargain: Chartists are for a fresh one . . .' The Convention, if nothing else, was a form of People's Parliament that was supposed to fill the vacancy left by radicals at Westminster where they seemed incapable of making any progress at all. These were called by Mrs Gaskell 'the terrible years'. In *Mary Barton* (1848) she states that 'this disparity between the amount of the earnings of the working class and the price of their food, occasioned, in more cases than could well be imagined, disease and death. Whole families went through a general starvation. They only wanted a Dante to record their sufferings.'

The calling of the General Convention caused some to take fright, and there was talk of arms. An organized police force was introduced to more towns, the army was increased and some Chartists were arrested. But, as a historian of the time put it, 'we are become a sober people'. There was no prospect of any armed conflict and, indeed, as so often happened, the conflicts between the radicals themselves were more ferocious than any outer agitation. What should be the methods used? Moral force? Intimidation? Physical force? Or some mixture of the three? Everything was planned for a march upon parliament and the presentation of a National Petition on the Six Points. Mrs Gaskell added that 'they could not believe that government knew of their misery . . . yet the idea that their misery had still to be revealed in all its depths, and that then some remedy would be found, soothed their aching hearts and kept down their rising fury'.

The National Petition was to be issued at a mass convention of 1839, and then to be taken up by a variety of reformist clubs in a great march to Westminster. The petition was 3 miles long and contained 1,280,000 signatures. But a million more signatures would not have been enough. It was presented to the parliament, which on 12 July voted even against considering it. There were rumours of a national strike but the working men were not ready for it. Local activists then turned to the notion of a national uprising, but that had even less of a chance to stir England. Riots and strikes were irksome enough, but no one had the appetite for an armed uprising which no leader could properly direct or control. A 'sacred month' devoted to the cause was truncated to three days of strikes, during the course of which the more militant Chartists were arrested. Some of them were bound over while others were given prison sentences of several months. There was no general attempt at repression. Yet nothing seemed right. The presence of misery and starvation in the north was known but barely understood. Some people called it 'the condition of England question'. It was a question, perhaps, without an answer. Thomas Carlyle wrote, in the opening sentence of *Chartism* (1839), that 'a feeling very generally exists that the condition and disposition of the Working Classes is a rather ominous matter at present; that something ought to be said, something ought to be done, in regard to it'.

The Chartists in their zeal had nothing to do with the members of the Anti-Corn Law League, whom they called 'a party comprised of avaricious grasping money-mongers, great capitalists and rich manufacturers'. Nothing could be more conducive to angering the lower classes than the network of financial and political considerations which used popular causes for their own benefit. They looked upon the Anti-Corn Law League as another special interest group destined to help the manufacturers who wanted cheaper bread for their workforce to keep wages down. It should not be forgotten that it was precisely in this period that Engels was considering the causes of working-class revolution. J. A. Froude, the historian and man of letters, said that 'all round us the intellectual lightships had broken from their moorings . . . the lights all drifting, the compasses all awry, and nothing left to steer by except the stars'. The members of the Anti-Corn Law League paid a subscription of 5 shillings per annum which, although it could just be afforded by the rising members of the middling class, was quite beyond the reach of the ordinary working people.

So there was very little ground between the two major groups who opposed the ministry for political or economic causes. It was a nice question whether the priority should be universal suffrage or the repeal of the Corn Laws. But that division ensured that the working classes never became a 'movement' in any revolutionary sense, and that the enemies of the Melbourne ministry remained separate from each other until its surcease. There was no class war in the orthodox sense. Sometimes the Chartists and the Leaguers would come together for a demonstration or a protest against the authorities, but their association was temporary and limited.

Melbourne was in any case busily occupied in guiding and educating the young queen, and paid even less attention to matters of public business. This, he might have said, *was* his public business. But there were other items. The Police Acts of 1839 might have been drawn up in an age of calm, with their prohibition of drinking at fairs and in coffee-houses and a ban on carrying 'any cask, tub, hoop or wheel, or any ladder, plank, pole, showboard or placard upon any footway'. Another offence consisted in 'the circumstance of obscene words being written or chalked on the walls of building, gates of houses and palings etcetera'. The police 'will in such cases deface the words quietly in the night time when it is possible to do so'. Some of these words would have contained the slogans of the radical agitators who were always at work in the great city.

A political fracas occurred in the spring of this year, however, when Melbourne was brought down on a bill concerning Jamaica. The sugar traders had no wish to liberate the slaves of the region, but a Jamaica Bill to suspend the constitution of the island passed by only five votes. It was more or less a defeat, a humiliation that could be repeated at any time through want of confidence or want of power. The prime minister had no choice but to resign rather than confront more such blows. He wrote to Victoria that he expected her to 'meet this crisis with that firmness which belongs to your character'. With the resignation of her loved minister, it would seem as if she herself had been voted out by the parliament, She could not eat or sleep; she cried continually. She wrote to the duke of Wellington asking him to take the place of Melbourne, but he gently refused. Sir Robert Peel was the next to face his mistress, but she found him 'odd' and 'cold'. They had discussed the aspects of the new administration and at one juncture he mentioned that the ladies of the queen's household, altogether Whig in persuasion, should accommodate Tories as well. On the following day she sent him a flat refusal; she could not have her intimate circle breached. She wrote to Melbourne, in disregard for the protocol of the court, that: 'I think you would have been pleased to see my composure and great firmness: the Queen of England will not submit to such trickery. Keep yourself in readiness, for you may soon be wanted.' It became known as the 'Bedchamber Crisis', although the queen herself had added to it the elements of high drama.

Peel retired from the fray with ill grace, and there were many contemporaries who believed that Victoria had in fact overruled the unwritten laws of regal conduct. Others, most of them Whigs, applauded her independence in such a sensitive matter as the royal household. So Melbourne was persuaded to rescind his resignation and remain prime minister for another two years. The duke of Argyll decided that he was 'an excellent head of a party dying of inertia'. It was simply a question of getting through. A vote of no confidence in the spring of 1840 was lost by a majority of ten votes, and soon enough the Whigs lost three seats in disparate areas – one in a country borough, one in a cathedral town and one in an industrial town. Robert Peel waited for the moment.

The failure of the national convention of Chartists, and the almost contemptuous rejection of the petition by the members of parliament, had characterized the summer of 1839, sowing the seeds of violent retribution which took place in the early winter. Many of the most prominent Chartists were under arrest or on bail, but the strength of Chartism lay not in its leaders but in the communities from which it sprang. The village tailor or the village shoemaker, the innkeeper or the hand-loom weaver, were part of the fabric of the movement just as much as they were part of the community. That was its power, but also its weakness. For that reason alone they were not ready or prepared to fight against the police, against the magistrates or against the men at Westminster. Melbourne was once more in charge and earned a verse tribute from Winthrop Mackworth Praed:

> To promise, pause, prepare, postpone
> And end by letting things alone:
> In short, to earn the people's pay
> By doing nothing every day.

On 4 November the miners and ironworkers of South Wales, led by well-known Chartists, marched on the town of Newport. This was the season of the year, marked by Guy Fawkes and his plot, when riot and disorder were commonplace. It is not clear what the men of 1839 wished to achieve, but a crowd of demonstrators surrounded the Westgate hotel where some of their Chartist colleagues were being guarded by a small military contingent. In this tense situation it takes only one man to lose his nerve. Shots were heard. The army fired into the crowd, which fled, leaving twenty or more dead. The three leaders of the Chartists were identified, arrested, tried and sentenced to death. But then, at the urgent instigation of the Lord Chief Justice, they were all reprieved. If they had been hanged further rioting might bring chaos; as it was, the fire of the Chartists seems to have been quenched by the bloodshed. The movement was suspended to discuss tactics and to initiate some internal reforms. It was the end of the first stage of their activity, and the Whig government congratulated itself on getting through the worst.

At the same time, in a land far, far, away, named Kensington Palace, Victoria met her future husband and was entranced by him. She was by nature highly sexed, and naturally longed for a husband. Albert was all she could desire. 'Oh to feel I was, and am, loved by such an *Angel* as Albert *was too great a delight to describe*! He is *perfection* . . .' Her liberal use of italics is entirely characteristic. Her use of exclamation marks was also red-hot. On parliament voting to cut Albert's allowance, on their marriage, she fired away: 'I cried with rage . . . Poor dear Albert, how cruelly are they ill using that dearest Angel! Monsters! You Tories shall be punished. Revenge! Revenge!' Their wedding was less Shakespearean. After the ceremonies were over, on 10 February 1840, and the couple put to bed, Prince Albert suggested to his new wife that their honeymoon at Windsor might be extended. This was the occasion for more italics and exclamation marks. 'You forget, my dearest Love,' she replied, 'that I am the Sovereign, and that business can stop and wait for nothing.' If he had had plans to rule alongside his wife, he was quickly disabused. He was fortunate if he was allowed to blot her page. Only during the queen's confinement, and the birth of their first child, did Prince Albert come into his own. He began to act as her private secretary, with the key to all the official boxes. He was no longer blotting the ink but holding the pen.

This might in fact be called the great age of pen and ink, since it was the first age of the penny post and what was known as the 'pillar letter box'. Rowland Hill, an inventor and social reformer, had done the sums and calculated that the best system was that of pre-payment beginning with the rate of one penny. He also recommended the use of 'the little paper bags called envelopes'. The first penny black went on sale in May 1840. This in itself created a social revolution equivalent to that of the electric telegraph; it promoted social cohesion and advanced national consciousness, prompting Henry Cole, one of the most ingenious of the nation's civil servants, to write in his memoirs that 'of all the events of which my career has been connected no one I feel surpasses or, indeed, is equal in value to the world at large as the adoption of uniform penny postage . . . the glory of England for all time'. The first official report on the post office system remarked that the postage system evinced 'the stirring industry and energy which is the national characteristic of all'. The stamp was such a symbol of national pride that no legend, only the head of the sovereign, ornamented it. It was greeted by 'the innumerable friends of civil and religious liberty' as 'a conveyance of thought' which would assist national self-determination and self-awareness. For more informal occasions the exchange of photographs by post was a significant token of friendship.

There are some vignettes of what became Melbourne's last days in power. After one lengthy cabinet meeting the ministers were proceeding to the door when they heard Melbourne calling to them. 'Stop a bit,' he said. 'What did we decide? Is it to lower the price of bread or isn't it? It doesn't matter which, but we usually all say the same thing.' Melbourne did not take very well to Prince Albert. He felt a natural jealousy that he had been supplanted in the queen's mind by a young and handsome foreigner. But he had grave doubts about Albert's earnestness as an instrument of policy. 'This damned morality', he had once said, 'will ruin everything!' At a cabinet meeting in the autumn of 1840 a possible war between France and England was discussed or, rather, not discussed. Charles Greville, clerk to the Privy Council, noted the intervention of Russell. 'I should like', he interposed, turning to Melbourne, 'to know what is your opinion upon the subject?' Nothing however could be got from Melbourne, and there was another long pause which was not broken till someone asked Palmerston, 'What are your last accounts?' On this Palmerston pulled out of his pocket a whole parcel of letters and reports from Ponsonby, Hodges and others, and began reading through them. In the middle of Palmerston's reading someone happened to look up and perceived Melbourne fast asleep in his armchair.

When parliament reopened in January 1841, the prime minister was effectively still asleep. Parliament had become a debating chamber to which petitions were addressed. The unreformed chamber had been more of a theatre where Edmund Burke and others practised their oratorical skills. Those days were soon to disappear, a transition anticipated by the Westminster fire of 1834. It was now a more earnest and more partisan assembly, congregating under the watchful eye of the press who devoted much space to its dealings. The parties were not yet disciplined or controlled in any modern sense; they were essentially coalitions of like-minded members who could go their own way when they so wished. They were distinguished by the inclinations of their leaders but there was no such thing as party policy. 'All is confusion,' Greville wrote in this decade, 'intermingling of principles and opinions, political rivalry and personal antipathy.' Melbourne was still living and working in the eighteenth century, even if this was really the age of Robert Peel.

But by the beginning of 1841, having lost four by-elections in succession, Melbourne was aware of the shadow of the sword about his neck. The crash came when a motion of no confidence in Melbourne's administration at the beginning of June 1841 passed by one vote. The subsequent general election confirmed the wide-spread belief that the Conservatives under Peel had become the party of government; their majority on their return to Westminster in the summer of the year, was more than ninety. Peel, having been cheated of office in the Bedchamber Crisis, now acquired a large enough party to do his best or worst. He became the first truly Conservative prime minister, the epithet 'Tory' now being considered a little old-fashioned.

The election did not pass without riot and general bravado. That would be too much to ask of a nation which had a tradition of popular protest. There was a large party, outside parliament, of brick- and stone-throwers who were eternally dissatisfied with the state of politics. They comprised the elements of the 'mob' which haunted public discourse. But the new masters of England – the middle classes in an alliance with the old ruling class – still had some reason for satisfaction. In its editorial on 29 July *The Times* claimed that 'until now the world has never known an instance of a party being installed in power expressly by the vote of a great people'. The stance of Victoria was not influential in the election but her preference for the Whigs was well known and well publicized. Lord Ashley wrote: 'I much fear that, in her total ignorance of the country and the constitution, her natural violence, her false courage, her extreme and ungovernable wilfulness, she will betray a disposition and a conduct which, while they will do no harm to us [the Tories] will be injurious to herself and to the Crown.' Victoria was not, then, universally respected. Even her husband had some reservations. Albert told his German adviser, Stockmar: 'Victoria is too hasty and passionate for me to be able often to speak of my difficulties. She will not hear me out but flies into a rage and overwhelms me with reproaches and suspiciousness, want of trust, ambition, envy etc. etc.' The new queen was not making a good impression.

It was a political revolution, but it was a relatively peaceful one. The Whigs had taken relief from the woes of government, according to Lord Clarendon, 'in a kind of apathetic acquiescence . . . which looks as if all energy and intention were extinct'. They had once been the commanding party of the nation, self-selected rulers who came from great families utterly accustomed to power; they were now powerless and seemed set for a vast decline and eventual extinction.

The new parliament met for its second session on 3 February 1842, and all the formal conversations were animated by the financial condition of the country. Expenditure was still too high, but how, in particular, would Peel deal with the taxes still imposed upon foreign corn? This was the heart of the matter. The Whigs had gone to the election on the slogan of 'cheap bread', but nobody believed them. Peel's intentions were still not clear, perhaps even to himself. Half his job was done for him by a bountiful harvest in 1842, succeeded by three more good harvests. His immediate actions were to reduce the tax on corn and to lower the tariffs on a wide range of goods; and, to balance the budget, he decided to reintroduce income tax. It had been dropped after the Napoleonic Wars but a fresh look was necessary at the nation's revenues. He may not yet

1. Robert Banks Jenkinson, 2nd earl of Liverpool, by Sir Thomas Lawrence.

2. George IV, king of the United Kingdom and Hanover.

3. 1815 Bread Riot at the entrance to the House of Commons caused by the implementation of the Corn Laws.

4. The 1819 Peterloo Massacre at St Peter's Field, Manchester.

5. Robert Stewart, Viscount Castlereagh
and 2nd marquess of Londonderry.

6. Caroline of Brunswick,
consort of George IV, 1820.

7. The arrest of the Cato Street conspirators in 1820.
The name comes from their meeting place near Edgware Road in London.

8. A model of the analytical engine, a calculating machine
invented in 1837 by Charles Babbage.

9. *Above, left*. Mary Anning, pioneer fossil collector and palaeontologist of Lyme Regis, Dorset.

10. *Above, right*. The Rt Hon. George Canning, MP.

11. *Left*. Arthur Wellesley, the duke of Wellington.

12. William IV, king of the United
Kingdom and Hanover.

13. The Rt Hon. Earl Grey.

14. An illustration of Daniel O'Connell for
The Imperial Dictionary of Universal Biography.

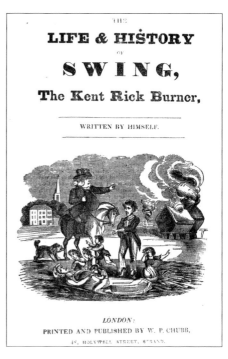

15. The title page to *The Life and History
of Swing, The Kent Rick Burner*, 1830.

16. A young Queen Victoria in 1842.

17. Prince Albert in 1840.

18. William Lamb,
2nd Viscount Melbourne.

19. Robert Peel.

20. A photograph of Lord John Russell.

21. *Left*. Lord Palmerston.

22. *Below, left*. The Rt Hon. W. E. Gladstone.

23. *Below, right*. Benjamin Disraeli.

have been determined to abolish the Corn Laws altogether, but the thought of it cannot have been very far from his mind.

Peel wished to simplify the tax system, revise all the arcane duties and tariffs and generally to discipline the finances of the country. 'I propose', he said, 'that for a time, to be limited, the incomes of this country should be called on to contribute a certain sum' for the purpose of reducing the deficit. The amount was set at 7 pence in the pound for incomes over £150 per annum. To use one of his own phrases, 'we cannot recede'. It came as an entire shock to his opponents, who took two or three days before crafting a reply. He had effectively initiated a financial revolution by which the entire system of revenue was changed. It was to be the predominant tone of his ministry.

He had a strong cabinet, however, to support him. Aberdeen replaced Palmerston at the Foreign Office and at once promoted cordial relations with England's principal allies and eschewed the rougher tones of Palmerston. The duke of Wellington became leader in the Lords, but without a specific ministry to control. Gladstone was promoted to the vice-presidency of the Board of Trade; in the following year he became president of the Board and thus in a powerful position to indulge his appetite for statistics and numbers. Thomas Carlyle described him as a 'most methodic, fair-spoken, purified, clear-starched, sincere-looking man', which was, for Carlyle, praise indeed. Edward Stanley (Lord Stanley a little later) had once been chief secretary to the lord lieutenant of Ireland but was now promoted to colonial secretary; as the earl of Derby, in a subsequent reincarnation he would rise much, much higher. Benjamin Disraeli remained, much to his chagrin, on the back benches; he had believed that his pre-eminent abilities would be as visible to others as they were to himself, but Peel had no room for him.

Peel came to office as a doctor approaching a sick patient. He did not do much at first; he was too busy observing the symptoms and accustoming himself once more to prescribe. It was the worst year to begin a new rule. It was reported to the Commons by Sir James Graham, the new home secretary, that 1 million out of a population of 16 million were receiving poor relief. The cotton mills fell silent and the cost of food rose. The banks themselves were in serious difficulties, and investment had dwindled. It was perhaps the lowest point of the century. The spinners of Bolton had a myriad grievances, 'namely, in the reduction of our wages, unjust and unreasonable abatements, in forcing upon us unhealthy and disagreeable houses, in charging us unreasonable and exorbitant rents . . . the above evils arise from class legislation, and we are further of the opinion that misery, ignorance, poverty and crime will continue to exist until the People's Charter becomes the law of the land'.

These were the conditions that once more roused the spirit of Chartism in an outpouring of pamphlets and addresses to working people, placards and demonstrations. 'Suffering caused by law', John Bright wrote, 'has made the whole population a mass of combustible matter, and the spark now ignited may not easily be quenched.' Members of the Anti-Corn Law League vied with the Chartists for the support of working men, although the latter were more squarely on the side of the workers. The Leaguers were still in some quarters dismissed as laissez-faire ideologues who were on the side of employers in the great battle. In the Midlands and in the north, in Lancashire and the West Riding, the colliers walked out of their work. In May 1841, another national convention had assembled to create a petition of more than 1.3 million signatures seeking a pardon for certain Chartist prisoners. 'They came pouring down the wide road in thousands,' W. M. Cudworth concluded in *Rambles Round Horton* (1886), 'a gaunt, famished-looking desperate multitude armed with huge bludgeons, flails, pitchforks and pikes, many without coats and hats, and hundreds with their clothes in rags and tatters'.

A radical journalist noted at the time that:

> The spectacle attracted great attention, from the ragged street sweeper to the duchess with the golden eye glass. The city police behaved very favourably, but the metropolitan blues were very indifferent. The omnibus drivers were very rough and violent. We marched down, slow march, through Fleet-street, the Strand, past Charing Cross, the Horse Guards, and to the Parliament House. The windows of the public offices were particularly crowded, and great curiosity seemed to prevail.

Parliament was not to be turned, and the petition was once again rejected on the casting vote of the Speaker. This created a fury that had not been seen before. The strikes intensified, and there was speculation once more that it might lead to a general uprising. Police stations were destroyed, prisoners released and the houses of prominent magistrates or mine-owners were put to the torch. The spring had turned into a hot summer. Another petition was carried to parliament in the following year; the demonstrators were like waves of the sea forever beating against the rocks. The petition was claimed to contain more than 3 million signatures but yet was overwhelmingly rejected by the Commons.

This was the catalyst for the 'Plug Riots' or 'Plug Plot Riots' of 1842, when the steam-plugs on boilers were removed so that no industrial work could be done. It began in the collieries of Staffordshire and soon spread. With the coalfields closed, the whole of industrial England suffered privation. London, too, was feeling the pinch of want and unemployment. In Clerkenwell Green and Paddington, two centres for urban radicals, large crowds assembled. A report in the *Sun* of 23 August noted that the leaders of the crowd 'were proceeding to condemn the conduct of the "Bluebottles" [police] when a loud cry was raised of "the Peelers! the Peelers!" On turning round it was discovered that about a dozen of the horse-patrol, armed with heavy cutlasses and backed by several divisions of police were rapidly advancing upon the crowd.' The result was broken heads, broken limbs, and worse.

The wreckage was doubly damned since the 'time-spirit', as Carlyle put it, was behind the machine. There was still an aura of mystery and secrecy about machinery and its workings. It was in a sense thought to be beyond human control. One 'disconsolate radical', as he termed himself, wrote that 'one rarely finds anybody who ventures to deal frankly with the problem of machinery. It appears to infuse a certain fear. Everybody sees that machinery is producing the greatest of all revolutions between the classes, but somehow nobody dares to interfere.'

If contemporaries did not interfere, they tried to ignore the problem altogether. This may help to explain the genesis of 'the Young England Movement' launched into life by the young Disraeli, still dissatisfied that his apparent genius was not appreciated by Peel and the other Tory leaders. What better course than to launch a party of his own? It turned its back upon industry and industrialism, preferring to dwell in an imagined feudal, hierarchical and pre-industrial age where the poorer folk and the nobility shared patriotic and Christian longings. It rejected utilitarianism, political economy, rationalism, Malthusianism and all the other early Victorian remedies for social ills. It was perhaps no accident that in 1842 Tennyson's *Morte d'Arthur* was published, inspiring a range of short and narrative poems that celebrated Lancelot, Arthur, Guinevere and the other august figures of national myth. In a paean to the 'Time Spirit', Carlyle hailed the Man of Letters as the Hero. 'I say of all Priesthoods, Aristocracies, Governing Classes at present extant in the world, there is no class comparable for importance to the Priesthood of the Writers of Books.'

So the Round Table had once more become one of England's icons. Young England was a young man's creed. It was an idealist creed, but it was also an avenging creed damning all that had come before. In the spring of 1845 Disraeli announced that 'a Conservative government is an organised hypocrisy'. The home secretary, Sir James Graham, took the trouble to write to a colleague that 'with respect to Young England the puppets are moved by Disraeli, who is the ablest man among them . . . I consider him unprincipled and dishonest, and in despair [without office] he has tried the effect of bullying.'

Peel was nothing if not a reformer when vital interests were under threat, but it was usually necessary to bring his party with him. Corn was just such an issue at a time when bread was cheap but people were still starving. It might have been expected that the Conservatives would continue their support of farmers and landowners. To deny protection to corn, and thus to risk the danger of cutting agricultural livings, was emphatically not Tory doctrine. But Peel had set his mind to the problem and followed his convictions wherever they led him. He was now sure that the Corn Laws, which had the effect of raising the price of imported corn, had to be changed.

Peel was a reforming prime minister quite different from his predecessors. He familiarized himself with every department of state; he had an appetite for statistics and details of policy. He mastered his colleagues with his administrative fervour and general toughness of approach. 'Peel has committed great and grievous mistakes', Lord Ashley wrote in 1843, 'in omitting to call his friends frequently together to state his desires and rouse their zeal . . . men would have felt they were companions in arms; they now have the sentiment of being followers in a drill.'

Disraeli may have been a singular figure but, in opposition to Peel, he was not a solitary one. He joined forces with George Bentinck in the fight for Protectionism and for what was known as 'the Anti-League' specifically opposed to the Anti-Corn Law League. It organized meetings and protests, in imitation of its successful opponents; it enlisted sympathetic MPs in its support of the values and principles of the landowners. It stood in line with those mild Conservatives who would negotiate between the various classes and interests in order to form a firm and just national settlement. They compared 'the prosperity, growing wealth and full employment under the old trade' with the vicious cost-cutting under 'victorious free trade'.

Nevertheless, the proponents of the Anti-Corn Law League had the strongest speakers and perhaps the most compelling proposals. It was widely argued that those against the Corn Laws were on the side of science; this can be called quite simply the argument of the age, joining the intellectual merits of free trade with the Victorian faith in progress and efficiency. The adherents of the League introduced lessons of political science to those who had no inkling of such things; they lectured on profits and wages to merchants and artisans and clerks. Nine million pamphlets and tracts were distributed through a network of agents. A great meeting was held at the Drury Lane Theatre in 1843, where Cobden used the most contemporary imagery to describe the power of free trade. 'There was a circle of continuous links which could not be injured in any one point, but it would like electricity pervade the whole chain [*great cheering*].'

It is hard to disentangle the various Tory policies that Peel had to consider. The Young England men were discussed by ministers, but they had very little effect on policy. The Tories of 'the old school' might be said to go back to James II and the Exclusion Crisis for whom reform of any kind was considered unnecessary and obnoxious. Orthodox Toryism was less pugnacious but maintained the settled conviction that the working population were of necessity inferior and that the patrician or governing classes were in effect born to rule. Liberal Toryism, as it were on the left-hand side, emphasized the powers of individual responsibility and held up the central image of 'the market' as balancing human values. They were on the whole in favour of parliamentary reform. Radical Toryism was a form of paternalism which was designed to sustain the morality and the well-being of every stratum of society. This was still considered to be a Christian country.

Very few members of parliament would have disowned Christian doctrine, whatever form of Christianity they espoused. A Whig radical and an orthodox Tory might choose the same church or chapel, and it was widely believed that by the early 1840s the moral and physical health of the nation was improved. Pauperism and crime had their climacteric in 1842, for example, and from that time forward they had gradually diminished in size and scale. An analysis of tax duties demonstrates that, from 1840, legislation had the effect of making spirits more expensive and thus of reducing their consumption. This may have been in part the result of Evangelical and Nonconformist missions that maintained their presence in East London and other deprived quarters. The success of the Salvation Army, after its foundation in 1865, may be a case in point.

The social renewal had taken fifty years. The clerk of Bow Street magistrates' office knew of what he spoke. 'I have no doubt', he told one commission of inquiry as early as 1816, 'that the manners of the lowest classes of society are much better than they were ten years ago, those excessive scenes of drunkenness which I have formerly observed are not by any means so frequent'. He was supported by the curate of St Giles, which had been the church on that pile of rottenness which was known as 'Rats' Castle' in Holborn. 'I think the face of the general appearance of the parish has improved within that time; there is not so great an appearance of vice as there used to be.' 'Yesterday,' a German traveller wrote in 1835, 'I wandered into Regent's Park. Of eating, drinking, singing, music, dancing, not a trace – they walk up and down and lie on the grass which is growing bare and yellow.' It was a remarkable transformation. No dancing. No drinking. No public sex. No ribaldry and blasphemy.

The public authorities, largely through the efforts of persistent reformers like Wilberforce and enlightened statesmen like Peel, modified the rigour of earlier decades. The worst punishments for felons and transported convicts were alleviated; imprisonment for debt was discontinued; some of the early Factory Acts were passed; children were banned from sweeping chimneys and dogs were prohibited from drawing vehicles like horses. The first public baths and wash-houses, established in 1845, admitted almost 80,000 people in the first year. Victoria Park in Bow became one of the lungs of London. Sir James Graham's Factory Education Bill of 1843 survived a stormy passage in which the various denominations fought the brave fight over their right to supervise the moral and religious guidance of the working classes. A cumbersome compromise was reached among people who did not relish compromise. Separate classrooms were set aside for Anglican instruction, and Dissenting ministers were invited to attend the schools once a week. It was not enough for the Nonconformists, however, who objected to a permanent Anglican schoolmaster and a majority of Anglicans on the school boards. Eventually the bill created such dissension that it was abandoned altogether. Lord Ashley wrote to Robert Peel: 'let this last trial be taken as a sufficient proof that "united education" is an impossibility. It ought never again to be attempted. The Dissenters and the Church have each laid down their limits which they will not pass; and there is no power that can either force, persuade, or delude them.'

This was also the period when self-help took on a political aspect with the growth of political societies dedicated to social reform. Trade unionism, Chartism and factory reform vied with benefit societies, secular societies and temperance societies in maintaining the social fabric at a time of perceived stress. The Vigilance Association for the Defence of Personal Rights can be placed beside the National Association for Women's Suffrage, the Moral Reform Union beside the London Society for the Abolition of Compulsory Vaccination and the Royal Society for the Prevention of Cruelty to Animals beside the Lord's Day Observance Society. Chartism may have been the light that failed, but it illuminated the way for working men's associations and eventually the Labour party.

No distinction was drawn between moral and physical hygiene or between moral and physical training. Indeed, the physique of the English seems to have been admired. Ralph Waldo Emerson, in *English Traits* (1847), remarked that 'they are bigger men than the Americans. I suppose a hundred English taken at random out of the street, would weigh a fourth more than so many Americans. Yet, I am told, the skeleton is not larger. They are round, ruddy, and handsome; at least the whole bust is well formed, and there is a tendency to stout and powerful frames.' This is the period when the word 'manliness' was introduced as a new definition of 'gentleman'.

11

City lights

If a traveller entered the heart of the kingdom, St Paul's Cathedral, in 1841 he would have discovered, according to an official report of that year, that 'the cathedral is constantly and shamelessly polluted with ordure, the pews are sometimes turned into cabinets d'aisance [toilets] and the prayer books torn up [for toilet paper]; the monuments are scribbled all over, and often with grossest indecency'. This was at the height of England's power and wealth. There were other types of gloom. In November 1841 the darkness of London thickened in the fog where 'hackney coaches drive up against church windows, old men tumble down cellars; old women and children stand crying up against lamp-posts, lost within a street of their own homes . . .' The fogs of London were famous then. White, green, and yellow fogs were the exhalation of coal fires and steamboats, factories and breweries. Torches were lit to find the way. The smell and taste of the fog were of particular concern; it was known as 'miners' phlegm'.

Here is a London scene. On London Bridge, in the fog, two entangled lines of cabs are shrouded in darkness; the silhouette of the broad-shouldered driver of an omnibus can just be seen, as well as the red face of the conductor who seems to have shouted himself hoarse; the omnibuses fight for space among the cabs and the coal carts and the beer wagons. All is mist and dust, with the cacophony of London sounds – the crack of the whip, the snorting of the horses, the cries of the children, the shouting out of destinations.

It may act as a prelude to the theme of anxiety and the strain of life in Victorian London. It was believed with some reason that whole societies of people, rich and poor, privileged and outcast, suffered from nervous maladies of one kind or other. The *Edinburgh Review* noted that 'throughout the whole community we are called to labour too early and compelled to labour too severely and too long. We live sadly too fast.' For those of religious temper the strain of conscience was greater than that of any physical suffering; there were many, sitting in small rooms, who believed themselves to be doomed to hell. Insanity often followed.

Walter Pater, in turn, later wrote of 'that inexhaustible discontent, languor and homesickness, that endless regret, the chords of which ring all though our modern literature'. This is a genuine strain of the Victorian temper that should be placed with all others. It was an age in which all the sustaining props of belief began to crumble. When insecurity and doubt began their insidious work, together with the suspicion, as the English divine Frederick Robertson put it, 'whether there be anything to believe at all'. It was the panic at nothingness which the Victorians did their best to exorcize. Were we simply, as Charles Kingsley feared, 'wheels of a vast machine'?

The following year was a time for contrast. On the night of 26 May 1842, Victoria and Albert were driven in a carriage to Her Majesty's Theatre in the Haymarket for a royal ball. Two weeks before, the royal couple had graced a costume ball at Buckingham Palace where they had dressed as Edward III and his queen, Philippa. This was the same month in which the Chartist marchers presented their second great petition to parliament only to see it contemptuously rejected. It was on this occasion that a member later to be revered for his learning, Thomas Babington Macaulay, declared that 'universal suffrage is incompatible, not with this or that form of government, but with all forms of government, and with everything for the sake of which forms of government exist'.

This was also the year when Edwin Chadwick published his *Report on the Sanitary Condition of the Labouring Classes of Great Britain*. In the course of this momentous report, largely financed and prepared by Chadwick himself, it was revealed that in the majority of the towns there were no attempts at sanitation. There was no drainage, and the refuse was simply thrown into the streets, where it would fester and rot; the courts and alleys were blocked by ordure and other filth, while there were no public pumps for the poor to find water. Fever was a powerful foe in all the metropolitan parishes, so that the poorest sickened and died before being carried to the workhouse.

In the same year Lord Ashley, who had already found fame for his factory reforms, persuaded parliament to appoint a royal commission on the state of employment in the mines. The details of the women, and the children, of the underworld were revealed to a nation previously unaware of what was essentially a domestic slave trade. The report also included illustrations and woodcuts of the workers – the women half-naked, the children almost completely so – bearing coal and dragging wagons like beasts of burden. They were beaten, stunted, malnourished and diseased. This was an aspect of the Victorian world – of Victorian civilization – that the public did not care to see. Almost at once the Commons passed a Mines and Collieries Act which prohibited female labour in the mines and raised the age of eligible children to ten. Yet the report had been salutary as well as severe. To know that English women and children had been reduced to a state only a little above savagery, to labour for long hours in filthy surroundings, to be exposed to all the opportunities of sexual licence, and to be injured or killed by the perils of defective machinery; all this was intolerable to the mass of people. The act was passed in the summer of 1842, but only after being severely curtailed in committee. Acts of mitigation had a thousand explanations without even mentioning the world of profit. The coaling industry was rich and powerful; two thousand collieries could not properly be investigated. What large body of men could examine them?

Conditions varied with each pit. How could standard measures of ventilation be used? Many questions were left unanswered. But why was no other industry being picked out in this fashion for remonstrance? What about needle-making or cobbling or work in the distilleries? There was no real response to this, which led many to despair of the whole industrial system as it existed in England.

It was this despair which led directly to the agitation for better educational and sanitary provision. It seemed that some legislators would have to start from the beginning.

The report on the sanitary conditions of the towns and cities did not have a speedy resolution. Edwin Chadwick had numerous enemies who did their best to block his work when it was ready to be published early in 1842. The Poor Law commissioners, under whose imprimatur the report was commissioned, refused to sign it. So Chadwick's *Report on the Sanitary Condition of the Labouring Population* was published under his own name. However, this subdued introduction did not affect its readership, which was soon calculated in the tens of thousands. One quarter of a million people each year flocked to the gutters and sewers. Two thousand eight hundred and fifty people were crowded into ninety-three small tenements. The excrement 'was lying scattered about the rooms, vaults, cellars, areas and yards that it was hardly possible to move for it'. The living lay with the dead, both bitten by vermin. They could no longer be considered as human, merely the detritus left upon the shore. The average age of mortality in the capital was twenty-seven. Half the funerals were for children under the age of ten.

It could not be considered, therefore, easy reading. In the first pages Chadwick considered the case of a district of Tiverton:

> The land is nearly on a level with the water, the ground is marshy, and the sewers all open. Before reaching the district, I was assailed by a most disagreeable smell; and it was clear to the senses that the air was full of most injurious malaria. The inhabitants, easily distinguishable from the inhabitants of the other parts of the town, had all a sickly, miserable appearance. The open drains in some cases ran immediately before the doors of the houses, and some of the houses were surrounded by wide open drains, full of all the animal and vegetable refuse not only of the houses in that part, but of those in other parts of Tiverton. In many of the houses, persons were confined with fever and different diseases, and all I talked to either were ill or had been so: and the whole community presented a melancholy spectacle of disease and misery.

English society might not in fact have been on the brink of collapse, but it seemed to many people of the time that this was exactly what was happening. 'Certainly I have never seen, in the course of my life,' Charles Greville wrote, 'so serious a state of this as that which stares us now in the face, and this after thirty years of uninterrupted peace, and the most ample scope for the development of all our resources. One remarkable feature in the present condition of affairs is that nobody can account for it, and nobody pretends to point out any remedy.' It was nobody's fault.

But surely it was somebody's fault. There was an immediate clamour against the parish vestries and the speculative builders who had allowed these conditions to fester and to spread. The engineers were at fault for improper maintenance, and the doctors at fault for negligent reporting. The reaction was so strong and so vociferous that the home secretary, Sir James Graham, was forced to institute a Royal Commission on the Health of Towns which gave him a breathing space of two years in which to do next to nothing. The Whig opposition did not harry the ministers concerned, as they should have done; the shock of defeat seemed to have left them immobile. Peel and his supporters had come to the conclusion that free trade, and commercial freedom in general, were the best remedy for social ills. The 'blue books' or statistical inquiries of Chadwick only served to illustrate the partial response to this great social evil. Organizations such as the Town Improvement Company, which hoped to run at a profit, and philanthropic associations such as the Society for Improving the Conditions of the Labouring Classes were established to fill the emptiness of parliamentary response.

Yet the Victorian city was, in many stretches, still the city of dreadful night. Lord Ashley, having visited what was known as a common lodging house (with men, women and children mingled together), told the Commons that 'these houses are never cleaned or ventilated; they literally swarm with vermin. It is almost impossible to breathe. Missionaries are seized with vomiting or fainting upon entering them.' 'I have felt', said another, 'the vermin dropping on my hat like peas.' No city was alike; each one had ills and vices of its own. The 'city' was not itself a favoured term. Victorians preferred the circumlocution of 'large towns and populous districts'. Sheffield was essentially a congregation of small industrial districts.

Birmingham had a more unified sensibility which would eventually be brought by Joseph Chamberlain to life. In Birmingham the small workshop was the key, where in Manchester it was the factory. The workforce was more skilled in Birmingham than in Manchester; housing and sanitation were also better. It was said, in fact, that Birmingham was the best-administered city in England.

Some urban leaders preferred Gothic, Grecian or Italian architecture for their public buildings. Since each city was different, there was no single or central style. This was complemented by the rise in the quality of the architectural fabric of the larger towns with town halls, mechanics' institutes, churches, squares and public gardens. The *Builder* reported that 'one can scarcely walk about Manchester without coming across frequent examples of the *grand* in architecture. There has been nothing to equal it since the building of Venice.' Birmingham was, according to the *Magazine of Art*, 'perhaps the most artistic town in England'. Leeds boasted 'whole streets vibrating with colour'. The conscious monumentality of these buildings was particularly striking as the tokens of a new urban age.

Nevertheless, there were towns and cities which emanated Victorianism like a whiff of coal smoke. Of Wigston in Leicester one historian of landscape, W. G. Hoskins, later wrote, 'the sight of South Wigston on a wet and foggy Sunday afternoon in November is an experience one is glad to have had. It reached the rock bottom of English provincial life; and there is something profoundly moving about it.' It had identical brick cottages and an iron church. It bears its origins in the nineteenth century like a birth-mark, all the flatness and uniformity an eternal reproach to the facile optimism that characterized many Victorians.

In 1830 Henry Brougham, himself a baron, spoke out in the Cloth Hall Yard of Leeds. 'We don't now live in the days of barons, thank God, we live in the days of Leeds, of Bradford, of Halifax and Huddersfield.' These are the towns and cities that bear the stamp of the nineteenth century as surely as if by some trick of conjuration they had been manufactured out of steam. In Leeds a hundred woollen mills employed ten thousand people, and thirty firms spinning flax counted five thousand workers. Bradford was also a textile town, but Leeds leaped ahead with its burgeoning engineering industry. Of Sheffield an official report claimed that 'the population is, for so large a town, unique in its character, in fact it more closely resembles that of a village than a town, for over wide areas each person appears to be acquainted with every other, and to be interested in each other's concerns'.

In Manchester there was no such unity, but a gulf between masters and men, and a gulf between different types of working men. With its unruly people, its social divisions and its contrasts, the city was a seedbed of fiction. The most prominent among the Mancunian novels were Elizabeth Gaskell's *Mary Barton* (1848), subtitled 'A Tale of Manchester Life', and the same author's *North and South* (1855), where the fictional city of Milton is based upon Manchester. A French observer noticed 'the river Irwell, forming a kind of peninsula, and if one travels up and down it the whole neighbourhood looks like a grey colourless Venice. Instead of the black gondolas, coal boats glide up and down . . .'

Yet there was a kind of magnificence in its misery. Disraeli suggested in *Coningsby* (1844) that only a philosopher could understand 'the grandeur of Manchester', while Thomas Carlyle, who was just such a philosopher, suggested that the starting of the cotton mills at half-past five in the morning was as 'sublime as Niagara or more so'. The suburbs seemed to be lying prostrate along endless streets while the central city was ornamented and rendered magniloquent with public spaces and public buildings. There was in fact a 'Manchester school' unified in support of the principle of free trade, whether seen from a financial or social vantage; it included Quakers, philosophic radicals, merchants, political radicals and manufacturers. There was a ferment of activity, of which Peel was the most successful beneficiary, and it was not unconnected to a perception of Elizabeth Gaskell on the Manchester crowd: 'The only thing to strike a passerby was an acuteness and intelligence of countenance which has often been noticed in a manufacturing population.' The social divisions were a cause of excitement rather than conflict, however, and it was widely believed that Manchester was the model of the city of the future. The Anti-Corn Law League was built up in Manchester. On the site of the Peterloo Massacre there rose, in 1856, the Free Trade Hall. It was the monument to the idea that first expressed itself here.

In the later decades of the nineteenth century Birmingham

became the beacon of what was known as 'the civic gospel' and was proud of being known as 'the best-governed city in the world'. In Birmingham there was greater diversity of trade than in, for example, Leeds. The concentration of smaller workshops other than factories encouraged an intimate and easier air between masters and men. A local Chartist remarked that 'large manufacturers cannot shut up their men as they did in Manchester . . . for it was well known that [in Manchester] the working people were at the mercy of the manufacturers'. The labour force of Birmingham was more skilled, promoting more social mobility. Richard Cobden wrote that 'the state of society' was 'more healthy and natural in a moral and political sense . . . There is a freer intercourse between all classes than in the Lancashire town where a great and impassable gulf separates the workman from his employer.'

This may have been one of the reasons why Prince Albert decided that he would visit Birmingham in 1843, much to the disquiet of his ministers. This was just a year after some of the most bitter strikes in living memory. Robert Peel noted that 'the difficulty arose from the mayor of Birmingham being a Chartist, and the town council participating in the same violent and dangerous opinions . . . it would be accompanied by an immense physical demonstration of the trained masses of the second town in the country'. There had been riot in the air during the previous year when the Anti-Corn Law League prepared a declaration that 'the country is on the eve of a revolution, and that the wheels of Government should be arrested'. The Chartists called for a general strike.

Nothing of the kind took place. In truth Walter Bagehot, the constitutional historian, was always of the opinion that the English were a naturally deferential people. How could they have survived for so long with few bureaucrats and with the help of amateurs only, without a standing army or a secret service or any of the other appurtenances of government? There had not been a police force until recent years.

Birmingham proved to be no different. The prince's private secretary, George Anson, noted that the '280,000 population seemed entirely to have turned out on the occasion, the streets were literally jammed, but nothing could exceed the good humour and good feeling, and apparently excess of loyalty which pervaded the whole multitude'. Dire warnings and threats of revolution had in reality been followed by mass outbursts of loyalty and good feeling. We may take into account the well-known fickleness of crowds, but this does not seem to allow for the vast disparity between the revolutionary slogans and the loyal crowds. It may perhaps be wise to repeat Edmund Burke's analogy of the grasshoppers and the cattle: the grasshoppers are small in number, but they make the worst din; the cattle murmur only, but they remain the solid life of the country. A report from Manchester completes the more settled picture on a more pathetic note: 'Yet these poor people are of remarkably peaceable habits, and would have been glad to have work if they had been allowed.'

One incident of the previous year is an example of unsuccessful urban revolution. On Sunday, 3 July 1842, John William Bean, a sixteen-year-old boy, stood in a dark coat on the fringes of the crowds at the Mall waiting for the queen and her cortège to make their way from Buckingham Palace to St James's and the Chapel Royal. He was described later as a 'hunchback' with a twisted spine and the lurch of a confirmed cripple. The more refined Victorians categorized him as one of the unfortunate victims of malign fate; to most of the London populace he was merely a freak, to be whistled at, spat at and stoned by the younger boys. He had sold his small collection of books, one of them a Bible, and bought a cheap pistol for threepence. At that day on the Mall he waited for the coach carrying the queen to pass by; then he aimed his pistol and pulled the trigger. Nothing much happened. The weapon did not fire. Another boy in the crowd, Charles Edward Dassett, saw what had happened and pulled the gun away from Bean. But he was too slow. A crowd had gathered around the small incident while a rumour spread that the queen had been shot. In the confusion Bean managed to slip away while Dassett was caught holding the pistol. It took some time for the confusion to be dispelled and the facts to be ascertained. Eventually a poster was put up with the description of a male 'thin made, short neck, and humped back, walks a little on one side, long sickly pale face . . .' The police leaped into action and hauled into their local stations any young hunchback they could find. It was reported that the number of 'little deformed men detained' was 'astonishing'. But Bean was finally identified and arrested, sentenced to eighteen months' hard labour. 'It is worth being shot at', Victoria said later, 'to see how much one is loved.'

The cities of the north and the Midlands had one significant similarity. The slums of the poor were still areas shunned, meanly built with dilapidated houses leaning over the narrow and dirty lanes. For all the spacious streets and commodious houses of 'Woolborough' or Bradford, there were quarters where dwelt only wretchedness, misery and disease. The lower depths of English towns and cities had no drains, no sewers, no toilets, no water. The mills and factories, the pride of the north, spilled noxious fumes and corrupted water into the nearby streets. 'In the manufacturing towns of England,' one health inspector wrote, 'most of which have enlarged with great rapidity, the additions have been made without regard to either the personal comfort of the inhabitants or the necessities which congregation requires'. And then there was the smoke, the Bradford smoke, the Leeds smoke, the Manchester smoke, each of a different colour and intensity, and each of a different odour; sometimes it condensed and congealed, falling as black rain or what was known as 'blacks'. The mayor of Middlesbrough asserted that 'the smoke is an indication of plenty of work – an indication of prosperous times – an indication that all classes of workpeople are being employed, that there is little necessity for charity and that even those in the humblest station are in a position free from want. Therefore we are proud of our smoke.' If it was set at the right tempo and cadence, this could be a significant Victorian hymn.

A hymn too, might have been formed out of what was known as the 'associative principle' which grew up in the cities as part of the common interest and common dependency. This 'principle' of mutual interest also covered the various voluntary organizations and social groups which made up the cultural and spiritual life of the cities; choral societies, debating clubs, social clubs and sporting associations all formed the close-knit fabric. A respectable citizen, or his wife, might join The London Philanthropic Society for Providing the Poor with Bread and Coal in Winter or The General Domestic Servants Benevolent Institution.

But a different form of enterprise was reaching out. In 1844 twenty-eight flannel weavers, calling themselves the Rochdale Society of Equitable Pioneers, amassed a capital sum of £28 and opened a co-operative store in Toad Lane. Their plan was to sell goods at current prices and then retain the surplus cash as the common property of the membership. Their success was evident, their profits useful, and their reputation spread until it became the Co-operative Wholesale Society. Its members attended meetings after hours in which they discussed the topics of the day. In seven years they had made a gross profit of £900 and there was already talk of schools and housing for their workers. It was one of the most formidable legacies of the nineteenth-century world. It had a tenuous line with Chartists, also built upon solidarity and class interest, but by this time Chartism was in rapid decline. Other forces would have to take its place. At the heads of their articles was the promise that: 'The objects of this Society are the moral and intellectual advancement of its members. It provides them with groceries, butchers' meat, drapery goods, clothes and clogs.'

The city implies crowds, grim and monotonous as they make their way to and from their place of work with the steady tread of shoes or boots upon stone; sometimes light and rapid in pursuit of some street entertainment or diversion; and at other times stolid and purposeless like a vagrant without a home. All these and a thousand others make up the nineteenth-century crowd. 'As we pushed through the crowd,' Charles Kingsley wrote in 1850, 'I was struck with the wan haggard look of all faces; their lack-lustre eyes and drooping lips, stooping shoulders, heavy, dragging steps, gave them a crushed, dogged air which was infinitely painful, and bespoke a grade of misery more habitual and degrading than that of the excitable and passionate artisan.'

The politics of town and city soon became the politics of the nation. One radical pamphlet of 1885 noted that 'the great towns as they now are constitute the source and centre of English public opinion. It is from them that Liberal legislation receives its initiatives; it is the steady pressure exercised by them that guarantees the political progress of the country.' They had developed their momentum in a very short time. In the 1830s Manchester was still organized by a manorial court, and Middlesbrough was barely a name. Yet their new men came forward with their own remedies for social ills. They formed a new urban bourgeoisie, and the editor of the *Leeds Mercury* remarked of these new cities that 'although they cannot boast of the historic glories of the great capitals of Europe . . . are even now superior to many of them in wealth and population and are laying broad and deep the foundations of a future destiny which may vie in interest and importance with some of the most famous cities of the ancient world.' In the first fifty years of the nineteenth century Manchester's population rose from 75,000 to 303,000, Birmingham's from 75,000 to 247,000 and Leeds's from 53,000 to 172,000. Between 1841 and 1901 the population of England and Wales more than doubled, and it was clear enough that the rising population came from urban surroundings.

The seaside towns, such as Brighton, Weymouth and Torquay, also flourished beyond their respective bounds. Spas and watering places, already with a decidedly dubious reputation, became more and more popular. William Cobbett noted that 'to places like this come all that is knavish and all that is foolish, and all that is base; gamesters, pickpockets, and harlots . . .' The example he mentions is now the genteel Cheltenham.

12

Charitable government

Those who were against government provision on principle summoned up visions of financial malfeasance and economic manipulation in England itself that proved quickly to be baseless. In fact something of an economic 'boom' had begun in 1844 and lasted for twenty years, during which period the railway system was more or less completed and the costs of production in cotton mills fell significantly. The impact of new technology and freer trade was now becoming part of public consciousness. In 1844 Gladstone, as president of the Board of Trade in the ministry of Peel, proposed a bill that would allow the government to buy out any railway after fifteen years. Peel did not favour the change, however, and instead proposed a scheme whereby every company would have to run a 'third-class' train every day at a penny a mile. These cheap trains had previously been open carriages, with holes in the floor to let the water run through, but the new bill insisted that they were fitted with roofs. Gladstone resisted the idea that cheap trains should run on Sundays on the grounds that 'the working respectable mechanic would not choose the Lord's Day for travelling'. First- and second-class passengers, however, were allowed the privilege of defying the Lord under the terms of the Railway Regulation Act.

In the same act provisions were made for the use of the electrical telegraph on every line. Three years before, the first telegraph system for commercial purposes was installed on the Great Western Railway between Paddington and West Drayton; it was only 13 miles in length but it heralded a new world of communication. A newspaper advertisement proclaimed: 'The Wonder of the Age!! Instantaneous Communication . . . The Galvanic and Electro-Magnetic Telegraphs on the Great Western Railway . . . The Electric Fluid travels at the rate of 280,000 Miles per Second.' The prospect of instant communication across vast spaces was considered to be a feat almost beyond the credible. In previous years the declaration of independence by the American colonies did not reach London for six weeks, while news of Trafalgar did not reach Westminster for twelve days. Within a relatively short time the electric telegraph became the means of mass communication, and was often described as the nervous system of Victorian culture. It controlled information and of course disciplined the railway network. It had a hundred uses. By annihilating time and space the telegraph revolutionized the control of the British empire, for example, and it was widely realized that 'towns at present removed some stages from the metropolis will become its suburbs'. You could also play long-distance chess. Some years later, in 1889, Lord Salisbury described the telegraph as 'a discovery which operates . . . immediately upon the moral and intellectual nature and action of mankind'. A quotation from Job was often employed: 'Canst thou send lightnings, that they may go and say unto thee, Here we are.' It was also understood in terms of fairy story and enchantment. But Ali Baba had never stumbled upon anything so wonderful.

Samuel Smiles dated the start of 'railway mania' to 1844, the year of the Railway Act, when 'the public outside the stock exchange shortly became infected with the same spirit, and many people, utterly ignorant of railways, knowing and caring nothing about their great national uses, but hungering and thirsting after premiums, rushed eagerly into the vortex of speculation . . . Shares! Shares! Became the general cry.' Soon 'the madness spread everywhere. It embraced merchants and manufacturers, gentry and shop-keepers, clerks in public offices and loungers in the clubs . . . No scheme was so bad that it did not find an engineer.' Hasty and slipshod building was the result; tunnels were made of half-baked clay instead of bricks, and rubble was used for the foundation of bridges. There were already one hundred and four separate railway companies, and six years later the number had doubled. A popular writer of the time, Dionysius Lardner, wrote: 'it is impossible to regard the vast buildings and their dependencies which constitute a chief terminal station of a great line of railways, without feelings of inexpressible astonishment . . . And then the speed!'

In this same year, the steam train reached its apotheosis in J. W. M. Turner's *Rain, Steam and Speed – The Great Western Railway*. An artist need have no opinion, and it is not at all clear whether Turner celebrated or demonized the locomotive. Any number of interpretations have been offered on the theme and composition of the painting; it has been described as a lament for the passing of the old ways or an enthusiastic rendition of the new force of steam that was changing the environment. Turner liked to travel, and it may have been his response to the new possibilities afforded by the train. The painting depicts a locomotive crossing the Thames over the Maidenhead railway bridge between Taplow and Maidenhead, but it is essentially an experiment in the vaporous sublime in which the material world of the train, the bridge and the outlying fields are wreathed in a veil of majesty and the laying down of pure colour elicits the most powerful and profound responses. Mist mixes with steam to show how two forms of reality mingle. The Great Western was already being called 'the most gigantic work', and Turner was moved to add the sublime to the grandeur.

Thackeray commented in *Fraser's Magazine* that 'the world has never seen anything like this picture'. The immediacy and energy of the painting are conveyed in his description that 'there comes a train down upon you, really moving at the rate of fifty miles an hour, and which the reader had best make haste to see, lest it should dash out of the picture, and be away up Charing Cross through the wall opposite'. He notes that the rain 'is composed of dabs of dirty putty slapped on the canvas with a trowel; the sunshine scintillates out of very thick smeary lumps of chrome yellow'. That one of the pinnacles of Turner's late art should come in the depiction of a new form of transport confirms the phenomenon of the railway as a form of genre painting. The overriding impression is that of speed. Some painters were more interested in the machine itself, while for others the terminus was depicted with vivid intensity as the architecture of a new way of life.

It is always wonderful to discern the patterns and alignments that manifest themselves in any period. The building of the railways, for example, also satisfied the Victorian passion for geology as the rock face was cut out of the land. One painter's view of the cuttings for the Manchester and Leeds Railway, for example, afforded 'a rich treat to the geologist, exhibiting numerous beautiful sections of strata, consisting of alternate beds of rock, shale, sandstone and coal, in which the parallelism and thickness of each is preserved'. So the railway connects with the deep interests of Victorian scientists. It is also significant that at the time of cutting, tunnelling and excavation, the nineteenth-century interest in fossils and the imagined prehistoric worlds became of paramount interest. Lyell's *Principles of Geology* (1830–33) became the work consulted for the nature of Creation and of the Flood, and the railway could become an instrument of Christian revelation. The nineteenth century began to explain itself and its concept of 'deep time'. So the earth was believed to have been created on the night before Sunday, 23 December 4004 BC.

Those who did the cutting, and the shovelling, and the embanking, were the 'navvies' or 'navigators' who were dreaded by the communities through which they passed. They were dirty, ribald and not at all inclined to politeness. Many were Irish, while others came from the Midlands and the north. But they had a universally recognisable uniform. The navvy would wear a white felt hat with the brim turned up, a velveteen square-tailed coat, a scarlet plush waistcoat and brightly coloured kerchief about his neck; his trousers were of corduroy and were tied at the knee, with sturdy high-lace boots. They were wanderers, moving individually or in groups from one set of works to another. The police or the officials of the railway company did not try to discipline them. It would have been futile.

It is a hard irony that, however much the policy of Peel prospered, the enemies in his own party flourished. In February 1845 he brought forward what was called 'the great Budget' in which import duties were abolished or reduced. Yet his obvious supporters were disaffected by his further embrace of free trade, especially since he insisted on maintaining the income tax; it was no longer considered to be a temporary measure. There was another flurry of Tory outrage in the spring of the year when Peel was instrumental in granting taxpayers' money to a Catholic seminar at Maynooth in Ireland. Not only was he against farmers, but he was on the side of the Roman Catholics! Rumours of treachery were everywhere. The Maynooth Bill was passed only with Whig support. Peel had wanted to tempt the Irish Catholics into friendship with the promise of real equality, but he seemed only able to infuriate the English. Yet the real betrayal, as it seemed to many Tories, was about to begin.

By the middle of October 1845, the dire news from Ireland upset all calculations. The potato crop had failed. This was a matter of life and death for a whole country where the potato was the only food. The duke of Wellington recorded Peel's suffering at a calamity that should have been considered: 'I never witnessed in any case such agony.' He added later to a colleague that 'rotten potatoes have done it all. They have put Peel in his damned fright.' The duke's tone is a measure of the standard response to the Irish calamity, leaving aside the fact that he himself was Anglo-Irish of Dublin stock. The English just wished it would go away. But the famine prevailed and lingered. Over the next three years 650,000 died; in the next three years a further 1,100,000 followed them into the grave. It was believed to be a form of genocide brought on by negligence and indifference.

The policy of England towards Ireland had always been characterized by a kind of shifty ignorance, and this was particularly true of the Famine. The government had no precedent on which to build. Mass starvation on such a scale was a disaster for which it was unprepared logistically and – even more to the point – ideologically. That it was the business of government to alleviate famine in an entire nation was a thought that occurred to no one in power at the time. As far as many in England were concerned, the sufferings of the Irish during the Famine were of the same kind as those they endured even in good years, just in greater degree: semi-starvation was the order of the day whenever the Irish had to wait for the next potato crop to ripen every year. And it is easy to forget that the progress of starvation and disease as a result of the Famine was, though terrible, relatively piecemeal; it was easy for British officials to point to the fact that the harvests were not uniformly disastrous. England and Scotland were not comparably affected. Nevertheless, corn was almost impossible to obtain either from the Continent or from America, a problem the British government could do little to remedy when it cast about for alternatives to the potato.

Two other intractable difficulties bedevilled the question: absentee landlordism and the tenancy system. Though both can ultimately be traced to English oppression and bigotry, they had acquired a distinctively Irish character. Most Irish landlords lived in England, and so when the better-intentioned among them returned to Ireland they discovered, to their horror and shame, that the sixty or so tenants on their lists had mutated into several thousand, clamouring feebly at their door. Simply in terms of finance, they were quite unequal to the demands made of them by the situation itself and, increasingly, by the government.

There was also the peculiar nature of Irish tenancy arrangements. In Ireland, tenancy was a Byzantine system of subletting which ensured that the smaller tenants could be hidden from the landowner by unscrupulous middlemen. They had, moreover, no rights worth the name. Owing to the urgent need to use all possible land for potato cultivation, acres in Ireland could be as dear as acres in Mayfair. The comparisons do not end there: rent in Ireland was effectively ground rent – the peasant paid for the privilege of living on the land. There was thus no ethic of reciprocal obligation such as obtained in England. With all this said in mitigation, however, it was widely felt in political circles that the Irish were guilty of lack of initiative or energy, and their supposed unimaginative attitude poisoned and weakened English fellow-feeling. One example will suffice. A priest from the west of Ireland, begging that a grain store be opened for his starving flock, was informed that such a gesture would go against the principles of free trade and upset the 'mercantile interest'. The priest's response was properly fierce, but the chilling obtuseness in the official he encountered was quite typical. While the Irish fell dead in their fields, beef, pork, lamb and a host of other necessaries were still being exported in bulk.

Free trade was Ireland's Shiva, lord of destruction. The bitter irony is that the Irish were killed not by negligence or indifference, but by a fanatic application of free-trade dogma to an economy that was simply not ready for it. The foods imported were almost useless, the foods exported essential to the exporting country – yet import and export had become sacred nostrums. It was characteristic of Victorian England that once it had found a new toy it must wave it about at every opportunity. Free trade was the new toy, but Ireland was in no condition to play with it. Where the charge of 'genocide' has more force, however, is in the policy openly known as 'extermination' (though the word still carried its old sense of 'mass eviction'). It was informed by much the same blithe indifference to Irish needs and realities as fuelled the mania for exporting. The land, it was felt, could not support the people, therefore the people must be driven from the land. English policy towards Ireland may be compared to a magnate suggesting to a beggar that his real problem was not starvation but short-sightedness.

Peel announced emergency measures to provide imported corn and to put the people to work on public projects. But still the people were dying by the roadsides before they were built. It was said that when they died they made no noise nor gave any sign. This was true of the western highlanders, too, when their potatoes rotted in the ground. Henry Kingsley noted from observation that 'the oldest of the able-bodied men began to lie down, and to fall asleep in a strange quiet way'. A French observer, Gustave de Beaumont, noted that 'in every nation there are poor people, more or less numerous. But an entire nation of paupers is something never witnessed before.'

At a cabinet meeting of November 1845 Peel proposed two measures which might help to assuage the hunger of Ireland and the anger of England. He proposed to suspend the Corn Laws as they were presently administered in order to alleviate the chronic shortages across the Irish Sea. He also proposed that parliament should consider the Corn Laws as a whole with a view to their repeal. The first measure was broadly accepted, even though many ministers considered it to be too late. The second measure was the occasion of fierce anger and debate, as a result of which Peel resigned. But he was not gone for long. His Whig opponent, John Russell, had recently pledged himself to repeal the Laws; and so he naturally took up the queen's commission. He took about a fortnight to realize that without the commanding authority of Peel he did not have the power to act. He did not even have full control of his proposed cabinet, when Palmerston refused to hold any office other than that of foreign secretary. So Peel returned to the battle. The newspapers now sensed that the moment had come.

When parliament met once more, in January 1846, Peel made a speech in which he announced his conversion to the cause of free trade and the repeal of the Corn Laws. 'I will not withhold the homage which is due to the progress of reason and to the truth, by denying that my opinions on the subject of protection have undergone a change.' The back benches behind him were silent. The debates continued until May, when a third reading was passed by ninety-eight votes. The salient feature of the result, however, was that 222 Tories voted against Peel's measures. He had won the vote but had lost his party somewhere along the way. Now there were Peelites and anti-Peelites, the larger flock being shepherded by Disraeli and Bentinck. The Tory rebels had their revenge on the next day when they voted against Peel's Protection of Life (Ireland) Bill, a measure which in ordinary circumstances they would have supported. But the circumstances were not ordinary. Disraeli had already dipped his pen in the darkest ink when in *Sybil*, published the year before, he had argued that there were 'two nations'; everybody knew what he meant but he spelled it out in capital letters: 'THE RICH AND THE POOR'. He could make a novel, but not a programme for government, out of the truism.

The Conservatives never loved Peel, and they never forgave him. Disraeli in particular brought his energies to bear on Peel's destruction. 'I love fame', he said, and for the rest of his life he acted on that assumption. He hardly needed to repeat the obvious. It was already clear that the days before Peel's departure could be numbered.

There was much rejoicing at Peel's belated defeat and Peel was obliged to resign; he was followed by the appointment of Lord John Russell as the head of a minority Whig government. But the deed had been done. The Corn Laws were gone. The middle-class shopkeepers and artisans cheered at the news. The Tory party may have withdrawn in smoke and confusion but, as Richard Cobden said, 'the intelligent middle and industrious classes' would be the beneficiaries.

Now that the Corn Laws had been removed there was an almost palpable sense of relief that an unjustified oppression, born out of social inequality and a self-interested legislature, had been lifted. Cobden addressed one of the last meetings of the Anti-Corn Law League and stated:

> there is no human event that has happened in the world more calculated to promote the enduring interests of humanity than the establishment of the principle of free trade – I don't mean in a pecuniary point of view, or as a principle applied to England, but we have a principle established now which is eternal in its truth and universal in its application . . . it is a world's revolution and nothing else.

His exuberance may be justified by the occasion but it is also testimony to the high principles of the politics of the day.

The repeal of the Corn Laws also put aside any remaining talk of revolution on the French model. As Cobden wrote a few days later to Francis Place, 'bless yourself that you live in times when reform bills, steamboats, railroads, penny postage and free trade, to say nothing of the ratification of civil and religious liberties, have been possible facts'.

The liberal Conservatives now followed Peel, although he disclaimed in any sense a Peelite faction; yet eventually Peelites joined with the Whig free-traders. The Protectionists, now bereft of leaders except for Disraeli and Bentinck, had all the appearance of having missed the omnibus. They seemed to be aware of the fact, and Bentinck was observed in the chamber making a bitter attack upon the government. 'His voice was raised to a screaming pitch – his eye gleamed like a wild animal at feeding time and his whole demeanour was so excited that no man out of Bedlam ever came near it.'

The same sensation of unanticipated liberty had followed the Reform Act of 1832. Now, as then, was another chance to clear away the dead wood that had accumulated over the generations. John Stuart Mill wrote to his French philosophical counterpart, Auguste Comte, in 1847:

we have embarked on a system of charitable government . . .
Today all the cry is to provide the poor not only with money
. . . shorter hours of work . . . better sanitation, even education.
That is to say they are to be governed paternally, a course to
which the Court, the nobility and the wealthy are quite agreeable. They forget that what is done for people benefits them
only when it assists them in what they do for themselves.

And so there passed a twelve hours bill and other salutary factory
reforms (by which was primarily meant the textile industry), a new
mines act and progress both with the poor law and public sanitation.
The working day for women and children was steadily reduced from
twelve hours in 1844 to ten hours in 1847; the hours for factory
children were reduced to six and a half to make way for education;
and the power of factory inspectors was significantly increased.

The process took some years and was accompanied by fiery
speeches and reproaches. In his *Memoirs* Charles Greville notes of
the furore accompanying one Ten Hours Bill which failed that there
was 'such intermingling of parties, such a confusion of opposition
. . . so much zeal, asperity and animosity, so many reproaches hurled
backwards and forwards'. It was in part the rage of Caliban looking
in a glass. By 1847 the 'system' had emerged or, as Disraeli wrote
in *Tancred* (1847), 'men obey a general impulse, they bow before an
external necessity' which was also known as 'the powers of society'.
Six years later, however, Dickens declared that 'our system fails'.

In 1847 itself there was already general talk of failure. One of
the great motors of investment in the railway was the opposing
tendency between 'mania' and 'panic'. Those who have studied the
madness and exhilaration of crowds are quite familiar with the
phenomenon. There was in 1847, for example, a sudden 'panic' in
the financial markets. A fall in the price of corn in the summer,
prompted by the repeal of the Corn Laws, caused the bankruptcy
of many dealers; a significant number of banks found that they were
burdened by so many bad debts that they had to suspend dealing.
The shortage of basic food supplies was responsible for a rise in
prices, as well as trade deficits which created a drain of bullion from
the Bank of England. The turmoil worked through the 'system' at
precisely the time when 'railway mania' increased the demand for

circulating capital. In America the cotton crop was less bountiful than usual at a time when England took 80 per cent of its cotton from the southern states. Turmoil and fear fed one upon another. Did the railways starve the country of capital or did they provide income and employment? But the panic subsided almost as soon as it arose, and became part of the general fluctuating and erratic nature of the business cycles which seemed to defy rational explanation. In the dark womb of time recovery seemed to come from nowhere. That is why some people related economic cycles to the phases of the moon.

Despite the interest in social reform there had been little progress in the education of the people. Even by 1870 only one child out of three attended a school of even the most rudimentary kind. Many people disputed that there was any progress to be made. Children were meant to work and to sustain their families in the unequal battle for survival. What was the point of stuffing their little heads with facts when they had no earthly use for them? Let them learn to work in a pin factory or cotton mill. And what was the point of universal literacy? The lower orders would only learn to read salacious propaganda, radical pamphlets and Whig tracts. The experiment of the 'ragged schools', meant for the children of the street, was not altogether a success; they were accused of spreading lice and bad habits.

Yet the educational reformers persisted. Their work took two forms. The 'national schools', established in 1811, used a model devised by Andrew Bell whereby older children acted as monitors and taught the younger children. Joseph Lancaster, another prominent educational reformer, used a broadly similar system but with more rigid discipline. When in 1833 parliament made an annual grant of £22,000 the amount was equally distributed between the two schemes; it could hardly be said to have been a generous provision. There were deep pits of ignorance which no funds could reach, abysses among the poor where no light could be seen. The Church and Dissent fought over the spoils of the little children, with the result that 75 per cent of the children who had gone through 'the system' only knew the letters of the alphabet and had little or no understanding of the words they uttered by rote.

The Whigs, together with assorted radicals, now governed

Britain with any number of compromises, conditions and caveats. The leader of the party in the Commons, John Russell, was a natural debater without being a natural politician. Peel himself, in opposition, was withdrawing to the margin of visibility. 'The fact is,' he told a colleague:

> that the state of public business while Parliament sits is becoming in many ways a matter of most serious concern. I defy the Minister of this country to perform properly the duties of his office – to read all that he ought to read, including the whole foreign correspondence; to keep up the constant communication with the Queen and the Prince; to see all whom he ought to see; to superintend the grant of honours and the disposal of civil and ecclesiastical patronage; to write with his own hand to every person of note who chooses to write to him; to be prepared for every debate, including the most trumpery concerns; to do all these indispensable things, and also sit in the House of Commons eight hours a day for 118 days. It is impossible for me not to feel that the duties are incompatible, and above all human strength – at least above mine.

Peel did not leave parliament. He thought it enough to resign his leadership of the party and forsake any further ambition. But he had to remain even if only to support the demoralized Whig party that had come into office as a result of his defeat. He could not contemplate the possibility of the Protectionists or radicals coming to power, and so he did all he could to prop up John Russell and his colleagues. He made it plain that he would support the Whig administration so long as they maintained the conditions of his policies. It was now believed that Peel essentially stood 'above party'. While some still continued to speak of his betrayal there were many who applauded his rigour and determination to maintain the state and to protect Reform.

Everyone talked about Ireland. No political conversation could do without it. It was on every politician's mind. Gladstone wrote to his wife in the autumn of 1845: 'Ireland! Ireland! That cloud in the West! That coming storm! That minister of God's retribution upon cruel, inveterate and but half-atoned injustice! Ireland forces upon us the great social and great religious questions. God grant that we may have the courage to look them in the face!' The Almighty was invoked for a number of reasons. For many it was the punishment for espousing Roman Catholicism or, in an alternative eschatology, the divine rebuke for sloth and fecklessness. More secular souls believed that providence had nothing to do with it, and that the failures were biological and mechanical. The harvests had in fact begun to improve by 1847, but they had left sickness, debility and fever in their wake.

13

The salamander

Peel's resignation speech at the end of June 1846 was notable for its unaccustomed oratory. 'It may be', he said, 'that I shall leave a name sometimes to be remembered with expressions of good will in the abodes of those whose lot it is to labour, and earn their bread daily by the sweat of their brow, when they shall recruit their exhausted strength with abundant and untaxed food, the sweeter because it is no longer leavened by a sense of injustice.' He was escorted from Westminster by a cheering crowd. When Lord John Russell took office after Peel in the summer of 1846 he offered cabinet posts to Wellington and other Conservatives, but all of them refused. Peel remained the most prominent politician in parliament, and Cobden congratulated him as 'the *Idea* of the age', the word doubly underlined.

Lord Palmerston joined Russell's cabinet as foreign secretary, thereby detonating some explosions of ill will in foreign capitals. It was a minority cabinet in the sense that the Whigs, radicals and Irish under Russell by no means represented a majority of the parliament. But Peel had no intention of leading a determined opposition against him. The Peelites were not so much a party as a fellowship of Peel's former supporters. *The Times* noted that 'their present difficulty is that they are not a party; they have not its ties; they have not its facilities; they have not its obligations'. But they still possessed Peel's ideals of free trade and economic stringency; and perhaps most importantly they retained Peel's independence of mind. It did not seem likely that they would be open to the bribe of cabinet posts.

In fact over the next twenty years squalls and tempests followed doldrums. Eight administrations followed each other, and for some years there was no party with a stable majority. There was at one stage a patched-up government between Whigs, radicals and Peelites, but this ill-starred coalition was directly responsible for the Crimean War. The general feeling was one of immobility, and if it had been hoped that the subsequent general election in the summer of 1847 might galvanize the electors and the elected, the expectation was largely unfulfilled. The result was much the same as before, with John Russell and his light cavalry dashing through the divided ranks of the Protectionists under Bentinck and the free-traders under Peel. But what exactly did it mean to call yourself a Whig or Tory? Nobody seemed to care very much, one way or the other.

It is significant that the new chancellor of the Exchequer, Sir Charles Wood, asked for and accepted Peel's advice on financial matters. In a debate Peel outlined what became his position for the rest of his life – that he would not encourage 'a factious or captious opposition' and that 'I cordially approve of the general principles of commercial policy set out by the administration.' John Russell was recognized as the leader of the Liberal party but he knew himself to be, at bottom, an old-fashioned Whig. So the Factory Act, passed in 1847, was an attempt at social amelioration, although the prime minister gave it only passive support. Women and young people were now allowed to work only ten hours a day in the textile mills; it was the result of a fifteen-year campaign. It has been described as a victory by the people against the government, and this may partly be true; it issued from a groundswell of support among operatives with encouragement from labour reformers such as Lord Ashley and John Fielden, a cotton manufacturer and MP for Oldham. It has also been described as a victory for landowners against the free-traders who had helped to repeal the Corn Laws. Those who supported laissez-faire were not inclined to support state intervention in traditions of employment.

John Russell took on his role as first minister with caution; his reforms were modest and moderate without a hint of revolutionary change. He had tinkered with the edges of the Irish famine, although it is not clear that any immediate changes would have made any difference to the suffering nation. It was left in the hands of God, who could not be criticized or blamed for His ministrations. Yet there were measures which had all the traits of what once would have been called Whig government. A Poor Law Board was established in 1847, and in the following year a parallel Central Board of Health was able to create local boards with statutory powers on public health from water to cemeteries. State control over education was strengthened, and the parliamentary franchise widened. A public welfare service was slowly coming into place. All these measures were manna for the quondam Whig aristocrats who had inherited a political sensibility which encouraged relief for all classes. The great landlords were, or thought themselves to be, the guardians of the nation who had a permanent interest in the welfare of all the people. Russell himself governed much as his Whig ancestry would suggest, with a waspish dominance, but he was not an inspiring prime minister; he was one of those who attain their eminence only by degrees.

The administration inaugurated by the ministry of Lord John Russell, had other consequences. The radical or Nonconformist members of parliament were now often businessmen or urban professionals; they sat for urban industrial seats, and the prosperity of commercial and industrial interests encouraged the rise of what might be called a professional class in suits of black and stovepipe hats. The great landowners could still ride this wave of new men, but gradually the temper and tenor of the Commons changed. It was no longer a congregation of the rich landlords and their dependants. It was now being affected by what eventually became known, by Disraeli and Salisbury, as 'industrial' Conservatism. There had been before the 'landed interest' or the 'local interest', composed of loyalty and patriarchy, but this was now diminished. The ubiquity of the railways meant that many on the land were displaced, and that many landowners became more interested in industry than agriculture. The lawyers of the railway companies were more than a match for the farmer, and the individual members of the 'landed interest' were on their own. So the lawyers also came into parliament.

The politicians and agitators knew all about Protectionism and free trade, but those who were dependent on agriculture were woefully ill-equipped to deal with the issues of the day. Inevitably their influence waned. Various attempts to set up Protectionist societies fell apart; farmers and labourers alike were loath to engage in popular demonstrations, even if they could have been organized.

Rural depopulation, however, was something of a chimera. Some of it was the result of a steady stream of emigration to North America, and in each of the three years after 1847 more than half a million emigrants crossed the ocean. Yet such was the energy or fecundity of the people that the population continued to increase. We can speak of depopulation only in terms of the number of families involved in agriculture, which did diminish, but the overall population of the countryside remained the same. In the country areas, too, improved agricultural techniques and more labour-intensive crops increased the workload for those who stayed on the land. The pattern of movement from fields to the local town was significant enough, but the outline of rural change over fifty years was a sequence of small-scale migrations over a limited territory. There was a continuity, even though a cursory reading of William Cobbett's *Rural Rides* (1830) would cure the reader of any illusion of rural comfort or tranquillity. The lives of the labourers were often dirtier and not less wretched than those of their dogs. They worked on the land because they feared and hated the spinning mills or, even worse, the privations of the poor house. The unknown was also the father of fear; when some manual labourers were being moved from north Devon to Kent, at the fiat of some landlord, they asked if they were 'going over the water'.

In 1846 Harriet Martineau wrote to Elizabeth Barrett:

> I dare say you need not be told how sensual vice abounds in rural districts . . . here is dear good old Wordsworth forever talking of rural innocence and deprecating any intercourse with towns, lest the purity of his neighbours should be corrupted. He little knows what elevation, self-denial and refinement accrue in towns from the superior cultivation of the people.

Yet the rural population had performed its duties. The King of Brobdingnag believed that 'whoever could make two ears of corn or two blades of grass to grow upon a spot of ground where only one grew before, would deserve better of mankind and do more essential service to his country than the whole race of politicians put together.' In 1816 the population of the British Islands had numbered 19 million; forty-five years later it had reached 29 million. But they were still being fed.

The attention of the nation turned again to the generally forgotten fields of foreign policy. Eighteen forty-eight became known as the 'year of revolutions', much to the dismay of those who wished for a century of peace. It was perhaps fortunate that the most formidable member of the Whig cabinet was Viscount Palmerston, who once more reigned over the Foreign Office. Reign is the word, because he was the sole monarch of his domain. He was a consummate man of business, a tireless worker, and a man whose apparent recklessness concealed cunning and, on especial occasions, high seriousness. The temperature had been raised at the beginning of 1847 when the duke of Wellington rose up and prophesied gloom. He wrote privately to a fellow officer on the unprotected state of Britain and, as such things happen, his letter was leaked to the press. It was revealed to the public that there was 'not a spot on the coast on which infantry might not be thrown on shore at any time of tide, with any wind, and in any weather, and from which such a body of infantry, so thrown on shore, would not find within a distance of five miles, a road into the interior of the country'. Immediate panic was the inevitable consequence. The fact was that Britain had for some time seemed to be uninterested in foreign affairs until they came too close for comfort.

The prospect of disorder loomed nearer when revolution touched France, Germany and Italy. In February fire and street-fighting filled the avenues of Paris, after Louis Philippe banned certain private meetings of the opposition parties; the troops shot at the crowd, and the riots followed. When Louis took off his wig he was, according to Victor Hugo, 'but an ordinary tradesman'. He fled to England under the name of Mr Smith just as the Second Republic was proclaimed. In March the people of Berlin rose up, as a result of which William, Prince of Prussia, fled to England. Ludwig I of Bavaria followed the procession by abdicating in favour of his son. The emperor of Austria, Ferdinand I, left Vienna for Innsbruck and then Moravia. The Hungarians demanded independence from Austria. The Czechs of Bohemia demanded their own parliament. Venice and Lombardy also rose against their old imperial enemy. The pope left Rome in disguise. But then the balloon burst.

One by one the rebel forces were defeated by the old guards; ethnic tensions were exploited as the Magyars turned upon Slavs instead of their common imperial enemy. One by one the rulers crept back upon their thrones. It might be described as a moment of madness in what *Punch* called 'the Asylum of Europe', but Lewis Namier described it as a 'turning point at which history failed to turn'. It is perhaps better to say that the ambition for change and freedom outstripped the resources available. The coming men of 1848, at the head of the middle classes and working people, became the martyrs and shackled prisoners of 1849.

The temporary surge of freedom had remarkably little consequence in Europe. It put Louis-Napoleon at the head of France, where he conducted a moderately successful regime as the president of the French Second Republic before he inaugurated the Second Empire. The year of revolutions also prompted the Russians to intervene more powerfully in Hungary, where they faced the indomitable spirit of the republican hero Lajos Kossuth. The cabinet and the royal family did not wish Kossuth to call upon Palmerston during his subsequent wanderings in exile; but the politician who was now the idol of the people replied that he would invite anyone he liked to his house. Charles Greville, clerk to the Privy Council, complained of Palmerston that 'the ostentatious bidding for radical favour and the flattery of the democracy, of which his speeches were full, are disgusting in themselves and full of danger'.

Palmerston, like the salamander, lived in fire, sending robust diplomatic missives to every court and every capital; this was not to the taste of Victoria and Albert, who were constitutionally inclined to the older order which Kossuth, for example, was intent upon undermining. The complaints against the foreign secretary by the royal family were constant and demanding, but he had a habit of ignoring them or shrugging them off. 'He was easy and obliging and conciliatory in little matters,' Disraeli wrote of Palmerston as the lightly disguised earl of Roehampton in *Endymion* (1880), 'but when the credit or honour of large interests were concerned, he acted with conscious authority . . . He was a man who really cared for nothing but office and affairs . . . but he was always playful and ever taking refuge in a bantering spirit.' This is not the Palmerston that Victoria knew. She told Russell that 'he was not always straightforward in his conduct'. This was the regal manner of calling him a liar and a hypocrite.

The nearest the nation ever came to the revolutions of 1848 occurred in the spring of that year when some latter-day Chartists organized a demonstration on Kennington Common. Their purpose was once more to deliver a petition to parliament on the need for universal suffrage and the secret ballot. Their numbers are not known for sure, but it was not the half-million of Chartist mythology. They were forbidden to march with their petition to Westminster and their leader, Feargus O'Connor, took a hansom cab instead to parliament while the crowds dispersed. It had not been a famous victory.

Such was the panic in advance, however, that the authorities had taken extraordinary measures. The cavalry and infantry were posted on both sides of the bridges that spanned the Thames; boats were made ready and cannon were stationed outside Buckingham Palace and the Bank of England; 170,000 volunteers were enrolled as special constables with truncheons and white armbands. It was clear that the fear of revolution, like those in Europe, was real. But the crowds simply melted away. This effectively ended the prospect of any revolutionary party in England.

Yet the trouble was not over. In the summer of 1848 an ill-judged and ill-timed revolution in Ireland was mounted by the Young Ireland movement in imitation of the revolutions in Europe. It degenerated into a shooting match between the rebels and the police which continued for some hours until the rebels were wounded or retreated. They had been trapped in the house of Mrs McCormack, and the fracas became known as 'The Battle of Widow McCormack's cabbage plot'. It is perhaps only surprising that the rebellion collapsed as suddenly and as completely as it did. The instinctive reaction of the English government was still one of rage. Russell wrote in 1849 that 'we have granted, lent, subscribed, worked, visited, clothed the Irish; millions of pounds of money, years of debate etcetera – the only return is calumny and rebellion'. These were the predictable but unjustifiable remarks of one who in the heat of the moment had forgotten the contempt and savagery which the English had lavished on the Irish for centuries. The English found it easy to forget or to excuse their own barbarity; the Irish never did.

The year 1848 was when the first two volumes of Macaulay's *History of England* were published, the preface of which declared that 'the history of our country, during the last hundred and sixty years, is eminently the history of physical, of moral and of intellectual improvement'. It is a salutary instance of the fact that formal history can be quite at odds with the reality of the world. This 'Whig interpretation of history', as it has universally been called, acted as an intellectual comfort blanket for those who otherwise might harbour serious doubts about the future of the country.

Here we may justifiably substitute Liberal for Whig. The new term was first used in the mid-1830s, but its meaning was not clear. The Liberals suffered from weak leadership of which John Russell was the latest example, and their avidity for office was matched only by their inability to do anything much with it. Russell knew as much himself, and confessed that his party needed Peel and an injection of Peelites to give them strength and confidence. When in 1848 a group of fifty or sixty MPs decided to identify themselves as Radicals with their own political programme the Liberals were in a quandary. Were these Radicals potential allies or potential rivals? No one seemed to be sure. As a result Russell's reputation gradually dimmed. The election of 1847 had only served to emphasize the fact that he was first minister only because the Conservative opposition remained fatally divided between the Protectionists and free-traders.

The Liberals were not democrats in any proper meaning of the word, and half of their elected members were landlords or the sons of landlords. They thought themselves to be the principal ruling party on the basis of past experience rather than present politics. As late as 1886 the *Fortnightly Review* could write that 'only a few years ago the name [Whig] was a proud boast, an hereditary recollection, the appanage of a great party; now it is an historical recollection, recalling colours and cries, buff and blue . . .'

There is one other phenomenon closely associated with 1848. This was the year when spiritualism, with its panoply of levitations, ghosts, spirits, table tappings, automatic writing, telepathy and shadow photographs, became the popular version of the learned discourses and experiments on electricity. Utopian socialists were some of the earlier students of these methods, but scientists and politicians were touched by the new beliefs. Many of the first founders of the Labour party were occultists. It would be a nice question to interpret these waves of feeling – whether electrophysical or mesmeric or spiritual – which passed over the country (and indeed other countries) in this period. The Theosophical Movement of 1875 was part of this yearning towards the spirit, as was the rise of the Oxford idealists in the work of T. H. Green and the spell of J. H. Stirling's *The Secret of Hegel* published in 1865. From where did this wind of idealism and awakening derive? It is impossible to say, but it might have been some sort of reaction to the 'hard facts' theory of education as parodied by Dickens in Mr Gradgrind and to the fixity of purpose and meaning in such Victorian shibboleths as free trade, profit and loss, and factory hours. In the same spirit, and in the same period, Christian Socialism sprang up among the determined or devout young men in plain opposition to Victorian materialism. It was suggested that the conventional tenets of Victorian Anglicanism were in direct opposition to God's law. The law of life should be above the law of labour. The cash nexus was the work of the devil.

There was one figure who stalked the corridors of the House of Commons who might have been conjured by a djinn. Disraeli walked silently, looking neither right nor left; he walked with a permanent stoop, his eyes cast down to the floor. 'See him where you will,' a journalist from *Fraser's Magazine* remarked in 1847, 'he glides past you noiselessly, without apparently being conscious of the existence of externals and more like the shadow than the substance of a man'. The reporter added that 'when he is speaking he equally shrouds himself in his own intellectual atmosphere, concentrating on the idea burning in his mind'. If he is interrupted he pays no attention or averts the speaker 'with a gesture of impatience, or with something like a snarl'. When he sat in the chamber he did so 'with his head rigid, his body contracted, his arms closely pinned to his side, as though he were an automaton, like one of those stone figures of ancient Egypt that embody the idea of motionless quiescence for ever'. Yet, in contrast, his speech often seemed careless or supercilious. He gave the appearance of not caring a damn for anybody. In reality he was always cautious, always calculating.

With the withdrawal of Peel, Disraeli, still in theory the Protectionist, was the leader in waiting. He was not everyone's first choice. His unusual looks, his very precise way of enunciating English, gave him the false reputation of being a foreigner. And of course the word on everyone's lips was Jew or 'the Jew'. He knew it and did not mind it. He might have preferred it to his other nickname of 'Dizzy'. With a leading Protectionist, Lord Edward Stanley (to become Lord Derby in 1851), consigned to the Lords, Disraeli was obliged to bear the heat and the dust of parliamentary combat. He was a realist by instinct. That is why the favoured theme of Protectionism was in fact losing its savour for him. He could do nothing, and go nowhere, with it. He was, to put it kindly, lukewarm on the matter. It had lost its savour, now that free trade had become the creed of the kingdom; it was a positive encumbrance.

Yet Disraeli was optimistic. In February 1849 he announced to his sister that 'after much struggling I am fairly the leader'. The few words accounted for a multiplicity of past deals, compromises and broken promises. Disraeli was in the end the most astute and eloquent of any Tory. He also had the inestimable support, if not admiration, of the leading Tory in the Lords. Lord Edward Stanley came from a revered and noble family. He would do his duty to his colleague, but it was not clear whether he would go any further.

The tapestry of the time grew more complex. In August 1849, Victoria visited Ireland to great acclaim, despite the horrors that the country had only recently endured. When she stepped ashore at Cork an old man shouted: 'Ah, Queen dear, make one of them Prince Patrick, and Ireland will die for you.' The queen wore Irish linen decorated with shamrocks. She had purchased Osborne House on the Isle of Wight, which was even then being rebuilt. 'I was brought up very differently,' she said. 'I never had a room to myself. I never had a sofa, nor an easy chair, and there was not a single carpet that was not threadbare.' This was a time when all England was drowning in cholera, reaching up to 2,000 fatalities each week. The diagnosis of a 'zymotic' fever, whereby the disease spread by fermentation, was anyone's guess. It took the physician

John Snow to trace the source of the cholera outbreak to a polluted water pipe in Soho.

At the end of June 1850 Sir Robert Peel's horse slipped on the road of Constitution Hill. Peel lingered for a while but his injuries were too severe. This was a severe blow to the body politic, even though Peel had more or less given up party politics. He had agreed to save the administration from Protectionism, but his ambitions did not stretch beyond that. Prince Albert had greatly admired him and tried to manage the royal administration with the same efficiency and what might now be called modernity.

In his death lay a puzzle. Who had the right, and presence, to take his place as the leading free-trader? Gladstone had remained a 'Peelite' in Peel's lifetime and said that Peel 'had a kind of authority that was possessed by no one else'. He added significantly that 'the moral atmosphere of the House of Commons has never since his death been quite the same and is now widely different'. Peel had brought a certain astringency and steady intellectual power that no one could contest or perhaps even emulate.

In fact, Peel suffered his fatal accident three days before one of the most redoubtable of English statesmen enjoyed what was arguably his greatest triumph in the 'Don Pacifico Affair'. Pacifico, a Jewish businessman born in Gibraltar (and therefore a British citizen), had his house in Athens pillaged and fired by an anti-Semitic crowd. Another minister might have cooled heads with conferences and compromises. After few months of fruitless negotiation, Viscount Palmerston ordered British gunboats to secure Greek shipping to pay an indemnity and to organize a blockade. It was not the usual procedure. The queen had been furious that she had not been warned or advised about the matter, and that Palmerston had put the country at risk for the sake of one man; in short, the foreign secretary must resign. Prince Albert understood events more quickly. He wrote to Russell in the spring of 1850 that 'his boldness pleases and his dexterity amuses the public; if his case be ever so bad a one he can represent it and dress it up to his own advantage'.

The sangfroid of Palmerston was below freezing point. He did not need to resign just yet; he had no particular regard for the queen, and never knowingly pandered to her feelings. He spoke for five hours in the Commons in his own defence, expatiating on the fact that it was the duty of the British government 'to afford protection to our fellow subjects abroad . . . as the Roman, in days of old, held himself free from indignity when he could say *civis Romanus sum*'. This was the peroration that Lords and Commons, already bewildered and nervous about the growing extent of the British empire, needed to hear. He won the debate by forty-six votes.

Towards the end of 1851 the president of the Republic, Louis-Napoleon Bonaparte, took over the state machinery of the Republic and imprisoned many of his rivals to make way for the inauguration of the Second French Empire under his rule as Napoleon III. In England the royal couple, and the ministry, had concluded that nothing whatever should be done to praise or to blame the French action. But this was not Palmerston's way. He let it be known that he approved of Louis-Napoleon's action as the inevitable outcome of the situation in France. This was more than the royal couple could bear, the matter made infinitely more grave when Palmerston actually congratulated Louis-Napoleon on his success without first consulting them. This was Pilgerstein, or pumice stone as Albert contemptuously called him, at his worst. As first minister Lord John Russell considered that the die had been cast and, calculating that he might survive with a new foreign minister or without any foreign minister all, he ordered Palmerston to resign.

But he may have misjudged the man. Palmerston was not going to leave quietly. He crossed the floor with his allies and joined the Conservatives under Lord Derby, who was still better known for exercising horse flesh. 'Palmerston is out!' Charles Greville confided to his diary on 23 December 1851, 'actually, really and irretrievably out. I nearly dropped off my chair yesterday afternoon . . .' Lord Granville was his chosen successor and the queen instructed him to lay out a set of general instructions with the help of Lord Russell.

Peel's sudden death had left men bewildered. Would X take over the leadership of the Peelites, leaving Y high and dry? Or would M dish the lot of them by going to the Lords? And, if so, what would N do? 'Such was the confusion of the Ministerial movement and the political process,' *Punch* wrote, 'that everybody went to call upon everybody.' After Palmerston was dismissed following constant royal pressure he promised to have his tit-for-tat with 'Johnnie' Russell as soon as may be. In February 1852 Russell introduced a Militia Bill and, when Palmerston successfully introduced an amendment, Russell resigned. This was Palmerston's revenge. Lord Derby succeeded in the very slippery position of first minister of an unstable Conservative administration divided between Peelites and Protectionists.

Another crisis had already presented itself. In the autumn of 1850, after the pope had been restored to the Vatican by his French allies, he issued a brief for 'the re-establishing and extending the Catholic faith in England'. England and Wales were converted into twelve sees, with Henry Edward Manning, soon to be archbishop and then cardinal, at the top of the procession in London. The furore was immense; the queen considered it to be an affront to her rule while the then prime minister, Lord John Russell, dismissed Manning as an ambitious convert.

In a letter to the comfortably orthodox bishop of Durham, Russell condemned the pope's intervention as 'insolent and insidious'. Russell knew very well that the queen considered him to be a small man in every sense, and needed some great cause to raise him higher. Now he had found it, and he was not about to let it go. In the queen's speech, on the opening of parliament in 1851, she announced her 'resolution to maintain the right of her crown, and the independence of the nation against all encroachments, from whatever quarter they may proceed'. All eyes turned to the papal apartments in the Vatican. Russell then issued a motion banning Catholic priests and prelates from claiming any territorial titles and ordering that lay gifts to them should be returned.

This pleased the people, not least the electorate, just as Russell had planned and hoped. It was in truth a minor storm in the baptismal font which caused no great alteration. But the cry of 'No Popery!' was one which united Englishmen, whether rich or poor, religious or neutral. The hawkers and the sweepers on the street knew all the words of the protest songs. It was clear that the pope would head the victims on Bonfire Night.

The missive from the pope coincided with mounting dismay in the ranks of Anglicans. Old-fashioned churchmen were not happy about the progress of ritualists within the Church of England; their vestments and thurifers belonged to Baal. Lord Shaftesbury remarked that he 'would rather worship with Lydia on the bank by the riverside than with a hundred surpliced priests in the temple of St Barnabas'. The newly built church of St Barnabas, in Pimlico, was a treasure house of Catholic ritual, including a wooden screen to separate the participant clergy from the congregation. It contained fair cloths and jewels, all of them condemned by Nonconformists as the trappings of Satan. The outcry against papal intervention was therefore more bitter. 'What a surprising ferment,' Lord Shaftesbury wrote. 'It abates not a jot, meeting after meeting, in every town and part in the country . . . it resembles a storm over the whole nation . . . All opinions seem for a while submerged in this one feeling.' Benjamin Disraeli was an acute observer. He wrote to Lord Londonderry: 'what do you think of Cardinal Wiseman? Even the peasants think they are going to be burned alive and taken up to Smithfield instead of their pigs.'

Catholicism in England was tainted by association with Ireland, adding to the sentiment of anti-popery. 'In former Irish rebellions,' one of Gladstone's political allies, Sir William Harcourt, wrote, 'the Irish were in Ireland. Now there is an Irish nation in the United States, equally hostile, with plenty of money, absolutely beyond our reach and yet within ten days of our shores.' It was believed also that the Irish migrants were a threat to their English neighbours. A supposed humorist in *Punch* noted the 'missing link' between the gorillas of the jungle and 'the Negro' in the presence of the 'Irish Yahoo' in the lowest areas of London. The *Birmingham Star* remarked of the Fenian brotherhood that 'numbers of insane people, of the very lowest class, get together stealthily in out of the way places for the purposes of drill. "Death to the Saxon" is of course supposed to be their watch-word and their object, but of what they would do after the killing, neither they, nor anyone else, have the least idea.' This is one of the most powerful anxieties of nineteenth-century England, and it was reinforced by statistics that purported to show the connection between the Irish and criminality. The fact that the Irish-born population in England rose by some 30,000 from 1841 to 1861 only served to increase hostility. The people did not need statistics but relied upon native observation. South Lancashire and London were the areas most affected. By the latter part of the century, however, xenophobia was being directed against the Jews of the East End. There was always an enemy somewhere.

The Ecclesiastical Titles Bill, as Russell's measure was called, passed with a large majority. It was repealed twenty years later after altering nothing whatsoever. William Ewart Gladstone travelled to Rome during the parliamentary recess of 1851, but not to kiss the fisherman's ring. He had come to investigate the troubled politics of the region. He had also come, according to his first biographer, John Morley, 'into that great stream of European Whiggism which was destined to carry him so far'.

He had gone down to Naples ostensibly for a pleasure trip but he seized the opportunity of visiting the prisons and prisoners there. He was appalled by what he saw. Here were filth and misery, 'the sick prisoners, almost with death in their faces'. He was determined to bring the merciless injustices of Naples to the attention of the British press, thereby to mend them or end them. It was his first manifestation of the moral earnestness he would now carry with him everywhere; he possessed a passionate purposefulness combined with an angry will for improvement.

So the tit-for-tat by Palmerston against Russell had succeeded, with the earl of Derby as the bewildered Conservative victor. Disraeli had called Palmerston 'an imposter, utterly exhausted, and at best only ginger beer, and not champagne, and now an old painted pantaloon'. Yet Pantalone might turn into Harlequin, and a vengeful Harlequin is to be avoided. Russell had therefore fallen from grace and favour.

14

A most gorgeous sight

By now public attention had moved on to the crystal palace in the park. There had been nothing quite like it, a transparent palace filled with marvels mechanical and electrical. It was considered by some to be the eighth wonder of the world, and London itself now greater than Athens or Rome.

On the first day of May 1851, some half a million people gathered in Hyde Park to witness the opening of the Great Exhibition by the queen. She wrote in her diary that 'the glimpse of the transept through the iron gates, the waving palms, flowers, statues, myriads of people filling the galleries and seats around, with the flourish of trumpets as we entered, gave us a sensation which I can never forget and I felt much moved'. Her husband had helped to supervise the funding and the construction of the great palace, perhaps with the idea of uniting the monarchy with the people in a joint celebration of England's power and inventiveness.

It was reported that there were 100,000 exhibits and marvels on display from all over the world. The exhibition itself was devoted to four great schemes, the first a survey of the raw materials of the earth and the second of machinery and mechanical inventions. The third section was given to manufactures, and the fourth to sculpture and plastic art. More than 2,000 men worked on 2,000 cast-iron girders, 3,000 columns, and 900,000 square feet of glass; the vast glittering edifice was created out of 4,000 tons of iron and 400 tons of glass. The building itself was 1,851 feet in length from east to west and 408 feet in width from north to south, with an interior height of 128 feet. The language used to describe the architectural detail, of vault and transept, nave and aisle, was taken from the great cathedrals to which this was the closest relative. Almost 300,000 panes of glass glittered in the light and motion of a crystal fountain some 27 feet in height. It was built on the summit of a gently rising slope so that the entrance from the west would display the interior all at once.

The Exhibition attracted 6 million visitors, and thus set the tone of profusion and extravagance which the Victorians felt most keenly. Twenty-five thousand season tickets were sold in advance, and the average entrance fee was at first 5 shillings, with 'shilling days' eventually introduced for the 'poorer sort'. On show were locomotives, microscopes, air pumps and cameras. But the spectacle of elm trees rising up at the sky within the great glass house seems to have been the first wonder. In the mid-nineteenth century there was no clear division between mythology and material progress. 'Technology' was too recent to have its own category and so was seen as the sister of Art. The 'vulcanizing' process came from Vulcan, the god of fire. The new techniques of manufacture were themselves the object of wonder. Cast iron was the material of the age, but here were also corrugated iron and zinc for those in the vanguard of the modern.

The colours were striking – blue, white and yellow for the verticals, blue, white and red for the curving girders and red, white and yellow for the roof bars. This was a thoroughly modern design, and the photographs of the interior reveal a surprising contrast with the usual dim and fudged Victorian interiors. In these photographs, also, the impression is of a bazaar or department store rather than an exhibition. It might almost be the work of Fortnum and Mason. To other visitors it resembled a vast railway terminus where in fact new locomotives were on display. It is possible to sense the context, or the conditions, of the 'mass market' which flourished in the next century.

The visitors participated in the universal excitement banishing the apocalyptic ferments of the 1790s, the rural unrest of the 1830s and the political controversies of the 1840s. They could forget the famines of Ireland and the Chartist meetings of the day before. A spell of peace and security seemed to hold the capital. Entire parishes, led by their clergymen, arrived in London; colonels came with their soldiers and admirals with their sailors; schools came with their pupils en masse, and manufacturers with their workers. The *Illustrated London News* had a cartoon of 'Country Folk Visiting the Exhibition' but it was not sardonic or cynical; it showed young and old wandering in wonder. The average Londoner, too, knew very little about the industrial and technological changes which generally occurred within workshops out of sight; the Exhibition, if nothing else, was a huge surprise.

A contributor to the *Cyclopaedia of Useful Arts* wrote:

> the state of the metropolis throughout the whole period of the Great Exhibition will be remembered with wonder and admiration by all . . . Instead of confusion, disorder and demoralisation, if not actual revolution, which were foretold by some gloomy minds, instead of famine and pestilence confidently predicted by others, London exhibited a wonderful degree of order . . . it was like a gigantic picnic.

That can be seen as a further meaning of 'exhibition', as a way of 'exhibiting' the essential peacefulness of the British people. And this was the marvellous thing – 6 million people and barely a hint of violence. When the Victorians thought of crowds they thought of mobs, but the spectacle of Hyde Park, untouched, exorcized many of the panics that had been created out of thin air in previous decades. It seemed that 'the people', en masse, were not dangerous at all. Soldiers and policemen were ready for the call to arms, but it never came. This is perhaps the single most important aspect of the enterprise. It was also the context for the manufacture of glass beehives, also on display, in which the observer might reflect upon the discipline and cooperation of large numbers.

It is possible that the large crowds were overawed by the vision of a crystal palace never before dreamed of. They had a glimpse of the future and of progress as if they were a vision on a hill. It was related to that endemic optimism which accompanied the ardent endeavours of the time. Charles Kingsley put it best in his novel

Yeast, published in volume form in the year that the Exhibition opened.

> Look around you and see what is the characteristic of your country and of your generation at this moment. What a yearning, what an expectation, amid infinite falsehoods and confusions, of some nobler, more chivalrous, more god-like state! Your very costermonger trolls out his belief that 'there's a good time coming' and the hearts of *gamins* as well as millenarians answer 'True!'

The glass palace also acted as a giant machine for classifying and dividing the products of the earth and of the individual nations. A wig-maker complained that his product had been removed from 'Art' and placed in 'Vegetable and Animal Substances chiefly used in Manufacture, as Implements, or as Ornaments'. Was a wig art or ornament? The question has never been settled. Many groups and subgroups grew up like the elm trees in the Exhibition Hall, and some unlikely combinations proved the variety and diversity of the enterprise. Just outside the Hall was placed a block of coal weighing 24 tons, as a symbol of England's material wealth, and beside it stood a huge equestrian statue of Richard I as a symbol of the nation's greatness. The Roman marble of the 'dying gladiator' was beside Nasmyth's steam hammer, a penknife beside a graphic telescope. The visitor might be awed by the triumphs of British machinery, from a cigarette machine which produced eighty cigarettes a minute, to the copying telegraph which produced facsimiles of documents at the other end of the line and the 'silent alarm bed' which pitched the sleeper onto the floor at any given time. Ribbons were piled on silks, tapestries on carpets; ornamental plate and elaborately carved furniture, bowls of porcelain and ivory, were all gathered together. There were critics as well as admirers. Here, according to an article in *Papers for the People*, 'we have sham-classic . . . sham stone-mouldings and tracery; sham-stone pillars . . .' This was one of the nineteenth-century maladies, condemned by Carlyle, Ruskin and others who saw in their century the appetite but not the capacity for great work. Despite the mechanical and technological accomplishments there was a sense of something missing, something wanting, which no steam hammer or electric telegraph could assuage.

It was of course attacked by those who detested novelty of any kind. Some said that the Hall would collapse under the weight of its own glass or that a lightning storm might shatter it to fragments. What if people were baked alive in this giant greenhouse? Some said that it was simply an advertisement for free trade and therefore a gigantic fraud on the public. Others lamented the effect on one of the most important London parks, where the grass might never grow again. Might not the masses of people congregated together create an epidemic illness? But the major source of controversy was the sheer vulgarity of display which shocked some contemporaries. It was the kind of criticism that became vocal in the early part of the twentieth century when Victorianism was considered out of date. Lytton Strachey caught the mood in *Eminent Victorians* (1918).

But the seeds of the disenchantment can be found even before the time of the Great Exhibition itself. As Philip James Bailey puts it in his *Festus* (1839):

> What England as a nation wants, is taste;
> The judgement that's in due proportion placed;
> We overdo, we underdo, we waste . . .

When William Morris visited the Exhibition he remarked that the objects within it were 'wonderfully ugly'. Other observers were less than impressed by the English contribution to the extravaganza, the French and the Americans in particular regarded as having supplanted Britain in various manufactures. The French had more taste and refinement, and the Americans more energy and gusto.

It was observed that many of the visitors were working men with their families, and the Exhibition may have reconciled many to the industrial culture all around them which they treated with due suspicion as the destroyer of employment. Charlotte Brontë also found herself among the crowds in Hyde Park. 'Its grandeur', she wrote, 'does not consist in one thing, but in the unique assemblage of all things. Whatever human industry has created you find there . . . It seems as if only magic could have gathered this mass of wealth from all the ends of the earth.' Once again the language of magic and enchantment came easily to the Victorians. It was a mark of their sentimentality but also of their susceptibility to a world of novelties. 'I made my way into the building,' Macaulay wrote, 'a most gorgeous sight . . . beyond the dreams of the Arabian romances. I cannot think that the Caesars ever exhibited a more splendid spectacle.'

It was the immensity of the collection that astounded the visitors. Individual objects might not satisfy the taste for sublimity. But one of the great Victorian imperatives was innovation. One of Victoria's favourite exhibits was an envelope-making machine which could fold and gum sixty envelopes a minute; it fascinated her, perhaps, as a homely version of the ever-encroaching machine age. For better or worse, this was a peep-show into the soul of Victorian England. A dream of mechanical ingenuity and expertise, prompting some to ascend even further into the reaches of the imagination. A positive craze for the exhibition of novel inventions accompanied the event. A hall erected on the east side of Leicester Square included a diving apparatus, a 'vacuum coated flask', the 'Aurora Borealis Apparatus', the 'Gas Cooking Apparatus', the 'Patent Ornamental Sewing Machine' and 'the Manufacture of Paper Hangings'.

The year 1851 was also the year of the national census which confirmed the impression that the middling classes were growing. The clerk, the shopkeeper and the man of business were part of an expanding constituency; the plumbers, house-painters and glaziers joined with the cabinetmakers, upholsterers and printers in their increasing numbers. The 'railway servants' had almost tripled in numbers in twenty years, as had the puddlers, forgers and moulders in the iron trade. It seemed that there could be no end to the expansion. This was also the first year in which the majority of the English lived in cities. And so, if the Exhibition was a way of exorcizing domestic and social fears, perhaps that was achievement enough for the moment.

15

Blood lust

After the fall of Lord John Russell at the hands of Palmerston, in February 1842, there followed one of those apparently interminable attempts to make a government. None of the candidates seemed capable of forming a coalition that would last longer than a day. Lord Derby, a Tory who had inherited the title from his father, was recommended to the queen as the least worst person to lead. He took the post eagerly enough, but found it difficult to create a cabinet of quality. He had intimated to the queen that he might have Palmerston, but she replied: 'If you do it, he will never rest until he is your master.' It was the kind of direct advice that her ministers might usefully employ.

Derby was scrutinizing a list of possible candidates for the cabinet when he is supposed to have said: 'These are not names I can present to the queen.' He had moved so far from the old Conservative leadership that none of Peel's cabinet were called forth. Eventually, after another short spell in opposition, he managed to perform the trick. When the names were read out in parliament the duke of Wellington, now growing deaf, questioned in a loud whisper the names of those chosen. 'Who?' he asked. 'Who?' So it became known as the 'Who? Who? ministry'. It is perhaps best known for the fact that Benjamin Disraeli was appointed chancellor of the Exchequer. When he admitted that he had no expertise in finance he was told not to worry because 'they give you the figures'.

Derby adumbrated a programme quite different from Palmerston's, principally by 'not indulging vituperation and intemperance of language'. Its purposes were clear. The times themselves seemed out of joint, and Derby was determined to safeguard the present institutions from the threat of an increasingly radical world. The *Quarterly Review* stated 'we humbly but most earnestly' desire the new government 'to avert a democratic and socialist revolution'. The duke of Wellington confided to Croker, an Irish politician, that 'it is some consolation to us who are so near the end of our career that we shall be spared seeing the consummation of the ruin that is gathering about us'. It is curious that even the most experienced observers will interpret politics through the peep-show of their own fears and illusions. It cannot be denied, however, that in a society so deeply divided between great wealth and grinding poverty there was bound to be resentment and anger on one side with fear and trembling on the other. One Tory, Robert Cecil (later to become Lord Salisbury), wrote: 'the struggle, however, between the English constitution on the one hand and the democratic forces that are labouring to subvert it on the other, is, in reality, when reduced to its simplest elements, and stated in its most prosaic form, a struggle between those who have, to keep that they have got, and those who have not, to get it'.

One publication of the time added fuel, if not flame, to the fire. Henry Mayhew's *London Labour and the London Poor*, published in volume form in 1851, anatomized the horrors of the city in terms of sheer pain, punishment and epidemic plague. Many children suffered death in squalid and pestilential conditions; the ordinary victims of London's filth and stench knew that death came just as certainly and with little enough to assuage it. Mayhew included terrible stories of the urban poor. 'When I went back to the lodging house they told me she was dead. I had sixpence in my pocket but I couldn't help crying to think I lost my mother. I cry about it still. I didn't wait to see her buried, but I started on my own account. I have been begging about all the time till now. I am very weak, starving to death. I would do anything to be out of this misery.' This was really more terrible than anything in

Dickens. There was a state within the state, a community of persons who had no real connection with the external world of events and characters which is chronicled by history. These are people who had no religion of any kind, no sense of their country, no knowledge of their rulers and indeed no sense of their real selves. They are our forebears, the unknown people who lived and died in a world which offered them little but misery and disease. Another deadly bout of cholera stirred Charles Dickens to fury, and in his periodical *Household Words* he declared that the incompetence of the authorities meant that 'they are guilty, before GOD, of wholesale murder'. One more such attack 'and you will see such a shake in this country as never was seen on earth since Samson pulled the Temple down on his head'. All his rage, his pity, and his impotence to force action, are visible.

Food riots were endemic in the early 1850s, largely in areas like the West Country where no adequate railway service was yet in use. Other grievances grew and grew. Factory operatives joined with miners in dispute with their employers, but perhaps the main issue was their under-representation in the Commons. The clamour for parliamentary reform returned as soon as it was realized that the measures of 1832 were barely adequate for a new electorate. Continental reforms following the 'year of revolution' added salt. Napoleon III instituted universal male suffrage for the workings of the Second French Empire, but it was not an example which the grandees of Westminster necessarily wanted to follow.

Nor was it a period of parliamentary calm. None of the ministries that fell apart in the fifteen years from 1852 to 1867 was ever despatched by a popular vote; they had all foundered on the rock of internal disagreement and division. Pressure from without was less deadly than pressure from within. The new parliament met on 4 November 1852, but it took a further two weeks to prepare the funeral car of Lord Wellington and to order the obsequies; he had died in September but it was considered not quite fitting to put the old man into the earth without proper parliamentary respects.

It was widely believed that the new administration could not last very long, and Derby decided to end the suspense with a summer election. The duke of Argyll had written that:

the year 1852 was a highly critical one among parliamentary parties, and yet singularly destitute of the nobler interests which ought to belong to them . . . The moment it became certain that all danger of a return to protectionism was a thing of the past there remained nothing but personal feelings and the associations of long antagonism to prevent all the free trade sections from uniting to form a new and a strong government. The whole year was spent in attempts, by endless interviews and correspondence, to realize the aspiration.

The election of that summer was once again an inconclusive contest, with the Whigs gaining more votes and the Conservatives more seats, but the general consensus seems to have been the continuation of the same policies under Derby. In one of his election speeches Palmerston adverted to the fact that in France an innkeeper would attract custom by christening his inn 'The New White Horse' or 'The New Golden Cross', whereas in England it would no doubt be called 'The Old White Horse' or 'The Old Golden Cross'. It was an astute observation of the English character. It is often believed that Derby was simply a figurehead, but it did not seem like that at the time. Victoria told the queen of the Belgians that 'our acquaintance is confined almost entirely to Lord Derby, but then *he is* the Government. They do *nothing* without him.' She was not so sure of his colleagues. She told King Leopold that Derby had 'a very sorry Cabinet. I believe, however, that it is quite necessary they should have a trial and then have done with it.'

Disraeli, as chancellor of the Exchequer in Derby's government, had to remove the yoke of Protectionism from Tory necks. He did so cautiously and deliberately with a series of proposals to reduce the land tax and thus conciliate the agricultural interest to free trade. He had to plead and explain and exonerate; his entire effort according to Lady Dorothy Nevill was 'to drag an omnibus full of country gentlemen uphill'. His central financial policies of low taxation and low government expenditure were not too far away from those of his great opponent in the Liberal party, William Ewart Gladstone, but he reached them by different means. Gladstone was in essence a moral leader whose robust principles were matched by a ferocious intelligence. Disraeli's policies on taxation were driven by questions of political calculation. Gladstone's principled vision encouraged a policy in which financial, foreign and military matters were closely related; the policies of Disraeli, with a whimsical touch here and there, did not materially add to them. They had once belonged to the same party, even though Peel had favoured Gladstone.

The appointment of Disraeli as chancellor came as a distinct surprise. The *Edinburgh Review* commented that 'his appointment to this post was one of the most startling domestic events which have occurred in our time. People seemed never tired of talking and speculating on it. He glittered in the political horizon as a star of the first magnitude.' Disraeli was never one to lower expectations and was eager to impress the English people with his major budget of December 1852.

'Yes, I know what I have to face,' he told the Commons. 'I have to face a coalition.' By which he meant Peelites, free-traders and various Irish representatives. Disraeli spent some hours in explaining and defending his measures, but all his efforts were in vain when Gladstone launched a bitter invective against them as frivolous and opportunistic. The duel between the two men took place in lightning and storm, with peals of thunder interrupting the cheers and counter-cheers that rang through parliament. Disraeli had planned, by means of his budget, to steady the national Exchequer after the inoculation of free trade had threatened some kind of nervous collapse, and at the same time he wished to install a more favourable system of taxation. The agricultural interest, for example, was to be rewarded a 50 per cent cut in the malt tax. As he sat down Gladstone, against all precedent, jumped to his feet. 'My great object', he wrote to his wife, 'was to show the Conservative party how their leader was hoodwinking and bewildering them, and this I have the happiness to believe that I effected.' The correspondent for *The Times* noted that Gladstone's speech was 'characterised throughout by the most earnest sincerity. It was pitched in a high tone of moral feeling – now rising to indignation, now sinking to remonstrance . . .' This was the Gladstone style, which did not really change over twenty-five years. It was described by one colleague as 'Oxford on the surface, but Liverpool below'.

Derby's son, Stanley, recorded that 'Gladstone's look when he rose to reply will never be forgotten by me. His usually calm features

were livid and distorted with passion, his voice shook, and those
who watched him feared an outbreak incompatible with parliamentary rules. So strong a scene I have never witnessed.' Disraeli's budget
was defeated by nineteen votes, and Derby went down with it. It
is usually believed that Gladstone delivered the significant stroke,
but in truth Disraeli's budget was fatally flawed. 'Now we are properly squashed,' Derby said. 'I must prepare for my journey to Osborne
to resign.'

On another occasion he would have been succeeded by Russell
and a Liberal ministry, but after the 'tit-for-tat' with Palmerston
they hardly possessed the confidence of the country, let alone each
other's. Instead the queen sought out the former followers of Peel
who, standing apart from both sides, had acquired the reputation
of being 'statesmanlike'; they also happened to be the most accomplished members of the Commons. The Liberals were the larger
party, but the erstwhile followers of Peel had most of the talent.

Some would not serve under Russell, and others would not serve
under Palmerston. The earl of Aberdeen was the natural choice. He
was the leader of the 'Peelites' and had been foreign secretary for
five years under Peel himself. And the queen liked him. He took
over the administration towards the end of the year on the clear
understanding that he would reconcile Liberals and Peelites. His
audience with the queen lasted an hour, primarily because they had
already reached agreement of a kind. Aberdeen was willing to create
a cabinet and then withdraw from the proceedings. It would be a
farewell gift to his country. The proposed cabinet had a dispropor-
tionate number of Peelites, members of Aberdeen's old party, and
a few last-minute adjustments were required. *The Times* was enthusiastic: 'If experience, talent, industry and virtue are the attributes
required for the government of this empire . . .' then the political
experiment had been a success.

Russell, forever eager to maintain Whig or Liberal honour, was
nominated for the Foreign Office, and Palmerston to the Home
Office, realizing only too well that the queen herself would deter
him from returning to the Foreign Office. Palmerston confessed to
his brother-in-law: 'I have for the last twelve months been acting
the part of a very distinguished tight-rope walker and astonishing
the public by my individual performances and feats . . . So far, so

well; but even Madame Saqui, when she had mounted her rope and flourished among her rockets, never thought of making the rope her perch, but prudently came down again to avoid a dangerous fall.' It is interesting to note that he compares himself with a star-spangled female circus performer. The new cabinet held their first dinner on 29 December 1852, where Palmerston was all smiles.

Leaving Madame Saqui aside in the green room, this was in theory the most talented and most experienced cabinet of the century, with its members in favour of moderate progress and free trade. Gladstone joined them at the Exchequer, and proved to be one of the better chancellors of the nineteenth century. He was in a different league from Disraeli, who tended to prefer bright ideas to solid policy. Gladstone may have picked the knave of spades when he opted for the Treasury. He knew that it would be a heavy burden, but he did not flinch from it. He had already developed the habit of self-flagellation after his conversations with the women of the streets, the prostitutes whom he was keen to 'rescue' from their calling, and never more obsessively than in the 1840s and 1850s. Various biographers have diagnosed 'emotional distemper', 'near despair' and 'private torments'. He was filled with repressed energy and repressed anger, quite unlike the demeanour of the 'grand old man' of later reports.

Gladstone's subsequent budget of 1853 was most singular for its maintaining income tax but lowering or abolishing duties on all foodstuffs and on items from soap to life insurance, from dogs to tea. He spoke for almost five hours, the longest budget speech on record, and declared at the close:

> these are the proposals of the government. They may be approved, or they may be condemned, but I have at least this full and undoubting confidence, that it will on all hands be admitted, that we have not sought to evade the difficulties of our position – that we have not concealed those difficulties either from ourselves or from others; that we have not attempted to counteract them by narrow or flimsy expedients; that we have proposed plans which, if you will adopt them, will go some way to close up many vexed financial questions.

He had, as one peer put it, 'made a long and flying leap in his ascent to power'. The earl of Clarendon declared that 'it was the most perfect financial statement ever heard within the walls of parliament, for such it is allowed to be by friend and foe'. It was remarkable that Gladstone could look at one year in advance, in distinction from his predecessor, who knew about as much arithmetic as would calculate his publisher's earnings.

It was a time of modest prosperity, encouraged by Gladstone's homage to the ideals of free trade. British exports never grew more rapidly than they did in the seven years after 1850. The rate of growth of cotton exports doubled in the same period. Economic liberalism and the growth of free trade created an unprecedented demand and maintained the condition of what was essentially a financial new world; Henry Hyndman, a Marxist who managed to combine his creed with Victorian capitalism, compared the years from 1847 to 1857 with the great era of world discovery by Columbus and Cortez. This was also the period when mid-Victorian England witnessed the birth of '*la semaine anglaise*', the Saturday afternoon of leisure, at least for the industrial labour force. Factory workers now passed their Saturday afternoons in the musical hall or at the market, in the pub or in the parks, shopping, exercising, drinking, flirting, socializing. Many dedicated their free time to sport, and especially to football, which was played and watched in industrial towns and cities across the country. Going to see the football on a Saturday afternoon became one of the most important of Britain's male-bonding rituals. 'It is now a stock saying', commented one working-class engineer, 'that Saturday is the best day of the week, as it is a short working day, and Sunday had to come'. After the factory bell rang, the men downed their tools and gathered outside their workshops, eager to 'devote themselves to the business of pleasure.'

It was said by Disraeli that the British people did not like coalitions – a surprising aspect of a nation that favoured compromise above all else. But there was also the favourite metaphor of 'drift', There was a feeling abroad in 1853 that events were getting out of control and that a looming war between Russia and Turkey over the collapsing Ottoman empire was becoming inevitable. These are moments when the prophets of fate and destiny are at their loudest. 'We are drifting towards war', Aberdeen wrote in June 1853, and only a month later he declared again: 'we are drifting hopelessly' towards war. So drift was the word on everyone's lips. Why, then, did sober, rational men feel themselves to be hopelessly swept along? 'If the country might be roused,' Derby told a colleague, 'it might be well; but we are falling into the fatal sleep which precedes mortification and death.' It could be that the pressures of life encouraged blankness or fatalism, and that even the most experienced elder statesmen threw up their hands in despair and preferred to be lost in the maelstrom of events.

Aberdeen might have been made for the arts of peace, but fate decreed otherwise. He was in many respects an elusive figure, marked by the early deaths of both his parents and of his first wife. As a result, perhaps, he was disinclined to play a leading part in the world. 'You look for interest and amusement in the agitation of the world,' he told a noted contemporary, Princess de Lieven, 'and the spectacle it affords, now I cannot express to you my distaste for everything of the kind . . . but I have had enough of the world . . . and would willingly have as little to do with it as is decent.' Fourteen years after writing this, he became prime minister. He had an awkward manner and a diffident or difficult temperament. Disraeli had the most damning verdict when he described 'his manner, arrogant and yet timid; his words insolent and yet obscure; his sneer, icy as Siberia; his sarcasms drear and barren as the Steppes'. Yet he also earned affection and admiration. Gladstone called him 'the man in public life of all others whom I have *loved*. I say emphatically *loved*. I have *loved* others, but never like him'. He was in politics for most of his life but he never became a victim either of cynical self-regard or hypocritical self-abasement. He was not an oily man, to use a phrase of the day. He was bone-dry. It would perhaps be fruitless to investigate his foreign policy, apart from his need of 'doing the job' or 'seeing it through'.

When at the end of 1852 Louis-Napoleon Bonaparte proclaimed the Second French Empire and became the Emperor Napoleon III, the world groaned. The tsar, Nicholas I, raged at the assumption of this parvenu ruling dynasty, but the lightning flash came out of the Holy Land. This sacred area, comprising Palestine and the shrines of Jerusalem, as well as the present Israel and Jordan, was under the control of the Ottoman empire. The new French emperor, ever in search of glory, threw his protection over a group of Catholic monks and placed a silver star with the arms of France in the sanctuary of the church of Bethlehem. He also seized the keys to the doors of the church and to the sacred manger of Jesus Christ. Nicholas I was now directly threatened. He was the self-appointed protector of the Eastern Orthodox Church, and sent an ultimatum that the Orthodox monks and worshippers should be placed under his protection.

The Ottoman empire could not allow its space to be contaminated in such a conspicuous fashion. Having obtained the support of France and Britain, its Sublime Porte or central government declared war on Russia in October 1853. The manger of Jesus Christ might have had little to do with it. 'Really and truly,' Palmerston wrote, 'this is a quarrel more for times long gone by than for the days in which we live.' It could perhaps be interpreted as a crisis between Orthodox monks and Roman Catholic monks over who should guard the Holy Places; Richard I might have ridden out on his charger, but it is hard to see Disraeli or Gladstone in such a martial posture. In truth the Russians and the Turks were essentially fighting over territory and the 12 million people inhabiting it.

Some believed that it would be a short war, others were convinced that it could extend indefinitely. It was commonly believed that it would be a great war that would redefine the map of Europe. The *Register* believed that it was a struggle 'which may change, ere it closes, the destinies of the civilised world'.

At the beginning of the war the tsar attacked and occupied the two regions of Wallachia and Moldavia which now, with Transylvania, comprise Romania. Every thought of Aberdeen was for peace and compromise, but other members of his cabinet disagreed. Just as the war was beginning Aberdeen told John Bright that 'his grief was such that he felt as if every drop of blood that would be shed would rest upon his head'. His son would later recall how he left an abandoned church on his estate to be rebuilt by a successor in deference to a sentence from Chronicles: 'thou shalt not build an house unto my name, because thou hast shed much blood upon the earth in my sight'.

In February 1854 more than five divisions of infantry and one of cavalry made their way via Malta to the north of the Crimea in the expectation that two or three short battles would determine the issue. England was the master of the world, was it not, with the railways and the electric telegraph, the screw-propeller steamship and perhaps most importantly a muzzle-loading rifle known from the name of its French inventor as the Minié. In comparison the Russians were still considered primitive.

So the people were with the soldiers, marching alongside as they made their way to their barracks, cheering and singing. But the singing was soon to stop. Eight days after the announcement of war, Lord John Russell withdrew a proposal for further electoral reform legislation, in the light of more significant events, and at once fell prey to what was called 'an hysterical fit of crying' on the floor of the Chamber. This was not the time to look for indulgence. The ensuing war destroyed the peace that had lasted since 1815, and inaugurated a period when every great power was at war with another great power. From 1853 to the 1880s, England was engaged in a European war once, France thrice, Austria thrice, Russia twice, Germany (Prussia) thrice, Italy twice, Denmark once and Turkey twice. It is little wonder that Europe was sometimes compared to an armed encampment and that the periods of peace were as hazardous and fragile as the periods of war. It was disconcerting too, that former enemies were now allies. The French experience of the English had been at the wolf's throat, but now they were obliged to greet them as long-lost relatives.

Palmerston had no responsibility for foreign policy in these months, but he strongly opposed the Russians and argued that Britain, if necessary, should ally itself with Turkey. It was a contest between two less than lovely despots, but the English public (as the newspaper-reading classes might be called) supported Palmerston and his horror of the Russian bear. Aberdeen was still steering a middle course when the Russians set sail from their port at Sebastopol in the Crimea and sank the Turkish fleet at Sinope on the Black Sea. That finally decided British and French policy. It would be war against Russia which, for the French, might be a belated revenge for Napoleon's fate in 1812. For the English it was an instinctive matter. For a foreign power to sink a foreign fleet was to trespass on Britain's empire of the waves. On 14 December Palmerston resigned from the government, only to resume office ten days later. It was all very mysterious, unexplained and perhaps inexplicable. Was he pursuing his feud against Russell, or was he opposed to Aberdeen's lukewarm war policy? Public opinion does not love a vacuum. This was the year when realpolitik was first coined.

It was soon believed that a Russian conspiracy was active within the inner circles of the administration. Who was, as the *Morning Advertiser* put it, 'the interpreter of Russian wishes and the abetter of Russian purposes'? The suspicion soon fell upon the one foreigner who reigned at court, Prince Albert, who by every standard of speech and custom was indeed a 'foreigner'. Did he not speak with a pronounced accent? It was whispered finally that he had been placed in the Tower for treason. Husband and wife became prostrated with nervous illness as the rumours mounted. 'Since yesterday I have been quite miserable,' he wrote to a companion, 'today I have had to keep to the house.'

It was said that the Russians had long been preparing for war, made even more certain after the events at Sinope and the British demand that Russian ships leave the Black Sea. There was a feeling in the early weeks of 1854 that events were gaining a momentum of their own. 'We have on our hands', the tsar told the English ambassador in St Petersburg, 'a sick man, a very sick man: it will be, I tell you frankly, a great misfortune if one of these days he should slip away from us, especially before all necessary arrangements are made.' The 'sick man' was Turkey and the Ottoman empire. These portentous words are perfect for the period – vaguely threatening, a hint of menace and danger, a sense of steel somewhere behind it. So the Russians seemed to have been set for this moment. Lord Shaftesbury told the Lords that 'this was a long-conceived and gigantic scheme, determined on years ago, and now to be executed, for the prevention of all religious freedom, and so ultimately of all civil freedom, among millions of mankind'. The more inflated the rhetoric, the more readily it was believed.

Palmerston feared that Russian power might supplant the Turks, while Aberdeen was sceptical of Turkish rule over Europeans. The cabinet was divided, and just before England entered the war Disraeli had told the Commons: 'I would like to know how the war is to be carried on with efficiency and success by men who have not settled what the object of war is.' There was growing impatience with the English high command, who did not seem to know when or where they were going. When was the fighting going to begin?

The Turks believed that they were fighting for their survival, while the Russians were determined to augment and defend their empire. The forces of the Turkish allies, France and England, had turned their attention to the port of Sebastopol, from which the Turkish fleet had been detached to Sinope. In the middle of September they landed at Calamita Bay, on the western coast of the Crimean peninsula, and a few days later the first battle was fought near the banks of the river Alma. It was a case of hard pounding and heavy fighting, but the British infantry regiments and the Highlanders, in particular, eventually routed the Russians. One of the British colonels said: 'and we have to do the same thing on new ground tomorrow, and perhaps once more before we reach the port of Sebastopol'. Lord Raglan, overall commander of the British army, wrote a despatch to the foreign secretary in which he stated that 'all our anxieties point to the last scene at Sebastopol'. It was on everyone's mind.

The battle at Alma was a foretaste of the larger war. A contemporary traveller surveyed the dead shrouded in linen cloths. 'What did these fellows know about the Turkish question? And yet they had fought and trembled, they had writhed in agony, and now father and brother, maid and mother, were weeping and breaking their hearts, and all about the Danubian principalities.' It had been hoped that the soldiers of two mighty powers would make short work of the Russians. It was not quite like that. In front of a group of interested observers with bottles of champagne and opera-glasses, approximately 5,000 men died. This was quite a new sensation for the spectator, a real battle with all the blood and detritus flying in all directions. They had read accounts of the Napoleonic Wars but they could not have been prepared for the screams and the stench. Forty years of peace had prepared no one for war.

From the battle of Balaclava, fought in the next month, came two phrases of fire, 'The Thin Red Line' and 'The Charge of the Light Brigade'. Both of them were in essence ambiguous; they could be redolent of triumph but they could also be tokens of disaster. The charge has effectively been taken out of time by Tennyson's poem. 'The Charge of the Light Brigade' is at once a ballad, an ode, and a memorial of an event that would otherwise soon have been forgotten. It was written at a gallop, as soon as the news of the event reached England. Tennyson even uses the dactylic metre which has the cadence of a gallop to echo the horses. The charge of British light cavalry was led by the earl of Cardigan against Russian arms and forces; they consisted of the 4th and 13th Light Dragoons together with the 17th Lancers and the 8th and 11th Hussars. Their horses were unarmoured, therefore light and fast; the men were armed with lances and sabres to effect swift and massive shock. In charge of the British cavalry was the 3rd earl of Lucan. Cardigan and Lucan were brothers-in-law who despised one another. The British army was in the overall command of Lord Raglan.

Raglan ordered Lucan to deploy his cavalry to prevent the Russians from withdrawing captured naval guns from the redoubts in the valley between Fedyukhin Heights and the Causeway Heights. This was named by Tennyson as 'the Valley of Death'. But the lie of the land around Lucan meant that he could not see the movement of the Russian troops in the vicinity. The Light Brigade could see the danger, but not one of them questioned the order to gallop unto sudden death. The English were on the left and the Russians on the right; and so the English charged them almost blindly. They were only obeying orders. The French forces were more sagacious and cleared the Fedyukhin Heights of the Russians.

The Light Brigade descended for three-quarters of a mile before they came under showers of shells and shot which surrounded them with a ring of fire: 670 men succeeded in getting through the Russian cavalry, but on their subsequent ascent of the hill 118 men were killed and 127 injured. Two-thirds of the brigade were destroyed. It had been a massacre. News of the disaster did not reach England for three weeks, and Tennyson read a leader on the affair in *The Times* of 13 November. The newspaper reported that 'some hideous blunder had occurred'. In his poem Tennyson wrote:

> Not tho' the soldier knew
> Someone had blundered . . .

But the poem is not a lament or criticism; it is couched in the language of heroism and of magnificence, as if the Light Brigade had been so many life-size statues suddenly come to life.

For Tennyson's contemporaries it was a catastrophe, too, but on an heroic scale; it was a tragedy but at the same time a triumph. This was how the English characteristically understood their defeats. That is why they were considered by others to be almost obtuse in the face of imminent peril, to be valorous beyond the call of duty, and to be almost negligent about deaths and casualties. A French cavalry commander remarked that 'the British cavalry officer seems impressed by the conviction that he can dash or ride over everything as if this sort of war were precisely the same as that of fox-hunting'. The ill-starred charge has quite obliterated the charge of the Heavy Brigade which took place earlier on that same day; under the command of James Yorke Scarlett, the brigade ignored the conventions of warfare and charged uphill against a much larger formation of Russians. In this it was triumphantly successful, and the Russians were routed. Unlike the humiliation of the Light Brigade, however, this victory has been forgotten. It might seem that the British prefer heroic failure to heroic success.

In truth Balaclava was an unnecessary battle notable only for misunderstanding, arrogance and blunder. The valley of death into which the cavalry rode was no more and no less than an abattoir. But the theatre of war is not an area for shrewd or patient judgement. The charge of the Light Brigade may be considered by some as glorious, if costly. Others will still consider it to have been ill-timed, ill-judged and ill-conducted.

Balaclava led to the third of the infernal trio of battles, Inkerman, where once more the individual soldiers were lost in the mist of strife. One brigadier general recalled that 'on our part it was a confused and desperate struggle. Colonels of regiments led on small parties, and fought like subalterns, captains like privates. Once engaged, every man was his own general.' The Scots Guards could smell the Russians in their vicinity, a 'peculiar strong leather-like smell'. When the fog lifted with the winter sun the dead and dying lay in heaps.

For every hundred men in the battalions, seventy-three were killed by hunger or by cold; and these were the troops from the richest country in the world. All that could be said was that they had done their duty, much more than the country which despatched them into the Crimea. The new recruits were often the first to die.

There were no roads. Fuel was in short supply. There were no ambulances and the hospital ships were overcrowded. In one hospital more than half the patients died in one month. In another, where 2,000 were suffering from dysentery, only six shirts were washed. The Crimea was a festering sore. Albert wrote in a memorandum that 'we have no generals trained and practised in the duties of that rank; no general staff or corps; no field commissariat; no field army department; no ambulance corps; no baggage train; no corps of drivers; no corps of artisans . . .' The battle of Inkerman became known as 'the Soldier's Battle', since it was fought one against another like any battle between Briton and Anglo-Saxon. The soldier lost in the fog of the battlefield is one of the enduring images of the Crimea.

Winter was now settling in. All battles ceased and the primary concern was the siege of Sebastopol itself with its Russian defenders. It was now heavily fortified, its defences very hard to pierce, and the difficulties of communication further hampered by bad weather and bad field control. The arena around Sebastopol became a place of suffering and pestilence. A fierce storm descended that did not blow itself out for three days. The story of the dying and wounded was transmitted to London and elsewhere by means of the electric telegraph. The correspondent of *The Times*, William Howard Russell, sent candid and uncensored reports of the chaos and inefficiency that are the handmaids of war. The dead were left unburied and the injured left untreated; there was no hygiene to speak of, and the medicines were in woefully short supply. The flies alighted on the festering wounds, and more died from filth and privation than from injuries sustained in battle.

The siege of Sebastopol has only indistinct links with that of Troy, but the idea of a siege had more than martial associations. It was always a sign of endurance, of individual heroism and ingenuity. But Sebastopol did not fall. The year was late, and winter came early to the Crimea; the troops were not adequately fitted, clothed or fed. Amoebic dysentery had already begun its work. As for the defenders of Sebastopol, they were reported to be in high spirits, confident that they could outlast any siege. The allied commanders were bereft of information, and did not even know the number of Sebastopol's defenders. The earl of Clarendon wrote: 'It seems to me, God grant I may be wrong, that we are on the verge of a monster catastrophe.' He was not alone in his forebodings. The memory of the Great Exhibition was now hopelessly lost in the fog and fury of a war the English did not believe they could win.

At the end of 1854 Charles Greville wrote in his diary:

> The last day of the most melancholy and disastrous year I ever recollect. Almost everybody is in mourning and grief and despair overspread the land. At the beginning of the year we set forth an army of joyous and triumphant anticipation . . . and the end of this year sees us deploring the deaths of friends and relations without number, our army perishing before the walls of Sebastopol, which we are unable to take, and after bloody victories and prodigies of valour, the Russian power hardly is yet diminished or impaired.

A world of suffering lay behind the words.

A British army surgeon reported that 'we say here that "We did not take Sebastopol because the French would not fight by day, the English would not fight in the dark, and the Turks won't fight at all."' There was a morsel of comfort. By the beginning of 1855 a railway, 'The Grand Crimean Railway with Branch to Sebastopol', was being built, notable for the speed of its construction and the fact that it was the first attempt to organize mechanized warfare. But Raglan, the commander of the British troops, had died – some say of disappointment, others of a broken heart and others of strain. The point was that everybody wanted the war to end. It had gone on too long, and had been responsible for the loss of too many lives, to be endured. The tsar emphasized in a despatch to a Russian commander, Michael Gorchakov, 'the necessity to do something to bring this frightful massacre to a close'. This is what it had become, a massacre and not a war.

Another inglorious battle was fought in the spring of the year when the English forces attempted two sieges of the Great Redan, one of the fortresses guarding Sebastopol; they were forced off and were obliged to retreat, a signal contrast to the successful French assault of the fort at Malakhov.

The war had already engulfed Gladstone and his budget of 1854 which reversed much that had been decreed in 1853; income tax was doubled, and additional revenue was once more derived from sugar, spirits and malt. It was Gladstone's belief that war costs should be borne out of revenue and not out of borrowing. 'The expenses of war', he told the Commons, 'are the moral check which it has pleased the Almighty to impose on the ambition and lust of conquest that are inherent in so many nations.' The combination of piety and belligerence was not to everyone's taste, especially since Gladstone himself would soon enough have recourse to borrowing.

The real crisis of the Crimean War occurred towards the end of January 1855. A radical member of parliament, John Arthur Roebuck, was able to pass a resolution demanding a committee of inquiry into the mismanagement of the war. It was essentially a motion of no confidence, and almost at once John Russell resigned from the cabinet, saying that Aberdeen's government was 'the worst I ever belonged to'. His abrupt departure was considered by some to smack of ambition. The queen sent him a note expressing 'her surprise and concern at hearing so abruptly of his intention to desert the Government on the motion of Mr Roebuck'. Russell had thoroughly disgraced himself in the eyes of most observers, and the queen never forgave him, but he attained office again after a few months. The parliament agreed to a committee of inquiry into the debacle by the surprising majority of 157 votes; the result was followed by silence, not cheering, and a few derisive laughs.

Aberdeen resigned his post into the hands of the queen after surviving for two years. 'The country was governed for two years', Disraeli wrote, 'by all its ablest men, who by the end of that term had succeeded by their coalesced genius, in reducing that country to a state of desolation and despair that they could hear their heads thump as they struck the ground.' The committee of inquiry itself was not a success. 'I felt corruption all around me,' Roebuck wrote, 'but I could not lay my hand on it.' The same discontent and frustration affected the public reaction. The Administrative Reform Association was established as a direct response to the mismanagement in the Crimea; it comprised City men and London professional men but it was slow, cumbrous, and achieved very little.

Someone had to take the blame, or at least to take the helm. It might be thought that no sane man would wish to take on the duties of a prime minister in wartime, but who will necessarily believe that politicians are altogether sane? It was thought that Derby, as leader of the Conservatives, might step forward; but, much to Disraeli's fury, he refused to do so. Disraeli had an affection for the Levant and was bitterly disappointed that his leader in the Lords had shirked the fight against Russia. But you could never know what Disraeli was really thinking. Sir William Gregory, once on the fringes of the Young England movement, remarked: 'that he was a man of immense talent not even his greatest enemy can deny; but even I, his personal friend, must confess that from his entrance into public life until his last hour he lived and died a charlatan'.

There seemed only one viable candidate, however he may have been disliked by the queen. Palmerston's bravura and assertive patriotism, together with his ambition to crush any despot within reach, had endeared him to the working-class radicals who might otherwise have abhorred the war. He felt that he had the support of the people, too. There was another way of looking at it. 'I object to Lord Palmerston on personal grounds', the queen said. 'The Queen means', Prince Albert explained, 'that she does not object to Lord Palmerston on account of his person.' It might have come from Lewis Carroll, if he had been writing at the time. 'Pam', as he was widely known, cobbled together a ministry, or, rather, he preserved the same ministry without the embarrassing presence of Aberdeen, Newcastle, former secretary of war, and of course John Russell, who like a jack-in-the-box returned later as colonial secretary. He could not be kept down. If it had not been for the occasion of a war, this particular ministry might have endured the course, but it did survive long enough to seal the peace. Palmerston had stepped forward, no doubt with a spring in his step. The old warhorse was pawing the ground but, more importantly, he elicited the support of the nation as a defender of its vital interests.

All the combatants were tired of the bloody and messy war fought over a small territory, but Palmerston did not wish to end it until England and France had taken Sebastopol. Once that was achieved, with the retreat of the Russians, the peace negotiations could begin in earnest. On 9 September 1855, the Russians eventually abandoned the fortress of Sebastopol. It was a victory of sorts for the English and French, but they hesitated to follow the enemy any further. Under the circumstances this was considered to be a famous victory. It is estimated that 300,000 Russians lost their lives in Sebastopol, which had by the end of the hostilities become a smoking ruin. One of the burial places was known as the Cemetery of the Hundred Thousand. A great storm tore down the huts and tents used by the allies. The British forces were reduced to shreds and patches.

The English public had become acutely aware of the imbecility of the military command, or what *The Times* on 13 December 1854 described as 'the incompetency, lethargy, aristocratic hauteur, official interference, favour, routine, perverseness and stupidity which revel and riot in the camp before Sebastopol'. Nonetheless the British people expected a spring campaign to finish off the enemy. The blood of two years might otherwise be shed for nothing; the commanders had already lost a third of the army. There was a hunger for news. The first national penny daily, the *Daily Telegraph*, emerged on the streets on 29 June 1855. The walls of the wooden huts that sheltered the besiegers of Sebastopol were covered with engravings torn from the pages of the illustrated papers. Some inglorious fighting muddied the issue before its close. An attempt to storm the fortress of the Redan was aborted when the British refused to leave the safety of their parapet. One of their commanders, Colonel Windham, complained that it was the 'greatest disgrace that had ever fallen on the British soldier'. It had not been a lovely war.

The English army was prevented from finishing its mission by the terms of the treaty of Paris, signed at the end of March 1856. The participants had become ever more determined to escape the quagmire of the Crimea, but they had conflicting purposes. The Russians wished to snatch what profit or dignity they could from their humiliation. The French and British wished to preserve the Ottoman empire from all possible harm, as a bulwark against the Russians, while at the same time renewing their own ancient and almost prehistoric rivalry. But the terms of the treaty lacked any sense of determination. The integrity of Turkey was guaranteed, the Danube was opened to shipping, and the Black Sea was neutralised. That was all. The treaty of Paris was disconcerting and disappointing to those who believed that England had been fighting a moral as well as a military battle. The English were shocked, and in many cases horrified by what they considered to be an inconclusive and ineffective peace. The heralds who announced it were hissed as they stood by Temple Bar, and no one was sure whether they should illuminate their windows in celebration. They might have been smashed. All the patriotism, all the expectation and fervour, all the ideas of a just cause, had come to nothing.

The expansion of Russia would be checked for fourteen years, but this was scarcely the victory the home crowds had been seeking. The conflict did not assist or make any military reputations, and the war itself had emanated from the fear of an attack which was never contemplated and a threat which barely existed. Lytton Strachey remarked that 'its end seemed as difficult to account for as its beginning'. It was a war of foreboding, neither just nor necessary, but it was hurried on by public opinion in one of its moods of foolish optimism. The peace itself was premature and too partial to the enemy, with concessions over neutral shipping and trade with Russia. Diplomacy, not battle, won the day where the English had expected a significant victory. Aberdeen had drifted into war, and Palmerston drifted into peace. The fate of the European peoples still under the Ottoman empire would have to wait for another day.

The other effects of the war are difficult to determine. The disappointment of the peace had been too sudden, and too unexpected, to trace many more subtle consequences. It helped to sustain the movement for military reform, with a greater level of efficiency observed in the 'Scientific Corps'. A Staff College was also established. It is said that the example of the soldiers encouraged a cult of heroism, such as that embodied in the Volunteer Movement of 1859 to strengthen the defences against a proposed but illusory threat from Napoleon III. This is hard to believe. This was the period when the cigarette – or, as it was first known, the paper cigar – was introduced to England by the soldiers coming home from abroad.

Palmerston had a 'good war' primarily because he had little to do with it. Gladstone had become more isolated in the heady atmosphere, and described parliamentary business at the time as 'the tossing of a ship at anchor', where there was 'motion but no progress'. Disraeli, in turn, described the Tory task as 'to uphold the aristocratic settlement of this country'. The aristocracy had indeed faltered, and in some cases been disgraced, but they came back fighting in later decades. All in all, nothing much had happened on the domestic front. One moment from a state visit to England by Napoleon III in April 1855 may leave an appropriate impression. At the end of the national anthems the French empress quickly looked behind her to make sure the seat was in place; Victoria sat down at once without turning. She was born to rule without hesitation.

Nevertheless, the war in the Crimea had become a national shame, more than humiliation, to which the efforts of Florence Nightingale and her cadre of nurses brought much relief. Her devotion to the soldiers, her selflessness in her duty, her courage in the face of difficulties, helped to soothe the suffering spirit of the nation with an embodiment of clear-headed and efficient administration. It could be achieved, after all. A report in *The Times* on her conduct perhaps gilds the lily a little but was what people wanted to read after the empty bravura of Raglan and Cardigan:

> She is a 'ministering angel' without any exaggeration in these hospitals, and as her slender form glides quietly along each corridor, every poor fellow's face softens with gratitude at the sight of her. When all the medical officers have retired for the night and silence and darkness have settled down upon those miles of prostrate sick, she may be observed alone, with a little lamp in her hand, making her solitary round.

Nightingale was not the only woman to devote herself to the sufferings of the soldiers. One other such was Mrs Mary Seacole, a 'quadroon' from the British West Indies who confronted prejudice against her sex and her race simply by knocking it down. Like many formidable women (Lady Hester Stanhope is another shining example from a period just before), she had a confirmed and powerful wanderlust. 'I have never wanted [lacked] inclination to rove', she wrote, 'nor will powerful enough to carry out my wishes.' This was the antithesis of the Victorian idea of a woman, immured in the house as a domestic prisoner. How much is 'the angel in the house' a masculine illusion foisted upon frustrated wives who may have had adventurous spirits as powerful as that of Mary Seacole?

She acquired many of her skills at the British Army Hospital in Jamaica, where yellow fever in particular led to many deaths. Of her decision to minister to the soldiers of the Crimea, she remarked that 'heavens knows it was visionary enough'. But she recalled that in 'the ardour of my nature, which carried me where inclination prompted, I declared that I would go to the Crimea'. She was not at first welcome, since Florence Nightingale had doubts about a non-white nurse, and she was also rebuffed by the War Office and the Medical Department. Eventually she decided to make her own path and to bypass the authorities by opening a hotel for invalids. Cards were printed and distributed in the war region, announcing a 'BRITISH HOTEL' where she intended 'to establish a mess-table and comfortable quarters for sick and convalescent officers'.

The fame of her skills as a healer and nurse soon spread. She called her patients 'sons' and she was universally known as 'Mother Seacole'. As soon as she arrived on the Crimean peninsula she learned that 'the hospitals were full to suffocation, that scarcity and exposure were the fate of all in the camp'. She built up a cadre of female nurses of whom she said that 'only women could have done more than they did who attended to this melancholy duty; and they, not because their hearts could be softer, but because their hands are moulded for this work'. It may not be going too far to suggest that without the unacknowledged assistance of the women the men would not have survived. Mary Seacole returned to England and died in May 1881.

Aberdeen's fall after his humiliation had proved that 'the public' was now too great a presence to be ignored. It was what Carlyle sarcastically called 'The Wonderful Face of Public Opinion'. This new 'reading public' wanted news and more news. Speeches were read out from the newspapers at social meetings and Lord Rosebery recalled that when he was a boy his family sat down after breakfast also to read the speeches. The street ballads, so much a part of nineteenth-century life, were often snippets and precis of news in rhyme and rhythm.

At the end of the Crimean War the nation was more than ever split by class consciousness. The numbing complacency and incompetence of the aristocratic military elite destroyed any confidence that the working classes possessed in their leaders. In the summer of 1855 a Sunday Trading Bill had just passed its third reading in the Commons, by which the licensing laws were restricted and Sunday trading forbidden. An immediate and furious reaction followed. A Chartist poster, in large print, was displayed over all London

> *New Sunday Bill* prohibiting newspapers, shaving, smoking, eating and drinking and all other kinds of recreation and nourishment both corporal and spiritual, which the *poor people* still enjoy at the present time. *An open-air meeting* of artisans, workers and '*the lower orders*' generally of the capital will take place in Hyde Park on Sunday afternoon to see how religiously the aristocracy is observing the Sabbath and how anxious it is not to employ its servants and horses on that day, as Lord Robert Grosvenor said in his speech. The meeting is called for three o'clock on the right bank of the Serpentine, on the side towards Kensington Gardens. Come and bring your wives and children in order that they may profit by the example their 'betters' set them!

The carriages of the wealthy were 'mobbed' on three successive Sundays in Hyde Park. Those without carriages mobbed those with carriages; this is not quite the same thing as the poor mobbing the rich, but it came somewhere close to it. The repressive legislation was withdrawn, a sign of changing class consciousness in the 1850s and also of the nervous fear that beset the administration after the Crimean debacle.

It had been widely believed that the war would banish all the materialism and selfishness that had afflicted the nation and that a new mood of national unity and purpose would purge the 'condition of England question' which had been so much part of the periodical press. But the most promising hopes are the first to die. In 1859, five years after the end of the war, *The Times* delivered its judgement: 'That ill-starred war, those half million of British, French and Russian men left in the Crimea, have discharged to the last iota all the debt of Christian Europe to Turkey. Never was so great an effort made for so worthless an object. It is with no small reluctance that we admit a gigantic effort and an infinite sacrifice to have been made in vain.'

Yet war expedited the process of invention and improvement, continued step by step in the directions suggested by earlier inventions and previous improvements. These, too, were largely created, as Isambard Kingdom Brunel put it, in correlation with 'a demand which circumstances happen to create'. In 1856 the first approaches to the age of steel were made with the patenting of the Bessemer technique; a powerful blast burned out the carbon and silicon from pig iron which, when manganese was added, became steel. Steel rails eventually became cheaper than iron rails and were far more durable. In the same year a chemistry student discovered the process for creating mauveine, the first synthetic dye, which changed the clothes and the interiors of the world.

The ill-fated Administrative Reform Association, established in 1854 following the disaster in the Crimea, was merely a token of the fact that efficiency and modern organization were far more significant than personal bravery or heroics. War was a practical business to be run on business principles. This could have been the lesson of the Crimea. A tendency to preach lofty ideals was combined with disgust at existing political institutions. In the same year the Northcote–Trevelyan Report urged that open and competitive examination was the best way to find proper recruits for the civil service. It was in other words an implicit recommendation that the middle class should play an active role in the administration of the country. It was significant, perhaps, that Samuel Smiles's *Self Help* (1859) became popular after the Crimean War. 'At this moment,' Nathaniel Hawthorne wrote at the beginning of 1855, 'it would be an absurdity in the nobles to pretend to the position which was quietly conceded to them a year ago. This one year has done the work of fifty ordinary ones; or more accurately, it has made apparent what has long been preparing itself.'

The apparent thing was the emergence of a country organized by the middle classes on the virtues of thrift, self-help and businesslike efficiency. Local self-government was still seen to be the key to administrative progress. In 1855 the Metropolitan Board of Works was established, and three years later an act was passed for the cleansing of 'that noble river' the Thames, the state of which was 'little creditable to a great country, and seriously prejudicial to the health and comfort of the inhabitants of the Metropolis'. So the businesslike work was being done. In 1863 the first section of the Metropolitan Underground Railway was opened, and in 1862 the Board of Works was authorized to build an embankment on the north side of the Thames from Westminster to Blackfriars Bridge. And business needs statistics. Between 1876 and 1884 the Board began schemes to displace 22,000 people and rehouse 28,000.

Within months of the treaty of Paris, Palmerston, who had become prime minister following Aberdeen's resignation, once more made sacrifice to the god of war over a minor incident in the harbour of Canton. A ship manned entirely by Chinese seamen, the *Arrow*, flew the British flag for convenience; it had an English captain, too, and so sailed in the shadow of Viscount Palmerston. The captain of a passing cargo ship recognized one of the crew of the *Arrow* as an erstwhile pirate and called in the local authorities to arrest him. The ship was boarded and, apparently, the British flag was hauled down. The incident had become an insult and the governor of Hong Kong, Sir John Bowring, ordered the immediate bombardment of Canton. The English newspapers took his side as if in some way he were countering the disappointment of the Crimean campaign. It has been called the Second Opium War, the first having been fought fourteen years before over the Chinese blockade of trade. This earlier incident was granted the soubriquet of 'gunboat diplomacy', and as a result the British confiscated Hong Kong and signed an 'unequal treaty' allowing them extensive trade privileges. But they were not enough. The second war, started on a pretext, was designed to garner larger and larger profits from opium by opening up China to foreign merchants.

It was essentially the conflict between a modern industrial power and an ancient system of civilization which considered its assailants to be nothing but barbarians. In turn the Chinese were caricatured as wife-murderers and child-beaters. *Punch* had said: 'What do the Chinese matter to us? They are faraway and good for nothing.' Never had two civilizations less in common. When Lord Elgin travelled to Shanghai in January 1859 he noted that 'uninvited, and by methods not always of the gentlest, [he had] broken down the barriers by which these ancient nations sought to conceal from the world . . . the rags and rottenness of their waning civilisations'. But he had done more than that; he had introduced to the West one of the great powers of the world.

The first battle of Canton took place in 1857 and the allies, Britain and France, retained the city for three years. The Conservatives with a sprinkling of Radicals, ever ready to topple Palmerston from his popularity, drew up a motion against the Cantonese imbroglio. When Palmerston lost the vote he promptly dissolved parliament in the spring of 1857. By astute management and confident self-promotion he had become the hero of the hour, and the subsequent general election gave him for the first time an overriding victory over the Conservatives with a clear majority of eighty-five seats. Cobden and Bright, both illustrious pacifists, were rejected by their constituencies. It seemed that international morality would never beat national patriotism. The Emperor's Summer Palace was burned down. This was the result, as Lord Derby put it, of 'a Conservative minister working with Radical tools and keeping up a show of Whiggism in his foreign policy'. Palmerston, in other words, was following the tradition of British diplomacy.

The English were moving forward on another front. The great Moghul empires of India were beginning to break apart. In 1613 the 'Company and Merchants of London were granted a trading station north of Bombay'. This was the beginning. In 1707 the last great Moghul left a divided country partitioned among sons, grandsons, Moghul governors and Hindu nobles. The English were not long in following and under the aegis of the East India Company became the predominant military and commercial power in the region. In 1849 the earl of Dalhousie, as governor general, annexed the Punjab to British India; this was followed by Sikkim, due north of Bengal, and Pegu in lower Burma. This was in turn succeeded by the colonization of the Muslim kingdom of Oudh. As a result 'new' British India was a third and a half larger than the previous colony.

'We are making', one British administrator said, 'a people in India where hitherto there have been a hundred tribes and no people'. There are various stories of massacre and treachery in this process, although it is worth noting that they are generally associated with native rather than British atrocities, while the tales of heroism all concern the European minority. The self-congratulatory tone in fact concealed much barbarity on the part of the British colonists to the native peoples. Dalhousie, on leaving India, struck a more sober note. 'No prudent man,' he said, 'having any knowledge of Eastern affairs, would ever venture to predict a prolonged continuance of peace in India.' Yet Dalhousie also wrote, 'We are perfectly secure so long as we are strong and believed to be so.' The ambiguous end in Crimea might suggest that the British were not so strong as they used to pretend to be.

The reasons for the Indian War of Independence, and in particular the events of August 1857, were various. They ranged from the evidence of the Crimean campaign that the English were no longer good at war to the reluctance of native troops to serve in Burma and Persia. The East India Company was both a military compound and a commercial power. After the battle of Plassey in 1757, Robert Clive, Commander-in-Chief of British India, took Calcutta, Madras and Bombay, the cities manned by the native infantrymen known as sepoys and controlled by the British. It was not an idyllic posting. The deadly heat burned down, and cockroaches as large as mice scuttled beneath the doors of the Residency in Calcutta. This was the background to the Indian War. Drink was the only solace.

In 1856 and 1857 rumours of mutiny soon spread about the country. The only thing that superseded railway mania in India was religious mania. Here was the problem. It was widely believed and reported in fact that the new cartridges for the Minié weapon had been greased with the fat of pigs and cows, displaying sublime disregard for native custom. The story was untrue but it is a measure of the distrust of the native population for their colonial rulers. The cow is sacred to the Hindu, and the pig is a pollutant to the Muslims. For the Hindu it was a matter of losing caste for ever, in this world and in the next.

On January 1857 a general reported an 'unpleasant feeling' among the native soldiers. At the beginning of May eighty-five members of the cavalry stationed in Meerut were sentenced to ten years' hard labour for having refused to touch the greased cartridges. The Muslims had sworn on the Koran, and the Hindus by the holy waters of the Ganges, that they would have nothing to do with the desecration. In the presence of the entire force the prisoners were stripped of their uniforms and were loaded with chains as if they were common felons. It was for some of them much worse than execution; it was degradation and worse than death. The sepoys erupted in rage, and were seen 'dancing and leaping about, calling and yelling to each other'. English women and children were the first casualties. The native infantry were heard to call out: 'Quick! Delhi! Quick! Delhi!' They were on their way to the old Moghul capital.

On the following Sunday the regiment mutinied, broke open the gaol and released its prisoners before going on to gut the bungalows of the British and to massacre all their inhabitants. The mutineers then made their way towards Delhi, only 40 miles distant. Fear and rumour flew like the wind. Bahadur Shah, king of Delhi, was an ancient pensioner of the British, but was now helpless in the face of several insurrections. The massacres took place in bazaars and cowsheds, on the flat mud roofs and at the bottom of deep wells.

Two miles north of the city were stationed three native infantry regiments, but they attacked their white officers, and hacked many of them to death. The commander-in-chief, General Anson, was far away in the north. He was told that nothing could be done since transport was unavailable. He died of cholera two days later. Trials and executions of Indians followed apace, but it was noticeable that the men met their unhappy fate with great aplomb.

The disturbances moved rapidly through the North West Province; some of the local officials were pursued by rebels, and the province quickly subsided into a state of anarchy.

Cawnpore, on the west bank of the Ganges, had been considered safe within the emollient rule of Nana Sahib, but he no longer felt much reason to support the British and began a policy of condign punishment over his former allies. The sun beat down through the hot days of June and July, and the European contingent were felled by famine and disease. At Cawnpore they were promised safe passage by the Nana, if they laid down their arms and marched to boats waiting for them on the Ganges. Their embarkation was, however, the signal for the slaughter of all the men, women and children that had taken to the water. Only four survived.

The massacre at Cawnpore was a flame that gave the signal to the rebels of Lucknow. In 1857 Sir Henry Lawrence drove into the Residency at Lucknow and came upon a most desperate situation where ill administration and foolish vengeance provoked unrest. The English forces were caught off guard by the native forces and were closely pent and besieged in the Residency. The Residency was well fortified, however, and those within repulsed the siege against them.

Everywhere the English went, blood followed them. It is customary to call the native Indians mutineers or rebels, but they were nothing of the kind. If they had any parallels it was with the forces of Hereward the Wake who fought for their territories against the Norman invaders. This did not seem, of course, a satisfactory or credible version of events at the time. The British public, its appetite for violence not sated by the casualties of Crimea, erupted in a blood lust. One pamphlet of the time declared that as a preliminary measure every single mutineer should be hunted down and killed, adding that 'India will not be secure so long as a single man remains alive'. The English were ready to create a wasteland and to call it good government. One Englishman suggested that those about to be executed should be forced to lick the blood of those whom they had killed or cut down, in the certain knowledge that the men 'should leave this world with the conviction that their vile souls were about to migrate into the bodies of cats and monkeys'. Thousands were hanged or mutilated or suffocated or otherwise despatched. Blood and smashed bones were found at the bottom of many local wells. We may say with an Intelligence chief, Henry Hodson, that the whole countryside became 'a steaming bog . . . scorpions like young lobsters crawled about in damp bedding', while the lips of the men were caked with flies.

Months of bloody repression, and of sporadic warfare, were necessary before the disorder was contained. It could not go on for ever. A young officer, John Nicolson, was sent to stiffen the resolve of the British in Delhi, and in the middle of 1857 the assault had begun on the Kashmiri Gate, the Lahore Gate and the Kabul Gate. Once the advance had been successful there was another glut of mayhem, drunkenness and death. Martial law was imposed in the course of which the three sons of the king of Delhi were shot dead. Lucknow, like Delhi, was a wasteland.

The East India Company was relieved of its administrative 'responsibilities' – perhaps another way of adverting to the taking of treasure and plunder – and the powers of the Company were transferred to the sovereign with the help of a secretary for India and a Council. Thus India and its people came under the control of Queen Victoria, a hegemony emphasized by her accession to the title of empress of India. The office of secretary of state for India was instituted, with a council of fifteen advisers. In 1861 the Indian and English armies were united.

The prevailing belief that conquest by a 'superior' power would lead to 'order' was one of the visionary clichés that came to nothing. The governor of Madras, Sir Thomas Munro, had stated in a note composed in 1824 that 'we should look upon India, not as a temporary possession but one which is to be maintained permanently, until the natives in some future age have abandoned most of their superstitions and prejudices and become sufficiently enlightened to frame a regular government for themselves and to conduct and preserve it'. So crumbled the hopes of a different world. The rebels still alive were forced into Nepal, and the sporadic risings in the rest of India were quickly suppressed. A day of thanksgiving was declared in July 1859 with the words 'war is at an end. Rebellion has been put down.' It had been contained. It had been put down. Most of the country remained loyal. The landlords had remained apart from the villagers. The army mutinies were confined to Bengal. The princes were content. Yet there was still a shuddering sense that the British empire had revealed its heart of darkness.

16

A dark world

The life of 1855 was the high water mark of mid-Victorian society. This was the period when Anglo-Saxon studies were revived, when Tennyson derived inspiration from the Arthurian epics and Pugin from the Middle Ages. All were looking backwards at earlier societies that were characterized by an organic unity, a collective will and a shared piety. Many of the most notable writers of the period – Ruskin, Morris, Carlyle – looked back with nostalgia to feudal or semi-feudal ages of England when hierarchy and authority were regarded with reverence. It was all a matter of myth, of course, but the myth mattered. Life mattered. Life was earnest. The High Church revival with John Keble and Edward Pusey shared a rapport with medieval England. At the opening of Macaulay's *History of England*, published in 1848, he states: 'I will relate . . . how from the auspicious union of order and freedom sprang a prosperity of which the annals of human affairs had furnished no example . . .' But the triumph of competitive enterprise and individual attainment was dismissed by Carlyle as 'Pig Prosperity'. No epoch was so beset by energy and by doubt.

Walter Bagehot, who never did cease to comment on such matters, said that 'in a period of rapid change such as is confronting men today, the preservation of such continuity with the past, with the standards they are used to, and the social world where they can find their way about, is essential . . .' The Victorians were not always talking about Malory or medieval monasteries, but they were still looking for the same permanence, the same security and the same stability. At the Royal Academy Exhibition in 1855 the paintings praised were resplendent with 'energy', 'passion' and 'feeling'. George Eliot was talking with a contemporary on God, Immortality and Duty, which may be considered the Holy Trinity of the period. She 'pronounced with terrible earnestness how inconceivable was the first, how unbelievable the second, and yet how peremptory and absolute the *third*'. We may think once more of the Crimean soldier fiercely slashing in the fog.

The picture of the family, at a dining table generally of mahogany, lingered well into the Edwardian age. There was no picture without a frame, no chair without upholstery, no screen or curtain without a tassel, no table without a cover, no box without its little objects, no maid without her pinny. Domestic servants became a necessity, and when Seebohm Rowntree completed a survey in York, he reckoned the keeping of at least one servant as a distinctive mark of the middle class as opposed to the lower class. There were visitings and dinings out, and when the moon was high they were known as 'moons'; hospitality was a social duty, and those who did not mingle with their neighbours were considered to be very odd indeed. You greeted acquaintances with two fingers of the outstretched hand; good friends and family were offered three. Choral societies and learned institutes, social clubs and sporting associations might be patronized by doctors, lawyers, accountants, senior clerks, owners of superior merchandise, company directors and civic officials. These were what we might call, in general, professional people, the whole swathe of middle Britain getting together and spending.

They were not devoid of admirers. The editor of the *Leeds Mercury*, which might be considered a representative middle-class newspaper, wrote that 'never in any country beneath the sun was an order of men more estimable and valuable, more praised and more praiseworthy, than the middle class of society in England'. James Mill wrote, as early as 1826, that 'the value of the middle classes of this country, their growing number and importance, are acknowledged by all. These classes have long been spoken of, and not grudgingly, by their superiors themselves, as the glory of

England.' Henry Brougham evinced the same sentiments. 'By the people I mean the middle classes, the wealth and intelligence of the country, the glory of the British name.'

But the slow process of social separation and division had begun early. In 1820 an anonymous contributor to *Blackwood's Magazine* noticed that 'it is too evident that the upper orders of Society have been tending, more and more, to a separation of themselves from those whom nature, providence and law have placed beneath them'. There were infinite gradations in these other orders. If we were to begin a disquisition on the upper middle class, the middle class, the lower middle class and the upper lower class we would need volumes which in the end would provide a complex stratification of manners that were in fact unique to each individual; any monolithic 'class' was a chimera made by doctrinaires and social statisticians. The movements between levels of class were intricate and, as one writer of the period observed, 'in the middle classes we note an almost universal unfixedness of position. Every man is rising or falling or hoping that he shall rise or fearing that he shall sink.' It can also be surmised that the struggle between the 'working class' and their supposed superiors was as nothing to the competition between workers who inhabited various levels of life and income.

Yet group activities do provide something of a group identity. Legal, medical and other professional institutions began to emerge, soon to be accompanied by civil and mechanical engineers, by architects and by accountants. In the previous century there had been five principal professions, but now there were twenty times as many constantly vying for status in the guise of dignity and decorum. The modern concept of public service was also becoming evident.

Social decorum was continued in the church where male and female sat on different sides; the more affluent had their own pews, and it was the custom of the poorer sort to remain after the service until their betters had left. Some women were daring enough to wear brown straw mushroom hats as part of their 'Sunday best' which became fashionable after 1856. The male of the house wore a tall hat and morning coat, and went to work in a horse-drawn omnibus. This is where he saw his neighbours, although they did not necessarily exchange greetings. Let us say that he worked in the City as an employer of one of those innumerable clerks in black who make so stiff a contrast with the street vendors and the local merchants.

The midday meal, costing from tenpence to one and six, consisted of beef or ham or veal with beer. If the customer was in a hurry he would pick up a pie from a street seller. Chicken bones were thrown into the gutter. If he had more time and money, he might visit a chop-house, from the windows of which he might on occasions be obliged to stare into the fog which was the breath of London. The street lamps were regularly turned on at noon. The American ambassador recorded: 'I could not see people in the street from my windows. I am tempted to ask, how the English became great with so little day-light.' The hours were long, up to fifty-two hours per week, but there was an 'English' half-day holiday on Saturday when the family might take a steamer or a tram to the parks or greener suburbs, while on Sunday, of course, the church called to the pious or the conventional. Others lolled in bed or made the pilgrimage to the local public house.

The life of the home was granted a less comfortable tone in the description of a cabinetmaker of the period:

> The vast majority of them [families] in the towns and cities have no room to be merry in. The bread winner has to be up and off early and home late . . . His little ones are fast asleep. He gets a peep at them . . . A look at the wife is a painful one. What is the matter dear, oh nothing. Poor dear she has been at work too. Trying to earn a bite to keep them decent. If this is the case in ordinary times when employ was regular and dad comes straight home and denies himself a glass of ale till he gets there, his shirt wet with sweat and tired with a long walk, where does the merriment come in?

The lower orders were also a besetting problem. Friedrich Engels considered the industrial system to be at the root of all evil, and Walter Scott blamed the steam engine, while Thomas Chalmers directed his anger against the poor laws. Lord Liverpool accused 'seditious and blasphemous publications' for weakening 'among the lower orders the attachment to our government and constitution'. 'Seditious and blasphemous publications' were the great cliché of moralists in the early age of mass reading.

To rest, and to do no work, however, was the great sin. The alluring adjective was 'conscientious'. The severe and steady detail of the pre-Raphaelite painters was conscientious. Painting itself was seen to be the product of labour and study. The patient work of the painter is of the essence, in the minute reproduction of detail and the evidence of arduous technique. Every figure is a study. Ruskin wrote in *The Stones of Venice* (1851–53) that the power of drawing was accessible to anyone 'who will pay the price of care, time and exertion'. One of the characters in Charlotte Brontë's *Shirley* (1849) is advised to look upon life and 'to study its knotty problems closely, conscientiously'. The Victorians were in love with the wrinkled brow and the clenched hand. Ruskin's moral scrupulosity ended in insanity; madness was for him, in that phrase from *The Stones of Venice*, 'the price of care, time and exertion'. The sprightlier minds of the latter part of the century took a different view of the matter. They were not averse to industrialism and science, but they were opposed to seriousness. Whether in the wit of Wilde, the high spirits of Gilbert and Sullivan or the absurdities of Lewis Carroll, knotty problems and conscientiousness are ignored. They are rejecting a world in which the imperatives of George Eliot concerning God and Duty are taken seriously.

The term 'Victorian' did not come into general circulation until 1851, the time of the Great Exhibition, as if it were only then that the fruits of civilization were revealed. To be 'Victorian' in that period was to be up to date, to take an interest in all that was mechanical and progressive; it was to accept an age in which everything was out of scale with the preceding era. The steam engine, the steamship, the buildings in the cities, were larger and grander than anything that had come before. 'Victorian' was modernity itself in the home, with striped wallpaper, patterned Brussels carpets, hour-glasses, wax flowers and wax fruit under glass. Harriet Martineau commented upon 'the spread of a spirit of peace – of a disinclination, that is, for brute violence'. The conditions of housing and sanitation were improving, and being poor was no longer confused with criminality. Duelling was now quite out of fashion. Our ancestors would have been astonished if they had known that 'Victorian' would come to mean constricted, brutal or unhealthy. The truth is that nobody can live in an age to which he or she is

not assigned. This is the paradox of gazing at Victorian painting or
reading Victorian fiction. The reality would be disgusting and un-
endurable, just as the early twenty-first century might seem to a
Victorian.

There are certain particulars which mark out the period. Holi-
days were coming into fashion, and are recorded in William Powell
Frith's painting *Ramsgate Sands* (or *Life at the Seaside*) of 1854. The
women are of course fully dressed in shawls and crinolines, together
with gloves and bonnets; it is a reminder that the lower classes had
neither the time nor the money to take an excursion and would not
arrive by the sea for another twenty-five years. The men wore their
usual dark suits, with waistcoats, and it was not rare to see top
hats between the sand and the sea. No one is swimming. It was
indecorous. The people did no more than paddle, but there were
entertainers and vendors to catch the attention. No one wanted the
sunlight. Even a blush on the cheeks would have been indelicate.
There is altogether a sense of defensiveness. It is the Victorian
paradox of self-confidence and energy in execution together with
the intimation or suggestion of tenuousness. The mingling of land
and sea was one of the great tokens of melancholy in the face of
eternity signified by Matthew Arnold's poem 'Dover Beach', when
the waves:

> Begin, and cease, and then again begin,
> With tremulous cadence slow, and bring
> The eternal note of sadness in.

The people are crammed together on the sands as if in formation. Yet they do not seem to be enjoying themselves; they are
tentative because they owe their hours to work. Work was the key.
Work was the appointed calling. They look as if they were ready to
return to it at a moment's notice. Carlyle noted that 'there is a
perennial nobleness, and even sacredness in work'. It may raise the
prospect of salvation.

The moral aspect of painting was never overlooked. Fault was
found in Frith's painting of the seaside, for example, because it
contained no vignette of a concerned mother overlooking a convalescent child. The Germans had already scoffed at English artists
for a certain nervousness or understatement in the presentation of

passion. The most that English painters managed in the depiction of human emotion was the representation of people in which something has been left unsaid, as in William Holman Hunt's *The Awakening Conscience* (1853) and Ford Madox Brown's *The Last of England* (1855). Some foreign artists appreciated the style. Théodore Géricault had achieved a triumph with *The Raft of the Medusa* but he left on record his appreciation of English (or Scottish) reticence in David Wilkie's *The Chelsea Pensioners reading the Waterloo Dispatch*:

> I will speak only of one figure which seemed to me the most perfect, whose pose and expression draw tears, however much one holds them back. It is a soldier's wife who, thinking only of her husband, searches with an unquiet and haggard eye the list of the dead . . . There is no crape or mourning; rather the wine flows on every table and the sky is unharrowed by any fatally presaging lightnings. But it reaches a final pathos like nature itself . . .

In regard to table manners, it is recorded that 'it is not done to take wine without drinking to another person. When you raise your glass you look fixedly at the one with whom you are drinking, bow your head, and then drink with great gravity.' Words and phrases also had a life of their own. 'Nice' was constant, as was 'you know'; 'spoony' suggested someone who was a bit of a weakling. In an era of rapid and remorseless change there was an abiding sentimentality for the past or 'bygones'. Very good was 'A1' and bad was 'shoddy' or 'very bad shoddy'; 'bunkum' was 'buncum' and 'in course' was used instead of 'of course'. A 'hobble' was trouble. Other topical words and phrases abounded: 'She would play old gooseberry', 'I think he is coming round to cotton to me'. 'Antediluvian'. 'Levanted'. 'A screw loose'. 'He is a Bohemian who hates the decencies of life'. 'In a blue funk'. 'There are moments when we try to give a child any brick on the chimney top'. 'Chaff'. 'Poltroon'. 'Ta-ta'.

The Victorians had their guides, however, in the presence of several writers who can be said to comprise the mind of the nineteenth century. In an age of prose they were considered to be more remarkable than the poets and, compared to them, the novelists were mere entertainers. Thomas Carlyle himself was considered to be a modern prophet who created a language of declamation and lamentation that was intense and original. He was not one to use the language of the herd; the discourse of parliament was for him the defining disgrace of the nation, while electoral reform was no more than 'shooting Niagara', with an abysmal conclusion. Why stop short at householders when the beasts of the field do not have the vote? 'Divine commandment to vote,' he wrote. 'Manhood Suffrage (Horsehood, Dog-hood ditto not yet treated of).' He was profoundly out of sympathy with the middle classes to whom he believed that power had been entrusted, and all the middle-class nostrums from freedom of trade to freedom of speech were anathema to him. His political heroes were strong men with a taste for decisive action and arbitrary rule. He believed that slavery was of no consequence, and that only the strong needed to survive. He was treated as a prophet by some because many in the nineteenth century shared his views and his detestation of 'Nigger Philanthropists' and other liberal voices. There was nothing of Shaftesbury or Wilberforce in him; he would no doubt have been horrified if he had known that these two eminent humanitarians would come to represent Victorian civilization more than he ever could.

He discerned correctly that his was a mechanic and utilitarian age based upon calculation and constraint which touched economic theory, religion, education and the physical sciences. The philosophy of the utilitarians would lead only to a 'greater perfection of Police'. Their network of sensible truths tied down the world and all the people in it. Laissez-faire, the philosophy of the moment, the truism of a thousand clowns, had replaced special responsibility with an impersonal 'cash nexus' which lowered human beings to the level of integers. 'Man's Unhappiness, as I construe, comes of his greatness; it is because there is an Infinite in him, which with all his cunning he cannot quite bury under the Finite.' His language is almost always heroic despite himself. He was fierce and eloquent and arresting.

In his deployment of the rhythm and cadences of prose he is not profoundly dissimilar to other writers of the great Victorian generation. Wherever we dig, we strike gold. There is the pellucid brightness of Thomas Macaulay's prose, which shines with an even light as he converts the disparate facts of the eighteenth century into a convincing if also convenient history. There is George Eliot, with her solemnity touched by tenderness and, as Lord Acton put it, 'a consummate expert in the pathology of consciousness'. John Ruskin will be of the same company; the structure of his thought reflects a particularly vibrant sensibility concerning architecture and stone. 'I notice', he wrote, 'that among all the new buildings . . . churches and schools are mixed in due, that is to say, in large proportion, with your mills and mansions, and I notice also that the churches and schools are almost always Gothic and the mansions and mills are never Gothic.' It may seem commonplace but it deserves some consideration for its analysis of the Victorian age.

Charles Darwin has appeared in this narrative more than once, since he of all writers embodies the purest Victorian spirit. The notion of evolution by natural selection is so fitting to its age that it resembles a great jewel found in a rock; the removal of special creation by a deity meant that the age of miracles had passed, leaving some more comfortless than ever. The imaginative landscape of *On the Origin of Species*, published in 1859, was equally compelling. It was a dark world indeed, dominated by the necessity of labour and the appetite for power. Even the bees 'are anxious to save time', and Darwin extols 'the more efficient workshops of the north'; nature itself is described as frugal and even miserly with a continual desire 'to economize'. Darwin also suggests the need for 'heavy destruction', with the subtext 'let the strongest live and the weakest die'. He celebrates the spectacle of violent death with his discourse on the bee. 'We ought to admire', he writes, 'the savage instinctive hatred of the queen bee, which urges her to destroy the young queens, her daughters.' Combat and slaughter become the principal components of this world. He imagines all life on earth to be derived from one 'common parent' or 'primordial form'; the offspring of this 'prototype' then develop into various species of animals or plants which in turn fight among themselves to 'progress towards perfection'. So 'evolution' can be interpreted as a suitable Victorian myth. This is what Charles Dickens, in *Dombey and Son* (1848), called 'competition, competition – new invention, new invention – alteration, alteration'. Everything is of a piece.

It carried very far. Beatrice Webb remarked of her mother's beliefs in *My Apprenticeship* (1926) that 'it was the bounden duty of every citizen to better his social status; to ignore those beneath him, and to aim steadily at the top rung of the social ladder. Only by this persistent pursuit by each individual of his own and his family's interest would the highest general level of civilisation be attained . . .' This returns the narrative to the world of work. A French observer remarked that: 'On entering an office, the first thing you see written up is "You are requested to speak of business only".' Carlyle emphasized 'that the mandate of God to His creature man is: Work!'

'Men of letters' were for the Victorians the epitome of a very broad band of learning, from social thinkers and political economists to philosophers and historians. It is something of a paradox that the century which produced the most elegant and voluminous prose should have only a small readership. It was estimated in 1861 that only 5 per cent of all pupils remained in school after the age of eleven; so we can confidently assert deep levels of illiteracy. Yet for the existing reading public the whole spirit of literature could be found in the morally useful where the essayist and the historian could be seen as preachers rather than scholars. In a world so permeated by religion the works of Ruskin, Eliot and Carlyle were prized for their moral exhortation and spiritual comfort. By the 1840s the Gothic novel and the histrionic romance had been super-seded by novels that explored spiritual problems of the modern world or inquired into matters concerning social structure and social status. There was no necessary disparity between realism (in the English rather than French mode) and moral elevation. The other grace notes of the Victorian world were seriousness and self-confidence, with a certainty that was close to dogmatism.

This quality of interest could not last in a society where literacy was steadily increasing and where the printed word would soon become ubiquitous. It had led to what John Stuart Mill described as 'the diffusion of superficial knowledge'. Matthew Arnold wrote to Arthur Hugh Clough that 'these are damned times – everything is against one – the height to which knowledge is come, the spread of luxury, our physical enervation, the absence of great *natures*, the unavoidable contact with millions of small ones, newspapers, cities, light profligate friends . . .' Here was a Victorian perception – the absence of great *natures* was keenly felt. It had always been said that the various Reform Acts would eventually create a world of the middle class and the lower middle class in which previous values would no longer apply. When one of the old Whig aristocracy criticized Prince Albert for attending a meeting of the Society for Improving the Condition of the Labouring Classes, the prince replied that 'one has a duty to perform to the great mass of the working classes . . .' This was the prevailing sentiment. The triumph of science and the rise of secularism effectively discontinued the tradition of Ruskin or of Carlyle; we know, even as we read them, that they are whistling in the wind.

17

Quite the fashion

One of the greatest contributions of the Victorian epoch to indigenous English culture is that of the music hall. There was a tradition of popular and often obscene entertainment that goes back to the jigs and comic songs of the Elizabethan stage and to the 'singing booths' of the fair. 'Harmonic meetings', taverns and 'free-and-easies' had their origin in the eighteenth century, but the true age of the 'halls' dates from the 1840s with the Canterbury Arms and the Surrey Music Hall, with their attendant aromas of gin, sweat and orange peel. The supper rooms of the 1850s added to the diversity, serving poached eggs on steak and devilled kidneys seasoned with red pepper. The attendant tavern concerts and 'night cellars' generally lived up to their reputations; the Cider Cellars in Maiden Lane and the Coal Hole on the Strand were two of the more notorious. The famous song of the Cider Cellars was 'Sam Hall', with its refrain 'damn your eyes!' The songs were as Victorian as the Crystal Palace.

From Store Street to Hungerford Market the music halls became the major form of popular entertainment. From the 1850s onwards they flourished particularly in the East End where the conditions of living were hard if not harsh. There were four such halls – the Rodney, the Lord Nelson, the Eastern and the Apollo – in Bethnal Green alone.

Specialized performers such as the 'Lion Comique', the female 'serio comic' acts and the 'heavy swell' were always in demand. They tended to cultivate 'coster songs' and songs written in a 'flash' or Cockney dialect. But much attention was paid to the 'chairman' who introduced the acts, made topical jokes and generally encouraged the audience to drink up and enjoy the same. This was known as 'wet money' when the price of admission included a drink. Their songs, such as 'Why Can't We Have the Sea in London' and 'My Shadow is My Only Pal', have no memorial, but they were the true token of popular sentiment. They were the songs of the poor, the songs of longing. No history of the nineteenth century would be complete without them.

One of the most celebrated of the artists was Dan Leno, born in 1860 in the neighbourhood of St Pancras. Like Charles Chaplin, he began his career as a clog artist. Clog dancing was a Victorian speciality, born out of life in the factories. The operatives in the textile mills tried to keep themselves warm by tapping their feet to the rhythm of the power mills, and soon enough it became part of a dance routine. Clog competitions became popular all over the north of England. Leno excelled with his speed and style to such an extent that he became in part identified with this eccentric form of dancing. He was on stage by the age of four, but did not create his individual act for another seven years, when he was billed as a 'Descriptive and Irish Character Vocalist'. It was not until 1885, however, that he perfected the act that brought him fame. His first 'turn' was that of a harassed woman who sang 'Going to Buy Milk for the Twins'.

No nostalgic evocation of the 'good old days' of the 1860s and 1870s is appropriate here, since the Leno family was often close kin to starvation and hopelessness. Leno's principal memories are of the long walks from town to town in search of employment. Yet, as in the best pantomimes, his fortune changed in a grand transformation scene. In 1880 he won the award for 'Champion Clog Dancer of the World' at the Princess's Palace in Leeds, beating off competition with his speed and precision. One critic noted that 'he danced on the stage, he danced on a pedestal, he danced on a slab of slate, he was encored over and over again, but throughout his performance he never uttered a word'.

His stature of 5 feet and 3 inches, his pallid and strained face, his pursed lips, his small husky voice and his sudden leaps backwards became the marks of his performance. He combined a curiously wayward 'patter' with sudden bursts of wild capering; he could bawl with the best of them before falling silent with a puzzled expression on his face. He was humanity personified, humanity in its essence, the object of pity and sympathy and exuberant hilarity. The few extant recordings of his act scarcely do him justice, because it was in communion with his audience that he became superb. He became the audience. He retained the utmost fidelity to ordinary familiar life. 'Whenever he is on the stage,' a dramatic critic wrote, 'be it theatre or music-hall, he literally holds the audience tight in his power. They cannot get away from him. He is monarch of all he surveys.'

Max Beerbohm put it best in the *Saturday Review*:

> I defy anyone not to have loved Dan Leno at first sight. The moment he capered on, with that air of wild determination, squirming in every limb with some deep grievance that must be outpoured, all hearts were his . . . that poor little battered personage, so put upon, yet so plucky, with his squeaking voice and sweeping gestures; bent but not broken; faint but pursuing; incarnate of the will to live in a world not at all worth living in . . .

In the latter part of the nineteenth century the halls became more ornate, with gilt and plaster, with balconies and stage boxes, just as the public houses of the period became more grandiose with mirrors and lights, so that they resembled the working-class notion of 'palaces' as they were soon called. Other halls were more enlightened. The Cambridge Music Hall in Liverpool, erected in 1866, contained frescoes of 'Science', 'Music' and 'The Seasons'. It opened at a time of typhus and an American cotton blockade so that entertainment of even the most puerile kind was welcomed. Drink and the music hall were the solace of the people. It was the will to live in a world not at all worth living in. When all else failed, put on a pantomime.

Dan Leno came to London in 1885 where he began a gruelling life by performing in Bethnal Green, Drury Lane and Westminster Bridge Road. Three music hall performances in one evening were not regarded as excessive (some managed six or seven) and the phrase 'I must hurry along to my next hall' became familiar. George Robey recalled that Leno was 'tearing from hall to hall, night after night. One would see him coming in from his brougham, still dripping with perspiration, and looking so tired.' But as soon as he appeared on stage with the audience in front of him he was transformed. He was always a busy, restless man, and one theatrical contemporary recalled: 'I can honestly say that I never saw him absolutely at rest. He was always doing something and had something else to do afterwards, or he had just been somewhere, was going somewhere else, and had several other appointments to follow.'

He played many parts, the majority of which were lower class or lower middle class; as was also said of Charles Dickens, 'he had the key of the street'. Four of his most familiar roles were as a waiter, shop-walker, muffin man and landlady whose boast or threat was 'Young Men Taken in and Done For'. They were part of the landscape of Leno's imagination that was lower-class London in essence, with its fried-fish shops, its public houses, its pawnbrokers, its shellfish stalls, its old-clothes shops and its markets. Nowhere else was he at home.

Dan Leno barely survived the Victorian era which he had so closely represented. His final part as Mother Goose may have contributed to his nervous breakdown, and he was taken to Peckham House Asylum, where he was diagnosed with a syphilitic disorder that had turned his mind. His constitution was not helped by the large quantities of alcohol which he had imbibed over the years since childhood. Alcoholism was the curse of the performing classes, and a large number of artists succumbed to cirrhosis of the liver and related complaints. He was released and, on the vague hope of recovery, continued to perform. In another period of mental confusion, towards the end of his life, he was seen queuing for one of his own shows. His largest audience of the period, however, was the one that accompanied his funeral cortège in the early days of November 1904.

The ribald and boisterous humour of the music hall was by the 1880s diluted by the growing respectability of the increasingly dominant middle class. The comic books and essays were written by what could be called the *Punch* school of writers that was ironic and even sarcastic without being subversive. The periodical itself was established as a weekly in 1841, nine years after the first Reform Act, and its contributors included Thackeray, Thomas Hood, Douglas Jerrold, Henry Mayhew and assorted members of the circle of humorists who had assembled around Dickens. It was more famous, however, for its multifarious cartoons which satirized the news and politics of the week.

One of its more enduring contributions, still in print more than 120 years later, was *The Diary of a Nobody* by George and Weedon Grossmith. It purported to be the intimate journal of a middle-aged clerk of lowly background, Charles Pooter, who has aspirations towards respectability and even gentility. The Grossmiths both began as stage entertainers, with George Grossmith a principal artist for Gilbert and Sullivan, but they stepped onto the pages of fictional history, in *Punch*, in the spring of 1888. The initial critical reception was not overenthusiastic, since in certain respects it was perhaps too close to home to seem comic. The references were always up to date. But gradually its reputation spread, so that by the 1890s it was regarded as one of the most important contributions to the late Victorian era.

The *Oxford English Dictionary* derives many of its phrases from the text, including 'I've got the chuck', 'dead cert' and 'a good address'. The actual address of the Pooters was 'The Laurels', Brookfield Terrace, Holloway (drawn by Weedon Grossmith as the last house in a two-storey terrace with a small front garden), an area of Islington which became heavily populated in the latter half of the nineteenth century. It could be described as a new suburb except for the fact that London soon surrounded it. The narrative could have been written there from observation. The fashion for spiritualism and table-rapping is faithfully recorded, as well as the newspaper question of the day: 'Is Marriage a Failure?' The domestic interiors of the suburban house are given in full detail, from the stags' horns of plaster of Paris painted brown to the blue wool mats on which the vases were placed. Chrysanthemums, bicycles and stuffed birds were the properties of the day. The Grossmiths also drew up an anatomy of 'home' as the lodestar of Victorian longing and contentment.

In a different light, *The Diary of a Nobody* might be considered to be a substantial contribution to the new fashion for 'realistic' fiction. George Gissing, the great master of English realism, had written that he wanted to record 'the essentially unheroic, with the day-to-day life of the vast majority who are at the mercy of paltry circumstances'. This is also the aim and object of the *Diary*. Here in this constricted circle Gissing and the Grossmiths introduced the same problems of upward mobility, of children and of marriage, and of the slow redefinition of class at the turn of the century.

Here are some apposite remarks from *The Diary*:

'Consequences' again this evening. Not quite so successful as last night, Gowing having several times overstepped the limits of good taste . . . Pa, at all events, was a gentleman . . . I had a fit of the blues come on, and thought I would go to see Polly Presswell, England's Particular Spark . . . as I am master of this house perhaps you will allow me to take the reins . . . I do not think such a style modest. She ought to have . . . covered her shoulders with a little lace . . . I feel as fit as a Lowther Arcade fiddle, and only require a little more 'oof' to feel as fit as a £500 Stradivarius . . . 'Oh, I'm going in for manicuring. It's all the fashion now'.

There were standard features – the one-price hat at three and six, the amateur theatricals, the hand-me-down frock coat, the fondness for fun and after-dinner games, the impromptu song recitals, the irate cab drivers, the annual week at Broadstairs (a little more select than Margate), the endless puns. And so the world went, in what was known as a right little, tight little, island. The phrases and expressions were all new-minted and bring the reader as close as possible to the language of the respectable classes of the late Victorian population, expressing the mild facetiousness and mild distaste, the clinging to standard conventions of good taste, the horror of anything approaching unorthodoxy, which prevailed among them. But *The Diary of a Nobody* suggests also that the conventions and phrases of the period were open to mockery even by those who employed them.

Wherever we turn we find new institutions and societies and clubs supplying what Dan Leno used to describe, concerning the

Tower of London, as 'a long-felt want'. The Reading Room of the British Museum was opened in 1857 for all those who wished to live in the shadow of the valley of the books. Anyone with any aspirations to scholarship and no other place to find it, from Karl Marx to Oscar Wilde, could acquire a ticket. There had been a reading room attached to the British Museum since 1759, but it was a 'damp and dark room' lined with stuffed birds. It emerged in its most familiar form in 1857 until its purpose was taken over by the British Library in 1973. Its circular shape represented by accident or design a giant cranium, but with a dome of 140 feet in diameter and a height of 106 feet, it was also a great feat of Victorian engineering. It is inferior to the Pantheon of Rome by 2 feet, and surpasses St Peter's and the church of Hagia Sophia in Constantinople.

It became, at the very least, a powerhouse of thought fuelled by all the calculations and results and theories that rose into the mid-Victorian air. Karl Marx came every day for thirty years, scrutinizing the floods and eddies of economic history. Stalin came, Lenin came, Trotsky came, all of them seeking the fount or origin of historical wisdom. The whole of Bloomsbury, in the immediate vicinity of the Reading Room, became magnetized by communist theory, with meetings and events and clubs and committees springing up in the vicinity of the great dome. The middle and late years of nineteenth-century England were capacious enough to tolerate a political enemy in their midst. It is appropriate, therefore, that George Bernard Shaw should leave a third of his estate to what he called a 'magnificent communistic institution'.

The Reading Room had an almost analgesic effect on the rest of the neighbourhood, since in the adjacent streets emerged theosophical, Swedenborgian, psychic and spiritualist organizations that became at once familiar and appropriate. This is another distinctive aspect of nineteenth-century England. The Hermetic Order of the Golden Dawn, for example, established its headquarters in London just opposite the Reading Room.

When the Reading Room was completed the books came flying in by means of donations, wills, outright purchase, but principally by means of copyright legislation which demanded each published book from every publisher. This was of course condemned as 'high-handed', but it exemplified the national movement towards bureaucratization and control. As a result the problem of storage was perhaps the greatest dilemma the librarians ever faced. The Reading Room itself could house 303 readers. Another great problem lay in its lighting. Artificial lighting was not allowed, and in heavy fog the Reading Room was closed, banishing its readers to the outer darkness. But in November 1879 a ripple of applause echoed around the dome when the first electric lights were turned on. George Gissing wrote of the 'sputtering whiteness of the electric light and its ceaseless hum'. But the atmosphere within the dome was heavy, and some people succumbed to what was known as 'museum megrims'. Algernon Swinburne collapsed and hit his head on his desk.

For many years it was supposed to be a library of last resort to which readers were only admitted if they could not find the chosen book elsewhere. A later century would relax the rules, to no very great advantage. But others crowded in. Charles Dickens remarked on the number of 'shabby-genteel' people who were attracted to the books; perhaps the warmth, perhaps the relative comfort, or perhaps the pleasure of participating in what might be called a universal mind, attracted them. It afforded the sensation of being engaged in some vast enterprise of which the individual readers were a part. It was a Victorian experience. George Gissing wrote in *The Private Papers of Henry Ryecroft* (1903) that 'at the time that I was literally starving in London, when it seemed impossible that I should gain a living from my pen, how many days have I spent at the British Museum, reading as disinterestedly as if I had not a care!'

Arnold Bennett described the readers as comprising 'bishops, statesmen, men of science, historians, needy pedants, popular authors whose broughams are waiting in the precincts, journalists, medical students, law students, curates, hack-writers, women with clipped hair and black aprons, idlers: all short-sighted and all silent'. However it was not altogether silent. The noise of books being opened and paged through, like an autumn rustling of leaves, was familiar. Coughs and sneezes and sniffles abounded in people who were not well nourished. Voices were occasionally raised on the question of a missing book or of a long delay in receiving one. Sometimes a book was dropped. But how were the endless footfalls muffled? There was a perfect Victorian solution. A material called kamptulicon, of cork and rubber, was laid down.

Fictional personages have also been seen here. In Max Beer-bohm's story 'Enoch Soames' (set in 1895, published in 1916), the eponymous hero, after making a pact with the devil, reappears a hundred years after his death to see if his name had entered the general catalogue of books. Jonathan Harker, in Bram Stoker's *Dracula* (1897), studied the maps of Transylvania under the great dome but could not find the location of Count Dracula's castle. The great period of the Reading Room has been variously estimated but it roughly coincided with the flourishing days of Mudie's Circulating Library.

Mudie's Lending Library was situated one minute's walk from the front gates of the British Museum, on the corner of Museum Street, and can be considered as a sort of commercial adjunct to the great library, where the customers could hire the latest fiction that was not yet available in the Reading Room. The demand was enormous and the latter decades of the nineteenth century were indeed halcyon days for the once great but now forgotten Victorian phenomenon of the three-volume novel.

Charles Edward Mudie opened his first shop in 1842, at the age of twenty-two, and charged his subscribers 1 guinea a year to borrow one volume at a time, and a 2-guinea subscription to borrow four books at a time. He soon discovered that fiction was the opiate of the people. The cost of novels was so high that Mudie's subscription selling was an immediate success, but his refusal to stock 'immoral' books or novels 'of questionable character or of inferior quality' made a singular impression on the new fiction offered for sale.

He did, however, have a more benign effect on the popularity of scientific books; he purchased, for example, 500 copies of Darwin's *On the Origin of Species*. His books were not taken in only by house-holds or individuals; they were delivered to institutes, reading clubs, book clubs, business clubs and others. About three and a half million volumes were in circulation at any one time, and the books travelled over most of Europe, America and the empire. By 1870 Anthony Trollope declared that 'we have become a novel-reading people . . . from the Prime Minister down to the last appointed scullery maid'.

Prose of course had also been the medium of first resort in the eighteenth century, but the nineteenth century became the home of fiction. Mudie has some claim to turning the art of reading into a mass market where before it had been a specialized pleasure. Theologians and philosophers, historians and biographers had always commanded attention, but it is possible that the flood tide of books released by Mudie and other circulating libraries helped them to move slowly upwards. Much of the fiction that Mudie delivered was not of the highest quality, and was dismissed by some as trash; nevertheless, the conveyance of the printed word throughout the country had some effect upon literacy and education. There eventually came into being a class known as 'the common reader'. Henry James described the onset of fiction in alarmist terms. 'The flood at present swells and swells, threatening the whole field of letters, as would often seem, with submersion.' Prose itself was linear, consequential, packed with meaning and reference; it could describe, command, elucidate, distribute and cancel. It was the language of power.

Mudie hired out the three-deckers of Thomas Hardy, George Meredith and Henry James even if it was not a form that any one of them would have chosen. It was simply a new way of making money for the publisher – three volumes instead of one, priced at 31 shillings and 6 pence for the set. It also encouraged bulk orders from the publishers and steady sales for the authors. His forms of moral censorship were always an irritant, however, with the assumption that he would stock nothing that could bring a blush to the cheek of a young lady. This disqualified much fiction, especially from the Continent, at a stroke. The single volume came to be considered a low form more fitted for a street stall than the three-volume dignity. The railway bookstalls sold cheap reprints known as 'yellow backs', and they made a killing out of 'shilling shockers'. Some of them were also known as 'sensation novels', which can be interpreted in a literal sense. The design of the sensation novel, after all, was 'to electrify the nerves'. Many of the characters in these novels seem to be in a nervous state and may communicate their fear to the reader. Wilkie Collins, for example, was concerned with doubles and double identity, with monomania and delusion, tracing the paths of unconscious association and occluded memories thirty years before Freud began investigating the subjects.

Yet it was not a format that appealed to other writers who had to wrestle with the three volumes in order to import long conversations, long descriptions, long moral reflections, as well as double plots, to make up the bulk. In 1853 Charles Reade, one of the most successful novelists of the century, complained that 'the three volume novel is the intellectual blot of our nation – it is the last relic of our forefathers' prolixity and damned digressive tediousness . . . The principle of the three volume novel is this – write not what you have to say only – but what you have not got to say as well.' Yet they were left on tables, draped over sofas, poised on the arms of armchairs and put on the bedroom table. They did not die of malnutrition until 1895, when other forms of literature were emerging.

18

The game cock

Palmerston's majority at the end of the Indian War of Independence was not as firmly based as it seemed, and his personality was not the cohesive force it once had been. The 'bundle of sticks', as his party was called, was no longer firmly in his grasp. United they were unbreakable; individually they could be easily snapped. There is a portrait of Palmerston in this period. 'He looked like an old gentleman, like a man who has used up his strength in fifty years of uninterrupted struggle but who knows how to cultivate his will power to a certain extent since it must serve instead of the rest of his strength as the whole once did. He looked like someone who is determined to rule to the end . . . there was no mirth on his lips, no gaiety on his brow.' At a Royal Literary Fund dinner Turgenev had observed that his face was 'wooden, hard and insensitive', an opinion he shared with Victor Hugo. But Palmerston had a strong sense of humour. He said of the Brazilian government that it resembles 'a Billingsgate fish-woman seized by a policeman for some misdeeds. She scolds and kicks and raves and calls on the mob to help her and vows she won't go to the lock-up house but will sooner die on the spot; but when she feels the strong grip of the policeman and finds he is really in earnest she goes as quietly as a lamb though still using foul-mouthed language at the corner of each street.' He still had the gift of turning foreign affairs into a Punch and Judy show, with himself as a frequently pugnacious Punch.

The counter-blow against him came from an unexpected source. In January 1858 an Italian nationalist, Felice Orsini, conceived a plan for the assassination of Napoleon III; largely as a consequence of lax police surveillance he gathered arms and men. Orsini himself travelled to England, where he persuaded a sympathetic gunsmith to build six bombs of Orsini's own devising. On the discovery of the plot the French people fell into one of their fits of hysterics, largely aimed at the perfidious English. Palmerston, fearful of the charge that the country had become a haven for revolutionaries, and wishing to save face with the emperor, caused a Conspiracy Bill to be introduced. It was defeated on a second reading and 'Pam' had a great fall. A journalist, William White, noticed that 'the "Great Minister", who but yesterday rode on the top-most crest of the waves of popularity, is sunk so low that there is hardly a man of his former friends to say, "God save him." Nor do men think of him in their speculations as to the future.' The pattern of politics was routinely called 'kaleidoscopic' after the invention of 1817.

It came as a shock to the opposition as well as to the administration. Disraeli and Derby – known colloquially as 'the Jew and the Jockey' – prepared themselves for an unanticipated rule, with Disraeli as chancellor of the Exchequer in the new Conservative administration. Their first step was faltering. Disraeli proposed his own India Bill, including the idea of an Indian council partly elected by the householders of the great English cities. Everybody laughed at him. A contemporary, William Fraser, wrote that 'no one can form the least idea, from looking at Hansard, of what took place. The cheering, groaning, laughing were beyond belief. We considered ourselves justified in using inarticulate means of rendering the eloquence of the other side nugatory'; rude noises and explosive shouts, in other words, were the order of the day. Derby had become prime minister, but he was still the leader of a minority.

In the summer of 1858, the sanitary health of the capital once more came into open view. It was the summer of the 'great stink', where the turbulent flow of faeces and other animal matter created a miasma over the Thames and the city. The effluent from all the houses ran down to the river, where it collected and stagnated; this was the water used for drinking and for washing clothes, which was described as having a 'brownish colour'. The smell permeated everything. Disraeli was seen in a corridor of the House of Commons doubled up with a handkerchief over his face. Victoria and Albert were about to take a leisure trip on the river but were forced by the smell to turn back. All smell was considered to be disease and recent outbreaks of cholera in London were blamed upon these gaseous eruptions. They rivalled in noxiousness the ubiquitous horse droppings which had for a long time been the characteristic smell of the city.

The foreshores were caked with excrement, and as far upriver as Teddington Lock the sewage was six inches thick and 'as black as ink'. Like the Crimean War, nobody claimed responsibility for it. It was nobody's shit. It was the system clogging itself. Yet someone, somewhere, decided that something should be done. An Act of Parliament in 1863 decreed that a vast and intricate network of sewers should be created. A civil engineer, Joseph Bazalgette, was chosen to be the saviour of London, which he duly became with his ingenious schemes of drainage.

The 'great stink' can be viewed beside another horror of 1858. The 'lunacy panic' of the year was aroused by the sudden awareness of the public, or the newspapers, that apparently normal people had 'disappeared' into lunatic asylums, generally at the instigation of greedy relatives. The ease with which it could be done was examined by Wilkie Collins, among others. 'It is easy to prove that an obnoxious relative is insane,' *Lloyd's Weekly* reported in August 1858, 'it is easier still to aggravate trivial symptoms by persistent bad treatment'.

In a world of privation and misery, madness could almost become epidemic. The apparent increase in cases of 'brain disorder' was widely noted. The *Edinburgh Review* speculated that it was the result of intense anxiety and competition in both social and commercial life; it noted that madness 'derived from the extreme tension to which all classes are subjected in the unceasing struggle for position and even life'. It was even rumoured that Victoria had succumbed to the illness of her ancestor and was so violent that she had to be restrained in a padded cell. It was a subject constantly reported in journals, novels and medical textbooks. Together with cholera it can be seen as the defining medical image of the nineteenth century. Its antidote was generally taken in the form of laudanum, known as 'Battley's Drops' or 'Mother Bailey's Quieting Spirit'.

Derby remained Conservative prime minister for fifteen months, but the larger action was behind the veil where Palmerston, Russell and other ambitious Liberal leaders vied for mastery. Russell condemned Palmerston for 'levity and presumption' but cautioned against any overt opposition to the Conservatives. Derby never had a majority, but he was not devoid of ambition. In March 1859, he and Disraeli introduced a parliamentary suffrage bill that would bring a form of equality to both town and country voters in an effort to bolster the Conservative constituency. But the Liberals and Peelites, working together, voted down the proposal (revived in 1884); Derby was obliged to resign and, at the subsequent April election, the Conservatives found themselves with thirty more seats but still in a minority.

Gladstone had already stated, four years before, that 'the great characteristic of this singular state of things is that political difference no longer lies between parties but within parties'. On 6 June 1859, the Liberals, Radicals and the rump of what were still known as Peelites came together for a definitive meeting at Willis's Rooms in St James's Street where the Liberal party was formally baptized. Nominally they came together over the 'Italian question', essentially in support of the Italians over their Austrian masters, but the substance of the meeting can be found in *The Times*:

> Lord John Russell next addressed the meeting and, after strongly deprecating the continuance of the Government in the hands of a minority, which he characterized as most unconstitutional and dangerous, expressed his hearty desire either to co-operate with Lord Palmerston, in the event of that noble Lord being called upon to form an Administration; or to avail himself of his assistance, in the event of his being required to conduct the affairs of the country himself. His Lordship adverted in the course of his speech to the state of the Liberal party, and expressed his opinion that in the event of a Liberal

Government being formed it was essential that the three great
sections of that party, the old Whigs, the Peelites, and the
advanced Liberals should each be represented in it.

From that time forward the Liberals became the dominant party
until the era of Disraeli. It can be said with some confidence that
there were now only two parties, Liberal and Conservative, the rest
of the Peelites dwindling away. The Liberal leaders, Russell and
Palmerston, were known by the queen as 'the two dreadful old men'.
The last of the true Peelites was, perhaps, her now ailing husband.

In the same month a vote of no confidence was passed against
Derby, and Palmerston became prime minister for the second time
at the age of seventy-five. He was a wonder. To some he seemed
to be no more than an aged pantaloon capering feebly in the corridors of Whitehall, but some called him 'Lord Cupid' for his youthful
looks. To them he represented a special kind of English verve,
vivacious until the end. He had become a 'fixture', a rock of ages.
He lured Gladstone into the Treasury, but they were hardly comrades-
in-arms. One member of parliament recalled that Gladstone would
come to the first cabinet of each session armed with suggestions
and proposals. Palmerston would stare down at his official papers
and, when Gladstone fell quiet, he would tap the table saying: 'Now
my Lords and gentlemen let us go to business.' He is also said to
have remarked to Lord Shaftesbury that: 'Gladstone will soon have
it all his own way and whenever he gets my place we shall have
strange doings.' It was not a question of policy but of personality,
which is the essential matter of politics.

Derby and Disraeli had no wish to deprive Palmerston of office
for fear of something worse, so they arranged a three-year 'truce'
with the prime minister without of course forfeiting the rights of
a loyal opposition. Derby advised Disraeli to encourage Palmerston
to rely on Conservative support 'and looking to Palmerston's
increased age and infirmities, the oftener these can be brought into
the same lobby in opposition to Radical moves, the better for it'.
He conveyed the message to Palmerston that he could rely on the
Conservatives whenever he was threatened by Radical demands. By
this stage, however, Palmerston's recovered popularity might have
seen him through. He was walking with a colleague by the Crystal

Palace. A contemporary observer, Viscount Ossington, noted : 'The moment he came in sight, throughout the whole building, men and women, young and old, at once were struck as if by an electric shock. "Lord Palmerston! Here is Lord Palmerston! Bravo! Hurrah! Lord Palmerston forever!"'

The principals at Westminster were in any case deeply bound together on the 'Italian question' and the perfidy of Italy's Austrian masters, although no one was very fond of the interested parties. That was always the way with foreign affairs. The general but often ignored rule was to stay out of the way of overseas imbroglios which seemed always to end inconclusively. One writer, John Trelawny, even suggested that foreign policy kept afloat the government in a world of threat 'with the great apprehensions most men now have of the effect of change at this moment. America, France, Italy, Poland, Hungary – danger everywhere. Who is to open the ball in this dance of death?' It was in fact Napoleon III who declared war on Austria; he had with him the new ally of Sardinia, which was eager to wrest more Italian territory from the maw of Austria; after defeats at Montebello and Solferino the Austrians were forced to come to terms, with the usual movement of territories from one overlord to another. These were the affairs of the world. The peasant still looked up at the sky in search of rain.

The year 1861 opened with the greetings of the *Annual Register*. 'The internal state of the country at the opening of the year 1861 was generally prosperous and tranquil . . . the state of the agricultural and manufacturing interests . . . was apparently sound. Whatever demand had temporarily existed for constitutional changes appeared to have now completely subsided.' Those who prophesied calm and contentment were, however, in a phrase of the period, 'destined to have the wind in their faces'. In the spring and summer of the year there was yet another French invasion scare which created panic among the more credulous and would have thrown the finances of the country into confusion if Gladstone had not been their implacable guardian. In this year he also abolished the excise duty on paper which, as Gladstone himself put it, propelled 'into vivid, energetic, permanent and successful action the cheap press of this country. To the most numerous classes of the community it was like a new light, a new epoch in life, when they found that the information upon public affairs . . . came to them morning after morning . . .'

The fear of France was succeeded, and superseded, by the fear of disruption with the United States. In May 1861 the Civil War broke out, dividing loyalties and counsel at Westminster. When seven slave-owning states seceded from the Union, the problem for the English administration became acute, rendered even more direct by the splits of public opinion. A significant body favoured the South, with whom trade was easy and profitable; the issue of slavery did not really enter the calculation. Others preferred to support the more 'modern' North with its business success and its instinct for economic and social progress. Yet perhaps a majority, or the largest minority, in the cabinet supported the South on the pragmatic grounds that the North would not be able to defeat the Confederacy.

Although the country professed neutrality that stance was seriously compromised when a Northern vessel detained two prominent Southern politicians on their way to England. It was fortunate that slow communications did not heat up the war. The opinion grew that it was imperative to keep out of the struggle, while conveniently forgetting that it was English statesmen and English parliaments who had helped to introduce slavery to those distant territories. The workers supported the North, and the manufacturers the South. The cotton operatives of Manchester and elsewhere were thrown out of work because of the fatal shortage of that commodity, and they might be said to have had mixed feelings on the matter. Palmerston, who himself favoured the Southern cause, was convinced that the North would never win, and made many jokes about the combatants. Dickens favoured the South, too, on the grounds that only its people could keep down the black population. Gladstone declared in one of his moments of mystic foolishness that: 'Jefferson Davis and other leaders of the South have made an army; they are making, it appears, a navy; and they have made what is more than either, they have made a nation.' The slow success of Northern arms, however, reminded Palmerston that he would be foolish to support a losing side.

Prince Albert did much to calm the tricky and ambivalent confrontation, but it was almost his last service to his adopted country. In December 1861 he died after a married life of twenty-one years. Only four years before, he had been made Prince Consort as if to solidify his position in English governance. It was said that they had behaved as if they were queen and king, although the queen would not have taken kindly to the suggestion. It would be fair to say that Albert took care of ministerial and managerial matters in which his wife was not wholly interested.

But she had regretted placing such burdens on what she called 'his poor dear stomach'. He had for many years had a nervous stomach which did not allow him to digest his food properly and provoked painful spasms. It is now suggested that he suffered from abdominal cancer or Crohn's disease; his teeth were painful and he suffered from gumboils. He may have known that the end was coming, but it was not the kind of news that could be intimated to the queen. 'I do not hang on to life,' he told her 'but you do – very much so.'

Victoria was called to the Blue Room of Windsor Castle where he lay. 'Oh yes, this is death,' she said. 'I know it. I have seen it before.' He faded slowly, fortified only by brandy. Melbourne had once said to her: 'English physicians kill you; the French let you die.' The English doctors were as always confused over symptoms, and used reassuring words as the palliative.

After her husband's death the queen promptly swathed herself in mourning from which she did not emerge for many years. It was the chrysalis for a black butterfly. She cancelled all her public and private engagements. The whole country was draped in black from the corner shops to the new department stores. Theatres, concerts and all public entertainments were cancelled. The queen totally withdrew from public life for two years, only venturing out to unveil statues or busts of Albert. It was an Arthurian mourning. It was a Tennysonian mourning. She lamented the fact that there was no one to call her Victoria now, and that she had lost the one prop upon whom she wholly relied. She was a little ball of black, of piteous face, to be glimpsed in the back of a landau. She would do nothing, appear nowhere, until there were some who wondered if she had any real purpose at all.

Her ministers faced insuperable difficulties if they ventured to suggest any public engagement. Victoria wrote:

Lord Russell and Lord Palmerston both strongly felt that as a lady, *without a husband*, with all the weight of Government thrown upon her, with weakened health, *quite incapable* of bearing the *fatigues* of representation, she could not be expected to entertain Princes *as* formerly. Consequently she cannot invite them. It makes *her* quite ill, to be *unable* to do the *right* thing – and yet she *cannot* do so.

She had an heir, Albert Edward or 'Bertie', whom she considered to be less than useless. On one occasion she felt moved to write in her journal: 'he is not at all in good looks; his nose and mouth are too enormous and he pastes his hair down to his head and wears his clothes frightfully – he really is anything but good looking'.

She would never turn to him for advice or comfort. She entered an almost cataleptic state of grief. If anyone dared to counsel her or advise her she responded with fury. Her only thought was of cherishing the memory of her husband with statues, parks and monuments. It would seem that the gentle training Albert had given her in the art and craft of ruling had largely been wasted, and by the mid-1860s the republicans of England were being given their second wind by virtue of Her Majesty's stubbornness. It would not be in any case correct to say that she had retired under a stone. Her family network established over Europe would have persuaded her, whether she liked it or not, to participate in the world. She had one reservation. She had written: 'I am also anxious to repeat *one* thing and *that one* is my firm resolve, my *irrevocable decision* viz that *his* wishes – *his* plans about everything, *his* views about *every* thing are to be my *law*!'

Gladstone was strengthening his position in the cabinet. He erred on the side of caution in his budgets, with strong rhetoric on the subjects of free trade and the defence of empire. He realized that he had no chance of ousting Palmerston but would have to content himself by waiting for his death, which surely could not be delayed for very much longer. As for further electoral reform, which was supported by Gladstone, the prime minister put it to one side for a while. There was no hurry. Reform had a vexed history. It had been attempted by Russell on two occasions without success, and Palmerston had not redeemed his pledge to introduce it. But it was probably wise to broach the matter once again when the public seemed apathetic, and no great issue would arise. The Reform Act of 1832 had produced none of the predicted effects, and there was no reason to believe that any new act would do so now. In any case it was not wise or expedient to continue to frustrate the industrial working class indefinitely.

Change must come sooner or later. Sooner was more politic. And so the pressure mounted slowly and gradually. In October 1858, Engels wrote to Marx that 'the British working class is actually becoming more and more bourgeois'. This was not necessarily a comfort to the authorities because it had been clear enough that the more 'bourgeois' the worker the more he demanded certain civil rights. Another observer of the mid-nineteenth century can complete the picture. Henry Mayhew wrote:

> the artisans are almost to a man red hot politicians. They are sufficiently educated and thoughtful to have a sense of their importance in the State . . . The unskilled labourers are a different class of people. As yet they are as unpolitical as footmen, and instead of entertaining violent democratic opinions, they appear to have no political opinions whatever; or, if they do possess any, they rather tend towards the maintenance of 'things as they are' than towards the ascendancy of the working people.

Palmerston made periodic visits to the regions in order to meet the people, and generally professed himself to be 'touched' and 'comforted' by their enthusiasm. He was the 'game cock', in boxing terms of the time, and had a few rounds still to win. But he was not ready just yet.

19

The unexpected revolution

Viscount Palmerston, and Lord John Russell as foreign secretary in Palmerston's administration, had observed the abiding principle of foreign affairs by keeping out of trouble. They kept out of Italy and, more important, they had kept out of the United States, where infinite difficulties threatened. When Napoleon III suggested that a European army should cross the Atlantic, there was a moment of horror in the Foreign Office before it was realized that the idea was thoroughly impracticable. The old certainties survived. France was still the enemy, and in any case there was a royal 'cousinhood' between England and Germany on a continent where everyone was related to everyone else. But the absence of English entanglement in any European war did not mean that the forces of the country remained entirely idle. There was scarcely a year in which troops and ships were not engaged in warding off threats to the empire from Afghanistan to Zululand. On this, there was a political consensus. 'The Tory party', Disraeli claimed, 'is only in its proper position when it represents popular principles. Then it is truly irresistible. Then it can uphold the throne and altar, the majesty of the empire, the liberty of the nation and the rights of the multitude.'

When Russia claimed its constitutional rights over Poland, in January 1863, the Polish revolutionaries provoked a fierce civil war on which England looked with horror. But it did nothing about it except to issue vague threats. When Russell mildly inquired of the Austrian ambassador whether Austria might use force against Russia, the ambassador returned the question. 'As I had foreseen,' he noted, 'Lord Russell told me that this eventuality had not been examined yet and that, not being ready to answer me, he begged me for the present to consider his question as not having been put.' Such was the dread of entanglements.

The situation did not change over the next two or three years as German and Austrian armies marched over Europe to proclaim their responsibilities. In an age when the world seemed to be utterly transformed by scientific and commercial advance, Europe itself achieved tumultuous change. Otto von Bismarck was a problem without necessarily being a threat. The kingdom of Italy was united in 1861, anticipating the creation of a united Germany by the controlling will of Bismarck, who forged together the multifarious German principalities and kingdoms under the control of Prussia. It is not the matter for a history of England, unless we engage in the grand game of consequences, but it is significant to note that Bismarck was the real master of the situation and that England played an almost negligible role in the creation of late nineteenth-century Europe.

The London workers had pledged their support to the Polish rebels, and the working-class solidarity with the various nationalists struggling to be free indirectly advanced their own domestic causes. One expression of this confidence came in the guise of cooperative production, a combination of socialism and self-help, and in 1863 the North of England Co-Operative Wholesale Industrial and Provident Society had been able to break the hold of the more exacting wholesalers. This was the period of friendly societies, building societies and savings banks which established their strength on the ideals of thrift, self-help and mutual security. In its beginnings it seemed to promise the slow and non-violent introduction of a socialist commonwealth, but these aspirations proved illusory. The working man and woman did not wish for social revolution, but rather for an improvement in their circumstances.

In the spring of 1864 the new demand for respectability became more influential in political counsels. On 11 May Gladstone explained to the Commons that 'every man . . . is morally entitled to come within the pale of the Constitution' unless incapacitated by 'some consideration of personal unfitness or of political danger'. Gladstone had raced ahead of the pack. He seemed to be proclaiming the vote as a right, not as a privilege. He went on to say that the union of all classes, so much to be desired, should be promoted 'by a reasonable extension, at fitting times and among selected portions of the people, of every benefit and every privilege that can justly be conferred on them'. Disraeli said that he sounded like Tom Paine. Palmerston accused him of promoting 'the Doctrine of Universal Suffrage which I can never accept'. Interestingly enough, Palmerston linked Gladstone's reform policy with his increasingly public role. 'It is to be regretted', Palmerston told him 'that you should, as you stated, have taken the opportunity of your receiving a deputation of working men, to exhort them to set on foot an agitation for parliamentary reform – the function of a government is to calm rather than to excite agitation.' At the end of May 1864 *Punch* published a cartoon in which Gladstone is the only rider on a racecourse. Palmerston, as the starter, is calling out: 'Hi! Gladstone! Democracy! Too soon! Too soon! You mustn't go yet!'

Gladstone had begun to recognize that the working classes were material which could be worked on. They might be tractable. He was beginning to see the possibilities of a wider public to which in later years he would appeal. To one delegation he stated that 'the franchise ought to be extended to the working classes'. In the autumn of the year he toured the manufacturing districts, slowly feeling his way into a new territory of democracy. Already the *Newcastle Daily Chronicle* was alluding to a 'Great Party of the People' with Gladstone as its leader. He liked to allude to the great cotton famine of 1862 when the American Civil War deprived the north of that necessary material. Gladstone praised the people of south Lancashire, in particular, for 'self-command, self-control, respect for order, patience under suffering, confidence in the law, regard for superiors'. These of course were the members of an ideal democracy. He was cheered and feted wherever he went. It is significant, therefore, that when Palmerston met a deputation of working men he was greeted with silence.

Palmerston was more successful in his proper home of parliament. He averted a vote of censure from the Lords on the question of ceding Schleswig-Holstein to the German Confederation, a controversy of infinite moment only to those who were directly involved. Palmerston had said that: 'Only three people have ever really understood the Schleswig-Holstein business – the Prince Consort, who is dead – a German professor, who has gone mad – and I, who have forgotten all about it.' In fact the betrayal of Denmark by Britain provoked a great deal of anger and disgust. Was this the way to deal with allies? As a result the Prussians became more confident, and the British lost much influence. Matthew Arnold argued that Palmerston had found the country first in the world's estimation, but left it badly diminished. The result may not have been as profound as this suggests, but the betrayal of Denmark did much harm.

Palmerston's survival of the vote of censure was greeted with relief by all sides. No one was yet ready for Benjamin Disraeli, who stood in the wings, awaiting the exit of Lord Derby. Richard Cobden taunted the Conservatives even for considering the departure of Palmerston, who was sometimes considered to be more Conservative than Derby himself.

> I think you are very wrong in trying to remove the noble Lord ... he throws discredit on reform; he derides the 220 gentlemen who are prepared to vote for the ballot. He spends more money and is far more extravagant than we would allow you to be if you were in office. Besides all this, I have always been of the impression that after he has thoroughly demoralised his own party, he intends, when he makes his political will, to hand over office to you as his residuary legatees.

After Cobden had finished speaking he followed custom by putting his top hat back on his head.

Two books of opposite tendency were issued in 1865. Walter Bagehot's *The English Constitution*, published in serial form between 1865 and 1867, was a treatise in favour of dullness. The eminent historian of Victorian England, G. M. Young, described Bagehot as 'the greatest Victorian' and 'a man who was in and of his age and who could have been of no other ... whose influence, passing from one fit mind to another, could transmit and can still impart that most precious element in Victorian civilization, its robust and masculine sanity'. It was a duty to be dull; it was a sin to be too clever by half, as the saying went. It bred suspicion. As Bagehot wrote, 'the most essential quality for a free people . . . is much stupidity'. Do not investigate too much; do not aspire too much. That was the way to preserve liberty. Bagehot believed that it was 'the dull traditional habit of mankind that guides most men's actions . . . that dullness in matters of government is a good sign and not a bad one – in particular dullness in parliamentary government is a test of its excellence, an indication of its success'. Excitement breeds excess. Innovation, let alone revolution, breeds anxiety, trouble and conflict. This is one of the keys to the general stability of Victorian England.

Yet there had been a change. In previous generations the gentlemen of parliament amused or abused their colleagues with speeches which resembled after-dinner conversations. Now the age of the newspaper had arrived, together with its conglomeration of facts and opinions. The orators of Westminster, if they could still be called such, relied upon what Bagehot called 'the patient exposition, the elaborate minuteness, the exhaustive disquisition' on such matters as chancery reform and the registration of companies. Bagehot speculated further: 'Regular business forms a regular statesman – quiet habits, sober thoughts, common aims are his obvious characteristics.' The great idea was to be, or to appear, ordinary. And 'if a steady observer really looks at actual life he will see that men never think if they can help it'. This can be taken as a fair summation of ordinary Victorian values.

Rare and singular exceptions can be found to that dispensation. In the same year as *The English Constitution* began its serialization, James Clerk Maxwell's *A Dynamical Theory of the Electromagnetic Field* also appeared. It is rarely mentioned in the histories of the period largely because it is still very difficult for the layman to understand. Maxwell's principal achievement was the promulgation of electromagnetic theory, which has been described as the 'second great unification theory', after Newton, in which electricity, magnetism and light were to be viewed as manifestations of the same phenomenon. This in itself might be seen as a quintessentially Victorian discovery, and one of great significance. A fellow physicist, Richard Feynman, wrote in the 1960s that: 'From a long view of this history of mankind

– seen from, say, 10,000 years from now – there can be little doubt that the most significant event of the nineteenth century will be judged as Maxwell's discovery of the laws of electrodynamics.' It can be argued that Victorian scientific theory will surpass all the religious and social tenets of its age.

We may note, however, that in the period of Maxwell's publication of his insights the greater fervour of the time – especially from the 1850s to the 1880s – was devoted to the problems of biblical criticism. The development of a more liberal theology, and freedom of doctrinal decision, made the world unsteady. Any number of causes célèbres provoked bitter fury and sarcasm, and the participants fought one another as if their life depended on it. Heresy trials and court cases were instituted which pitted Nonconformists against Anglicans, Presbyterians against Congregationalists, German against English theologians, bishops against priests. Was the biblical narrative inspired by the Word of God or was it the composite work of scholars in various periods? Was geology a savage assault upon the conventions of Genesis? The bishop of Natal, J. W. Colenso, published a series of examinations of the Pentateuch and the Book of Joshua in which he discerned inconsistencies, improbabilities and impossibilities. They could not have been inspired by a deity. Colenso wrote that 'our duty, surely, is to follow the Truth, wherever it leads us, and leave the consequences in the hands of God'.

The pious, who included the powerful body of Evangelicals and High Churchmen, were outraged. How could a bishop, of all people, propound such views? Bishop Lee of Manchester was afraid for 'the very foundations of our faith, the very basis of our hopes, the very nearest and dearest of our consolations'. There were calls for a heresy trial, although burning was not an issue any more. The bishop of Cape Town, Colenso's superior, convoked a synod in the course of which Colenso was deposed as bishop. Colenso then appealed to the Privy Council in London, which declared that he could not be so degraded. Nevertheless the bishop of Cape Town anointed another bishop while Colenso carried on regardless, creating a schism that lasted for decades. A similar pattern became evident in English dioceses where liberal clerics provoked ultra-conservative bishops and vice versa. The certainties of the past were in any case being eroded by what were seen to be 'objective' and 'scientific' solutions.

The decay of religious doctrine is in some subtle way linked with the observations of Thomas Hardy and Rider Haggard that village tradition came to an end in or about 1865. The last links of the old world, and of old England, were finally to be severed. It had happened almost without anyone noticing it. This was the year in which the *Fortnightly Review* was first published, with the mission (for such it was) to encourage 'Progress' and to further illuminate 'modern minds' with a broadly scientific and secular outlook.

In this year, also, Matthew Arnold, in 'The Function of Criticism at the Present Time', one of his *Essays in Criticism*, wrote that 'epochs of concentration cannot well endure for ever; epochs of expansion, in the due course of things, follow them. Such an epoch of expansion seems to be opening in this country.' For Arnold, then, the dissolution of traditional modes of thought promised 'expansion'. He wrote also that:

> in the first place all danger of a hostile forcible pressure of foreign ideas upon our practice has long disappeared; like the traveller in the fable, therefore, we begin to wear our cloak a little more loosely. Then, with a long peace, the ideas of Europe steal gradually and amicably in and mingle, though in infinitesimal small quantities at a time with our own notions. Then, too, in spite of all that is said about the absorbing and brutalizing influence of our passionate material progress, it seems to me indisputable that this progress is likely, though not certain, to lead in the end to an apparition of intellectual life; and that man, after he has made himself perfectly comfortable and has now to determine what to do with himself next, may begin to remember that he has a mind, and that the mind may be made the source of great pleasure.

It is interesting, perhaps, that material progress is regarded as 'passionate'.

An election, based upon the premise of economic stability and very little else, was held in the spring of 1865. The result was to be expected, with the Whigs under Lord Palmerston gaining a majority over Derby and his Conservatives. 'I trust God will look mercifully on His poor overburdened creature', Gladstone wrote of himself, 'as he trips and stumbles along the road of life.' He did in fact stumble on this occasion. He was rejected by the electors at Oxford, for being an earnest liberal with a touch of radical about him, and had to hurry north in order to be elected; he had always been in favour among the people of south Lancashire. He was greeted by a crowd of 6,000, whose enthusiasm soothed the wound of Oxford. 'At last, my friends,' he said, 'I am come among you . . . I come among you "unmuzzled".' The interpretation was that Gladstone now was ready actively to promote Reform. Whatever he meant, the word did not appeal to his prime minister.

It was now clear enough that Palmerston could not continue indefinitely, and the observers of the political scene noted that Gladstone was in the process of spreading his wings over the electorate. Yet Palmerston seemed to have been given a magic potion. One dinner companion, Lord Ossington, observed how:

> He ate for dinner two plates of turtle soup; he was then served very amply to a plate of cod and oyster sauce; he then took a paté; afterwards he was helped to two very greasy entrées; he then despatched a plate of roast mutton; there then appeared before him the largest and to my mind the hardest slice of ham that ever figured on the table of a nobleman, yet it disappeared, just in time to answer the inquiry of his butler. 'Snipe, my lord, or pheasant?' He instantly replied 'Pheasant!'

It might just have been too much. By the spring of 1865 he was beginning to look his age, and by the autumn he was dead.

He cannot be accused of any startling innovations; he stood by no great cause except, of course, for the prosperity of the country. He was part of the furniture of his age, a solid position which he gained by caution (as a wolf is cautious when stalking prey), good fortune and astute judgement. He has suffered, perhaps, in comparison with Gladstone and Disraeli – without the moral gravitas of the one or the serpentine flexibility of the other. *The Education of Henry Adams* (1918) describes the political situation more floridly:

The years of Palmerston's last cabinet, 1859 to 1865, were avowedly years of truce – of arrested development. The British system, like the French, was in its last stage of decomposition. Never had the British mind shown itself so *décousu* – so unravelled, at sea, floundering in every sort of historical shipwreck. Eccentricities had a free field. Contradictions swarmed in State and Church. England devoted thirty years of arduous labour to clearing away only a part of the debris . . .

Trollope put it more succinctly in *Phineas Redux* (1873) when he observed that 'it is the necessary nature of a political party in this country to avoid, as long as it can be avoided, the consideration of any question which involves a great change'.

The death of Palmerston was considered to be a grave national calamity, but it did take the block away from any form of political or social advancement. Once again political reform was in the air. It had been bottled up and stored for so long that it seemed that it might now explode. 'The truce is over,' Disraeli wrote. 'I foresee tempestuous times, and great vicissitudes in public life.' A National Reform Union was established in 1864, and next year the Reform League promoted the policy of manhood suffrage. The tight bonds of legislation and conformity had been gradually released. The reduction or abolition of certain privileges, and the removal of religious disabilities, had lightened the atmosphere and freed the way for more humane legislation. Trade unions were slowly accepted as part of the world of work, and municipal reform helped to provide parks, schools and public baths. Sanitary hygiene, after the 'great stink' of 1858, had become a national imperative.

Palmerston died in harness, as the saying went. The premiership went from a man of eighty-one to one of seventy-three. Earl Russell, as John Russell now was, accepted the challenge. Some people were surprised that Russell would take up the old burden again but, as the king of Belgium told Victoria, 'these politicians never refuse'. In any case the sky did not fall, and it was almost as if nothing had happened at all. Derby and Russell carried on like the old partners of rival firms and, naturally enough, the interest moved to the next generation of leaders. Gladstone and Disraeli were in the dressing room, preparing for their parts.

On the day of Palmerston's death Gladstone had written a letter to Russell acknowledging that the older man was the obvious successor. 'Your former place as her minister, your powers, experience, service and renown, do not leave room for doubt that you will be sent for.' In turn Gladstone remained chancellor of the Exchequer and leader of the House of Commons. He had become the most formidable chancellor in English history, and among his cabinet colleagues he was *primus inter pares*. His fiscal policy was one of undeviating caution. He kept down military expenditure, reducing taxes and tariffs wherever he could prudently do so, and managed to create annual surpluses. He had emphasized 'the essential and vital connection between the growth of the industry of the country and the legislative process pursued within the last quarter of a century'. It was all part of the programme he had espoused in his speeches across the country. He was the right minister to introduce a new Reform Bill as one of the new administration's first measures.

Reform was a jack-in-the-box. Whenever you opened the box of change, out it sprang with a grin upon its face. Its motto was 'Here we are again!' The atmosphere for change seemed to become more urgent when in March 1866 the bill-broking firm of Overend, Gurney and Company collapsed, setting off a financial panic. Even though Gladstone had been charged with putting forward a bill, he was uncertain how to steer the course. John Bright wrote to him: 'you have had three months in which to form a bill which any man knowing anything on the subject could have done in a week'. Gladstone finally unveiled his proposals in March 1866, but they pleased nobody; he floundered in debate. Besides, they looked suspiciously like reheated porridge. The nominal majority of the Liberals plunged and the Russell government resigned in June. There were members of his party who suggested an immediate general election, but others believed that it would be unpopular. So the cabinet agreed to a resignation without a dissolution. The Conservatives were in without a fight.

The administration had been outvoted in what had become suspiciously like a game of tit-for-tat. Disraeli had been joined by a group of Liberals who were firmly and almost viscerally opposed to Reform; they were called, and eventually called themselves, 'Adullamites', after the cave of Adullam where David sought refuge from Saul. A 'cave' became the name for a party within a party. The Conservatives, long starved of office, took over power in the prevailing public expectation that Reform was now out of the question. They had not reckoned on Benjamin Disraeli, who seemed to have an uncanny ability to anticipate and even to shape the political weather.

The government of Russell and Gladstone had fallen on 18 June, and nine days later approximately 10,000 protesters gathered in central London, complete with brass bands and red flags, to protest at this rejection of Reform with shouts and slogans such as 'Gladstone and Liberty!' and 'Gladstone for ever!' It was clear that he was the central figure of popular hope and expectation.

Mass demonstrations continued in Hyde Park, Victoria Park and Lincoln's Inn Fields. Marches were organized in Manchester, Liverpool, Birmingham and elsewhere. The police attempts to control the protesters met with only partial success, and of course handed the cup of moral victory to those on the streets. But they were nothing like the previous demonstrators of London. The Gordon Riots were a distant memory. These were respectably dressed Londoners who behaved with sobriety and decorum. A few crushed flowers in Hyde Park, and some broken railings, were the extent of the carnage. Matthew Arnold had witnessed the scenes from a balcony along the Bayswater Road and was inspired to write *Culture and Anarchy* (1869). But the news of anarchy rather than culture spread, causing needless panic. If the public had recalled how peaceable the crowds of Hyde Park had been at the time of the Great Exhibition, they might have rested more easily. Those who had once been drill sergeants now organized the lines of the demonstrators with precision. Some of the protesters wore top hats. Their call was for 'manhood suffrage' or 'household suffrage', which was not at all the same thing as democracy for all. These were the old measures proposed for half a century. They were really associated with the idea of property, in particular of a house, so that the propertied classes would have a much larger stake in the direction of the country. The women, the poor and the vagrant were implicitly excluded from the process. The sober and well-organized marches and speeches for electoral reform impressed Gladstone, who was more than ever sure that the time for Reform had come. Yet the fact was that he had been defeated over Reform and was out of office.

The earl of Derby, however, also believed that the moment of the Conservatives had come. Standing with him was the arch-manipulator of the time, Benjamin Disraeli. It was Derby's third minority Conservative government, but he informed his colleagues in the Lords 'that he did not intend for a third time to be made a mere stop-gap until it should suit the convenience of the Liberal Party to forget their dissensions'. By some act short of magic he was determined to take his minority into a majority, and perhaps conjure together a scheme of reform measures that would attract a large number of adherents.

He was not yet sure from where support for Reform might come. He consulted the leading Adullamites, who were his enemies' enemies, but they were not about to oblige him; they were, after all, still Liberals, even if they were not reformers. Lord Shaftesbury, who had acquired a reputation as a supporter of humanitarian causes, also declined to assist him. The Conservatives themselves were a heterogeneous assembly including liberal conservatives, conservative liberals and conservative radicals who might or might not be bound together. Yet Reform was a necessity. The failed measures, the false starts and the delaying tactics of those against change had created an opposing momentum which could not be denied for much longer. Derby wrote to Disraeli: 'I am coming reluctantly to the conclusion that we shall have to deal with the question of Reform.'

Disraeli was not so sure. He had seen other ministers, including Gladstone, come to grief over a question which seemed to have no definite solution. It would require mature consideration but could not be avoided altogether, or else the Tories, Disraeli said, 'must have dwindled away like the Jacobites or the non-jurors'. 'I was determined', he added, 'to vindicate the right of the party to a free hand, and not to allow them to be shut up in a cage formed by the Whigs and Radicals, confined within a certain magic circle which they were not to step out of at the peril of their lives.' But the public was apathetic. Nine out of ten cried out: 'We must have a reform bill!' but eight out of nine whispered to each other: 'Does anybody want one?' This was Bulwer-Lytton's perception.

Derby would not avoid the issue, however, since as he told

Disraeli, 'the Queen spoke to me about it the other day. She said she is very anxious to see it settled, and that if she could do anything personally to bring opinions together, she would most readily do it.' This was not quite a royal command, but it could not be easily overlooked. Disraeli dismissed the royal proposal of bringing Conservatives and Liberals together as a 'phantom', but he also knew the dangers of advancing upon Reform legislation in unknown territory. No one would believe that the Conservatives were serious unless and until they put forward a scheme bolder than anything Gladstone and Russell envisaged. They could not afford to be 'outbid' by the opposition. They had to propose legislation which would put Gladstone and the others in the shade.

Disraeli, however, would eventually emerge with the greater credit, together with the implicit assumption that he would replace Derby whenever the time came. His political agility and astuteness may not have been to the taste of some, but he dazzled or bewildered many others. It was not at all clear what his ulterior plan might be, except that he wanted to stay in power for as long as possible; he surrendered and fudged some positions, in order give the reform legislation a clear path. His goal seems to have been simply to succeed and, in a phrase of the period, 'to dish the Whigs' – to beat the Whigs at their own game of widening the electorate. Once the gate had been opened it would never be closed again, and from the muddle and confusion there eventually emerged a working democracy that has never been seriously threatened.

Disraeli was a great improviser, a master of the unexpected and a superb tactician. He proposed a much larger franchise by accepting household suffrage, and with the help of some recalcitrant Whigs batted away any attempt to restrict or hamper the extent of the new electorate. Amendments were added to enlarge the estimate of voters, and in the early summer private members' bills added to the franchise. The residence requirement was reduced from three years to one. Lodgers 'of ten pounds value' were given the vote. In February 1867 Derby addressed the Lords on maintaining good relations with 'the great Republic on the other side of the Atlantic', with the obvious implication that republics are not all made up of wolves and hyenas. He announced that Disraeli would be putting forward certain plans that would require 'mutual forbearance'. On the day that Disraeli was to put forward his proposals Viscount Cranborne, the secretary of state for India, did his sums and concluded that 60 per cent of the constituencies would be given to new voters.

On receiving Cranborne's message Derby wrote at once to Disraeli that 'the enclosed, just received, is utter ruin! What on earth are we to do?' A compromise was reached that satisfied nobody. Yet Derby, strengthened by Disraeli, rejected the compromise. He would introduce household suffrage at whatever cost to the party. It was a matter of honour rather than of principle. Plans were drawn up that any man who could claim two years' residence and had paid poor rates would be entitled to vote. But this was only the first of several amendments and corrections that steadily widened the scope of the franchise, so that, in the end, Derby had no idea of the number who had been affected. What had begun as a plan to alter the borough franchise had concluded as a scheme for household suffrage.

Disraeli had become the guiding agent of the legislation. He knew or sensed that the Conservatives would follow him as long as he regained the political initiative and refused to be cowed by Whig objections. Gladstone was ignored, therefore, and Disraeli seemed receptive to radical proposals to extend the vote. As the Conservatives had nothing to lose by extending household suffrage, they might as well endorse it with enthusiasm.

Derby was gradually weakened by ill health, but the Conservatives were in any case experiencing a semi-fevered fit of radicalism. They wanted to out-Gladstone Gladstone, a feat they had been longing to perform, and in any case they were bored with the details and the statistics. Disraeli was succinct and sharp, but above all he was unpredictable. Gladstone bored many of his colleagues. They wanted to get it over with, and in the process turn the Conservative party into an infinitely more attractive force than it had been before. 'No doubt we are making a great experiment and "taking a leap in the dark",' the prime minister said after the Reform Bill had passed, 'but I have the greatest confidence in the sound sense of my fellow-countrymen.' In fact that 'sound sense' meant that the number of Radicals in parliament did not vary between fifty and one hundred; they were not particularly interested in the masses or in manhood suffrage, but in promoting industrial and commercial reform.

This is not unprecedented. Out of a chaos of cross-purposes, mistakes and misunderstandings some of the most enduring legislation has emerged, just as misinterpretations and false conclusions have been more responsible for wars than even the lies of statesmen. So of course there were no identifiable culprits or causes; everything took place in a fog of surmise and speculation. The most successful politicians are those who are able to ride the flood tide of conjecture and false claims. 'It is a privilege to live in this age of rapid and brilliant events,' Disraeli once wrote. 'What an error to consider it a utilitarian age! It is one of infinite romance.' The Victorian passion for fairy tales never had a better exponent. A contemporary described him 'as unlike any living creature one has met . . . The face is more like a mask than ever and the division between him and mere mortals more marked. I would as soon have thought of sitting down at table with Hamlet, or Lear, or the Wandering Jew.'

Nathaniel Hawthorne also sketched a pen portrait of Disraeli at this time.

> By and by there came a rather tall, slender person in a black frock [coat], buttoned up, and black pantaloons, taking long steps but I thought rather feebly or listlessly. His shoulders were round, or else he had a habitual stoop in them. He had a prominent nose, a thin face, and a sallow, very sallow complexion, and was a very unhealthy looking person; and had I seen him in America I should have taken him for a hard-worked editor of a newspaper, weary and worn with night-labour and want of exercise, shrivelled and withered before his time. It was Disraeli, and I never saw any other Englishman look in the least like him.

In the end some 938,000 voters were added to the electoral roll in a mixture of last-minute consultations, misunderstandings, mistakes, obstinacies, cowardice and a small amount of plotting. It was the most unexpected revolution in English political history.

It is appropriate that Viscount Cranborne, soon to be known as Lord Salisbury, should enter the narrative at this juncture. He had a command of figures but, more important, he knew how to use them to party advantage. He was short sighted, tall, with a slight stoop; he was not a gloomy man, but he was not sentimental. He never subscribed to the facile notions or the 'quick fix' attitudes of Disraeli. He was too intelligent to be charmed by him. Cranborne is one of the few Victorian grandees who can be introduced by his journalism, his pursuit before entering the Commons. He was on common ground with the quarterlies and he admired Palmerston against all the odds, for example, as one 'of those cynical philosophers who look upon Parliament as more useful for what it prevents than what it performs'. He was admirably blunt in his social and political opinions. 'The state did not relieve the poor on the ground of philanthropy,' he said, 'but on the ground of general order.' He abhorred parliamentary games and squabbles. He detested the opinionated and the self-important. He was firmly opposed to wider suffrage, with the belief that 'the laws of property are not very safe when an ignorant multitude are the rulers'. He had no very high opinion of others, which made the familiar methods of electioneering a positive horror; in campaigns he was shy and withdrawn.

Instead, he was a great believer in doing nothing, when nothing seemed the better course. He was for example more and more dismayed as the arch-Liberal, Gladstone, embarked for distant and wilder shores. In any case he would have been happier beside Pitt and Wellington than Disraeli or Derby. He considered most of his celebrated contemporaries to be little better than political charlatans, mouthing the received wisdom with all the conviction of the recently convinced. The doorkeeper of the House of Commons noted in 1863: 'he is haughty and proud, of intractable temper. He cannot submit to party discipline . . .' Another contemporary observed: 'he had small respect for the opinions of the house of Commons'.

It was whispered that Cranborne might make an ideal prime minister. Just before Salisbury travelled to an international conference Gladstone wrote to him: 'You should personally know the men who are governing the world, and it is well to know them in circumstances which will allow you to gauge their character, their strength and their infirmities.' This might be known as diplomacy of the old school, which Salisbury infinitely preferred to the reliance upon bold schemes and duplicitous enterprises. He once told Bulwer-Lytton that 'English policy is to float lazily down stream, occasionally putting out a diplomatic boat-hook to avoid collisions.'

At the end of 1867 Russell, at the age of seventy-five, relinquished his role as leader of the Liberals. As an unreconstructed Whig, he had outlived his time. He had been out of sorts with the leading principles of the age. He had, according to *Punch*, 'no particular test of ability, but *Debrett's Peerage*, and never knew that to fail'. Now in 1868 Gladstone might have come into his inheritance. In the cause of Reform, however, Disraeli had already outmanoeuvred him with the 'romance' of the extended franchise. Gladstone was humiliated by the debacle, and for a while considered retiring from the leadership itself. He seemed genuinely to have feared that Disraeli's enfranchisement would give the vote to what was called the 'residuum' or lowest level of the people. He considered Disraeli capable of anything in pursuit of power. Disraeli had no such qualms, however, and was merely concerned to maintain the Conservative electoral hold upon the counties, where the vote was granted to £12 householders rather than the rural poor. Disraeli knew that he had favoured the most deferential electorate of all. He was not concerned if redundant votes piled up in the cities. His nominal superior was thoroughly in agreement with him. Stanley wrote in his diary that his father, Lord Derby, was 'bent on remaining in power at whatever cost, and ready to make the largest concessions with that object'.

Both parties would have agreed on this, however. The balance of political power must be maintained at all costs; every version of Reform had been designed to stabilize the political structure, not to overturn or replace it. Yet it was not perhaps as simple as that. One of the consequences of the new Reform was to increase the number of urban representatives in the Commons, overturning centuries of rural predominance. A second and unintended result was the gradual politicization of the towns and cities. Soon enough the parties began to appeal to what they considered to be the urban vote. The Conservatives, in particular, began to organize working men's associations. With the larger electorate, politics became a sport and a spectacle. Gladstone's visage appeared on vases and on spoons; Disraeli jugs were placed beside octagonal plates bearing his image. He also became the darling of the cartoonists who could perform endless variations on his distinctive features. Portraits of these newly discovered heroes were to be found on teapots and coffee pots, jugs and snuffboxes. The essence of politics became diluted.

By gradual degrees a new prospect revealed itself. Parliamentary reform had been connected with the rise of what were often known as 'the masses'. It was not necessarily alarming. Some observers had always distrusted the conventional wisdom that the lower orders were by nature radical and subversive, and now was the occasion to prove them right. Edmund Burke had intimated, for example, that they were in fact instinctively conservative. To use a current analogy, they were the beasts of the field who were content to chew the cud. A phrase arose, under unknown circumstances, that the country was open to a 'conservative democracy'. At approximately the same time the idea of 'household suffrage' had become very appealing to those who wished to create as large an electorate as possible, on the supposition that householders would not be radicals. It could not be called a plan, but rather an instinct. As *The Times* put it, 'Disraeli discerned the Conservative working man as the sculptor perceives the angel prisoned in the block of marble.'

Derby took medical advice at this stage and it was advised that he could not survive under the manifold burdens of the office. He had not been faced by the agonies of Reform only. There were problems and outrages far more pressing and dangerous. A conspiracy had been discovered in Ireland, organized by the Fenians, a 'brotherhood' which believed that Ireland had a right to independence, and that armed revolution was the only way of achieving it. As a result the suspension of habeas corpus locked up a thousand supposed Fenians for a year. A Fenian army was gathered in the United States and attacked Canada with disappointing results; the battle of Ridgeway in June 1866 was their last stand.

Closer to home they made an attempt on Chester Castle in the search for arms and ammunition. They were not successful. Whenever the queen drove out, she was followed by two of her suite armed with revolvers. A now predictable bombing outrage was attempted at the end of 1867 when the Fenians tried to bomb the notorious prison at Clerkenwell where some of their colleagues were being held. It was again unsuccessful but managed instead to kill several Londoners; there were twelve deaths and over a hundred casualties. This may have been one of the incidents which persuaded

Gladstone 'to pacify Ireland' at a later date. Rumours abounded. It was reported that 'one informant speaks of 155 Fenians and republican clubs in London alone, all unknown to the police. Several announced projects for blowing up the houses of parliament and assassinating the queen.' It was said that a privateer filled with Fenians was coming from New York to kill her. Sticks of dynamite with clockwork mechanisms, known as 'infernal machines', were shipped from New York in crates labelled 'cement'. Alone as she was in spirit, she became frustrated and nervous; she asked that the militia be made ready for any insurrection.

For many, there was worse to come. The rinderpest or cattle plague was spreading through the country. It is noted in a farmer's diary of 1866 that:

> W Carson, Foulsike, has not one of his stock left alive. They are all either dead or destroyed. Sir R Brisco and Captain James insists on destroying all the cattle where the disease breaks out whether they are healthy and well or ailing or recovering. I doubt they are taking the power out of the Almighty hands. I think the Lord will have some compassion on us and leave some alive but Sir R Brisco and Captain James will leave none alive.

In a country which according to the most recent census was still predominantly agricultural, the cattle plague was a catastrophe about which little could be done. It was worse than a plague out of Egypt, and several leading clerics called for a day of prayer and fasting to placate the Almighty.

A violent controversy had also fallen upon the empire when Governor Eyre of Jamaica had been accused of unremitting barbarity in his treatment of the black population. For every man or woman who decried Eyre's disgusting treatment of the slaves, there was another to cheer him on. 'We are too tender to our savages; we are more tender to a black than to ourselves,' Tennyson told Gladstone, 'niggers are tigers, niggers are tigers.' This is precisely the kind of comment, from a great man of letters, which emphasizes the extent to which the empire was permeated with racism. What went on in the backstreets of Calcutta, the alleys of Bridgetown or the farmland of south Nigeria could not bear examination. Could it really be said that the empire was under the rule of law? That was one of the reasons why in February 1868 Derby resigned his office under medical advice. He had retained his leadership of his party for twenty-two years, a record that has not yet been rivalled.

It could only be Disraeli now. The queen wrote to her daughter, the crown princess of Prussia: 'Mr Disraeli is Prime Minister! A proud thing for a Man "risen from the people" to have obtained!' It might be questionable whether he had in fact risen from the people, as if he had just wiped the coal dust from his face, but the princess knew what her mother meant. In any case he had inherited his minority government from Derby and was obliged to hang on until a general election might improve his fortunes. 'Yes,' he said, 'I have climbed to the top of the greasy pole.'

One of the doorkeepers of the House of Commons described Disraeli's presence in that assembly. He 'comes up the members' private staircase, marches across the lobby, solemnly and slowly, generally alone, and speaking to no one as he passes'. On entering the chamber he 'sits down, folds his arms across his breast and keeps immovably in this position, with his eyes fixed upon the ground until he rises to speak'. He never wore a hat in the chamber, unlike most of his colleagues, 'for he neither winces nor laughs and seldom cheers; in fact he sits like an imperturbable statue . . . Though in the midst of his party, he appears not to be one of them, but as separate and as distinct as his race is from all the world.' When he spoke he always began badly but soon warmed up. His theory of premiership, if such it was, is suggested in his portrait of Lord Roehampton in *Endymion* (1880): 'Look to Lord Roehampton; he is the man. He does not care a rush whether the revenue increases or declines. He is thinking of real politics; foreign affairs; maintaining our power in Europe.' He rarely met his opponent in verbal combat. When Gladstone performed his perorations Disraeli often pretended to be asleep; but he was ever alert. If Gladstone committed an error Disraeli quickly corrected him.

He did manage to pass some congenial legislation. Public hangings were abolished. The railways were improved. The first act of nationalization was passed when the Post Office was given permission to purchase all the telegraph companies; this was an important stage in the structural unification of the country. Yet when Henry James first arrived in London, in 1868, he saw little sign of progress:

> The weather had turned wet. The low black houses were as inanimate as so many rows of coal scuttles, save where at frequent corners, from a gin-shop, there was a flare of light more brutal still than the darkness . . . A sudden horror of the whole place came over me, like a tiger-pounce of home-sickness which had been watching its moment. London was hideous, vicious, cruel, and above all overwhelming.

Disraeli would no doubt have known of such dark, far-off things but they did not enter his calculations. He said that, in his audiences with the queen, he never denied nor did he contradict but he sometimes forgot. He was particularly attentive to her majesty. Victoria told her daughter that 'he is full of poetry, romance & chivalry'. The new prime minister did in any case woo and flatter the queen in ways only he knew how to do, and his regular missives to her on parliamentary affairs were written in a style that combined *Coningsby* with the *Lays of Marmion*. He said later that 'to keep in good humour the Queen is in itself an occupation'. Wilful, self-preoccupied and inherently nervous, she was what all queens should be. So he poured on the charm with profusions of loyalty and obedience. He treated her as the representative of England on earth, which in one sense she was. There were some who believed their relationship to be too congenial. Derby wrote to him that 'nobody can have managed the lady better than you have; but is there a not just a risk of encouraging her in too large an idea of her personal power and too great indifference to what the public expects? I only ask, it is for you to judge.' Some called him Mephistopheles. A later generation might have called him Svengali. In any case his only competitor was Gladstone, whom the queen found profoundly un-sympathetic.

Time was pressing. He was prime minister and the old unreformed parliament would pass away in May 1868. Yet to leave with the old electoral register still in place would be a parliamentary and political embarrassment. His administration had only been in place for three months. The advice poured in. He consulted the queen, whose distaste for Gladstone or a further dose of Gladstone was well known. He decided to stay as long as circumstances permitted; there was also much parliamentary business to conclude. At the beginning of May, Disraeli moved to adjourn the House and advised the queen to dissolve parliament 'as soon as the public interest will permit' This in effect meant that they would wait until the electoral register was completed, which was now expected at the beginning of November. Despite the changes wrought by Disraeli it was widely believed that Gladstone and the Liberals would win again.

The election of November 1868 was hard fought, and the *Annual Register* declared that 'it is to be feared that the corruption, drunkenness and demoralization' were as evident as before. The wealthy member of parliament from Bristol was obliged to address his constituents from behind an open umbrella. The dead cats and dogs of the hustings were not yet finally buried. Nor were the bribes and the blackmail. The result was as expected, with a Liberal majority of 112 votes. Disraeli resigned at once, thus creating a precedent in which the wisdom of the electorate was more important than the procedures of parliament. It was clear enough that Gladstone had captured the loyalty of the public. He appealed to their sense of fair play. 'Do not wait to continue from year to year the painful – the ignominious, I would almost say, the loathsome process of suspending personal liberty in order to keep large portions of the Irish people down by force.' He also appealed to the new-found responsibilities of the reformed electorate, 'now that you are invested with the privileges by which you are to govern yourselves'. That probably clinched the matter. When he was informed of the result he was felling trees on his country estate at Hawarden. He ceased for a moment and declared: 'My mission is to pacify Ireland.'

20

She cannot go on

Disraeli did not believe that Gladstone was the man of the future. The two men did not believe in one another at all. Their rivalry may have risen in part from the fact that both leaders were members of the House of Commons, but a deeper division was manifest. Gladstone was a man of conviction and principle, while Disraeli was a man of convenience and practicality. That is how it seemed on the surface, and to their contemporaries, but we may be doing an historic injustice to both men by relying on conventional wisdom. Behind Disraeli's flippancy was a deep devotion to his Jewish faith, or at least a profound belief that he was one of the chosen people. He rated himself as highly as any English aristocrat, and behaved himself as such. He did not try to ape the manners of the aristocracy; he decided to make himself unique. Gladstone, too, had a share of practical and opportunistic politics – however hard he tried to disguise it – and it can be said that he framed his politics with one eye on God and Redemption and the other on the main chance. On taking office Disraeli had speculated on the greasy pole, while Gladstone remarked: 'I ascend a steepening path, with a burden ever gathering weight. The Almighty seems to sustain and spare me for some purpose of His own, deeply unworthy as I know myself to be. Glory be to his name!'

Gladstone had won a surprisingly easy victory. The results in

England were in balance but Scotland and Ireland put the result out of doubt. Disraeli could have given up his political career with honour, but he declined to leave the stage. The death of Lord Derby in the autumn of 1869 seemed only to steady his hand for a long career. There was a puzzle doing the rounds. 'Why is Gladstone like a telescope?' 'Because Disraeli draws him out, looks through him, and shuts him up.'

The Liberal party had indeed been in confusion after Disraeli's triumph with Reform, and Gladstone himself was baffled by the turn of the events before he came upon another cause that would unite his party. Ireland had become the mother of discontent and violence. But if his 'mission' was indeed to pacify the country, he had to proceed gradually and slowly with his new government. He could start with the religious question. 'The time has come', he said, 'when the Church of Ireland as a Church in alliance with the state must cease to exist'. Unlike the Church of Rome, which held the faithful in its grip, the Church of Ireland was almost supernumerary. It took the tithes but did very little in return. All the religious duties and ceremonies of the people were performed under its aegis, but it had precious little authority.

Beyond Ireland, the British seemed more successful and confident. This happy condition was confirmed in 1868 when a British force under Sir Robert Napier invaded Ethiopia and rescued some British hostages. It was considered an affair of honour, but it also provided an intimation of the imperial instinct. This was in fact the period in which a relative indifference to empire changed gradually into positive enthusiasm. The establishment of telegraphic communications with Australia helped to instil a new sense of unity. It also became clear that other countries were struggling to fashion empires of their own, with Germany the prime mover. Germany, Italy and the United States had themselves created a national unity. Why should not Britain and the empire together form a similar union? The extension of the franchise in 1867 created a large mass of urban voters who were fledgling imperialists. One member of the Commons regretted that the new administration did not recognize 'the great interest which the majority of the people, and especially the working classes, felt in the subject of the relations between the mother country and her colonies'. Another member regretted the implication 'that the Government were indifferent to the wishes and aspirations of the colonists, and that the House of Commons had no sympathy with their wants and requirements'.

It was in fact widely believed that Gladstone and his colleagues wished to shake off the colonies as an impediment to their domestic demands and to their Irish concerns, but a great petition from working men to the queen stated that 'we have heard with alarm and indignation that your Majesty has been advised to consent to give up the colonies'. 'Imperialism' was not coined until 1878, but it was anticipated a few years before. The Colonial Society was established in the summer of 1868 to counter any move towards separatism, and it was much encouraged by a policy of state-aided emigration to Australia and elsewhere. W. E. Forster, one of the prime agents of the administration, stated: 'I believe the time will come when by some means or other statesmen will be able to weld a bond together which will unite the English-speaking people in our colonies at present – unite them with the mother country in one great confederation.' Ruskin delivered a lecture in 1870 in which he emerged as another arch-imperialist. 'This is what England must either do or perish: she must found colonies as fast and far as she is able. Formed of her most energetic and worthiest men; seizing every piece of fruitful waste ground she can set her foot on, and there teaching these her colonists that their chief virtue is to be fidelity to their country and their first aim is to advance the power England by land and sea . . .'

Edward Cardwell, Gladstone's secretary of state for war, was tasked with the reform of the army, which he did by imposing professional standards upon its officers and insisting that promotion should depend upon merit rather than money. This further soured the relationship between queen and prime minister, however, since Victoria considered them to be *her* soldiers. Cardwell abolished flogging in peacetime and prepared an Army Enlistment Act so that men could join for shorter periods. Just as Cardwell was administering the army, Hugh Childers was reforming the navy by a similar process of economy and efficiency. He reduced the strength of squadrons in distant stations and brought the fleet closer to home.

Gladstone was still something of an enigma in office. The writer Emily Eden provided a succinct portrait of him:

I dare say he is very clever, and he is good-natured, doing his best to bring his mind down to the level of mine, but he fails. He is always above me; and then he does not converse – he harangues – and the more he says the more I don't understand. Then there is something about High Church people that I can't define, but I feel it when I am with them – something Jesuitical – and they never let themselves go . . . In short he is not frivolous enough for me. If he were soaked in boiling water and rinsed until he were twisted into a rope, I do not suppose a drop of fun would ooze out.

He stage-managed a debate of four days to discuss three Irish resolutions, one of them bringing the repeal of compulsory Church rates. He forced through an Irish Church Bill which did not only disestablish the Church of Ireland but also disendowed it. Complicated and controversial as the act was, it helped to placate Ireland by removing grievances from both Roman Catholics and Presbyterians. It was designed, also, to begin a process of reconciliation with the Irish. He spoke for three hours and, according to Disraeli himself, not a phrase was wasted.

In truth he did not know much of Ireland, and had never visited it, but he did have a good sense of timing, or perhaps of occasion. He once said that 'the most striking gift entrusted to me is an insight into the facts of a particular era and their relation to one another'. He had in other words a highly developed and profoundly intuitive historical sense, and relied upon it to choose the time to act.

In 1870 he prepared an Irish Land Bill of true Gladstonian complexity, but he had remained faithful to his promise when tree-felling. The tenants could now achieve recompense for any improvement they made to their dwellings, and could claim compensation if they were evicted for reasons other than non-payment of rent. It made very little difference in the long term, but it cost Gladstone much power and ingenuity to get it through the Lords, who were naturally hostile to any measure in favour of tenants. But it is significant that Disraeli made very little noise about what might have been considered as anti-Tory legislation. He had covered his eyes, ears and mouth. Gladstone had also suggested to the queen that her family should establish a royal residence in Ireland to please the Irish people. Victoria rejected the idea with horror; she had too many gloomy and draughty palaces.

Other acts were passed in the first Gladstone administration, among them W. E. Forster's Education Act, which allowed a revolution in educational practice as profound as it was beneficial. It would have been unthinkable to have removed the Church schools; they were the primary and often only source of education. The educational system was run by voluntary schools funded by two main religious bodies, the British and Foreign Schools Society (Nonconformist) and the National Society (Church of England).

Instead Forster increased state grants to voluntary schools, but more importantly he established a system of board schools or schools run by local boards of a non-denominational character. The local boards were set up to establish state schools, and in these establishments a daily act of worship of a non-denominational kind was introduced. They were financed by a local rate and, where appropriate, they were subsidized. This was as far as Forster and Gladstone could go, given the fact that a national school system would be inordinately expensive. But they had gone a long way. In 1870, when the Elementary Education Act was passed, there were fewer than 9,000 schools in England. Twenty years later 20,000 schools had been established. A national education system had finally been agreed. It was inevitable. One of the most bitter opponents of Reform, Robert Lowe, confessed: 'I believe it will be absolutely necessary that you should prevail on our future masters to learn their letters.' But they had to learn more than letters. They had to learn deference. They had to learn obedience. They had to learn literacy and numeracy or, as Lowe also put it, 'an education that may fit them for business'. They had to have sufficient schooling, as Tawney said, to understand a command.

Other ameliorative measures were taken by the Gladstone administration. University religious 'tests' were abolished. The secret ballot was introduced, so that each voter could cast his vote in confidence, and another bill was passed against municipal corruption. A Mines Regulation Act was also passed, and imprisonment for debt was partially abolished. Much was achieved relatively quickly, despite John Bright's warning that 'you cannot get twenty wagons

24. The 'Rocket' locomotive designed by George Stephenson in 1829.

25. *Rain, Steam and Speed – The Great Western Railway* painted before 1844 by Turner.

26. The royal family in 1846.

27. The Great Exhibition of 1851 held in a purpose-built Crystal Palace in Hyde Park.

28. *The Relief of the Light Brigade*, 25 October 1854.

29. Mary Jane Seacole.

30. *On Strike*, *c.*1891, by
Hubert von Herkomer.

31. An illustration of music-hall performers
for *The Illustrated Sporting and Dramatic News*,
1876.

32. *Ramsgate Sands* (or *Life at the Seaside*) by William Powell Frith.

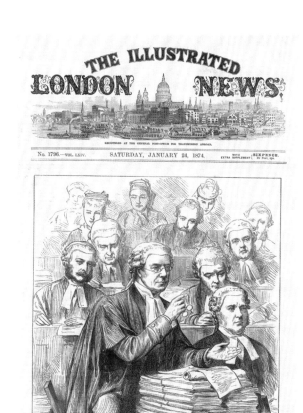

33. The cover of *The Illustrated London News* depicting Mr Hawkins addressing the jury during the trial of the Tichborne Claimant.

34. Annie Besant, from *Bibby's Annual*.

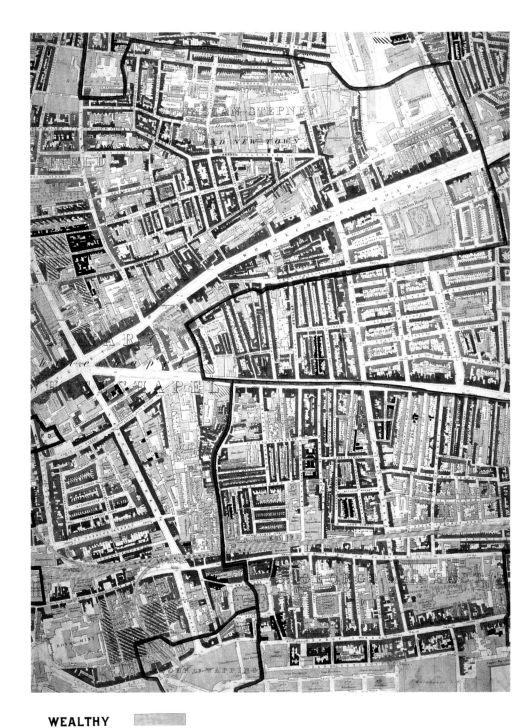

WEALTHY	
WELL-TO-DO	
COMFORTABLE	
POOR & COMFORTABLE (MIXED)	
POOR	
VERY POOR	
SEMI-CRIMINAL	

35. A descriptive map of London poverty, compiled and coloured by Charles Booth.

36. The key for Charles Booth's poverty map.

37. A photograph of Lord Rosebery.

38. A group of Boer commandos armed with the German Mauser rifle, 1895.

39. Oscar Wilde.

40. Queen Victoria, empress of India, and Abdul Karim (*munshi*), 1894.

at once through Temple Bar'. The answer was to remove Temple
Bar. (Its actual removal took place in 1878.)

With the slow dissolution of the ice of ages, other reforms
followed. The civil service came under the aegis of a competitive
examination system to help extirpate the nepotism that was still the
bane of England. The three common law courts were replaced by
a single Supreme Court of Judicature together with the Court of
Appeal; the Court of Chancery was also abolished, thus blowing
away the burdens of *Bleak House* (1853) and *Jarndyce v. Jarndyce*. A
Local Government Board took the place of the Poor Law Board;
in time this would become the Ministry of Health, as the state
consolidated its hold. From this time forward, in fact, local authorities were established to administer local services. The Local
Government Board Act of 1871 set up a central department which
was responsible for all the affairs of local government from public
health to public improvement; there would follow at a later date
various housing officers, sanitary reformers and education inspectors.
In an epilogue to this list of acts, some of which proved successful
and some not, we may add an extract from a letter Gladstone wrote
in March 1868: 'But above all, if we be just men, we shall go forward
in the name of truth and right, bearing this in mind – that when
the case is proved, and the hour is come, justice delayed is justice
denied.'

New bureaucratic offices and new administrators, after 1870,
could not but help the formation of a fully fledged state. By the
1880s the word was in full bloom. How far the 'state' would interfere with the liberties of the individual was still an open question.

The term was lent more resonance in the summer of 1870 when,
in a whirlwind campaign, Prussia thoroughly defeated France. This
was what a highly organized and efficient state might be able to
do. Bismarck, preparing for a decisive victory over its old enemy,
had set a trap for the French by squabbling over the southern
German states. In July 1870 the French declared war on Prussia
but were thoroughly overmatched by their militarized enemy; the
highly professional Prussian army made short work of the disor-
ganized French. Within six weeks victory was assured. At the
ultimate battle in Sedan, at the beginning of September, Napoleon
III was captured and his wife Eugénie fled to England for exile.

The Germans proceeded to elect an emperor of Germany and to take money and territory from France (including Alsace-Lorraine) as the spoils of war. So did the German empire arise from the ruin of France, with the English simply spectators on the side. The fact that Victoria favoured the Prussians, and adduced them as an example of glorious nationhood, did not improve matters. The myth of France as *la grande nation* had gone for ever. Now, after the collapse of the Second Empire, the Paris Commune of radicals and working classes might be a source of contagion for the working classes of England. But the important fact was simple: the new Germany held the hegemony in Europe, and no one could or would do anything about it.

In the Place de la Concorde, in Paris, the statue of Strasbourg was covered in black crepe and surrounded by garlands as a token of eternal mourning at its ingestion into the German empire. This 'new world', as some called it, was a spectacle worthy to be watched by Thomas Hardy's President of the Immortals.

It had been a hot summer and, as Trollope remarked, 'people were beginning to complain of the Thames'. Half the cabinet was unwell. 'Gladstone', Earl Granville remarked, 'told Bessborough yesterday that he sometimes felt alarmed for his own head. Cardwell at the last Cabinet sat close into the fire, looking as if he wished to cut his throat.' Spirits were very low. The historian Froude declared that 'English opinion is without weight. English power is ridiculed. Our influence in the councils of Europe is a thing of the past.' Bismarck joked that if the English army invaded Germany, he would send the Berlin police to arrest them. Lord Salisbury put it differently: 'The fault really lies in the change in the nature of the spirit of the English nation. They do not wish, as they formerly did, for great national position, and they are glad to seclude themselves from European responsibilities by the protection which their insular position is supposed to give them . . .'

Gladstone wrote an anonymous article in the *Edinburgh Review* on the European problem. He spoke for a 'moral empire' or 'a new law of nations' that might afford 'Public Right as the governing idea of European policy'. As so often with Gladstone the high road did not lead anywhere in particular, and was in any case quite unsuited to circumstances. But he had already emerged as the

'People's William'. Some still small voice within him had whispered: 'William, be a leader.' He was already aware of the power which the press had acquired, and as early as October 1862 he had embarked on the first of his public speaking tours in the north where his personal presence, his command over large crowds, and his theatrical delivery, worked wonders. If the crowds did not hear anything, they could read it in the following day's newspapers, made all the more valuable if the reader had been there in person. John Bright had said that a 'public speech was more read and told more on opinion than a speech in a debate in the House'. Gladstone's speeches were carefully stage-managed and meticulously planned, taking their cue from Covent Garden and the Haymarket as well as the music halls. These were the spectacles the Victorians understood.

Gladstone could not get enough of it; he revelled in the cheers, shouts and applause in a way that Disraeli, for example, did not. He was sometimes called 'Mr Merrypebble' as opposed to a glad stone. Mrs Gladstone was equally impressed. 'Oh I shall never forget that day!' she said of a speech in Tyneside in 1862. 'It was the first time, you know, that *he* was received as he deserved to be.' He explored the phenomenon in his study of Homer: 'The orator's work', he wrote, 'is an influence principally received from his audience (so to speak) in a vapour, which he pours back upon them in a flood . . . He cannot follow nor frame ideals; his choice is, to be what his age will have him, what it requires in order to be moved by him, or else not to be at all.' It is the finest description of how a politician can step forward in the spirit or shape of a people.

He gave the impression of supporting the cotton workers. He gave support to the representatives of trade unions and to the 'junta' of trade union leaders. He identified himself with the moral and upright working man. Yet it was not until 1871 that a Trade Union Act was published which removed from unions the threat of a charge of conspiracy and granted their funds the protection of the courts.

So much still remained to be done. In 1871, the Medical Officer for Health found a child of three making the notorious Lucifer matches in a hovel in Bethnal Green. Matches provoked a different kind of furore when in the spring of this year the chancellor of the Exchequer, Robert Lowe, proposed an indirect tax on them. This created mayhem, particularly among the match-workers of Bryant and May, whose unhealthy working conditions were not in any case well rewarded. This was the last straw. The tax was hastily withdrawn at the instigation of Gladstone, but the whole issue came to a head seventeen years later.

It was not an easy time. The Liberals were still composed of fragments and they were confronted with a hostile enemy in the House of Lords. Gladstone's hope for unifying his party still lay in Ireland. But he had perhaps invested too much of his popularity and his credit in that nation, about which the English were largely indifferent. The efforts over disestablishment and land seemed to make very little impression on the Irish, who remained, as English politicians saw it, perpetually ungrateful. Gladstone felt that the best days of his administration were now over. As he told Clarendon, he felt 'as a bee might feel if it knew that it would die upon its sting'. In the spring of 1872 Disraeli remarked of the Liberal front bench: 'You behold a range of exhausted volcanoes.' In the previous year *The Times* had commented that 'the conduct of public business in the House of Commons during the present session has been more injurious to its reputation than the shortcomings of years full of passionate incidents. Nothing is done, legislation is at a deadlock.' The burden of summer had grown too much; two cabinet ministers suffered nervous breakdowns and Cardwell, who had been seen by Earl Granville staring into the fire, was declared to be insane.

Gladstone and the queen were more at odds than ever. Her 'repellent power', as he described it, was generally directed at the prime minister. The depths of her own unpopularity were plumbed at the time of the birth and death of the Prince of Wales's third son. His birth was greeted by *Reynolds' News* as 'Another Inauspicious Event' but the death of the boy on the next day was heralded as 'A Happy Release'. 'We have much satisfaction', the newspaper reported, 'in announcing that the newly-born child of the Prince and Princess of Wales died shortly after its birth, thus relieving the working classes of England from having to support hereafter another addition to the long roll of State beggars they at present maintain.'

The *froideur* between statesman and monarch extended further when he suggested that she might spend more time in London, 'as likely to be of great utility in strengthening the Throne under circumstances that require all that can be done in that sense, if indeed we can make it a new means of putting forward the Royal Family in the visible discharge of public duty'. She responded with one of those hysterical explosions to which she was prone. Gladstone's influence was

> really abominable . . . What killed her beloved Husband? Overwork & worry – what killed Lord Clarendon? The same. What has broken down Mr Bright and Mr Childers & made them retire, but the same: & the Queen, a woman, no longer young is supposed to be proof against all & to be driven and abused till her nerves and health will give way with this worry & agitation and interference in her private life.

There is a hint or implication here that Gladstone himself was responsible for the wreck of ministers, let alone of herself, but that was not really a fit and proper subject with which to accuse the old man. She concluded: 'she *cannot* go on'. But of course she could, and did. Her accusations did have some merit, however. Bright, Childers and Clarendon were only the most recent public servants who had died or broken down at a relatively young age; among their predecessors were Pitt the Younger, Castlereagh, Fox, Liverpool and Canning, all of whom expired under sixty. It had much to do with the enervating and feverish atmosphere in which they were obliged to live. They had no rest, and were perhaps the early victims of the Victorian sense of duty and hard work. Their successors were in no better condition. The new burdens of empire, the new competitiveness among the industrial nations and the decline of agriculture all added further anxiety to already anxious public servants.

Queen Victoria relied upon the comfort and support of a much esteemed royal servant, John Brown, who treated her as an anxious father might treat a wayward daughter. As she grew more and more alienated from her family, including the heir apparent, she came to rely more and more on the kindness of those around her. It was said that John Brown was almost too kind, and there are unconfirmed reports that they were unofficially married, but these are tales for children.

Gladstone's own self-imposed moral duty was to rescue Victoria from the depths of inactivity and unpopularity into which she had fallen. His efforts were not welcomed. 'She looked very well at me and was kind,' he reported, 'but in all her conversations with me she is evidently hemmed in, stops at a certain point, & keeps back the thought which occurs.' Reports had also reached her of her prime minister's nocturnal encounters with fallen women. For him they seem to have been part of his mission, or vocation, but for an observer they might carry a very different significance.

Her own condition was not perhaps as serious as she imagined. Her private secretary, General Grey, wrote to the Prince of Wales that 'neither strength nor health are wanting, were the inclination what it should be. It is simply the long, unchecked habit of self-indulgence – that now makes it impossible for her without some degree of nervous agitation to give up even for ten minutes the gratification of a single inclination or whim.' She certainly could not bear the boredom of Gladstone's explanations. 'He speaks to me', she said, 'as if I were a public meeting.'

Gladstone himself was seriously contemplating resignation. He told Victoria that he did not wish to spend his old age 'under the strain of that perpetual contention which is inseparable from his present position'. The failure of his Irish University Bill in 1873, which in effect would have placed Catholic institutions under the control of Dublin University, was simply the last burden. He signalled his intention to resign, but there was the problem of Disraeli. She had called for him to form an administration in place of Gladstone, but he demurred. He would have been more than happy to accept his sovereign's wish, but not in the circumstances of the present House of Commons. He did not wish to lead another minority government and, privately, he wanted to give more time for his opponents to split even further. He wanted them to carry on, ever more desperate. Gladstone had no choice but to resume his yoke.

The queen had already recovered much of her popularity. What saved her was her son. It might have ended in a long-drawn-out disaster but for the sudden and dangerous illness of 'Bertie' on the tenth anniversary of his father's death. At the end of November 1871, the Prince of Wales contracted typhoid fever at the very time that his father had been stricken with the same sickness. He seemed to be progressing, but then relapsed to the extent that Victoria hurried to Sandringham where he lay. On 11 December a newspaper wrote ominously: 'The Prince still lives, and we may still therefore hope.' Three days later, on the anniversary of Albert's death, the nation waited in suspense. He came through. As he slowly recovered the country was inclined to support the queen. It might be asked how an irate nation intent on criticizing the monarchy should turn into a nation filled with pity for her. Was it because she was no longer seen as a queen but a mother? As a phrase it sounds well worn, but as a human truth it may have some resonance. We must also remember the fickleness and madness of crowds.

Victoria had also come out of hiding. She was driven to St Paul's with her son and daughter-in-law in an open landau to deliver her thanks. From this time forward she was celebrated as the 'mother' of the people. Another consequence seemed to follow. At the Thanksgiving service Gladstone was coolly received by the assembled crowds; Disraeli, on the other hand, was widely applauded. Reasons could be found. Disraeli had begun the forward march to 'Tory democracy'. Gladstone, despite or because of his victory in the general election, was considered unfairly as a bulwark against change. Disraeli was a 'character', considered something of a card, larger than life. A Conservative saw him in the Carlton Club a little while later, as still as marble and staring into space 'as of one who looks into another world'. 'I will tell you what he was thinking about,' another member said to him. 'He was thinking that he will be Prime Minister again.' At a speech at the Crystal Palace, in the spring of 1872, he proclaimed that the newly enfranchised voters were Conservative 'in the purest and loftiest sense'. They were 'proud of belonging to a great country, and wish to maintain its greatness'. His purpose was to create a coherent political programme at the very moment when Gladstone was in difficulties. He spoke of 'the three great objects of the Tory Party or, as I will venture to call it, the National Party'. The established institutions of the country were to be maintained; the empire must be sustained and the conditions of the people improved. Imperialism and the status quo were his principal themes. Disraeli cleverly knotted the nation with the monarchy in domestic circumstances. 'England is a domestic country. Here the home is revered and the hearth is sacred. The nation is represented by a family . . . and in the hour of public adversity, in the anxious conjuncture of public affairs the nation rallies round the Family and the Throne, and its spirit is animated and sustained by the expression of public affection.'

The affection for Victoria herself was further heartened by a failed attempt on her life just as she returned from the Thanksgiving at St Paul's to Buckingham Palace. As her carriage made its way through the Garden Gate a young man by the name of Arthur O'Connor brandished a pistol and called out in a weak voice: 'Take that from a Fenian'. Uncharacteristically Victoria lost her equanimity on this occasion. 'I was trembling very much, and a sort of shiver ran through me.' She grabbed the arm of a lady-in-waiting and called out 'Save me!' John Brown, the devoted servant, grabbed the boy and held him fast, for which service he was awarded a gold medal. But the threat of assassination only increased the queen's popularity, despite her confessing that 'the fright caused by the attempt, the Queen felt for *long afterwards*'. The boy was taken and sentenced to a period in Newgate. She seemed to be impregnable.

It may be the merest coincidence that the balance of the parties began to swing in favour of the Conservatives. Growing dissatisfaction with the Liberals was manifest when the Liberal chief whip alluded to the danger posed by 'the apathy and political discontent which is now so prevalent in our majority'.

In this year the postcard was introduced.

21

The Tichborne affair

He was known as 'the claimant' in headlines or on newspaper placards. His was the most famous trial of the nineteenth century, eclipsing those of Queen Caroline and Oscar Wilde; he was not only the talk of the town but also the talk of the world. Roger Tichborne was heir to a wealthy baronetcy. In the spring of 1853 he disappeared from England and eventually sailed to South America. In the following year he took ship from Rio de Janeiro, and after surviving a shipwreck he made his way to the Australian outpost of Wagga Wagga. According to the story he maintained, he set up as a butcher under the name of Tomas Castro. It was a good story. The transition from an heir of a baronetcy to a butcher was sufficiently startling in a world where even the slightest gradation in status was a matter of deep controversy.

The Dowager Lady Tichborne, after the death of her husband in 1862 and her younger son in 1866, grew disconsolate. Roger Tichborne, missing, was now the eleventh baronet. She advertised for her eldest son in *The Times* and elsewhere, her appeal even reaching the inhabitants of Wagga Wagga. Here all became known. Tichborne, or Castro, had already dropped hints about his past, and he was urged on all sides to sail to England and claim his inheritance. On 25 December 1866 he arrived in London. His mother seems to have known him at once. 'He looks like his father,' she said, 'and his ears look like his uncle's.' Other members of the family were not so sure and denied any connection with the man. How could close relatives differ so much on the question of identity? Was it a question of inheritance? And why had Tichborne come so late to claim his share? It was a conundrum, made more complex by a report that 'Roger Tichborne' was in fact Arthur Orton, a butcher from Wapping. Confusion had been further compounded.

In London the law courts were never far away, and the funds for Tichborne's claim began to be contributed. A putative baronet was a good investment. But he had also elicited public sympathy. The 1860s was the high point of what was known as 'sensation literature', which specialized in money, wills, murder and the dark secrets of apparently respectable families. It exploited the melodrama of the living room. The Tichborne case might have come from the pages of a 'shilling shocker', and part of its notoriety came from its coincidence with one of the most powerful fictional fashions of the time. Roger Tichborne, as he was now generally called, brought suit against Colonel Lushington, who was then resident at Tichborne House. The trial was so popular that it had to be moved from the Court of Common Pleas to the more commodious Court of Queen's Bench, wherein it lasted from March 1871 to May 1872. The *Era* complained that 'no one can go into any company whatever without being asked to discuss the matter'. The image of the claimant was modelled by Madame Tussaud and the queue to see it stretched down the street.

Matters other than notoriety were also at stake. The case of the claimant was taken up by radicals and what were known as the 'artisanal' class. Here was a poor man, a quondam butcher, who was now being cheated out of his inheritance by a band of aristocrats, landowners and property agents. The fact that he was now a baronet by his own admission did not make any difference. A phrase of the day was 'Fair play's a jewel'. As in the case of Queen Caroline, a victim was being hounded by the authorities for the sole reason that he or she challenged their power. The case was discussed in mechanics' institutes and popular debating societies, at mass meetings and public houses; it became the object of humour in comedies and music-hall acts. A network of publicans set up a fighting fund for him, while the members of other trades from cab drivers to cabinetmakers contributed what they could. Two newspapers were devoted to his cause. The 'claimant' himself gave a series of public addresses around the country. He did not wish to be recognized as Sir Roger Tichborne. He claimed only the right to fair trial; he added that he was the victim of a conspiracy. He even led a large march to Wapping, where he was once supposed to have been a butcher.

The trial at bar of the 'claimant' for charges of perjury lasted from April 1873 to February 1874 in front of a panel of three judges. The populace, largely in favour of Tichborne, set up a fresh clamour. 'Never was there a trial in England, I believe, since that memorable trial of Charles I,' Lord Chief Justice Cockburn said in that year, 'which has excited more the attention of the English than this.' Ruskin was more contemptuous. 'Just think . . . of that floor of idiotism that spent a couple of years or so of its life in writing, printing and reading the Tichborne trial.' The claimant was eventually found guilty on two charges of perjury and was sentenced to two periods of seven years which he served in an exemplary manner, winning converts within the prison service itself. That might have been the end of the matter, but the interests of others were now at stake.

The claimant's barrister, Edward Kenealy, had been disbarred for his behaviour in the courtroom; but his career then took a turn. He established 'The Magna Carta Association of Great Britain', invoking the ancient liberties of the English people; he was styled 'the People's Friend and the Champion of Poor "Sir Roger"'. He was duly elected as a radical member of parliament for Stoke. The entire episode contradicts the claims that radicalism was dead between the death of Chartism and the birth of socialism. The Tichborne claim had awakened the sympathy of those who opposed compulsory vaccination, the Lunacy Laws and the Contagious Diseases Act, where the duties of the state were supposed to override the rights of individuals. His name was deployed wherever the freedoms of the people were challenged. A banner at one Easter Monday demonstration spelled out 'Release Tichborne, secure triennial parliaments and the prosperity of the people'.

When he came out of prison he opened a tobacconist's shop but, popular acclaim having slowly dissipated, he did not succeed in the enterprise and died in poverty near Baker Street. Yet what had created the furore in the first place? The Tichborne case did attract for a while the fugitive interest of the crowds because it represented all that was wild and strange. The most sensational crimes of the period involved fraud or blackmail, and the case of Tichborne brought them into prominence. The reigning obsession was with what lay just below the surface, a world of nervous tension where the conventions of ordinary life concealed the burden of secrets and of irregular relationships. This was a world of confused identities where no one had a secure home. This was the world of Tichborne.

The case was of further interest because the Victorians were preoccupied by theories of heredity and of inherited characteristics. It filtered through the pages of Darwin into the most scandalous weekly. Could a butcher really be a baronet, or a baronet a butcher? It transgressed all the lines of respectable society, if anyone now knew what respectable society was.

22

The angel

'Men! They are the enemies of our innocence and our peace . . . they take us body and soul to themselves and fasten our helpless lives to theirs as they chain up a dog to his kennel. And what does the best of them give us in return?' Thus spoke Marian Halcombe in Wilkie Collins's *The Woman in White* (1860). Wives had no property rights and, as mere spouses, were deprived of their previous identities; at the same time they were incarcerated in the domestic world. The very being or legal existence of the woman was suspended. The husband could take her dresses or her jewels and sell them. She had no rights in the matter. So how can it be that in much social commentary women were mistresses of the house while being legally invisible? In public discourse of the nineteenth century they were disregarded; it was quite a different matter in private. It was one of the great lacunae of the late nineteenth century.

At the close of the eighteenth century Mary Wollstonecraft, the first systematic feminist, had died leaving the world her *A Vindication of the Rights of Woman* (1792), which was essentially a plea to middle-class women 'to endeavour to acquire strength, both mind and body'. It had not gone unobserved; the then nascent trade unions, particularly those of the shopkeepers and box-makers, contained a large percentage of women. Women were of course active and even predominant in the still flourishing cottage industries of wall-hangings and lace-making. The notion of the married woman as keeper of the hearth and the husband as the bearer of the torch – indeed the whole notion of 'separate spheres' in the middle-class sense – was not yet born.

By the 1860s, however, the full outline of 'the working man' had developed. But what of his wife, his sister, his daughter and even his mother? Could they any longer be denied their identity? And what also of the unmarried woman? The spinsters and widows were objects of concern, but they had at least one advantage: they were, relatively speaking, free. At the beginning of the nineteenth century a married woman owned no 'real' property (land being the principal item), and, in principle, no 'moveable' property. She was herself the property of her husband under the law – in legal terminology, a *feme covert* rather than a *feme sole*. In cases of divorce, which in each separate instance required a special act of parliament, the husband was granted custody of the children as a matter of course. Any money the wife earned became the property of her husband. The very money in her purse was her husband's. She could not sue or be sued. Her husband could treat her with as much brutality as he wished, confident that the complacency of the courts would overlook this.

It had not always been so. Anglo-Saxon women, when married, had rights and freedoms which under the Normans and their successors they were not to enjoy again until 1870. On issues of property, however, working women were in a superior position to those of the middle or upper classes for the simple reason that they had little of it. In fact many working-class women availed themselves of the practical advantages of cohabitation, without marriage and with few questions asked, through the early decades of the nineteenth century.

Yet the notion of 'separate spheres' became more and more pronounced in public discourse. No one can say precisely when it was first coined, or by whom, but it proved immensely influential. The quintessential mid-Victorian image is of a man looking out of a window with his hands clasped behind his head, and of the woman, sitting in an over-elaborately decorated chair, absorbed in needlework with her head demurely downcast. For the woman the world was home; for the man the world was the outer world itself.

In many occupations, however, the work was separated by task and not by gender. On the Severn and in Shropshire, the men would build the frame for the coracle while the women would sew on the skin; in agriculture the men would cut and the women would gather, while in fishing the men would catch and the women would gut the fish and sell it. Other examples suggest that this duopoly reflected the sexual politics of the time. The butler and the housekeeper, the male coal digger and the female coal heaver, the housemaid and the footman, the male cotton spinner and the female weaver, are examples of separate but interlocking spheres. Male protest only arose when man and woman competed for the same role; hence the savage reactions to the first women doctors.

Victorian women were subject to any number of privations when they appeared in public. Enormous skirts were fashionable in the mid-1850s, and there were cartoons of men being pushed out of the windows of omnibuses by billowing fabric, and of women stuck in doorways. Many of them wore cumbersome crinolines on Sundays, but during the working day they resorted to any number of expedients. The pit girls, for example, wore men's trousers. The fishwives wore several layers of skirts which were fastened so that the lower legs and feet were left bare; when the time came to prepare the fish for market, they wrapped themselves in large oilskin aprons. The female inmates of the workhouses wore a standard calico chemise, a flannel petticoat and a grey linsey skirt; a shawl, an apron and a pair of wool stockings completed the cheaply manufactured uniform. It was not only cheap; it never changed, and through the decades grew more and more antiquated. They were interchangeable, too, and the women would simply be given the last out of the wash.

Other restrictions prevailed. In the *Girls' Own Paper* Mrs Jamieson wrote that in the morning young females must use 'pure water as a preparatory ablution; after which they must abstain from all sudden gusts of passion, and particularly eschew envy, as that gives the skin a sallow paleness'. The young woman (although the term 'woman' was not to be used in demure households according to Dickens) must not stay up late, play cards or read novels by candlelight. Callisthenics, essentially waving the arms about, was the only suitable physical exercise. Female factory workers were in fact prescribed callisthenics as one of the day's duties.

One of the other duties of the woman was doing the laundry,

a job so laborious and so time-consuming that, if females had the means, they paid someone else to do it. In the 1861 census, professional laundry workers numbered 167,607, of whom 99 per cent were women. Home medicine was also the prerogative of women; male doctors and male pharmacists sold the drugs but the women of the house prepared and administrated the dosages. The women were also responsible for preparing home medicines, generally of an herbal nature. It was as much a part of the woman's role as baking and preparing bread. The advertisements for patent medicines were largely directed at women and women's fears, as in 'the jeopardy of life is immensely increased without such a simple precaution as Eno's Fruit Salts'. Epsom salts and senna leaves were also recommended to keep the 'system' in full working order. Advertisements were displayed for small hand-powered electrostatic machines with a pair of contacts for any part of the body including a 'vaginal attachment', the latter often used for 'hysterical' women. It was part of the medical vocabulary of the age.

Three Contagious Diseases Acts were passed in 1864, 1866 and 1869 that permitted the forced arrest of women deemed to be prostitutes; they were detained in isolation hospitals, for a period of approximately six weeks, where they were exposed to vaginal examination and other internal inspections. This was quite contrary to any belief in individual freedom, or the rights enshrined in habeas corpus, and the loud protests have been said to inaugurate the movement for women's rights. It was said that young working-class females, in particular, were being taken off the streets and forced to undergo what seemed to be a form of legalized rape. The acts were repealed in 1884, having done nothing but instil anxiety and outrage in the working-class population. These were some of the attributes of male power.

The pressure on women increased as the towns and cities multiplied. Those turned off the livings on the land were forced to resort to hand-weaving just when it was challenged by the power loom. Neither poor diets nor hours of work nor conditions of labour managed to halt this movement into the towns. The plight of the women was aggravated by their situation. The men themselves encouraged many pregnancies, even if these augmented the exhaustion of their wives. This had primarily an economic purpose: the larger the number of children, the greater the eventual family income. The abolition of child labour, therefore, was only in part prompted by humanitarian concerns. Labouring children, blameless and exploited through they were, had the power to put their parents out of work, or at least to lower their wages.

The more respectable ladies of the middle-class house rarely had to deal with such conditions, although they were confronted by such forbidding texts as Mrs Beeton's *Book of Household Management* (1861) and Coventry Patmore's *The Angel in the House* (1854), books of vastly different tendency, but both of which helped to fasten the fetters on the home-bound wife. Patmore's verses were not directed at an angel, or woman, or girl, or matron, or matriarch – or indeed at anything that might be recognized as human. The 'angel of the house' is a bundle of superterrestrial attributes, about which the female reader can only read and dream or weep:

> And if he once, by shame oppress'd,
> A comfortable word confers,
> She leans and weeps against his breast,
> And seems to think the sin was hers.

Virginia Woolf said that it was the duty of any female author to kill the angel of the house.

Mrs Beeton began her famous domestic sermons at the age of twenty-one in *The Englishwoman's Domestic Magazine*, but appearances are deceptive. Most of her recipes were lifted from earlier cookery books. She wrote a good and lucid prose, however, and she performed the inestimable service of putting a list of ingredients before the recipes themselves. Mrs Beeton's *Book of Household Management*, first published in October 1861, contained the recipes but seasoned them with advice on such matters as servants and first aid. It was a vade mecum for any middle-class woman aspiring to respectability. In the opening she quotes from Oliver Goldsmith on the nature of separate spheres:

> The modest virgin, the prudent wife or the careful matron are much more serviceable in life than petticoated philosophers, blustering heroines or virago queens. She who makes her husband and her children happy, who reclaims the one from

vice and trains up the other in virtue, is a much greater character than ladies described in romances, whose whole occupation is to murder mankind with shafts from their quiver, or from their eyes.

Some might applaud, and others despise, the sentiments.

It would not be too surprising to discover, therefore, that hundreds of thousands of women signed anti-slavery petitions at the time when that cause excited maximum controversy. It could be inferred that they felt immediate or instinctive sympathy with the enslaved. One anti-slavery activist, George Thompson, stated in 1834 that 'where they existed they did everything . . . In a word they formed the cement of the Antislavery building – without their aid we never should have been united.' Wilberforce did not necessarily approve of their presence, however, and stated that 'for ladies to meet, to publish, to go from house to house stirring up petitions – these appear to me proceedings unsuited to the female character as delineated in Scripture'. In fact Scripture had nothing to say on the subject. Philanthropists could also be bigots.

Two waves of female petitions against slavery, in 1830–31 and in 1833, included those from 108 English, four Welsh, thirteen Scots and four Irish towns and villages. The female members of the dissenting chapels added 15,000 signatures. The Wesleyan Methodist anti-slavery petition in 1833 was signed by 100,000 women. The Sheffield Female Anti-Slavery Society represented the cause as 'not exclusively a political but pre-eminently a moral one; one therefore on which the humble-minded reader of the bible which enriches his cottage shelf is immeasurably a better politician than the statesman versed in the intrigues of Cabinets'. This is the measure of the Victorian woman, no less practical and earnest than her male counterpart.

Many men demanded equal pay for women not on the grounds of equality but for fear that they would undercut and steal their jobs. In power looming, for example, men were greatly outnumbered by women. Some weaving associations made it a rule not to accept any man unless all the female members of the family working in the trade were union members.

It could even be suggested that the working-class woman, though disadvantaged in most ways, had some consolations; she was as often as not the true mistress of the home. Having no prospects of a gradual amelioration of her and her family's position, she was spared the bitterness and frustration of her middle-class contemporaries, and with no land, money or portion to offer it was possible that she could even marry for love. The upper-class woman, on the other hand, though a mere counter in the marriage market, could console herself with the thought that once married she would move to a comfortable home, replete with amusements and distractions; she was spared the worst horrors of child-raising, and she might have the opportunity to travel, write or translate. The middle-class woman, for all her apparent comfort, was arguably the most constricted; she had no real authority, and upon her fell all the force of Victorian moral scrutiny, while the intellectual morsels that passed for an education often served to aggravate longing and resentment. These women often became the mettlesome pioneers of political and social liberation.

One notable opponent of women's freedom was the most liberated of females. Queen Victoria wrote that she was 'most anxious to enlist everyone who can speak or write . . . [against] this *mad wicked folly* of "Women's Rights" with all of its attendant follies on which her poor feeble sex is bent, forgetting every sense of womanly feeling and propriety . . .' We may still consider this to be the conventional wisdom of the period.

One of its most notable challengers, however, was Annie Besant. In 1877 she and Charles Bradlaugh were prosecuted under the Obscene Publications Act which had been passed twenty years before. Both of them might be described as professional agitators who delighted in turning the law and the world on its head. Bradlaugh was a professed atheist who would soon provoke uproar in the House of Commons, while Besant gained national prominence as a supporter of female workers. She was self-aware and self-confident from the start. 'I hate affectation of all kind,' she once remarked. 'I never could bear those ridiculous women who cannot step over a straw without expecting the man who is walking with them to offer his hand. I always said to the man, "No, no. I have got legs of my own. Don't trouble yourself.'" Her personal likes and dislikes were plain.

Besant was said to be absolutely insensitive to the feelings of others. This is unjust but, in the context of her pioneering efforts, it is understandable. She had soon become aware of the social evils all around her through the eyes of a radical lawyer, William Prowting Roberts, a notable Chartist who took on the cause of the coal miner. 'I have heard him tell how he had seen them toiling, naked to the waist, with short petticoats barely reaching their knees, rough, foul-tongued, brutalized out of all womanly decency and grace.' This was the horror world of the nineteenth century, the gulf into which all 'Victorian values' slipped. Besant married a young priest, but the marriage was not successful as she slowly crept closer to atheism. In the summer of 1874 she gave her first public lecture at the Co-operative Institute in Castle Street off Oxford Street on 'The Political Status of Women'. From that time forward, while speaking in public, she experienced power and pleasure which would uplift her through all the personal perils of her political life.

Besant and Bradlaugh established a publishing company, one of whose first pamphlets, *The Fruits of Philosophy*, was prosecuted as an obscene publication. It was a treatise on the methods and virtues of birth control, a subject hitherto so mysterious that 133,000 copies were sold between March and June 1887. The test of obscenity was 'whether the tendency of the matter charged as obscenity is to deprave and corrupt those whose minds are open to such immoral influences and into whose hands a publication of this sort may fall'. An excerpt from the transcript of the trial may be illuminating:

> SOLICITOR GENERAL: It is not whether work of this kind can be submitted to a college of philosophy, but whether it can be sold at the price of sixpence about the streets of London and elsewhere . . .
>
> ANNIE BESANT: Do you, gentlemen, think for one moment that myself and my co-defendant are fighting the simple question of the sale or publication of this sixpenny volume of Dr Knowlton's? . . . We have a much larger interest at stake, and one of vital interest to the public, one which we shall spend our whole lives in trying to uphold . . . there is no harm in

gratifying the sexual instinct if it can be gratified without injury to anyone else, and without harm to the morals of society . . .

The name of Malthus was brought into the proceedings as testimony to the fact that the population was growing too rapidly and should be curtailed.

ANNIE BESANT: I have put it to you as plainly as I can the meaning of the word obscene, which will govern your verdict: I have pleaded that our intent is good, because it conduces to human and social happiness. I have shown you from Malthus – and he has never yet been disproved – what the law of population is . . . I have seen four generations of human beings being crowded together in one small room, simply divided into two of three beds, and I will ask you, after such an experience as that, you wonder that I risk even prison and a fine if I can bring some salvation to those poor whose misery I have seen.

She then turned to the other Victorian misery, early death. She stated that the death rate in Manchester was 117 in 1,000, and in Liverpool it rose to 132 in 1,000.

Put before yourselves clearly whether it is either moral or right to allow children to be brought into the world inoculated with the predisposition to be attacked by these preventable diseases, instead of putting, as I believe you ought to do, a check which would effectively relieve the population so terribly overcrowded; and you have to consider whether by refusing to apply such a check, we are not, by the very refusal, making a large class of criminals . . .

The origins of many Victorian prejudices are here, both in those who attacked a sixpenny pamphlet for encouraging birth control and in those who saw large numbers of children as responsible for a range of deadly diseases, a burden on the world's resources and a terrible seed of crime. Certain crimes were, according, to Besant, specific. One was the practice of baby-farming, where unwanted children were given into the custody of men, women and even children quite unfit for the task. Besant referred to 'a child three years of age employed as a ganger over eight other children . . .'

The prospect here was of early death. Another practice was of 'overlying' children, or in other words pressing them or suffocating them to death. Besant told the court that 'when you consider that the number of these children who, if they had been born in a higher rank, would not have died, is calculated by Professor Fawcett as 1,150,000 you will see what a large and important question this is ...' Besant then cited John Stuart Mill's *Principles of Political Economy* on the need for 'plain language', especially when Mill 'pressed on all those who marry the duty of limiting their families'.

She continued then to describe the mother of a large and poor family who was labouring at the washtub three or four days after giving birth. 'What am I to do?' the woman asked her. 'There is another mouth to feed. The children are there and must be provided for, and I must get about.' I must get about. This was the Victorian imperative.

In his summing up the solicitor general, prosecuting the case, said:

> this is a dirty, filthy book and the test of it is that no human being could allow that book to lie on his table; no decently educated English husband would allow even his wife to have it, and yet it is to be told to me, forsooth, that anybody may have this book in the city of London or elsewhere who can pay sixpence for it! . . . The object of it is to enable persons to have sexual intercourse, and not have that which in the order of Providence is the natural result of sexual intercourse.

Besant and Bradlaugh were sentenced to six months' imprisonment and then deemed not guilty on appeal. There is a mingling here of Low Church piety, mid-century moralism, social prejudice and sexual hypocrisy which seems to be thoroughly Victorian.

23

The empress

Gladstone had been denied the chance of resignation by Disraeli's refusal to take up the administration. But there were other ways to skin a cat. Gladstone waited for an excuse or an opportunity. When his plans to reduce the army and naval estimates were blocked by the relevant ministers, on the grounds that they could be squeezed no further, it furnished as good a reason as any other. When he announced the dissolution of parliament to his colleagues, it came as a great surprise. The earl of Kimberley wrote in his diary that most of the cabinet 'had not heard a whisper previously of such an intention on his part'. It was a 'thunder clap'.

On the morning of Saturday, 24 January 1874, Disraeli opened *The Times* to read the news that Gladstone had called an immediate dissolution; the paper was filled with Gladstone's election address, together with his pledge to abolish income tax. Disraeli summoned his senior advisers and, working through the night and day, prepared a manifesto for the Monday newspapers.

Gladstone had not found an issue with which he could identify himself with the electorate. His immediate record had been lacking lustre. His fiscal policy of austerity seemed the last word of an exhausted government. His only slogan was 'the free breakfast table', by repealing duties on tea and sugar, but it was not enough. His skills failed him, and Disraeli sailed on with 350 seats (100 of them uncontested). Gladstone could muster 242, and he retired to the back benches.

It was a significant election for other reasons. The Irish nationalists of the Home Rule League became the third-largest party in the form of fifty-eight seats, causing many fervent calculations among the Lords and Commons. It was the first election that employed a secret ballot. This may also have had something to do with the Irish success. Some observers also complimented the liquor trade on its benefactions to the Tory party: where the Liberals and Nonconformists might migrate to the chapel and meeting houses, the Conservatives seemed to have a monopoly on the pubs. That at least is how a disgruntled Gladstone saw it. Lord Hartington, known as 'Harty Tarty', took over from Gladstone as leader of the Liberal party in the Commons and Earl Granville in the Lords. They were much closer in background and attitude to the old Whig party, and many Liberal MPs regarded Gladstone as leaning too far towards radicalism. They were glad to be rid of him.

The Conservatives, who had not possessed a majority for thirty-three years, had earned the right to be surprised. But certain things were in their favour. Gladstone had called the election at the worst time of year. Disraeli's Reform legislation seemed at last to be bearing fruit. The organization of the party itself was also greatly improved. The dominant voice and personality were of course those of Disraeli, and he took the opportunity of sending one of his more vocal opponents, Lord Salisbury, to the India Office. This seemed to satisfy everyone for the time being. Nothing was to be achieved by bluster or bullying. All was conducted formally and with dignity. He mastered his ministers by mood and manners, but not by his policies. His ministers assumed a fertile mind on his part but, as the new home secretary, R. A. Cross, put it, 'such did not prove to be the case; on the contrary he had to rely entirely on the suggestions of his colleagues and as they themselves had only just come into office, and that suddenly, there was some difficulty in framing the Queen's speech'.

Disraeli's métier was not in the detail but in the broad brush and the theatrical sweep. Victoria had long since tired of Gladstone's manner and matter. She bridled at his nervous formality, viewed his Liberal policies as anti-monarchical, and considered him to be a very dangerous and even mad old man. Disraeli was different. He could have flattered his way out of a condemned cell and stolen the axe. He laid on the praise and congratulation with a very large trowel, and made sure that their respective opinions never clashed. He was hyperbolical to the point of fatuity, and in his correspondence she could become 'princess of the Faery' or the 'Faery Queen'.

Where Gladstone's first ministry had sprinted forward as if the hurdles were rushing towards it, Disraeli's second administration at first managed few leaps. He was faced with a meagre opposition, with Gladstone taking what might have been seen as permanent retirement, but in any case he seemed averse to any kind of radical change on electoral reform or anything else. Disraeli was looking old, his pale and emaciated face contrasting oddly with his surprisingly dark hair.

The session of 1875 was more effective. A Public Health Act consolidated previous sanitary legislation on fresh water, street lighting and refuse collection. An Artisans' Dwellings Act provided the funds for local councils to buy up areas of slum dwellings and rebuild them. Two acts equalized the legal status of employers and employees. An Agricultural Holdings Act compensated rural tenants for the improvements they had made. This was known as 'suet pudding legislation', reassuring and necessary, if rather bland, but it was part of Disraeli's 'one nation' attempt to improve the conditions of the working people. The Conservatives under Disraeli did a signal service to the nation's welfare without gaining much praise, and were happy to continue in much the same vein for the next two years.

In June 1875, Disraeli told the Commons:

permissive legislation is the characteristic of a free people. It is easy to adopt compulsory legislation when you have to deal with those who only exist to obey but in a free country, and especially in a country like England, you must trust to persuasion and example as the two great elements, if you wish to effect any considerable change in the manners and customs of the people.

Government, in other words, was slow and difficult, but by 1876 the principal measures of public health and sanitation had been passed. And in truth Disraeli's heart was not wholly moved by domestic legislation. Berlin, Paris and Moscow were his orbit, not Manchester, Birmingham or Nottingham.

Inventions seem to have streamed forth in this period. A cable was laid across the Atlantic in 1876, and Graham Bell invented the telephone in the same year. The internal combustion engine was manufactured for sale in 1876. Electric light companies were established in the 1880s, and the turbine engine was invented in 1884. The first motor car drove out in 1885. The observer seems to be in the position of H. G. Wells's time traveller moving through the factory system into the machine age.

Gladstone seemed to have become more amiable. 'The Queen', Granville wrote to him, 'told me last night, that she had never known you so remarkably agreeable.' This was the period when he spoke of retirement, and the imminent withdrawal from the fray might have encouraged high spirits. He wrote to Granville: 'I see no public advantage in my continuing to act as the leader of the Liberal Party.' Yet he still maintained a formidable presence. Disraeli reported to the queen, on one parliamentary session: 'Mr Gladstone not only appeared but rushed into the debate . . . The new members trembled and fluttered like small birds when a hawk is in the air.'

Disraeli was also undergoing a change. Despite the legislative activity, for which he was nominally responsible, he had not proved to be as effective in government as in opposition, and a colleague complained that 'in the ordinary conduct of business Disraeli shows himself at every turn quite incompetent to guide the House'. He was a born oppositionist, and even his advancement of the Reform Act might be construed as a charge against 'the enemy'. The truth was that he was wearing out. He was often ill with bronchitis and gout, while the hours spent in the Commons were agony for him. Everyone saw the choice ahead of him – retirement or the House of Lords. Retirement was out of the question, and in 1876 he became earl of Beaconsfield. His last speech in the Commons was devoted to the loyalty owed to the empire. As he left the chamber he took one last look at the scene of his endeavours, and then passed quietly behind the Speaker's chair; he was wearing a long white coat and 'dandified' lavender gloves. A political opponent, Sir William Harcourt, wrote to tell him, that 'henceforth the game will be like a chessboard when the queen is gone . . .'

The year before, he had earned the distinction of purchasing a large interest in the Suez Canal from the khedive of Egypt. It was the passage to India, far superior to the Cape route, but it was unfortunately in the hands of the French and the khedive. With his flair for scheming and what his enemies called duplicity, he relied upon the imminent bankruptcy of the khedive himself. Disraeli set Baron Rothschild's son to expedite negotiations, which were sealed when the Rothschilds agreed to lend the required £4 million. Disraeli wrote to Victoria: 'It is just settled. You have it, Madame.' Then he wrote to a confidante: 'The Fairy is in ecstasies.' Many of his colleagues deprecated the manner and method of Disraeli's coup. Stafford Northcote, the chancellor of the Exchequer, remarked: 'suspicion will be excited that we mean to buy ourselves quietly into a preponderating position, and then turn the whole thing into an English property. I don't like it.' Others were more enthusiastic. Derby commented: 'so far as I can make out the purchase is universally popular. I might say even more, it seems to have created a feeling of something like enthusiasm far in excess of the real importance of the transaction.' Derby was not sure of the consequences, however, and it was becoming apparent that Disraeli did not have a purposeful foreign policy. It was said that Derby, at the Foreign Office, *would not* look ahead, and Disraeli *could not* look ahead. Disraeli's methods were fitful at best. He conceded to a correspondent that: 'Turkish and Egyptian affairs get worse every day . . . we have plenty of troubles ahead, but perhaps they will vanish when encountered.' This is another example of fairy-tale diplomacy.

Another episode of Disraeli's fairy tale was manifest in the spring of 1876. During the previous winter the Prince of Wales spent four months travelling in India, and such was the enthusiasm for his visit that it occurred to Disraeli that the queen herself might just as well become empress of India. In truth the suggestion might have come from the queen. It would be a new symbol of British power, making the queen the imperial equal of the tsar of Russia. She revelled in the appointment, and enjoyed wearing the jewels that the princes and princesses of her new acquisition bestowed upon her. To some of her subjects it seemed to be a kind of heathenism and only a fine line from Roman Catholic superstition. Others believed that it was a preparatory move for changing the title of queen to that of empress of the British Isles.

Another name must now be added to the sum of talent and ambition. Joseph Chamberlain came out of Birmingham like a railway train, with which he was contemporaneous; he was a screw manufacturer and a Liberal whose pre-eminent talents of oratory and organization made him mayor of that city in 1873. A few years before, he had joined the Birmingham Education Society, but soon enough he stepped out of that small circle, and in 1867 established a National Education League. Just as Forster was devising his own education bill, Chamberlain asserted that 'the vast numerical majority of the people of this country are in favour of national, compulsory, free and unsectarian education'. Chamberlain went into battle. His name spread widely enough, and one of his early biographers, Alexander Mackintosh, remarked: 'he is already hailed amongst working class radicals everywhere as the coming leader of democracy'.

Chamberlain was at this stage in his life a radical Liberal, a dissident who had little affection for what might be called the ministerial Liberals in the House of Commons. He was elected to represent St Paul's Ward in Birmingham, and began his campaign to change and cleanse the city. Once he had been elected as mayor he set out a programme of public works that was variously designated as 'municipal socialism' and 'gas-and-water socialism'. He promoted the resources of lighting and clean water; he advanced slum clearance and rebuilding, all of which granted him a national reputation as the civic amenities of Birmingham were transformed.

It was now inevitable that he would move towards Westminster. In 1876 he was returned unopposed for Birmingham, and soon enough his talent for, or obsession with, organization prompted him to bring together the radical Liberals in the Commons as a distinct body. He noted that 'the atmosphere is strange, unsympathetic, almost hostile'. There was soon a definite division between what might be called the conventional Liberals and the devotees of Chamberlain. At a later date Herbert Asquith, one of his opponents, said that Chamberlain 'had the manners of a cad and the tongue of a bargee'. His language could, in a word of the day, be 'choice'. He said that Disraeli was 'a man who never told the truth except by accident' and of Salisbury that he was 'the spokesman of a class – of a class to which he himself belongs – who toil not neither do they spin'. Salisbury described this as a 'Jacobin' attack.

But the matters of the outer world soon encroached upon private politics. Early in 1876 it became clear that the Balkans were in a state of revolt from the Turkish empire. The great powers of Germany, Russia and Austria brought pressure to bear on Turkey, which was accused of maltreating its Christian subjects. When in 1876 the Bulgarians rose against the sultan and his empire, the retribution was savage; it is estimated that some 12,000 Bulgarians were murdered by Turkey's irregular soldiers. Disraeli was inclined to take such reports lightly. They were a distraction, and no more. But Gladstone brooded on them, and when he brooded, a whirlwind together with hail and lightning might rise. He asked Disraeli, in his last weeks in the Commons before becoming earl of Beaconsfield, to institute an inquiry. Disraeli was concerned only to preserve British interests, and any talk of justice or humanity was essentially beside the point. 'What our duty is,' he said, 'at this critical moment, is to maintain the empire of England.'

These might have seemed unexceptionable sentiments at a different time and from a different prime minister, but the presence of Gladstone introduced a note of exemplary morality into the debate that could not be dismissed. 'Good ends', Gladstone stated, 'can rarely be attained in politics without passion and there is now, the first time for a good many years, a righteous passion.' It was almost as if he had been waiting for the moment.

He had for some years believed that politics could only be practised and irradiated by 'righteous passion'. That was essentially the reason he had become a politician and a minister. It might also have occurred to him that the moral outrage he evinced might also help to renegotiate his popularity with the irate electorate. He should strike while they were hot. The *Daily News* provided the necessary fuel with gruesome stories of sodomy, beheading, disembowelment and practically everything else. Disraeli dismissed the reports as the frothings of an anti-Tory newspaper and added that 'oriental people seldom resort to torture but generally terminate their connection with culprits in a more expeditious manner'. This was not one of his better observations.

Within four days, in September 1876, Gladstone had completed a pamphlet entitled *Bulgarian Horrors and the Question of the East*; and his daughter confirmed that 'the whole country is aflame – meetings all over the place'. Two hundred thousand copies were sold within the month, and Gladstone followed his triumph by an open-air meeting in Blackheath where in pouring rain he called out: 'Let the Turks now carry away their abuses in the only possible manner, namely by carrying off themselves.' Every pause in his speech was the occasion for shouts of 'Long life to you!' and 'We want you!' By the force of will and intelligence he was able to shape the vast populace into one highly sensitized human being. And at the end of the meeting people called out continually: 'Lead us! Lead us!'

Disraeli was not impressed. He called Gladstone one of the worst of the Bulgarian horrors, and threatened Russia with the consequences of invading Turkey. This inspired one of the most memorable of music-hall songs:

> We don't want to fight but by Jingo if we do,
> We've got the ships, we've got the men, we've got
> the money, too!

The acting leaders of the Liberal party, Hartington and Granville, feared that Gladstone might ignite a war between Russia and Turkey in which England would be obliged to take part. The queen described him as that 'half mad man'. But Gladstone had regained his moral public, and to be in touch with the nation once more was vastly exciting. In the spring of 1877 he entered the realm of controversy by aligning himself with Joseph Chamberlain at the first meeting of the National Liberal Federation in Birmingham. He declared that the Liberal party was alone 'the instrument' by which a 'great work' could be accomplished. He saw Chamberlain as a fellow worker in that enterprise, 'expecting to play an historical part, and probably destined to it'. Chamberlain might be described as a fellow missionary, but it was clear enough to Gladstone, as to Chamberlain, that the younger man wished to fashion the Liberal party in his own image. Gladstone was more intent on widening his own franchise by the evident moral challenge he put to his party.

The country itself was split into rival camps, those with Gladstone and the pro-Russians, while others supported Disraeli and Turkey. Disraeli told the queen that 'in a Cabinet of twelve members there are seven parties or policies as to the course which should be pursued'. Most of the discussion centred on the interests of the various foreign powers involved, but some also on the careers of the ministers engaged in the conversations. Derby said that 'to the premier the main thing is to please and surprise the public by bold strokes and unexpected moves; he would rather run serious national risks than hear his policy called feeble and commonplace'. The collapse of a conference at Constantinople at the beginning of 1877 led to a war three months later, and it became a matter of intervening in a fight between a serpent and a bear. The forces of the sultan were no match for the power of the tsar, and the Russians surged up to the walls of Constantinople. England, fearful of a wider war, was obliged to send the fleet to Constantinople. Disraeli was concerned with the Eastern Mediterranean and the route to India. He called up the reserves in England, a clear indication of an imminent war. As a result, Lord Derby resigned and Salisbury took his place as foreign secretary.

A treaty between the antagonists was signed at San Stefano in the early weeks of 1878, but as a result a much larger Bulgaria emerged that might threaten its neighbours. There followed more secret talks, more smuggled notes, more bribes and false promises, more betrayals. So in Berlin three months later it was arranged all over again, with a much diminished Bulgaria; England had agreed to defend Turkey against illegal violations, the sultan had agreed to effect necessary social reforms, and in the course of the complicated negotiations Britain was awarded Cyprus. She would return the island if Russia also gave back the land it had seized in Asia. It seemed to be, by the standards of the age, an honourable settlement. The prime minister returned to London as victor ludorum. The armistice was signed in March 1878. It was the first time that the queen had seen a telephone installed in Osborne House.

Yet for many it was not a matter of 'peace with honour'. Lord Rosebery, a rising Liberal in the Lords, castigated Disraeli and his allies. 'They have partitioned Turkey, they have secured a doubtful fragment of the spoil for themselves. They have abandoned Greece. They have incurred responsibilities of a vast and unknown kind . . .' He had forgotten that Disraeli preferred responsibilities to be as vast and unknown as possible.

The new foreign secretary, the marquess of Salisbury, had travelled with Disraeli to Berlin even though he did not wholly agree with the premier's Turkish inclinations. But he was even now one of the leading players who already had dreams of premiership. He watched with some scorn the theatrics of Disraeli in Berlin. He informed his wife that Disraeli 'has not the dimmest idea of what is going on – understands everything crossways – and imagines a perpetual conspiracy'. Of his colleagues in the cabinet he wrote: 'they are all middle-class men, and I have always observed throughout life that middle-class men are afraid of responsibility'.

That is perhaps why, as foreign secretary, Salisbury became entangled in a number of small wars. He seems to have been partly responsible for the Second Afghan War, which continued for two years and ended with the battle of Kandahar. A more serious conflict arose when English troops invaded the Zulu kingdom at the beginning of 1879. In January the massacre of an entire army column at Isandlwana prompted the dispatch of a further 9,000 troops; it was the largest single strike by a native army, and caused much consternation. Disraeli said: 'the terrible disaster has shaken me to the centre'. The massacre provoked an equally gruesome revenge which was only partly reported. The bloody crisis continued into the summer, when the Zulu army was beaten at Ulundi. It was generally assumed that they had been defeated by what Charles Kingsley had described in *Alton Locke* (1850) as 'that grim, earnest, stubborn energy which, since the days of the old Romans, the English possess alone of all the nations on earth'. But this was mere posturing and pretence, or rubbish derided in the phrase of the time as 'leather and prunella'. The Zulus had been the victims of greed, racial hatred and bloodlust.

This was not how the empire had been conceived or imagined. The colonies were proving to be graveyards, and not just for the armies hurled into conflicts which they hardly understood. In West Africa half the arrivals perished within three months. In Sierra Leone the mortality stood at 483 per thousand and at the Gold

Coast the level stood at 668 per thousand. In Ceylon the mortality was five times higher than that of Britain. Victoria understood the world better than most of her subjects or politicians. At the time of the worst fighting in Afghanistan she wrote that 'our position in India and in the Colonies must be upheld'. She informed Beaconsfield that 'if we are to maintain our position as a first-rate Power, we must with our Indian Empire and our large Colonies be prepared for attacks and wars somewhere or other, CONTINUALLY'.

In a letter to Lady Ely she declared: 'I wish to *trust my* Government whoever it is but they should be well aware beforehand I never could if they intended to *try* and *undo* what has been done.' According to the novelist Frank Bullen, 'no youth would dare enter a school and speak against the Empire'. Were he to do so, 'he would promptly be knocked down'. Adventure novels, short stories and illustrated periodicals continually strengthened the link between empire and heroism or adventure. Much praise was devoted to pride and prestige, but little to commerce, even though the inexhaustible search for trade and markets was the *primum mobile* of imperialism.

At the close of 1878 Gladstone confided to his diary that he believed in the battle for 'justice, humanity and freedom' and added: 'If I really believe this, then I should regard my having been morally forced into this work as a great and high election of God.' This would have been a high justification even in the latter half of the nineteenth century, and would no doubt now be regarded as a form of mania except by those who follow on the less regarded path of religious radicalism. Gladstone had the Nonconformists behind him en masse, a force considerably more powerful and significant than radical liberalism. It was of course the sort of sentiment which would alienate and enrage an expedient man such as Disraeli.

This was the spirit in which Gladstone entered the Midlothian campaign of November 1879. It was for him an aspect of his denunciation of Turkish villainy, but he ranged over the whole field of national policy as a fitting prelude to the general election of 1880. He began his campaign at the country seat of Lord Rosebery, which boosted Rosebery's career considerably, before he travelled between Liverpool and Edinburgh to initiate what were essentially a series of speeches that were part lectures and part sermons. He spoke at Carlisle, he spoke at Hawick and he spoke at Galashiels. It was perhaps the first proper political campaign. As Disraeli had said, 'we govern men with words'.

Rosebery was waiting for him at Edinburgh station in a four-in-hand carriage to the accompaniment of bonfires and fireworks. 'I have never gone through a more extraordinary day,' Gladstone said. He had always been moved by the excitement of crowds, and for two weeks he lambasted the government for financial misman-agement, for virtually purloining Egypt and for making impossible commitments to the Turks in Bosnia. 'From that time forward,' he wrote, 'until the final consummation in 1879–1880 I made the Eastern question the main business of my life. I acted under strong sense of individual duty without a thought of leadership; neverthe-less it made me leader again, whether I would or no.' Posters of him as 'priest-king' were pasted over the walls and windows; shop windows were devoted to his display.

So Gladstone was on the attack. He was now seventy-one years old and had seen the empire expand sporadically and haphazardly, obeying its own laws of growth through trade routes and across oceans, challenging here, bribing there, threatening elsewhere. For Disraeli it was all in a day's work, to be reported to the Fairy Queen, but Gladstone never had an easy conscience. He took a whip to himself after his famous nocturnal conversations with the women of the street, and there is every reason to suppose that his political excitement elicited similar responses. 'Let every one of us resolve', he said 'that he will do his best to exempt himself; ay, that he will exempt himself from every participation in what he believes to be mischievous and ruinous misdeeds.' There were according to his own letters wild cheers and storms of applause. The towns through which he passed were illuminated by torches and fairy lanterns, by arches and decorations. 'Remember that the sanctity of life in the hill villages of Afghanistan, among the winter snows, is as inviolable in the eye of Almighty God as can be your own.' For him, Disraeli was the violator of world peace who had offended against every canon of moral justice. Every word was disseminated to a nation that imbibed political campaigns as eagerly as stout. Disraeli professed himself to be tired of his opponent's rhetoric primarily because he was so often the subject of it. For her part the queen refused even to consider Gladstone to be a serious political figure. By 1879 the battering had begun taking its toll on Disraeli, for whom recent events were far from satisfactory. The trials of Afghanistan and Zululand have already been mentioned but there were grave difficulties closer to home. *Reynolds' News* announced that 1879 offered only a record of disaster, 'the dullest year we remember in trade and the most disastrous in agriculture'. Rising unemployment had coincided with bad harvests and had culminated in a great depression of trade and in industrial discontent. A wave of strikes from London masons to Lancashire cotton operatives was a token of the winter of 1878 and 1879.

An economic decline had been evident since 1870; unemployment rose by more than 6 per cent in three years. Income tax was raised to sixpence to pay for the mounting cost of Afghanistan and South Africa. Disraeli was worn to the bone after the Berlin conference and seemed to have lost much of his vital elastic power. The depressed agricultural prices in England spelled torment for Ireland. In 1879 the Irish National Land League was established, with Parnell as president and four Fenians on the secretariat. It was yet another tortuous combination in the labyrinth of Westminster politics. In the Commons itself the Home Rule League party Irish MPs who sat in Westminster under Parnell were the significant force. They could effectively hinder all legislation, but more particularly that which concerned Irish affairs.

Deluded by some stray good news, Disraeli dissolved parliament in March 1880, and marched into his own Valley of Death. Gladstone set off on another speaking tour, convinced that his living relationship with the electorate was the most potent tie. The queen described them as 'mad unpatriotic ravings'. Yet it seemed that nothing could save the Conservatives in the election of 1880. Nothing did. Gladstone's Liberals gained over a hundred seats, and such was his victory that he was chosen as prime minister once again over the nominal leadership of Hartington and Granville. 'The downfall of Beaconsfieldism', he said, 'is like the vanishing of some vast magnificent castle in an Italian romance.' The faery lore of the past was still part of the Victorian imagination.

Gladstone took power like some caliph with the combined will of the people. The Conservative grandee Lord Salisbury commented: 'I was not sorry for the prospect. But such a defeat as this is quite another matter. It is a perfect catastrophe – and may I fear break up the party altogether.' There was a diversion. One of the members of the new parliament was Charles Bradlaugh, who had combined with Annie Besant in the fight for birth control. He now caused further controversy by refusing to take the official Oath of Allegiance on becoming a member of parliament, and demanded to affirm as an atheist. His stance provoked scenes of mock outrage that would do honour to Gilbert and Sullivan. He lost his plea, and when a by-election followed he submitted successfully for reselection; he entered Westminster with a large crowd and forcibly made his way into the Commons before being ejected into Palace Yard. He tried again on four other occasions, was ejected and then re-elected. Bradlaugh was a self-publicist who thoroughly enjoyed his notoriety and even enjoyed his brief imprisonment when it generated further headlines. Having caused considerable embarrassment to Gladstone and the Liberal party, he finally took his seat in 1886. Two years later, in 1888, he secured passage of a new and more accommodating Oaths Act.

Disraeli did not seem to take his downfall too seriously. He must have anticipated it. His only burden was the number of begging letters he received for posts, offices, sinecures and appointments before his final departure from the stage. He was also aware the queen would miss him as much as he missed her; they had formed a warm friendship, and he knew how much she depended on her allies.

His political opponents, therefore, were hardly likely to receive a warm welcome from Buckingham Palace. Of Gladstone, Victoria wrote privately that 'she will sooner *abdicate* than send for or have anything to do with *that half-mad firebrand* who would soon ruin everything and be a *Dictator*'. She calmed down sufficiently to be persuaded by Disraeli that Gladstone was her only viable candidate and that in any case he was too old to last much longer. Actuarial prophecies did not in fact prevail. He survived in politics for another fourteen years.

Lord Derby played host to Gladstone in the autumn of 1881.

The general impression seems to be, and certainly it is that left on my mind, that he is more agreeable, more light and easy in conversation, than would be expected from his manner in public; no subject comes amiss to him, he is ready to discourse on any, great or small, & that with the same copiousness & abundance of detail which characterise his speaking. He has no humour, rarely jokes, and his jokes are poor when he makes them. There is something odd in the intense earnestness with which he takes up every topic. I heard him yesterday deliver a sort of lecture on the various different ways of mending roads, suggested by some remark about the Liverpool streets. He described several different processes minutely, & as if he had been getting up the subject for an examination . . . Since the days of Lord Brougham, I have heard nothing like his eager and restless volubility; he never ceases to talk, and to talk well. Nobody would have thought he had cares on his mind or work to do. His face is very haggard, his eye wild . . .

It is as good a contemporary description as you are likely to find.

Disraeli was no longer so animated or voluble. It may be that he suffered his election defeat with more anguish than he admitted. At a party meeting at his house in Curzon Street in February 1881, he seemed to be a 'lean, dark, feeble figure'. His last visit to the Lords was in the following month, but he is supposed to have declined a visit from the queen with the words: 'No it is better not. She would only ask me to take a message to Albert.' It is more likely that he did not want his sovereign to see him in so shattered a state. He did not rest from his labours, and his private letters are full of political rumours and advice; he attended dinners as before, and often resumed his old animation. But there were times according to his first biographer, G. E. Buckle, when 'he sat silent and death-like, a mummy at the feast'. He had conquered his opponents in the Commons many times, but what had it all been for? He caught a chill that developed into bronchitis and he fought with death for three weeks; but he knew intuitively that it was his final battle. 'I had rather live,' he said, 'but I am not afraid to die.' This he did at his house in Curzon Street in the spring of 1881.

24

This depression

In 1880 the queen's speech in the first parliament after Gladstone's victory noted that 'the depression which has lately been perceived in the Revenue continues without abatement'. Three years later on the same occasion Randolph Churchill, an unruly and rumbustious Tory, attacked the fact that no mention had been made 'of the marked, continued and hopeless depression of trade in this country'. The word was on everyone's lips, although no one seemed to know what it was. The House of Lords demanded a Commission on the Depression of Trade 'to ascertain what this depression is'. No neat solution was found, but the word entered the political vocabulary and has never since left it.

In the autumn of 1880 Gladstone wrote to the queen that:

> the state of Ireland is without doubt not only deplorable but menacing. Its distinctive character is not so much that of a general insecurity as that of a widespread conspiracy against property. The evils are distinct; both of them sufficiently grave. There is one most painful feature in the case, namely that the leaders of the disturbed part of the people incite them to break the law, whereas in the times of O'Connell there can be little doubt that in the midst of a strong political agitation they stoutly denounced agrarian crime and generally enforced observance of the law.

The 'Irish Question' and its *damnosa hereditas* was for Gladstone what the 'Eastern Question' had been for Disraeli, a perpetual source of mischief and anxiety. With Parnell inside parliament and the Fenians outside, what wolf should be kept from which door? The Home Rule politicians and the activists of the Land League posed a formidable threat that Gladstone only barely grasped. Between 1879 and 1880 agrarian violence and evictions increased threefold. The first man condemned for evicting tenants was called Captain Boycott, and his surname became the nature of his punishment. 'I am very anxious to see how Gladstone means to get out of this Irish mess,' Salisbury wrote. 'It looks very like a revolution. We shall have to reconquer Ireland if we mean to keep her: and is there stuff and fibre in the English constituencies – at present composed – for this? I doubt it.'

The problem of Ireland had never gone away – or was it, rather, the problem of England? There were English land-agents, there were English landowners, there were English absentee landowners, the administration in Dublin Castle was English. The truth was that the English had never gone away. So many acts had been passed, over so many years, but all of them had favoured the English.

The Land League had responded to evictions and the like with rural outrages; this inflamed the situation without remedying it. Perhaps that was its purpose. Yet Gladstone pursued a policy against 'landlordism' on the clear understanding that land reform was the panacea for most of Ireland's problems. His Land Act of 1881 enshrined the 'three Fs', fair rents, free sale and fixity of tenure; a judicial authority was established for fixing the fair rents, which cleared the air a little without changing the political weather. Joseph Chamberlain, then president of the Board of Trade, had made it clear that 'we are agreed that it is impossible to concede the present demands of the Irish party. It is therefore war to the knife between a despotism created to re-establish constitutional law and a despotism not less completely elaborated to subvert and produce anarchy as a precedent for revolutionary change.' When parliament met early in 1881 a Coercion Act was passed first before the Land Act. Coercion would consign to prison anyone suspected of violence or intimidation.

Parnell's attempt to stifle the Land Act, while at the same time vilifying Gladstone, earned him a cell in Kilmainham Prison, where he promptly assumed the role of martyr under the Irish Coercion Act. The problem seemed wholly insoluble except by underhand means. The tortuous process whereby Gladstone came to Home Rule would be worthy of Ariadne herself, but it seems likely that from his cell Parnell had offered to bring peace to Ireland on certain secret conditions. On 4 May Parnell and two others were released from prison on condition that they would support the Land Act and on the understanding that Gladstone would protect Irish tenants who had fallen behind in their rent. The Irish secretary, William Forster, promptly resigned in dismay, and Gladstone asked Lord Frederick Cavendish to take his place. Within a few hours of his arrival in Dublin Lord Cavendish was assassinated in Phoenix Park; the assassins hacked him and a companion with long surgical knives. The phoenix is the bird that is reborn in fire, and those of a mythical frame of mind might see the fate of Ireland fringed in flame.

The confusion in the cabinet was compounded in the last months of 1880 by an uprising of the Boers in the Transvaal, a territory that the British had annexed three years before. The dissension, as so often, had arisen over the question of fair or unfair taxation. An English force was caught in an ambush at the battle of Laing's Nek at the end of January 1881, followed by a thorough defeat in the following month. The small army under General Colley was either captured or killed. Gladstone, who was suffering from a head injury, took to his bed. In effect he surrendered. At a convention in Pretoria Transvaal was declared to be independent but under British 'suzerainty'. Words like that can mean little or nothing; they can also breed mischief, misunderstanding and eventually conflict. And so it proved in southern Africa.

The administration was acquiring a reputation for weakness, confirmed by the bombing of Salford army barracks in the middle of January by a group of Fenians; it was chosen because it had been the site of the execution of the 'Manchester martyrs' in 1867, when the members of the IRA were hanged for the murder of a police officer. It can be seen as one of the first 'terror bombs' in England. The 'Clerkenwell Explosion' at the end of 1867 must claim, if this is the right word, the primacy. Gladstone was now beginning to recognize the signs of ageing. He thought it could not be right that he 'should remain on the stage like a half-exhausted singer, whose notes are flat & everyone perceives it except himself'. He 'would be of no good to anyone'.

On New Year's Day, 1881, the queen entered her own misgivings:

A poor Government, Ireland in a state of total lawlessness, and war at the Cape, of a very serious nature. I feel very anxious and have no one to lean on. I feel how sadly deficient I am, and how over-sensitive and irritable, and how uncontrollable my temper is, when annoyed and hurt. But I am so overdone, so vexed, and in such distress about my country, that that must be my excuse. I will pray daily for God's help to improve.

God did not necessarily answer her prayers. Just days after the stabbings in Phoenix Park, Gladstone ordered a naval expedition to Alexandria. It was perhaps the most unlikely event of his political career, contradicting all his policies and beliefs on the blessings of non-intervention. The financial situation of Egypt was the fundamental cause. Their funds were under the dual control of the French and English, a humiliating position for Egyptian nationalists who instigated a series of small coups. In February 1882 the British government ordered the removal of a nationalist ministry, and as a result faced the wrath of anti-Western rioters. The fleet was sent in May and, since commanders abhor a vacuum, the bombardment of Alexandria began in July. It was then decided to send a military force, and the nationalist army was thoroughly defeated at Tel-el-Kebir on 13 September. The victory surprised the rest of Europe, and gave an illusion of success which the Second Boer War finally dissolved. The radicals under Gladstone's nominal leadership were appalled by the Egyptian action. 'Dizzy had never done worse than, or as bad as, this bombardment,' John Bright told Rosebery. Rosebery tried to defend the prime minister, but Bright cut him off: 'Say no more, it's damnable!' The opinion spread that Gladstone's conscience was a movable feast, settling wherever his self-interest led him.

Gladstone realized the advantages, and disadvantages, of winning what was plainly an unholy war. It was a squalid affair, conducted entirely for money, even though he had gall enough to lend it a sense of missionary purpose. But what was to be done now, with Egypt occupied by the British? 'We have done our Egyptian business' – he made it sound like going to the lavatory – 'and are an Egyptian government.' Soon enough all would be thrown in doubt by an uprising in the Sudan which caused Gladstone more damage than any other event of his life.

Disraeli's natural successor as Conservative leader in the Lords was always to be Lord Salisbury. Not that he welcomed the appointment. He told the editor of *The Times*:

> you are the first person who has come here to see me in the last few days who is not wanting something at my hands – place, or decoration, or peerage . . . Men whom I called my friends, whom I should have considered far beyond self-seeking, have come here begging for something, some for one thing, some for another, till I am sick and disgusted. The experience has been a revelation to me of the baser side of human nature.

At the election of 1880 the Liberals had gained 337 seats, with the Conservatives a distant second on 214 and the Home Rulers with a respectable 63. The size of the Liberal majority surprised all those who had not reckoned on the effects of the industrial slump and the agricultural distress. With no convenient benefit in mind, the Liberals turned to Gladstone as the harbinger of their good fortune, whereas Gladstone gave all the praise to God. It may have been piety, or determination, that obliged him to soldier on as prime minister for the next four years; for once, the phrase of soldiering is appropriate. Having attacked the Liberal grandees in his Midlothian campaign, he was obliged to include them in his cabinet for want of better; of the radicals, to whom his rhetoric appealed, only a few were chosen. Eight of the cabinet were tried and confirmed Liberals. Only Joseph Chamberlain and one or two others could be described as Radical. Chamberlain was an oddity. He sported a monocle even while he mocked 'gentlemen'. But as president of the Board of Trade he managed to guide an Employer Liability Act for industrial accidents even as his radical fervour continued to circulate around South Africa, Ireland and Egypt. These were the great causes to be addressed.

Change was also close to hand. In 1881 H. M. Hyndman formed

the Democratic Federation, which was soon known as the Social Democratic Foundation and can be described with only a little exaggeration as Marxism and soda water. But at least in a formal sense, Hyndman introduced socialism into England just at the time that land reform was being promulgated by the American reformer Henry George in *Progress and Poverty* (1879), where he announced: 'We must make land common property.' The spirit of reform spread. The Socialist League went its own way with William Morris in 1884, the year in which the Fabian Society was formed. George Gissing said of the Fabians that they were 'a class of young men distinctive of our time – well educated, fairly well bred, *but without money*'. Most of their names are now quite unknown to the public, but without their constant intercessions twentieth-century English history might have taken a different course. The transition, from old radicalism to new socialism, was as important as the change from Whig to Liberal. It can be said, for example, to have promoted and justified state intervention on a scale never previously seen.

The state had in any case slowly acquired new powers. It had come to regulate factories, mines and lodging houses. Food and drink were more closely monitored, and minimum standards for education and public housing were also promulgated. A large number of officials and administrators now entered the service of what was becoming, to all intents and purposes, a modern state. The managers of it were now professional rather than amateur. This of course meant the gradual eclipse of the principle of laissez-faire which had been in the ascendant for most of the century. The Cobden Prize essay for 1880, A. N. Cumming's 'On the Value of Political Economy to Mankind', reported: 'we have had too much laissez-faire . . . the truth of free trade is clouded over by the laissez-faire fallacy . . . we need a great deal more paternal government – that bugbear of the old economists'. A Radical programme of the time noted the growing intervention 'of the State on behalf of the weak against the strong, in the interests of labour against capital, of want and suffering against luxury and ease'.

Collective sports, with national cricket and football leagues, with public swimming baths, became the public pastime. Choral societies, and brass bands, and railway excursions, were the mood of the age in which the rules of collective conduct were paramount.

Collectivism can take many forms. In 1884 Randolph Churchill made a speech in which he declared:

> Gentlemen, we live in the age of advertisement, the age of Holloway's pills, of Colman's mustard and of Horniman's pure tea; and the policy of lavish advertisement has been so successful in commerce that the Liberal party, with its usual enterprise, has adapted it to politics. The Prime Minister [Gladstone] is the greatest living master of the art of personal political advertisement. Holloway, Colman and Horniman are nothing compared with him. Every act of his, whether it be for the purposes of health, of recreation, or of religious devotion, is spread before the eyes of every man, woman and child in the United Kingdom on large and glaring placards.

It is one of the first examples of the 'media politics' that emerged in the latter part of the nineteenth century, a tendency that might conceivably have had its origins in the granting of the vote to urban artisans in 1867.

Gladstone was not helped, however, by the group of Tories under the leadership of Randolph Churchill himself. Churchill and his cohorts combined the contempt and bad manners of youth with the vigour of unfulfilled ambition. They paraded the virtues of something known as 'Tory Democracy', but when Churchill was asked what it was he replied: 'to tell the truth I don't know myself what Tory Democracy is, but I believe it is principally opportunism. Say you are a Tory Democrat and that will do.' They were, in other words, painfully naive, and not even the name of Churchill could save them from obloquy.

They became known as the 'Fourth Party', and were eager to eject the 'Old Gang' of Conservative grandees such as Stafford Northcote, who liked nothing better than to cause a fuss. Still some bills struggled exhausted on to the Statute Book, among them a Bankruptcy Act and a Patents Act in 1883; the Corrupt and Illegal Practices Prevention Act of the same year was designed to eliminate fraud and intimidation.

There was one other piece of unfinished business to do with the franchise. It had been a slow process. Disraeli's wizardry with the Second Reform Act in 1867 was followed five years later by the

Ballot [or Secret Ballot] Act whose name is its nature. The Corrupt Practices Act of 1883 was followed, in 1884, by the Representation of the People Act which applied the same franchise to the counties as to the boroughs. The Third Reform Act, as it became known, extended the vote to agricultural labourers, thereby increasing the electorate threefold. Of course it did not imply universal suffrage; all women and 40 per cent of men were still excluded from the electoral process.

Nevertheless, a great political storm was rising over a new redistribution bill of the following year. A wider franchise was considered to be 'a good thing', but for the Conservatives it had to be guarded by a wholesale redistribution of seats to protect the Tory interest. Tory Lords and Liberal Commons fought like stags in the rutting season, yet after some discreet pressure from the queen the two sides met at a house in Arlington Street to ponder over the redistribution of seats, in which manoeuvres Salisbury was the master tactician. The franchise of some seventy-nine towns, with populations under 15,000, was swept away. The rule now was for single-member constituencies to be carved out from the larger towns and cities: 160 seats were abolished and 182 were created. Two million extra voters were enfranchised. The great metropolitan conurbations were divided into roughly equivalent constituencies and great swathes of suburban seats were grouped around them. It was considered to be hubristic. Was not a larger franchise enough? In truth very few people understood the arithmetic of the calculations. If it were done, was the common cry, let it be done quickly.

Salisbury had stood his ground. Gladstone agreed to his terms, and Salisbury's daughter recorded: 'My father's prevailing sentiment is one of complete wonder . . . we have got all and more than we demanded.' Salisbury proved himself to be an excellent negotiator, seat by seat. He managed a number of compromises, with consequences which could not have been foreseen. His philosophy was essentially a simple one. 'Whatever happens will be for the worse, and therefore it is in our interest that as little should happen as possible.' It may be placed beside another of his maxims: 'Parliament is a potent engine, and its enactments must always do something, but they very seldom do what the originators of these enactments meant.' The point was that Salisbury's conservatism was tacit or unstated. It was the Conservatism of silence as perhaps invoked in 'the silent majority'. The Redistribution of Seats Act of 1885 in fact created a flood of single-member seats which now dominated the parliamentary process. The country seat was now as potentially powerful as the town or the city seat; the miner and the agricultural labourer had now obtained the vote. As a consequence the landed proprietor lost much of his power of patronage. 'Media politics' was accompanied by the makings of a mass electorate.

An unexpected and welcome ally in nursing the new electorate was providentially found in the Primrose League, which had sprung up in 1883. The name was taken from Disraeli's supposed favourite flower (he probably preferred the orchid), and soon became the largest voluntary society in England, with half a million members by 1887. It was inclusive and heterogeneous, barring only 'atheists and enemies of the British Empire'. Members (who were known as knights, dames or associates according to the annual subscription fee they paid) swore allegiance to the sovereign, and declared their readiness to maintain 'religion . . . the estates of the realm, and the imperial ascendancy of the British Empire'. The league was largely organized by women and became notable for its tea parties, garden parties and bicycle outings. Summer fetes, held at stately homes and attended by prominent Conservative MPs, were the highlight of its social programme. MPs also contributed to the *Primrose League Gazette*, the organization's weekly newspaper. With its strong emphasis on hierarchy, honours, imperialism, archaic titles and rituals, the League inculcated in its members the values of deference, nationalism and respect for tradition. As the organization attracted a million less affluent, associate members, by the early 1890s, it might be said to have grafted the Conservative party upon the roots of the middle class and the lower middle class. It represented the growth of imperialist sentiment also, confirmed by the establishment of the Imperial Federation League in 1884. Imperialism, however, had its own disadvantages.

25

Frightful news

The domination of Egypt by Britain after the bombing of Alexandria created difficulties with that country's neighbours. An uprising in the Sudan was led by its religious leader, the Mahdi or 'Guided one', whose forces overwhelmed the British garrisons on two separate occasions towards the close of 1883. The better part of valour may lie in retreat, and the British government decided to abandon Sudan in company with the Egyptian soldiers they had recruited. It was a difficult feat to accomplish, and so Gladstone and his cabinet sent General Gordon to organize the evacuation. Gordon, however, elected to disobey orders, to stay and fight. He was a soldier of the old school – small, stubborn, and self-sufficient. The sword and the Bible were his not always reliable guides, and as a famous warrior he may not have been the best officer to administer a retreat. Evelyn Baring cautioned that 'a man who habitually consults the Prophet Isaiah when he is in a difficulty is not apt to obey the orders of anyone'.

Gladstone confessed that they had selected Gordon from 'insufficient knowledge of the man, whom we rather took on trust from the public impressions and from newspaper accounts'. Here is a new and timely account of the power of the press and the importance of 'impressions' gathered from the public. The situation would have been unthinkable thirty years before. It was accompanied by a general indifference to the imperial colonists who were treated somewhat as if they were country cousins. 'When a distinguished colonist comes to London,' E. G. Wakefield wrote in *A View of the Art of Colonisation* (1849), 'he prowls about the streets and sees sights till he is sick of doing nothing else, and then returns home disgusted with his visit to the old country. Nobody has paid him any attention because he was a colonist.'

Gordon's disobedience to his instructions from Whitehall did not bode well for his expedition to cow the Sudanese. When he arrived in Khartoum, the capital, in February 1884 he announced his intention of keeping and defending the city instead of evacuating it before ceding it to the Mahdi and his followers. When the Sudanese forces advanced and gave siege, he decided to stand and fight against all the odds. For two years he made his last stand in the city, bombarding London with plans to seize the initiative and capture or kill the Mahdi, while the feverish public demanded that a relief force be sent to rescue him from the fate he preferred to ignore. The country seethed. The cabinet could not agree on any action, and Gladstone reported in June 1884 that 'they have no fresh reason to anticipate the necessity of an expedition for the relief of General Gordon'. They could either reject his proposals and send him home, or they could accept them and send reinforcements. Neither course was chosen.

Gladstone dithered as he found the whole country turning against him. The newspaper placards were huge. When would a relief force be despatched? 'The Nile expedition was sanctioned too late,' Baring wrote in *Modern Egypt* (1908), 'and the reason it was sanctioned too late was that Mr Gladstone would not accept simple evidence of a plain fact which was patent to much less powerful intellects than his own'. On 26 January 1885, the besiegers broke into Khartoum, where General Gordon waited on the steps of the palace in his white uniform. They cut off his head and threw his body down a well. Two days later, the relief force arrived.

The outcry was immense. The queen sent an open telegram deploring the disaster. 'These news from Khartoum are frightful,' she wrote, 'and to think that all this might have been prevented and many precious lives saved by earlier action is too frightful.' The message could have been read by any postmaster, and was no doubt intended to be. The cabinet discussed resignation but came to no certain conclusions; they could not see beyond their individual careers, and resignation meant death. The G.O.M. – the Grand Old Man, as Gladstone had been called – became the M.O.G. – the Murderer of Gordon. There had been no more painful disaster for fifty years, and it did much to alienate the British public from the Liberal government. Gladstone himself was covered in anger and hysterical rebuke.

A general sense of instability prevailed. Every member seemed to think that he had been betrayed by one colleague or another over Sudan, over the budget, over Ireland, over the Coercion Bill. Gladstone confided to his wife that it had been 'a wild romance of politics with a continual succession of hair-breadth escapes and strange accidents pressing upon one another'. When in June 1885 the budget was rejected by the Commons, Gladstone took the opportunity to resign, whereupon Lord Salisbury took over as the Tory premier and remained prime minister for seven months. He had an idea. The Tories had a commanding majority in the Lords, and to act as radicals might not do them any great harm in the country. Disraeli had managed it once. So Salisbury, with the support of Gladstone, considered the possibility that the Tories were perhaps more likely to pass radical measures for Ireland. But it was no more than a chimera, and perhaps he knew as much. He was moved to comment on the nationalist proclamation that 'we are to have confidence in the Irish people'. He replied that 'confidence depends upon the people in whom you are to confide. You would not confide free representative institutions to the Hottentots, for example.'

In his short period of office, known by Chamberlain as the Ministry of Caretakers, Salisbury sent a laurel branch to the land across the sea by dropping a crimes bill and by passing a land purchase bill for Irish tenants. But it was not going to be enough. Parnell pressed Salisbury for more. He subtilized his parliamentary tactics to the point that he could effectively curtail all proceedings. His was a double game for the benefit of Ireland. In the subsequent general election of 1885 he was triumphant. The Liberals won 319 seats, the Conservatives 249 and the Parnellites 86, and the balance of power. The results pleased no one except Parnell. The Liberals were the largest party, but that was less singular than the fact that they did not possess a majority. Salisbury led a minority government, and he knew that it could not last long. 'Somehow I felt the whole thing melancholy,' Lord Rosebery wrote. 'Mr G was older, feebler, less victorious by much than in 1880, if victorious at all, and somehow one felt as if one was witnessing the close of that long & brilliant career.' Gladstone was hoarse and sat silent before the new ministers who themselves did not have very much to say. On Ireland they were bewildered and uncertain, fearing trouble to come. Salisbury explained the inactivity by claiming that by taking office they were fulfilling a duty of honour to the queen. They needed to do nothing more until the time of the general election. So he decided to carry on with the assistance of Parnell.

Gladstone mocked this Irish union with 'demoralized and dangerous Tories', but it was not long before he was considering schemes that might unite him with Parnell. Yet Gladstone was in a quandary. Whatever his thoughts about Home Rule, he could not confide them to Parnell alone; it would be unwise and dishonourable. But he could not divulge them to his party without dangerous disruptions and divisions. So he was obliged to remain silent.

In December 1885, however, the *Evening Standard* published a document that seemed on the face of it to be a plan for Home Rule composed by Gladstone himself. Many doubted its veracity, and others its validity. It became known as the 'Hawarden Kite' and it turned out to have been flown by Herbert Gladstone, Gladstone's son, as a way of diverting opposition. It included the statement that 'nothing could induce me to countenance separation, but if five-sixths of the Irish people wish to have a Parliament in Dublin, for the management of their own local affairs, I say, in the name of justice, and wisdom, let them have it'. How could he deny the Irish self-government when he had championed it for Italy and Bulgaria? It was necessary, but it was also inevitable. Gladstone would take up once more the cares of office for 'the creation of an Irish Parliament to be entrusted with the entire management of all legislative and administrative affairs, securities being taken for the representation of minorities and for an equitable partition of all Imperial charges'.

The varying reactions were immediate and profound. His multifarious enemies believed that he had betrayed England. He had betrayed Ireland. He had betrayed both. There was now no chance of cross-party allegiance, and he had painted himself into a corner. He had torn his party in half. He, or Herbert, might have claimed in defence that Gladstone simply wished to gain the initiative and assert his authority. But he continued his policy of obfuscation and silence.

While Salisbury ruled, Gladstone offered to support any Conservative attempt at a Home Rule Bill, but they were still not to be tempted into apostasy. Instead, with the tacit or complicit support of the Liberal Unionists, they adopted a new Coercion Act for Ireland. Parnell, of course, backed off and decided once more to support Gladstone. In a division of January 1886, Salisbury's Tories were defeated by a potent combination of Liberals and Irish Nationalists. Three days later Gladstone was once more in power. He was summoned to office for the third time, with the implicit declaration that he was to draw up a bill for Irish Home Rule. He declared that 'the hope and purpose of the new government in taking office is to examine carefully whether it is practicable to try some other method [than coercion] of meeting the present case of Ireland'. Everyone knew what he meant. For him, Home Rule had become inevitable.

One of his first actions was to send to anyone whom he suggested for cabinet office a proposal 'for the establishment of a legislative body to sit in Dublin, and to deal with Irish as distinguished from imperial affairs'.

But a large number of Liberal MPs, including those of the oldest faction who still liked to call themselves Whigs, abhorred the idea of minimizing the role of parliament and of national as well as imperial disintegration. They rebelled, and their defection provoked the great schism of the Liberal party.

Gladstone seemed to relish the task of drafting a Home Rule Bill over the next few months. One of his private secretaries, Sir Algernon West, wrote of him that:

> the intense enthusiasm with which he entered into the subject and the object of the moment was apt to dim, if not obliterate, the little loves and affections which crowd the life of smaller men. The execution of his great work was the one thing in his

eyes, and the instruments and tools he used were dearer to him than anything else; and the men associated with him at the moment were always greater than the men who had passed away.

A few trusted civil servants, and a few reliable members of the cabinet, superintended by Gladstone, worked in haste and silence.

When at the end of March the cabinet met to discuss his proposals, which included an Irish government with powers of taxation, Chamberlain and the Irish secretary, Sir George Trevelyan, left the room and did not come back.

On 8 April the Commons whipped itself into a fever of excitement. Every space was taken. Gladstone was greeted with cheers from his admirers, who watched him being driven to Westminster, and by many rounds of applause from his supporters in the Commons. He spoke for three and a half hours, and the ensuing debate continued for sixteen days. At the close of the debate Gladstone rose and exhorted his colleagues: 'Ireland stands at your bar, expectant, hopeful, almost suppliant . . .' He must have known that he would lose. In the event 93 Liberals voted against him and the Home Rule Bill was defeated by 343 votes against 313. There were now Liberals and Liberal Unionists, the latter taking as hard a line on the maintenance of the union as their Conservative colleagues. The Liberal Unionists and the Conservative Unionists were as one on the vital principle of the day, and it would not be long before they formed a party.

Gladstone was not in the least disheartened. He blamed vested interests for his defeat and declared not for the first time that 'the masses have been right and the classes have been wrong'. Many Liberals, however, blamed him for hitching his party to the wandering star of Irish nationalism which, as he told Rosebery, 'will control and put aside all other questions in England till it is settled'. He believed the chimera in his own brain to be the overwhelming question.

After Home Rule had been voted down, the queen was asked to dissolve parliament. Let the people decide. The ensuing election battle was fierce. Randolph Churchill derided the Home Rule proposals as 'this monstrous mixture of imbecility, extravagance and political hysterics ... the united and concentrated genius of Bedlam and Colney Hatch would strive in vain to produce a more striking tissue of absurdities'. This was the way many people understood the situation. The United Kingdom, not to mention the Liberal party itself, was to be torn apart in order to 'gratify the ambition of an old man in a hurry'. Even though he looked old, bent and infinitely wearied, he was engaged once more in a national speaking tour, as if only the balm of popular acclaim could heal his wounded spirit. He noted in his diary on a speech in Liverpool at the end of June that he had spent 'seven or eight hours of processional uproar and a speech of an hour and forty minutes to five or six thousand people ... I went in bitterness, in the heat of my spirit, but the hand of the Lord was upon me.' His biblical cadence suggests that he was beginning to adopt the role of an Old Testament prophet. The queen was dismayed. She said that it was 'grievous' to see a man of seventy-seven 'behave as he does, and lower himself to an ordinary demagogue ... if only he could be stopped'.

The electorate stopped him. 'Well, Herbert, dear old boy,' he told his son, 'we *have* had a drubbing and no mistake.' The Conservative Unionists and Liberal Unionists had a combined majority of 118 over the Gladstonians and the Irish Nationalists. At the end of the year he wrote in his diary:

> it has been a year of shock and strain. I think a year of some progress; but of greater absorption in interests which, though profoundly human, are quite off the line of an old man's direct preparation for passing the River of Death. I have not had a chance given me of creeping from this Whirlpool, for I cannot abandon a cause which is so evidently of my fellow men, and in which a particular part seems to be assigned to me.

He was, in other words, not going to give up.

To almost everyone's amazement, Gladstone seemed ready to carry on. He said that he remained at the disposal of his party and his friends while 'giving special heed to the calls of the Irish question'. It had become his great cause, the fruit of his moral being. He might be the justified sinner, identifying his existence with a greater good. His anger against the enemy became more pronounced. 'Ireland is perhaps the most conspicuous country in the world,' he said, 'where law has been on one side and justice on the other.' No government 'by perpetual coercion' could stand, when it had been erected by 'the foulest and wickedest' means 'that ever were put in action'.

Salisbury had in the interim created his Conservative cabinet, which Randolph Churchill dubbed 'Marshalls and Snelgroves' after the solid but uninspiring department store in London. Churchill was given the offices of chancellor of the Exchequer and leader of the House, from which eminence it was believed that he would catapult himself into the first office. Salisbury's duty, as he saw it, was to sit tight and ensure that Gladstone and Home Rule were no longer on the table. It was also his duty, as first minister, to keep his party whole and united. This was not necessarily an easy task, with Randolph Churchill firing off grandiose schemes, vilifying his colleagues and threatening resignation with every twist and turn of his fortunes. Eventually Salisbury decided to silence him by accepting the most recent of his letters and, much to Churchill's amazement, allowed him to resign. The menace was gone in an instant. Salisbury was now on his own, but he had a solid Unionist majority to comfort him.

Gladstone was still in good spirits, with his devotion to the cause of Irish Home Rule giving him the ballast to survive. He and Parnell had now a 'union of hearts' in the Irish cause. But there is always room for the unexpected. Parnell was fatally compromised by being cited in a divorce case; the evidence was overwhelming. John Morley, a Liberal statesman, had said once that 'Ireland would not be a difficult country to govern – were it not that all the people are intractable and all the problems insoluble.' Gladstone privately deplored 'the awful matter of Parnell', but for a time kept quiet until the public reaction forced his hand. Adultery and divorce were more heinous in Ireland even than in England, and even the most popular politician could not escape the fire. Yet it was Gladstone who threw the burning branch. He wrote to Parnell urging him to resign. Parnell refused, and almost at once Gladstone made sure that his letter reached the *Pall Mall Gazette*. As far as Parnell was concerned, the case was concluded. Gladstone had cast him into the outer darkness. Those who still voted for him were 'either rogues or fools'.

The Irish question was the most important for Salisbury's administration. Salisbury told the Lords that 'for the moment, the guardianship of the Union supersedes every other subject of political interest'. He had said that: 'The severity must come first. They must "take a licking" before conciliation would do them any good.' For that purpose he appointed his nephew, Arthur Balfour, as chief secretary for Ireland. Balfour had a languid and rather vague manner, in the style of the 1880s; with his wispy moustache and his juvenile good looks he could have been taken from the cast of a Gilbert and Sullivan operetta. But appearances can be deceptive. In Ireland he was known soon enough as 'Bloody Balfour'. He believed in the Tory policy of coercion, which he proceeded to apply without much remorse or doubt. 'There are those who talk as if Irishmen were justified in disobeying the law because the law comes to them in foreign garb,' he said. 'I see no reason why any local colour should be given to the Ten Commandments.' Balfour introduced his Crimes Act in the spring of 1887, making boycotting, intimidation and resistance to eviction a criminal offence with a minimum sentence of six months' hard labour. It was not considered to be a provisional or temporary measure; it was written in stone until such time as any future government might repeal it.

A contrary form of political action began to emerge in England. From 1886 a number of strikes took place in London. John Burns and Tom Mann, both of the Social Democratic Federation, were intent on organizing the engineers and promoting their claims for a fixed living wage. At the beginning of February 1886, the Federation also held a meeting in Trafalgar Square to demand the provision of public works for the unemployed. The crowd in the square grew in size, and on the advice of the police they moved to Hyde Park, but Pall Mall, with its clubs and emporia, lay along its route. The temptation was too great. Windows were smashed and shops looted. Burns told the waiting crowds at Hyde Park: 'We are not strong enough at the present moment to cope with armed forces, but when we give you the signal will you rise?' There were loud calls of 'Yes! Yes!' London heard the cries. The shops were boarded up and the banks were closed. Bernard Shaw put the response in context. 'They do not want revolution,' he wrote in the *Pall Mall*

Gazette. 'They want a job.' The 'unemployed' and the phenomenon of 'unemployment' reached the public vocabulary in this period.

In the autumn of the year demonstrations and parades were banned from Trafalgar Square, which had taken over from Clerkenwell Green as the centre for radical activity. A free speech demonstration took place in the Square on 13 November which became known as 'Bloody Sunday', with the police confronting the crowds. Skirmishes and scuffles occurred in Holborn and the Strand until the Life Guards cleared the Square; one hundred were injured and two were killed. It was the largest disruption of the period, though by continental standards it was relatively modest. In 1888 a group of radical agitators attending the annual Trades Union Congress at Bradford pressed for the foundation of an independent Labour party. In the same year Keir Hardie was instrumental in the establishment of the Scottish Labour party. There was no mention of socialism. That was considered too continental and redolent of revolution.

Nothing could be more paradoxical than the fact that the summer of 1887, when public discontent prevailed, marked the golden jubilee of Victoria. The little old lady insisted on wearing her bonnet (although garnished with jewels) as she drove in an open landau through the streets of London to Westminster Abbey. She was surrounded by her royal guards as well as seventeen princes, close relations from the Battenbergs to the Wittelsbachs, and innumerable imperial potentates. According to the *Illustrated London News* it was 'the grandest State ceremony of this generation; one, indeed, practically unique in the annals of modern England'. The less she had to do, and the more remote her life became from that of her subjects, the more she was celebrated.

The empire now extended to Buckingham Palace and Balmoral, where two new Indian servants took the place of John Brown. Mahomet Buksh and Abdul Karim were soon to be given the title of *munshi*, or clerk and teacher. Victoria had decided to learn Hindustani.

George Gissing's *In the Year of Jubilee* (1894) charts the temperature of the nation at this juncture, and it records a prevailing indifference over the state of the monarchy, despite an intense love of spectacle which the jubilee provoked. Gissing's characters are of

the middle class and lower middle class living in the environs of
Camberwell and Denmark Hill in south London, where the young
women are sighing for higher status and more income. It is not the
world of Anthony Trollope. It is the opposite. It is a world which
was largely taken for granted, mild grey like its atmosphere on the
borders of the great city. Gissing was a connoisseur of slovenly rooms
in these suburbs. 'The pictures were a strange medley – autotypes
of some artistic value side by side with hideous oleographs framed
in ponderous gilding.' An autotype was a photographic print popular
in the late nineteenth century; an oleograph was a photographic
print made to resemble an oil painting. On tables and chairs:

> lay scattered a multitude of papers: illustrated weeklies, journals
> of society, cheap miscellanies, penny novelettes and the like.
> At the end of the week, when new numbers came in, Ada
> Peachey passed many hours upon her sofa, reading instalments
> of a dozen serial stories, paragraphs relating to fashion, sport,
> the theatre, answers to correspondents (wherein she especially
> delighted), columns of facetiae and gossip about notorious
> people.

The children of a similar family 'talked of theatres and race-courses,
of the "new murderer" at Tussaud's, of police-news, of notorious
spendthrifts and demireps'. A demirep was a female of dubious
reputation. In a slightly more elevated household, 'on the table lay
a new volume from the circulating library – something about Evolution . . . Her aim, at present, was to become a graduate of London
University . . . to prepare herself for matriculation, which she hoped
to achieve in the coming winter . . . She talked only of the "exam",
of her chances in this or that "paper".'

The setting for the first part of the book was the great public
occasion of the year.

> She's going to the Jubilee to pick up a fancy Prince . . . These
> seats are selling for three guineas, somebody told me . . . Thank
> goodness everyone is going to see the procession or the decor-
> ations, or the illuminations, and all the rest of the nonsense . . .
> I want to go for the fun of the thing I should feel ashamed of
> myself if I ran to stare at Royalties, but it's a different thing

at night. It'll be wonderful, all the traffic stopped . . . And you know, after all, it's a historical event. In the year 3000 it will be 'set' in an examination paper, and poor wretches will get plucked because they don't know the date . . . What have I to do with the Queen? Do you wish to go? Not to see Her Majesty. I care as little about her as you do . . . I didn't think this kind of thing was in your way. I thought you were above it . . . You have heard that Nancy wants to mix with the rag-tag and bobtail tomorrow night? . . . Now I look at it this way. It's to celebrate the fiftieth year of the reign of Queen Victoria – yes but at the same time and far more, it's to celebrate the completion of fifty years of Progress. National Progress without precedent in the history of mankind.

Most people had a clear sense in which the direction of events was moving. 'Now, before the triumph of glorious Democracy . . . after all the people have got the upper hand nowadays.' The phrases of the period ring through the pages of the novel. 'Look sharp about it. Do you twig? . . . his temper was that 'orrible.' A boyfriend was a 'masher'. A fine man or woman was 'a great swell'. 'Oh what a silly you are. Go ahead! What's the latest?'

Gissing reports the nature of the Jubilee from the level of the streets: 'At Camberwell Green they mingled with a confused rush of hilarious crowds amid a clattering of cabs and omnibuses, a jingling of tram-car bells. Public houses sent forth their alcoholic odours upon the hot air.' You can hear the voices: 'A woman near her talked loudly about the procession, with special reference to a personage whom she called "Prince of Wiles".' An argument breaks out among the crowd: 'We're not going to let a boozing blackguard like you talk in that way about 'er Majesty.' The characters often break into the latest music-hall song, sometimes mixed with pathos rather than with humour.

'Ta-ta.'

26

Daddy-long-legs

The Salisbury government was held together more by Gladstone than by any other Tory grandee. As long as he pursued his dream or vision of Home Rule, and pursued it with determination, the administration would ensure that he remained locked out of office by staying in its place. That at least was the theory. Salisbury himself was still a remote figure, pessimistic or cynical according to taste, temperamentally averse to change of any kind and naturally appalled by social reform and social reformers. Yet it was his government that pushed through some legislation that seemed to Cardinal Manning to be the most radical since the 1830s.

The Local Government Act of 1888 set up popularly elected boards to run the counties and turned the cities into county boroughs. The squires and leaders of local society were at a stroke made redundant, replaced by administrators and bureaucrats who controlled everything from the police to the lunatic asylums. Thus was finally severed the link between the owners of the land and the powers of authority, even though England did not become a fully bureaucratized nation until the Local Government Act of 1894, which imposed elected local authorities for every village with over 300 inhabitants.

London had been an administrative chaos almost from the beginning of its existence, but the County Council Act, as the Local

Government Act was known, ordained that it should be administered and governed by the London County Council. The 'LCC', as it was everywhere known, became a formidable presence in the capital, beyond the range of government departments and national policy-making. It reflected the contemporaneous taste for municipal socialism in the provision of public baths and wash-houses, parks and allotments and public libraries. It was also responsible for the swathe of 'council houses' and 'council flats' that was erected in all parts of the metropolis, and thus changed the texture of life in London for the next hundred years.

The first chairman of the LCC was a Liberal. In some respects Lord Rosebery resembled Chamberlain, although he was not himself an advocate of municipal socialism. But he was in advance of his colleagues on social matters, and was part of a new generation approaching the characteristic sentiments of the early twentieth century. He waged war against slum landlords and declared that London was 'not a unit, but a unity'. His social radicalism was based on the principle of 'getting things done'. He was what was known as a 'coming man', but no one could have known how far he would go.

The perils of the times, in an age of bewildering change, seemed infinite. To reach adulthood was itself an achievement. No one, except a few of the highly favoured, was ever completely well. It was a highly nervous age in which even the huntsmen, in Anthony Trollope's *The Duke's Children* (1880), discuss

> the perils from outsiders, the perils from new-fangled preju-
> dices, the perils from more modern sports, the perils from
> over-cultivation, the perils from extended population, the perils
> from increasing railroads, the perils from literary ignorances,
> the perils from intruding cads, the perils from indifferent
> magnates . . . Everything is going wrong. Perhaps the same
> thing may be remarked in other pursuits. Farmers are generally
> on the verge of ruin. Trade is always bad. The Church is in
> danger. The House of Lords isn't worth a dozen years purchase.
> The throne totters.

It is in part a satirical account of the prejudices of a narrow section of society, but it does disclose the high anxiety, the fear and trembling, that afflicted the supposedly more robust and resourceful members of the Victorian public. Wilkie Collins described 'these days of invidious nervous exhaustion and subtly-spreading nervous malady'. John Morley stated: 'all is in doubt, hesitation and shivering expectancy'. In 1888 another writer, Elizabeth Chapman, wrote of 'a general revolt against authority in all departments of life which is the note of an unsettled, transitional, above all democratic age'. A journalist, T. H. Escott, had perceived 'old lines of demarcation being obliterated, revered idols being destroyed'. The seismic shift, the change of society, was felt before being properly understood. Among many it provoked nervous exhaustion, tremulousness and fear.

That is why one of the defining images of the age was the railway crash. The epitome of the new world, of time and speed, of ever-increasing momentum, was also the image of death and disaster. In Turner's *Rain, Steam and Speed* a hare is seen running before the Great Western Railway train as it crosses the viaduct at Maidenhead. Contemporaries would have known or recalled the old proverb that to see a hare running before you portends calamity. 'We have seen a hare. We shall have no luck.' The steam engine itself became a metaphor. There was journalistic talk of a 'new improved patent, steam-engine way of passing a bill through the Lords'. The new entrepreneur measured, according to John Stuart Mill, 'the merit of all things by their tendency to increase the number of steam-engines and make human beings as good as machines'. Yet it seemed that in the game of life it was necessary to train the mind and body 'like a steam-engine to be turned to any kind of work'. There was great admiration for the power of machines and for the people who maintained them. An early historian of the cotton trade, Alfred Wadsworth, wrote 'that the new machinery spread quickly in England because the whole community was interested in it'. Carlyle denounced the new respect for 'steam intellect'. The references are everywhere.

But there was another Victorian way of looking at the world. Even as George Stephenson surveyed the railway world of 1850, the power and extent of which had changed the English landscape for ever, he told friends in Newcastle: 'as I look back upon these stupendous undertakings it seems as though we have realised the fabled power of the magician's wand'. For many this was a world of fairy magic, of sudden transformations, of spells and enchantments; the mundane had grown marvellous. The burning down of parliament in October 1834 had been described at the time as 'a perfect fairy scene'. When Fanny Kemble visited the newly excavated Edge Hill tunnel she felt 'as if no fairy tale was ever half so wonderful'.

To recognize endless novelty and change demanded some resort to images of magic and enchantment, as if only by such means could it be understood. The lighting of the streets by gas, the building of the tunnel under the Thames, the factory machinery that could replace the work of a thousand hands, all were seen in terms of wonder. The age of electricity had become a rival to gas, too, although it was said by Arthur Young in his *Travels* of the 1880s that the new electrical telegraphs created 'a universal circulation of intelligence, which in England transmits the least vibration of alarm from one end of the Kingdom to the other'. Nothing seemed very far from chaos.

In her diary for 1882 Beatrice Webb pronounced the times as exemplifying the spirit of benevolence, where 'social questions are the vital questions of today: they take the place of religion'. Social reports and surveys now lay beside sentimental novels and sensation novels and, although most of the world passed by, some stopped to consider the ragged child or the lean and drunken mother. Charles Booth's *Life and Labour of the People in London* (1889–1903) provided a less idiosyncratic account than Henry Mayhew's *London Labour and the London Poor*, published forty years earlier, when individuals, rather than classes, were the object of study. The anecdote had given way to the statistic, representing a sea change in the representation of social history. Booth surmised, for example, that 30 per cent of the London population were in poverty, of whom about a third were 'very poor'. 'Very poor' in the 1880s meant one small degree above destitution. But he believed that if poverty was definable it might also be curable; he also intimated the conclusion that the government itself must incur the responsibility for removing the areas of 'occasional labourers, street sellers, loafers, criminals and semi-criminals', painted black, from the maps of London.

But he did not necessarily blame 'the poor' themselves for their

condition, which had been the standard response of earlier generations. They might be 'hard working' and 'struggling' but the
economic conditions of the period were fatally opposed to them. It
had nothing to do with laziness or drink, but the factory gates had
been closed against them. There was a growing recognition that the
poor were not an original or permanent part of society, and that
the conditions of many of them might be remedied. It was generally believed that the improvements of the nineteenth century, from
water provision to sanitation, had in fact ameliorated the worst
conditions. The poorer parts of town were known for 'glitter and
gas', with the chop-houses, the gin shops, the cook shops and the
burlesque shows together with the ballad singers, the organ grinders,
the travelling bands and the stentorian tones of the costermonger.

But a glance at one of Charles Booth's 'poverty maps' quickly
disabused any false optimism. Black marked 'lowest class, vicious,
semi-criminal', while dark blue registered 'very poor, casual. Chronic
want'. Even the people of the stratum above, coloured light blue,
were obliged to live on 18 shillings to a guinea a week. The East
End was the heart of darkness, over a third of its population living
below 'the margin of poverty'. Conditions may indeed have improved
since the 1840s and 1850s, but the very poor *felt* more deprived in
comparison with others. An economist, J. A. Hobson, wrote in 1891:
'the rate of improvement in the condition of the poor is not quick
enough to stem the current of popular discontent'.

If the problem was not one of individual fecklessness, or even
of bad luck, the blame was laid upon that increasingly popular term,
'the system', with a new recognition of, or concern for, 'unemployment'. Trafalgar Square became the centre of meetings and
demonstrations on behalf of this new element in the state. A
Mansion House fund for the relief of the unemployed was established, but it could do ameliorative work only. The 'unemployed'
became the shadow world to be regarded with trepidation. No one
knew what to do with them. There was an even lower category, 'the
residuum', which spread contagion everywhere. But the unemployed
remained at the forefront of public consciousness.

The plight of the 'labouring poor' or the 'deserving poor' was
not yet to be alleviated by collective means; there were some 700
philanthropic societies that worked in a generally uncoordinated

and ad hoc manner. Certain streets, certain districts, even certain individuals became the focus of concern in a society which had no 'safety net' to catch those who had fallen out of the system. Instead there had been in place since 1869 the Charity Organisation Society which Henry James believed to be 'so characteristic a feature of English civilization'. It was as practical and pragmatic as any other English society, but it did try to bring together the multifarious charities which were in danger of bumping into each other in the street.

Lothair, the titular hero of Disraeli's novel published in 1870, remarked that 'it seems to me that pauperism is not an affair so much of wages as of dwellings. If the working classes were properly lodged, at their present rate of wages, they would be richer. They would be healthier and happier at the same cost.' The same insight had occurred to other enthusiasts for 'model dwellings', some of whom were rich philanthropists who began a course of slum clearance and new building still to be found in English cities.

The queen travelled to the East End in the spring of 1887 to open the 'People's Palace', which was a concert room, a library and a singing gallery all in one. She heard what she called 'a horrid noise (quite new to the Queen's ears) "booing" she believes it is called'. Salisbury told her, in way of an apology, that 'London contains a much larger number of the worst kind of rough than any other great town in the island . . . probably Socialists and the worst Irish.'

The East End of London had also become in the popular mind a place of mystery and of darkness. It was 'the abyss'; it was 'darkest London' and 'the nether world'. It was the city of dreadful night. It came to represent the essence of Victorian London and has been seen as such in a thousand television dramas. In the summer and autumn of 1888, however, it became the object of more particular attention. Two industrial disputes made a powerful impression, as if they were heavy with the weight of the future like dark clouds prophesying rain. The girls who worked in the Bryant and May match factory in Bow walked out of their jobs when two girls were dismissed for insubordination at the beginning of July 1888. The girls went on strike, and achieved some very prominent support. Their dismissal drew attention to their working conditions in a positively unhealthy environment. White phosphorus used in the manufacture of lucifer matches, for example, provoked a debilitating condition known as 'phossy jaw'. They were the pale and unhealthy slaves of the industrial process. Seven hundred of them walked out of their place of employment, the Fairfield Works, and the factory was closed. They were vigilant for their cause, and their first protest march was to Fleet Street rather than to Westminster. They gained the support of journalists, MPs and the members of the various socialist parties that operated in the capital.

A prominent unionist, Tom Mann, wrote later:

> the girls were soon organised into a trade union. Their case was conducted with great skill. A club was formed, which was used as an educational and social centre, and a spirit of hopefulness characterised the proceedings. The girls won. They had a stimulating effect upon other sections of workers, some of whom were also showing signs of intelligent dissatisfaction.

Most of the girls were of Irish ancestry and their shared culture was of great effect in the East End. And it was a defining moment for English trade unionism itself, and set the terms for a great dockers' strike in the East End of the following year. Engels described the activity of the match-girls as 'the light jostle needed for the entire avalanche to move', soon to be demonstrated.

Meanwhile a shadow had fallen over the East End which claimed the nation's attention. The brief reign of Jack the Ripper, from August to November of that year, aroused popular terror on an unprecedented scale. It was as if all the presumed darkness of the area had become concentrated in this elusive anonymous figure, and the fact that he was not captured led to the fugitive suspicion that the neighbourhood itself had killed the women. It was a catalyst for the nervous worn-out excitement that characterized the period.

Strike followed strike in the context of popular socialism and the demand for 'democracy' of some form or other. By 1887 the various unions in the cotton trade came together. A strike for a nine-hour day among engineering workers was successful even without the intervention of trade unions. In the same year Ben Tillett, a working docker, formed the Tea Operatives and General Labourers Union at Tilbury Docks. These working men became central in the emergence of what became known as the 'new unionism'. It was designed to organize those trades which the old unionism had neglected or forgotten, under the principles of a legal minimum wage and a compulsory eight-hour day. The old unions, known as 'the aristocracy of labour', had ignored the poorer workers, the sweated labour, the unskilled workmen. John Burns and Tom Mann of the Social Democratic Foundation accused their own union, the Amalgamated Society of Engineers, of 'selfish and snobbish desertion' of the poor workers. In that year, too, the Labour Electoral Association urged: 'working men must form themselves . . . as centres to organise the people'.

In 1888 the Miners' Federation was formed. When Will Thorne started the National Union of Gas Workers and General Labourers Union at Beckton Gas Works in the early summer of 1889, he recalled that 'the news spread like wildfire in the public houses, factories and works in Canning Town, Barking, East and West Ham, everyone was talking about the union'. To their surprise their demand for an eight-hour day was conceded without a struggle. The Great London Dock Strike took place in the same summer, when the dockers walked out for the sake of the 'dockers' tanner'; they were part of the wave of action which had begun with the match-girls in the year before. Ben Tillett had organized the poorer-paid employees of the dock, and when he called them out on strike they were soon joined by workers on both sides of the Thames. Their demands were a wage of sixpence per hour and a minimum of four hours for those unloading cargo.

They were one of the most exploited groups of workers, who relied upon casual labour and an inhumane system of crowding around the dock gates to see who would be hired. Ben Tillett stated: 'we are driven into a shed, iron-barred from end to end, outside of which a foreman or contractor walks up and down with the air of a dealer in a cattle market, picking and choosing from a crowd of men, who, in their eagerness to obtain employment, trample each other underfoot, and where like beasts they fight for the chances of a day's work'.

It was one of the last aspects of an earlier era to remain beside the Thames. But it was soon removed. For the first time since 1797, the Port of London was closed. Cardinal Manning, and the

Salvation Army, became involved in the negotiation; Manning became a familiar figure in incidents of social dispute and G. K. Chesterton gave a memorable description of him resembling 'a ghost clad in flames' as the people in Kensington High Street dropped to their knees before him. We may presume that some of the kneeling crowd were the Irish poor, hoping for some measure of wage reform to alleviate their bitter poverty. The crisis was settled in September, with the unanticipated emergence of the dockers' union as a force for the new century. Once again the conscience of the middle class was awakened and £18,000 was contributed to the union funds. And then the strike was finally won when £30,000 was sent by the labour unions of Australia to their comrades in need.

Engels wrote in December 1889: 'the people are throwing themselves into the job in quite a different way, are leading far more colossal masses into the fight, are shaking society much more deeply, are putting forward much more far-reaching demands . . .' The *Annual Register* put it differently: 'For . . . almost the first time the representatives of the skilled workmen showed a readiness to throw in their lot with, and to support, unskilled labour . . .' This was essentially the face of new unionism. It was designed to assist those who obtained no help hitherto, and it combined an economic with a political message. The old union leaders dressed like the employers; they wore expensive overcoats, gold watch-chains and tall hats. The new unionists simply looked like workmen. It was said that it was easy to break one stick, but not fifty sticks in a bundle. And the cry went up, from Liverpool to London: 'Unionism for all!' The movement even affected life at Westminster. A group of seventy radical Liberals voted together on social issues and even elected their own whip. It was in the spring of 1890 that the first 'May Day' demonstration was held in England, with 'dense crowds as far as the eye could see marching up with music and banners, over a hundred thousand . . .' That, at least, is what Engels saw. This was the period, too, when Joseph Chamberlain recommended a united Unionist front against the threat of socialism as well as of Home Rule for Ireland, and by the time of the next general election he had formed a coalition under the Conservative leadership of Lord Salisbury.

The Gladstonian Liberals had compounded the confusion by

concocting a group of radical measures that was known as the
Newcastle Programme. They included an act for Employers' Liability
for Accidents, Home Rule for Ireland, triennial parliaments, a local
veto on the sale of alcohol, the disestablishment of the Church in
Ireland and Scotland, as well as various other assorted measures
which were designed to increase the Liberal vote for the election
of 1892. It was significant only in the sense that, despite Gladstone's
sense of righteous mission on the subject, Home Rule was only one
among other issues. It might seem, in fact, that the whole subject
had been forgotten by everyone except the immediate protagonists.
In a speech at the Mansion House Salisbury announced that he
had never seen Ireland so peaceful. The vigour and calculation of
Balfour's rule as Irish secretary impressed all, at least all those who
were ready to be impressed, as a great token of imperium in action.
The majority of the English, as usual, treated the whole business
with indifference.

In the 1880s and 1890s, too, the advent of socialist tracts and
pamphlets marked a change of political tone. Engels connected the
new dispensation to the gradual collapse of Britain's imperial power.
He insisted that the loss of Britain's industrial and trade monopoly,
so much a feature of the 1850s and 1860s, was 'the secret of the
present sudden emergence of a socialist movement here'. This was
by no means the principal or only explanation, but it was part of
the transvaluation of all values that characterized the years before
the First World War. The poorly paid or the unemployed were really
no longer viewed as a threat; they were being socialized, and those
who had become attached to a union were also becoming part of
the community. That may be one of the reasons why the middle
class furnished the new unions with funds; it may have been done
out of pity and charity but there may also have been an iota of
self-defence. This covert form of self-preservation was one of the
elements in what sceptics called 'clap-trap morality'.

In one of Gladstone's speeches an observer noted that 'his head
looked like a white eagle perched on a black stump'. He refused all
talk of resignation. He did, however, decide to migrate to the South
of France for a holiday. When Gladstone returned from Biarritz
in February 1892, his ministers were eager for news of his intentions, but he 'talked almost entirely of trees'. His ministers were

now impatient for him to be gone, as soon as possible, but he remained aloof. Rosebery said that he was in a condition of 'righteous wrath' and was still resolved to lead his party into the election of that summer. There were many, including the queen, who were astonished by the spectacle of a man in his eighties wishing to administer the nation and the empire – and this was for the fourth time. At the beginning of June 1892, Gladstone refused to take up the cause of legal eight-hour days because he was too busy with Irish affairs. Yet all was not well. He was being driven through the streets of Chester a few days later, when an old woman hurled a piece of hard gingerbread at him; it struck his left eye, and from the time of that blow his eyesight began to diminish. The election campaign was about to begin.

He did not win the election of July 1892, but he did not lose it; he gained the largest number of seats but did not command a majority without the support of the Irish Nationalists. Salisbury refused to resign and ensconced himself in the Commons waiting for a parliamentary vote of no confidence to eject him. In the middle of August he eventually received his quietus, and Gladstone returned with a minority government which he regarded as 'too small'. Victoria was in any case horrified at the result. She declared that the incoming government would be filled by 'greedy place-makers who are republicans at heart'. She could not yet bring herself to 'send at once for that dreadful old man . . . whom she can neither respect nor trust'. Of course she had to resign herself to the situation and to the constitutional proprieties, but she disliked him. She thought the relationship between them was a sham, and that he was a sham.

Nevertheless, his inner will, combined with external victory, seemed to revive him a little. A contemporary journalist, Henry Lucy, noted that 'in appearance he looks younger rather than older as the weeks pass. His voice has gained in richness and vigour, while his mind seems to have grown in activity and resource.' In effect Gladstone ran a government with Irish Nationalist support, a most difficult position to maintain. Yet this late bloom could not last. He grew angry and on more than one occasion threatened to resign.

Lord Acton described him as 'wild, violent, inaccurate, sophistical, evidently governed by resentment'.

One of the more significant results of the election of 1892 was the election of Keir Hardie to the seat of West Ham South. He stood as an independent but he soon became involved in the creation of an Independent Labour party which would stand apart from Liberals as well as Conservatives. He had already created a surprise at Westminster by arriving in a cloth cap and tweed jacket, and his clothes perhaps marked his sense of vocation. The inaugural conference of the Independent Labour party was opened on 14 January 1893. Its purpose was to create a party majority on the necessity of labour reform, which meant they were more intent upon alliance with the trade unions than with the myriad socialist parties which had really become talking shops.

Gladstone was still in the thrall of Home Rule. He had given his assent to the Newcastle Programme but his heart was not in it. Chamberlain pressed him for the details of the imminent Home Rule Bill: 'How long are you going to allow ducks and drakes to be made by the Irish party of all your British legislation?' Gladstone introduced his Second Home Rule Bill in February 1893. He and Chamberlain were now pitted against each other as in some tableau of age and relative youth. 'I say that never in the history of the world', Chamberlain declaimed, 'has a risk so tremendous been encountered with such a light hearted indifference to its possible results'. The Second Reading was carried for Gladstone, with the help of the Irish Nationalists, by a margin of forty-three votes. The members of the Stock Exchange marched in formation and burnt the bill in front of the Guildhall. The bill slowly went forward, but not without great bitterness and recrimination. A fist fight broke out on the floor of the Commons, much to the horror of the public gallery. The bill was already expiring but the House of Lords killed it by a majority of ten to one. There was no public outcry. English indifference effectively put the bill out of its misery, and Gladstone was heard to mutter: 'I can do no more for Ireland.' It seemed that he could do no more for anyone, and there were constant whispers that it was really time for him to go.

The final moment, for him, came when he delivered a letter of resignation to the queen at the beginning of March 1894. She accepted it in good spirits and seemed not at all perturbed by his resignation. 'Mr Gladstone has gone out,' she told the archbishop of Canterbury with a laugh. 'Disappeared all in a moment.' He was deeply upset by her lack of concern and of any attempt at commiseration or congratulation. He had stumbled a weary way and had become only the queen's donkey. At a melancholy and lachrymose cabinet meeting, whose tears he did not appreciate, he gave his colleagues notice of his decision. Without the captain of so many years the ship seemed to drift. No one seemed capable of command.

On 15 March Lord Rosebery travelled to Windsor and kissed hands with the queen. She liked him well enough, even though she had no time for the party he represented. Rosebery had the advantage of being, in the queen's eyes, the least objectionable Liberal. She said only that 'she does not object to Liberal measures which are not revolutionary & she does not think it possible that Lord Rosebery will destroy well-tried, valued and necessary institutions . . .' Rosebery was the Whig non plus ultra, regarding Conservatives as vulgar and other less aristocratic Liberals with only distant affection. He had also gained attention and admiration in the country for his handling of a long and complicated coal strike. So he became the chosen one. He had shown much promise in the cabinet but now, at the pinnacle of his career, he spoke with an uncertain voice. He was not sure what to do. His predecessor had so dominated the party that serious questions of policy had not been debated. Yet he was witty, and articulate, with an enviable ability to turn a phrase. In demeanour and dress he was of the 1890s. He was not Gladstone or Disraeli, or even Salisbury; he was not solid or necessarily reliable. He even looked flirtatious, and there were strange rumours about his relationship with his private secretary, the older son of the marquess of Queensberry.

When out of temper, he was irritable and impatient. The *Spectator* described him as a 'butterfly Prime Minister, ephemeral in his essence'. In fact the Rosebery administration lasted for only fifteen months. The burden of his office proved too much for him, and he made the unpardonable blunder of stating that 'the majority of Members of Parliament elected from England proper are hostile to Home Rule'. So the last eighteen months of frantic negotiation and political planning had in effect been for nothing. The new prime minister had no fire. He had no fight in his belly. He never really knew what he wanted, and the irritation he felt against other people was in reality irritation with himself. The cabinet was always in a state of indecision and disarray; he was now considered both too aloof and too flippant. He informed the queen, in the formal third person, that 'Lord Rosebery in the meantime is shut up in a House almost unanimously opposed to his ministry and, for all political purposes, might as well be in the Tower of London.' He could not have succeeded because he was oversensitive, resentful of opposition and inclined to paranoia. 'He is', Rosebery told the queen, 'as Prime Minister more unfortunately situated than any man who ever held that high office.' He could not sleep, and remained awake for nights at a time brooding and worrying. 'I am unfit for human society,' he told a colleague. This was not a good sign for a prime minister. Yet his sense of duty forced him forward.

On 19 February he summoned the cabinet and read out a prepared statement: 'I cannot call to mind a single instance in which any individual in the party or the Ministry has spoken even casually in my defence within the walls of Parliament . . . The difficulties to which I allude have been hard to bear, indeed I could not undertake to face another session like the last.' It was a strangely maudlin report from any prime minister, and confirmed his unfitness to govern. He was all bluster and self-pity. He was persuaded not to resign, for the time being, but a week later his body capitulated where his mind did not. He collapsed with influenza and the debilitating effect of the illness stayed with him. He said that he understood why people in public life committed suicide. On 21 June the secretary for War, Henry Campbell-Bannerman, was censured by the Commons over a shortage of cordite, and on the following day Rosebery persuaded his cabinet to resign en bloc as a matter of confidence. A few hours later the queen sent a message inviting Salisbury to form another administration.

At the subsequent election in July 1895 a Liberal majority of forty-three was transformed into a Unionist majority of 152, which must be recorded as one of the most considerable reversals in English political history. Rosebery and his colleagues felt nothing but relief. When Chamberlain joined the new government, the pact between the Conservative and Liberal Unionists was sealed, and a formidable coalition emerged. Rosebery admitted that the Liberal party had become 'all legs and wings, a daddy-long-legs fluttering among a thousand flames'. He always did have a talent for phrase-making. He had also invented a phrase, 'the clean slate', which might have been intended for Salisbury himself, who remained as prime minister for the next seven years.

27

Lost illusions

In the trials of Oscar Wilde in 1895, the heart of the late Victorian world was stripped bare. Wilde's Irishness set him apart in England, and ensured that he looked from a distance at the customs and conventions of his adopted country. Of all people he recognized the follies of Victorian society and the vices it concealed. *The Importance of Being Earnest* (1895) was so funny that English audiences forgot – at least for the duration of the play – that they were laughing at every institution and value they held sacred. But of course it is a mistake to reveal to your contemporaries that their ideals are illusions and their understanding all vanity.

Like many of his generation, as a young man he donned the cloak of aestheticism, commonly known then as 'art for art's sake'. Art was to be divorced from morality and, as a result, had no social or political content to convey. Since Britain was going through another phase of its long industrial revolution (some historians have referred to it as the second industrial revolution), in which objects were made by machines rather than by craftsmen or artists, the divorce or disengagement from social circumstances might have been predicted.

After achieving fame, in the 1880s, as the popular spokesman of the Aesthetic Movement, Wilde became the unofficial leader of the Decadent movement of the 1890s, which can roughly be dated from the publication of the first magazine version of *The Picture of Dorian Gray* in June 1890. He has been identified therefore as a writer of the *fin de siècle*, who delighted in artifice and parody, celebrated style and pastiche, and mocked the values of previous decades. In Wilde's time the end of Victorianism (and all it had come to represent) was in sight but nothing had taken its place. It was a time of spiritual, moral, social and artistic chaos, when even the most formidable conviction began to crumble, slide and eventually dissolve. It could be said that he lived in a worn-out society, theatrical in its art, theatrical in its life, theatrical even in its piety. The meanings of the nineteenth century had been hollowed out. Everything seemed to be on display, like the halls of Swan and Edgar's. Wilde knew by heart the lesson of Balzac's villainous hero Vautrin: 'There are no longer any laws, merely conventions: nothing but form'. He responded to the theatricality around him by turning his conversation into an art, his personality into a symbol, and his life into a mystery play.

The *fin de siècle* of the nineteenth century was in part represented by the *Yellow Book* which flourished in the 1890s as the leading journal for aestheticism, decadence and symbolism – a trinity of terror for those who maintained a solid mid-Victorian sensibility. In March 1894 its first editorial announced that the aim of the magazine was 'to depart as far as may be from the bad old traditions of periodical literature . . . It will be charming, it will be daring, it will be distinguished.' It was not greeted with any great enthusiasm, and was discounted by some as a pile of 'hysterical and nonsensical matter'. Its first art editor was Aubrey Beardsley, and he has been considered the progenitor of the startling yellow covers which were already associated with the more flamboyant French fiction of the era. Among the contributors in its short life were Max Beerbohm, Henry James, H. G. Wells and William Butler Yeats. It represented the gay death of the nineteenth century.

It might be presumed that Oscar Wilde was on the list of the *Yellow Book*'s contributors, but in fact he never took part in the enterprise and professed to despise it. Nevertheless Wilde remained, and still remains, the defining figure of the last years of the century, simply because he turned its values on their head. He was the 'Other' of late Victorian culture, dominated as it was by jingoism, John

Bullism, Pooterism and black and white Puritan morality. He was enamoured of 'beauty' and 'art' rather than 'truth' and 'reality', which he regarded as second-rate, and baneful fictions.

We could easily extend the list of binary opposites further – Wilde was queer, rather than straight, and through his openly homosexual lifestyle he boldly challenged middle-class domesticity. He was concerned with surfaces rather than depths, the body more than the soul, and aesthetics instead of ethics. He was 'serious' about everything Victorians regarded as 'trivial', and vice versa. His addictions to ambiguity, indeterminacy and inconsistency were no less subversive. Rather than excavating and expressing a single, monolithic self, in his life and writings he effortlessly invented and discarded identities, referring to insincerity as 'a method by which we can multiply our personalities'. His mercurial genius naturally expressed itself in the drama and the dialogue, in the paradox and in the parable, genres and forms in which he could perform a number of his selves and present a debate between doctrines rather than a single view. It is no surprise, then, that many commentators portray Wilde as a confirmed Nietzschean engaged in a furious war against Victorian morality, and in the transvaluation of late nineteenth-century middle-class Christian values.

Wilde was so much the master of his period that he could effortlessly adopt all its disguises and convey all its effects. He delighted in trying out and testing the limits of each literary form. He brought hilarious and provocative comedy back to the English stage, from which it had been exiled for many years. He invented the prose poem in English, and was a pioneer of symbolic drama. He was also one of the first authors to write a 'French' novel, *Dorian Gray* being French in subject and style, if not in language. That novel was fiercely satirical of English middle-class mores. The 1890 magazine version attracted outraged and outrageous reviews, in a large part because of its homoerotic overtones, which would have been even more pronounced had the publisher not censored Wilde's radical and explicit typescript. Yet the outcry did not stop Wilde adding new chapters to the story the following year, for its publication as a novel in book format, in which he characterizes England as 'the native land of the hypocrite', and the English as a race that 'balance stupidity by wealth, and vice by hypocrisy'.

In 1891 Wilde also composed his political essay 'The Soul of Man under Socialism' for the *Fortnightly Review*, in which he attacked the 'stupidity, and hypocrisy, and Philistinism' that pervaded English culture. Wilde rails against English public opinion, which, he says, exercises a 'tyranny' over art, politics and 'people's private lives' through the press.

'The Soul of Man' expresses Wilde's commitment to an anarchistic form of socialism. Its attacks on hypocrisy were however directly related to Parnell, and at the journalists and MPs who hounded him out of politics after his relationship with the married Kitty O'Shea became public knowledge at the end of 1890. Wilde's criticism is a token of his staunch support for Irish Home Rule and of his essential Irishness – something recognized by everyone who knew him well, from the English Alfred Douglas to his compatriots Shaw and Yeats. Wilde's Irishness allowed him to understand, and satirize, the English of the late Victorian period, because he was an insider-outsider, a man who shared their language but did not share the values and vision that informed and were propagated by that language.

On this language issue Wilde made some interesting pronouncements. 'French by sympathy,' he described himself in the winter of 1891, 'I am Irish by race, and the English have condemned me to speak the language of Shakespeare.' During his American lecture tour of 1882 he also declared: 'I do not know anything more wonderful, or characteristic of the Celtic genius than the quick artistic spirit in which we adapted ourselves to the English tongue. The Saxon took our lands and left them desolate. We took their language and added new beauty to it.' So English–Irish relations offer a political context for Wilde's paradoxes and his lush prose poetry. He was a colonial subject inverting and embellishing the language of the ruler, exposing its hidden prejudices and doublespeak. It is no coincidence that Wilde (like Samuel Beckett) wrote in French as well as English, and that in the early Nineties he contemplated becoming a French citizen when his French-language play *Salomé* was banned by the English censor from the London stage. 'I am not English,' he told a journalist at this time. 'I am Irish – which is quite another thing' – a pointed comment at a time when Ireland was nominally part of a 'United Kingdom'.

Even as an Irishman Wilde set out to defy late Victorian stereo-
types. On the English stage, and in the press, the Irish were often
presented as feckless, drunken, sentimental and dirty 'Paddies'.
Wilde, like Parnell, always presented himself as calm, urbane, impec-
cably dressed; he also discarded his native brogue soon after
matriculating at Oxford. Wilde's philosophical and historical
outlook, which was rigorously intellectual and scientific rather than
emotional and intuitive, can also be seen in this context. 'England
is the land of intellectual fogs,' he told Shaw, and he felt it was
Celts like themselves who, contrary to popular prejudice, were best
placed, because of their disinterested minds, to blow those fogs away.

In his 1895 appearances at the Old Bailey, Wilde seemed to
revel in presenting himself as the subversive 'Other' of the late
Victorian bourgeoisie, challenging, from the witness box, the 'seven
deadly virtues' so dear to their heart. Rather than being diligent, he
boasted in the courtroom of frittering his time away in restaurants.
Where the bourgeoisie were thrifty, he proudly announced he spent
£50 a week at the Savoy. Instead of associating with respectable
members of his own class he socialized and slept with young men
from the gutter. In preference to a noble life guided by notions of
duty and responsibility, he declared that pleasure was the only thing
one should live for, and self-realization the primary aim of existence.
The fact that Wilde realized himself through homosexual rather
than heterosexual relationships naturally made things much worse.
At his first trial, the Pooterish men who comprised the jury – there
was a stockbroker, a bank manager and several 'gentlemen' from
Clapton – must have thought that the seven deadly sins were being
paraded before them.

Wilde's eventual conviction for 'gross indecency' caused a moral
panic in late Victorian England. The nature of his offence was
abhorrent to the respectable; moreover the trials had suggested that
Wilde was a leading figure in a vast network of gentlemen who not
only loved other men, but preferred men from the lowest orders.
Only six years before Wilde's trial, in what became known as the
'Cleveland Street Scandal', a brothel of boys working for the Post
Office was revealed as the trysting place for members of the aristocracy, and even of the royal family. It was as if the hierarchies of
power and society had been subverted and made rotten to the extent

that aristocracy itself might be seen as a gigantic confidence trick. It was one of the first occasions, outside the enchanted realm of fiction, when the private lives of gentlemen, the staple of society, were investigated and found to be false and hollow.

These scandals and trials also represented, albeit in subliminal fashion, the overturning of sexual roles which the 'New Woman' and the loosening of the matrimonial laws pointed towards. It is no coincidence perhaps that Wilde himself was a supporter of the 'New Woman' to such an extent that soon after his conviction *Punch* announced: 'THE END OF THE NEW WOMAN – The crash has come at last.' The New Woman was the representative of advanced and adventurous ideas not unconnected in the public mind with decadent sexuality. The emancipated woman, as she was also known, challenged the conventional ideas of marriage, respectability, and legal and educational inequality. Cartoons in the satirical press were filled with images of women riding bicycles or wearing bloomers or sporting wire-framed spectacles; they were considered mannish or part of a 'shrieking sisterhood'. Many wanted careers rather than continuous childbirth. It is interesting to note then that it is women who are the true protagonists of Wilde's dramas, from Salome and Mrs Erlynne to Lady Bracknell and the Courtesan-Saint. They are witty and unafraid. They control the worlds Wilde portrays. They manipulate and dominate the men. So much has been said of Victorian patriarchy and the subjugation of women that it might be interesting to inquire into Victorian matriarchy and the subjugation of men. Females were the lawgivers of society – from the mansions of the West End depicted by Wilde to the back alleys of the East End – and their power was all the greater for being largely unacknowledged.

28

The terrible childbed

Salisbury's cabinet prompted the great war at the end of the century. The Cape of Good Hope, known familiarly as the Cape Colony, was a British colony whose inhabitants were largely Afrikaners. The Orange Free State and Transvaal were neighbouring republics established by the Boers, the first Dutch-speaking settlers in southern Africa, in their quest for self-defence and self-definition. This led directly to the First Boer War, in which the British were soundly defeated and were forced to accept Boer control of the Transvaal under British suzerainty.

The discovery of diamonds made the Cape Colony rich under its prime minister, Cecil Rhodes, but then, fifteen years later, gold similarly transformed the fortunes of the Transvaal. English settlers rushed in with so great a thirst for the gold stuff that they soon formed the majority of the adult white population of what was still a Boer republic under the presidency of Paul Kruger. The English, known as 'Uitlanders', were obliged to pay 90 per cent of the taxation. They were susceptible to hastily imposed taxes, but they had no role in the government and no equality with the Dutch. So two hostile white tribes lived in the midst of a much greater black population. The tensions grew apace as the mining of gold became more and more successful.

This was the scene when plans were formed to invade the

Transvaal and seize it for Britain. Leander Starr Jameson led a band of mercenaries into the territory in order to foment a rebellion among the Uitlanders and the rest of the British settlers. Five hundred men, with six Maxim guns, had invaded Kruger's republic in order to overawe his people of the rifle and the Book. News of them reached the Boer government of Pretoria within a day, and they were still nowhere near their destination of Johannesburg, approximately 34 miles away. The raid, at the very end of 1895, was a complete failure from the start. Jameson and the other conspirators were surrounded and captured by the Boers who dispatched them to London for condign punishment. On the news of the defeat the Kaiser sent a telegraph to Kruger, congratulating him on his victory. The British press reacted furiously against this German slight, with headlines like 'Get Ready', 'England Yet' and 'Hands Off'. The music hall refrain of the period was 'We're not going to stand it'. It served the German purpose, however, to whip up its own public opinion in response and to justify an increase in its naval power.

The Jameson Raid was financed and authorized by the magnate who had made a fortune out of diamonds, Alfred Beit, and by Cecil Rhodes himself. Yet it was generally believed to have been despatched at the instigation of the British politicians at Whitehall, particularly that of the colonial secretary Joseph Chamberlain. Salisbury, as prime minister, might have been suspected of knowledge if not of complicity, but it seems that he was only vaguely aware of the plans for the raid.

The lack of support for the British raid, which had all the characteristics of an invasion, and the universal obloquy which it attracted, emphasized what Arthur Balfour and others called 'our national isolation'. The isolation had suddenly become more intense. Kruger and the Transvaal were the heroes of the hour, and the British were condemned as mischievous, incompetent, weak and, more precisely, conspiratorial. It seems probable that, after all, Chamberlain and the Whitehall gang had been in close contact with Rhodes and Beit. They were everywhere denounced.

These were the conditions leading to the Second Boer War, which was waged from 1899 to 1902. Some were ready and eager for battle. Jan Smuts, for the Boers, declared: 'our *volk* throughout

South Africa must be baptized with the baptism of blood and fire before they can be admitted among the great peoples of the world'. Kruger realized from the logistics of the Jameson Raid that his military forces, largely volunteer, were not altogether adequate. So he set about creating a viable military presence in the Transvaal. He was buying arms from Germany and elsewhere; Chamberlain informed Salisbury that Transvaal 'had a stock of artillery, rifles and ammunitions of all sorts enough to furnish a European army'. The English were more conciliatory, and had appointed Alfred Milner as high commissioner for Southern Africa and governor of Cape Colony as a more sympathetic figure than his predecessor. Nevertheless, he was an English imperialist who considered himself to be part of 'a superior race' who ought to govern southern Africa.

His aspiration was strengthened with a petition of 21,000 British subjects, the Uitlanders, asking their home country to intervene in the tortuous affairs of Southern Africa. Milner and Kruger met at Bloemfontein to attempt to settle their differences. Milner's military secretary wrote: 'the conference goes on its rather weary way . . . meanwhile our Uitlanders will lose patience and upset the game'. Kruger, as rugged as an African hippo, remained obdurate; Milner believed that he would have to put more effort into 'screwing' Kruger. This was Chamberlain's word. He might draw inspiration from events elsewhere. The English military had recently enjoyed some success. At the beginning of September 1898, Kitchener destroyed the Mahdist army at Omdurman; two days later the British and Egyptian flags were flying over the palace at Khartoum, which for Kitchener at least was some revenge for the death of Gordon. The victory was followed by a successful confrontation with the French in Fashoda, where the French sailed away to avoid a fight. All this put some spirit into the military authorities, and they were growing increasingly impatient with the negotiations between Kruger and Milner. It was said that Kruger would 'bluff up to the cannon's mouth', a phrase of Cecil Rhodes; at the same time the typewriters of the English press were growing hotter in their calls for action.

The death of Gladstone, in 1898, intervened. He had returned to Hawarden Castle to entertain the colonial premiers who had come to England for the Diamond Jubilee. In his old age his major preoccupation had changed from Irish Home Rule to the prevalence of jingoism which swept the press and the music halls and filtered into streets with the orange peel and the bunting. He had never really been interested in imperial attitudes. He was suffering from facial neuralgia which soon metamorphosed into cancer. He died on 19 May 1898, at the age of eighty-eight, and in the spirit of the new age was taken on a London Underground train before his funeral at Westminster Abbey. For some he represented one of the last obstacles to the steady progress of the state, and for others one of the last memorials to a once resplendent nation.

The time had come to call Kruger's bluff. He had organized a 'foreign brigade', among them troops from Ireland, Africa, Germany and Prussia. In retaliation the British brought on the forces of the empire: Australians, Canadians, New Zealanders and Indians. Milner wrote in a memo that 'the case for intervention is overwhelming'. The British had become the white helots, 'Uitlanders' who had no rights. British regiments were despatched from Bombay and Calcutta, and Smuts sent a secret memorandum in which he stated: 'South Africa stands on the eve of a frightful blood-bath.' They would either be a defeated and hated race, the pariahs of Africa, or the sturdy founders of a United South Africa. Salisbury wrote in a memorandum: 'I feel convinced that the Dutch leaders in Transvaal, Orange State, and Cape Colony, have got an understanding together and have agreed to make a long pull and a strong pull to restore Dutch supremacy in South Africa. If that is their view, war must come; and we had better take it at a time when we are not quarrelling with anyone else.' He had written two months before: 'I see before us the necessity for considerable military efforts – and all for people whom we despise, and for territory which will bring no profit and no power to England.' For Salisbury it was largely a question of prestige rather than power. It was to determine the identity of what was known as 'Boss' in southern Africa.

The Boers delivered an ultimatum, but on the same day the British troopships made landfall at Durban before they moved inwards into Africa. War was declared on 11 October. The Boers, without uniforms and with precious little leadership, had the initial advantage. They knew the country; they knew the places for ambush and retreat which were denied to the 20,000 British and the 10,000

Indians who followed them. The Boers were also very good shots, accustomed as they were to hunting the springbok and the wildebeest. The same readiness and proficiency were not evident on the British side. The physical condition of the volunteers was appalling: when 12,000 came forward in Manchester, 8,000 were rejected as unfit. The most significant failure of the British in South Africa was the poor quality of the troops, at a time when army standards had been deliberately lowered. It was considered shameful and revived the 'Condition of England' question in the more direct terms. A correspondent in London wrote to Milner: 'People walked along speaking in whispers and muttering, while ever echoed round the shrill and awful cry of "Terrible Reverse of British Troops".'

As garrison commander Robert Baden-Powell, aware of the large number of Boer forces, set up his headquarters at Mafeking to facilitate the arrival of British ships and to deter the population from aiding the Boers. At the beginning of October 1899 it was surrounded and shelled. No one then believed that 'the Siege of Mafeking' would endure 217 days. There was bad news elsewhere. 'Mournful Monday' was followed by 'Black Week' at the beginning of December which claimed 3,000 lives. An epidemic of enteric fever was meanwhile killing fifty soldiers a day who occupied Bloemfontein. Nowhere was safe. 'What's them 'ere blokes on that bloomin' hill?' The English tents were on the slopes of Mount Impati, in the British colony of Natal, and now the Boers had crept out of cover to remove them. The English repulsed them, but at the cost of fifty-one dead and more than two hundred wounded. It was the beginning of a war played out to the accompaniment of drums, mountain guns, the Boers' 'Long Toms', rumbling carts, 94-pounders, the snorts and whinnies of the horses and pack mules.

When the English retreated into Ladysmith from the mountain it was reported that 'they came back slowly, tired and disheartened and sick with useless losses'. The siege of Ladysmith then began. It was not a little war. Mafeking, Ladysmith and Kimberley were for that period the arsenals of empire in an otherwise hostile terrain. It was a great war fought from an impossibly long distance. It riveted the attention of the world, much of which was wishing and hoping for the demise of the British empire. In the ensuing battle of

Ladysmith the British were driven back into the town, with many dead or injured, where they endured a siege of 118 days.

The bad news of Ladysmith, and subsequent defeats, shook the nation as it had never been shaken before. Victoria had said: 'we are not interested in the possibilities of defeat', but even her confidence was modified. 'No news today,' she wrote in her journal, 'only lists of casualties.' The public reaction was more severe. Something had gone terribly wrong. The prime minister, Salisbury, seemed sanguine and almost listless, feeling that from the start he had been outwitted by 'Milner and his Jingo supporters'. Yet he saw the point. Any defeat would cast a shadow over the country's imperial supremacy, to which, of all recent prime ministers, he most fervently subscribed.

As for the public, it was a calamitous awakening. The editor of *The Times* commented at a later date that 'our national life and thought never were the same again'. The veil of British mastery had been torn, revealing blunder after blunder. To the rest of the world it revealed that the British were as bad they had always believed them to be – blustering and hypocritical and essentially incompetent. One commentator, Karl Pearson, noted: 'the spirits of one and all, whatever their political party or their opinions might be, were depressed in a manner probably never experienced by those of our countrymen now living'. A diplomat, Cecil Spring-Rice, remarked in December 1899: 'One lies alone with a living and growing fear staring one in the face.'

One phrase, 'splendid isolation', had been taken up and circulated, but it steadily grew out of favour; it suggested an absence of policy rather than any positive contribution. In a speech to his Birmingham constituents in the spring of 1898 Chamberlain declared:

> Now the first point I want to impress on you is this – it is the crux of the situation – since the Crimean war, nearly fifty years ago, the policy of this country has been a policy of strict isolation. We have had no allies. I am afraid we have had no friends ... All the powerful states of Europe have made alliances, and as long as we keep outside these alliances – as long as we are envied by all and suspected by all – and as long as we have

interests which at one time or another conflict with the interests of all – we are liable to be confronted at any moment with a combination of Great Powers . . . We stand alone.

It was one of the most important speeches on foreign policy made by an English politician. He spoke the truth as he knew it, and it did not need an omniscient observer to realize that, to the rest of the world, England was in danger of being overwhelmed. Her isolation, and the insignificance of her relatively small army, were well known. The dissensions among her politicians and the dangers of her street-bred masses were discussed, and the perils of her navy in defending the British empire throughout the world were obvious. Germany was the virile European state, and Russia was making its way to China and to India. There was hostility between the United Kingdom and the United States, and a civil servant in Pretoria remarked: 'the fall of England shall be the crown of the end of the nineteenth century'.

At the end of January 1900 the two houses of parliament met for their last session in the reign of Victoria, who had been on the throne for sixty-six years. This was the parliamentary session in which Chamberlain, as colonial secretary, was almost universally reviled for the failures of the Boer War. He held back his head, and his eyes were closed. It was said that he looked like a soldier under fire.

Yet the mood of war soon changed. As in other recent British wars, initial defeats were succeeded by a national revival. Only a few days after Chamberlain's speech on foreign policy, Field Marshal Roberts swept on to Bloemfontein, and the advance continued to Pretoria and Johannesburg. Within forty-eight hours came the relief of Kimberley and the liberation of Ladysmith; on 17 May 1900, Mafeking, besieged by the Boers, was relieved. Baden-Powell had held out for 217 days. It was perhaps the greatest victory of the war, and Baden-Powell became a national hero. The church bells rang, the schools closed for the afternoon, and the people danced around makeshift bonfires. Much of the anxiety, which had been the most deleterious of all responses to the war, was lifted. It was a time of 'dancing, jumping, screaming in a delirium of unrestrained joy'. The effect was tremendous, greater than the celebrations of 1918 or 1945. London went 'maficking'.

No one then knew or cared about the camps that Kitchener had constructed for the women and children of the enemy, but they soon became known as 'concentration camps', and were reviled as a new horror of war. Even the new leader of the Liberal party, Henry Campbell-Bannerman, spoke out against 'methods of barbarism', a phrase which delivered a huge shock to the members of his own party and to interested observers who believed that the imperial path was the way to glory.

The guerrilla war itself, at which the Boers were supremely adept, ended at the Peace of Vereeniging in May 1902. The independence of the Orange Free State and the Transvaal were ceded to the British, but only with the promise of self-government and, in the immediate future, with copious funds for the restoration of the Boer farms, withered in the conflict, together with a general reconstruction and restocking of the two republics. England had been humiliated, its army had been ill-equipped and ill-trained, its policy of civilian incarceration had been condemned by the major nations. It was a terrible childbed for the twentieth century.

Salisbury had said: 'you may roughly divide the nations of the world as the living and the dying'. The living nations had enlisted science and industry, railways and weapons, that increased their range and power. The dying nations – well, they were obvious. Spain, China, Portugal, Turkey, were apparently all in the throes of senescence. Surely that could not be said of England?

In 1896 Lord Northcliffe established the *Daily Mail*; it boasted of a readership from Brighton to Newcastle, and at the same time there was some loss of interest in local or what were known as 'provincial' affairs. This was also the year when Marconi sailed to England to persuade the General Post Office to take his wireless. The first cinema picture was shown in the West End, and cars were no longer enjoined to bear a red flag in front of them. The world was winning through despite the best endeavours of its statesmen.

In the halls of the old establishment, however, gloom and monotony prevailed as the wheels of administration and empire seemed to grind slowly. Joseph Chamberlain, the most vigorous member of the cabinet, complained: 'There is little backbone in politics and the great majority are prepared to swallow anything and to stick to the machine.' The queen herself was perceptibly slowing down, and a visitor reported 'intense monotony' at court, where there was 'a curious charm to our beloved Sovereign in doing the same things on the same day year after year'. The prime minister, the marquess of Salisbury, was becoming more distant from his colleagues and from the affairs of state. He was generally aloof, unwilling to engage with his cabinet or to propose new policies. He had always supposed that new policies were bad policies and his generally weary and negative view of the war added to the twilight world. One backbencher noted: 'of all futile expedients, party meetings always struck me as being the most futile'. The voice of the Church was muted in the land. Lord Rosebery, stricken with inanition and a sense of failure, had finally abandoned the leadership of the Liberal party in the autumn of 1896. The parliamentary sessions of the next two years were recognized to be the dullest of a dull series. It culminated in the general election of 1900, known as the 'khaki election', based upon the ongoing Boer War. Lord Salisbury and his allies, the Liberal Unionists, returned once more to government.

Not everything revolved around politics. There was activity of every kind in other areas of national life. There was a vogue for the 'new' in implicit deference to the new century just below the horizon. There was the 'new woman' and the 'new humour', the 'new hedonism' and 'l'art nouveau'. The 'new' was embraced in every aspect of life, in the department stores, in bikes and bloomers. The Kodak camera appeared in 1888. Families became smaller; more space and time and money were left for popular luxuries and distractions from the working day such as theatres, racecourses, pleasure gardens, fairs and music halls. The first motor-car race was held between London and Brighton on Motor-Car Day of 14 November 1896. Seventeen out of thirty cars finished the course. The defining phrase of the period was 'we moderns', perhaps given an ironical emphasis, but it was a genuine reaction to the coming death of the century.

Three months before the Second, or Diamond, Jubilee of June 1897 the queen had travelled to the Riviera to meet the members of her multifarious family. But there was a problem. The familiar royal household refused to let the *munshi*, her Indian servants, dine with them. In one of those acts of fury of which she alone was capable, the queen swept everything off her desk in a gesture of anger; ink-pots, papers, pens and blotting papers were hurled to the ground. It was evidence of the violent fury that she was never able to shake off. The *munshi* went with her to the South of France.

Envoi

The queen returned from a visit to Ireland in the spring of 1900, and on her return to Windsor Castle she was greeted by the boys of Eton College singing patriotic songs. She leaned out of the window, repeating many times 'Thank you, thank you.' The boys were astonished to see one of her Indian servants handing her a whisky and water. On two separate days she reviewed from her carriage a march past from two of the regiments returning from South Africa. The stress of the war had burdened her, and those who knew her best noticed the change. Her lady in waiting, Lady Churchill, remarked to her maid that the queen looked to be 'a dying woman'. But Lady Churchill died first, of a heart attack, and the queen lamented: 'that it should happen here is too sad' and 'the loss to me is not to be told'. On New Year's day she had the strength to visit soldiers in a convalescents' home. They were some of the last of her subjects she ever saw. In the middle of January 1901 she seemed confused, and on the following day took to her bed. At about four in the evening the queen's doctor, Sir James Reid, announced to the family that she was slowly sinking into death. A little while later she opened her eyes and whispered: 'Sir James, I am very ill.' She was later heard to murmur, according to her daughter, Princess Louise: 'Oh I don't want to die yet. There are several things I want to arrange.' But there was no time left. There was nothing more to arrange. She died at 6.30 that evening, and with her died an era.

Bibliography

Adelman, P., *Victorian Radicalism: the Middle-class Experience, 1830–1914* (London, 1984)

——, *Peel and the Conservative Party, 1830–1850* (London, 1989)

——, *Gladstone, Disraeli and Later Victorian Politics* (London, 1997)

Altick, R. D., *The English Common Reader: a Social History of the Mass Reading Public, 1800–1900* (Chicago, 1957)

Anderson, O., *A Liberal State at War: English Politics and Economics during the Crimean War* (London, 1967)

Annear, R., *The Man Who Lost Himself: the Unbelievable Story of the Tichborne Claimant* (London, 2003)

Anthony, Barry, *The King's Jester* (London, 2010)

Aspinall, A., *Lord Brougham and the Whig Party* (Manchester, 1939)

Barbary, J., *The Crimean War* (London, 1972)

Baron, X. (ed.), *London 1066–1914: Literary Sources & Documents* (vols 2 & 3) (Robertsbridge, 1997)

Batho, E. C., Dobrée, B., & Chapman, G. (ed.), *The Victorians and After, 1830–1914* (London, 1938)

Battiscombe, G., *Shaftesbury: a Biography of the Seventh Earl 1801–1885* (London, 1974)

Beales, D. E. D., *From Castlereagh to Gladstone* (London, 1971)

Bédarida, F., *A Social History of England, 1851–1975* (London, 1979)

Bell, H. C. F., *Lord Palmerston* (London, 1936)

Bentley, M., *Politics without Democracy: Great Britain, 1815–1914: Perception and Preoccupation in British Government* (Oxford, 1985)

Best, G., *Mid-Victorian Britain, 1851–1875* (London, 1971)

Bew, J., *Castlereagh: Enlightenment, War and Tyranny* (London, 2011)

Biagini, E. F., *Liberty, Retrenchment and Reform: Popular Liberalism in the Age of Gladstone, 1860–1880* (Cambridge, 1992)

Black, J., *The English Press 1621–1861* (Stroud, 2001)

Blake, R., *Disraeli* (Oxford, 1969)

Bloom, C., *Victoria's Madmen: Revolution and Alienation* (Basingstoke, 2013)

Boase, T. S. R., *English Art, 1800–1870* (Oxford, 1959)

Bodelsen, C. A., *Studies in Mid-Victorian Imperialism* (London, 1960)

Bradford, S., *Disraeli* (London, 1982)

Brady, A., *William Huskisson and Liberal Reform: an Essay on the Changes in Economic Policy in the Twenties of the Nineteenth Century* (London, 1928)

Briggs, A., *Victorian People: a Reassessment of Persons and Themes, 1851–67* (Chicago, 1955)

——, *The Age of Improvement 1783–1867* (London, 1959)

——, *Victorian Cities* (London, 1963)

——, *Iron Bridge to Crystal Palace: Impact and Images of the Industrial Revolution* (London, 1979)

——, *Victorian Things* (London, 1988)

Brock, W. R., *Lord Liverpool and Liberal Toryism, 1820 to 1827* (Cambridge, 1941)

Brown, D., *Palmerston: a Biography* (New Haven, 2010)

Buckley, J. H., *The Victorian Temper: a Study in Literary Culture* (London, 1952)

Burn, W. L., *The Age of Equipoise: a Study of the Mid-Victorian Generation* (London, 1964)

Bury, J. P. T. (ed.), *The New Cambridge Modern History.* Volume X, *The Zenith of European Power: 1830–70* (Cambridge, 1974)

Buxton, S., *Finance and Politics: an Historical Study, 1783–1885* (London, 1888)

Cecil, H. P., & Blake, R., *Salisbury: the Man and His Policies* (Basingstoke, 1987)

Chamberlain, M. E., *Lord Aberdeen: a Political Biography* (London, 1983)

Chambers, J. D., & Mingay, G. E., *The Agricultural Revolution, 1750–1880* (London, 1966)

Checkland, S. G., *The Rise of Industrial Society in England, 1815–1885* (London, 1964)

Clapham, J. H., *An Economic History of Modern Britain* (3 vols) (Cambridge, 1926–1938)

Clark, J. C. D., *From Restoration to Reform: the British Isles 1660–1832* (London, 2014)

Coleman, B. I., *Conservatism and the Conservative Party in Nineteenth-Century Britain* (London, 1988)

Colley, L., *Britons: Forging the Nation, 1707–1837* (London, 1994)

——, *Captives: Britain, Empire and the World, 1600–1850* (London, 2002)

Collins, M., *The Likes of Us: a Biography of the White Working Class* (London, 2004)

Colloms, B., *Victorian Visionaries* (London, 1982)

Conacher, J. B., *The Aberdeen Coalition, 1852–1855: a Study in Mid-Nineteenth-Century Party Politics* (London, 1968)

——, *The Peelites and the Party System, 1846–52* (Newton Abbot, 1972)

Conrad, P., *The Victorian Treasure-House* (London, 1973)

Cookson, J. E., *Lord Liverpool's Administration: the Crucial Years 1815–1822* (Edinburgh, 1975)

Cowling, M., *1867: Disraeli, Gladstone and Revolution: the Passing of the Second Reform Bill* (Cambridge, 1967)

Crawley, C. W. (ed.), *The New Cambridge Modern History*: Volume 9, *War and Peace in an Age of Upheaval, 1793–1830* (Cambridge, 1965)

Crosby, T. L., *The Two Mr Gladstones: a Study in Psychology and History* (New Haven, 1997)

David, S., *Prince of Pleasure: the Prince of Wales and the Making of the Regency* (London, 1998)

Davidoff, L., & Hall, C., *Family Fortunes: Men and Women of the English Middle Class 1780–1850* (London, 1987)

Davis, H. W. C., *The Age of Grey and Peel* (Oxford, 1964)

De-la-Noy, M., *George IV* (Stroud, 1998)

Deane, P., *The First Industrial Revolution* (Cambridge, 1965)

Deary, T., *Dangerous Days on the Victorian Railways: a History of the Terrors and the Torments, the Dirt, Diseases and Deaths Suffered by Our Ancestors* (London, 2014)

Dodds, J. W., *The Age of Paradox: a Biography of England, 1841–1851* (London, 1953)

Egremont, M., *Balfour: a Life of Arthur James Balfour* (London, 1980)

Emerson, R. W., *English Traits* (London, 1906)

Englander, D., *Poverty and Poor Law Reform in Britain: from Chadwick to Booth, 1834–1914* (London, 1998)

Ensor, R. C. K., *England, 1870–1914* (Oxford, 1936)

Evans, E. J., *The Forging of the Modern State: Early Industrial Britain 1783–1870* (London, 1983)

——, *Britain before the Reform Act: Politics and Society, 1815–1832* (London, 1989)

Eyck, F., *The Prince Consort: a Political Biography* (London, 1959)

Feiling, K., *The Second Tory Party, 1714–1832* (London, 1938)

Feuchtwanger, E. J., *Disraeli, Democracy and the Tory Party: Conservative Leadership and Organization after the Second Reform Bill* (Oxford, 1968)

——, *Democracy and Empire: Britain, 1865–1914* (London, 1985)

Flanders, J., *Consuming Passions: Leisure and Pleasure in Victorian Britain* (London, 2006)

Fontane, T., *Journeys to England in Victoria's Early Days* (London, 1939)

Ford, B., *Victorian Britain* (Cambridge, 1992)

Francis, M., & Morrow, J., *A History of English Political Thought in the Nineteenth Century* (London, 1994)

Freeman, M. J., *Railways and the Victorian Imagination* (New Haven, 1999)

——, *Victorians and the Prehistoric: Tracks to a Lost World* (New Haven, 2004)

Garfield, S., *The Last Journey of William Huskisson* (London, 2002)

Garvin, J. L., & Amery, J., *The Life of Joseph Chamberlain* (6 vols) (London, 1932–1969)

Gash, N., *Politics in the Age of Peel: a Study in the Technique of Parliamentary Representation, 1830–1850* (London, 1953)

——, *Mr. Secretary Peel: the Life of Sir Robert Peel to 1830* (London, 1961)

——, *Reaction and Reconstruction in English Politics, 1832–1852* (Oxford, 1964)

——, *Sir Robert Peel: the Life of Sir Robert Peel after 1830* (London, 1972)

——, *Aristocracy and People: Britain, 1815–1865* (London, 1979)

——, *Lord Liverpool: the Life and Political Career of Robert Banks Jenkinson, Second Earl of Liverpool, 1770–1828* (London, 1984)

Gilbert, A. D., *Religion and Society in Industrial England: Church, Chapel and Social Change, 1740–1914* (London, 1976)

Gillespie, F. E., *Labour and Politics in England, 1850–1867* (London, 1966)

Gleadle, K., *British Women in the Nineteenth Century* (Basingstoke, 2001)

Goodway, D., *London Chartism, 1838–1848* (Cambridge, 1982)

Guedalla, P., *The Queen and Mr. Gladstone* (London, 1933)

Guedalla, P. (ed.), *Gladstone and Palmerston: Being the Correspondence of Lord Palmerston with Mr. Gladstone, 1851–1865* (London, 1928)

Gunn, S., *The Public Culture of the Victorian Middle Class: Ritual and Authority and the English Industrial City, 1840–1914* (Manchester, 2000)

Halévy, E., *A History of the English People in the Nineteenth Century* (6 vols) (London, 1949–52)

Hall, C., McClelland, K., & Rendall, J., *Defining the Victorian Nation: Class, Race, Gender and the British Reform Act of 1867* (Cambridge, 2000)

Hamer, D. A., *Liberal Politics in the Age of Gladstone and Rosebery: a Study in Leadership and Policy* (Oxford, 1972)

Hamilton, J., *London Lights: the Minds that Moved the City that Shook the World, 1805–51* (London, 2007)

Hammond, J. L., & Hammond, B. B., *The Age of the Chartists, 1832–1854: a Study of Discontent* (London, 1930)

Hanham, H. J., *Elections and Party Management: Politics in the Time of Disraeli and Gladstone* (London, 1959)

——, *The Nineteenth-Century Constitution 1815–1914: Documents and Commentary* (London, 1969)

Harris, J., *Private Lives, Public Spirit: a Social History of Britain 1870–1914* (Oxford, 1993)

Harrison, J. F. C., *The Early Victorians, 1832–1851* (London, 1971)

——, *Late Victorian Britain, 1870–1901* (London, 1990)

Hay, W. A., *The Whig Revival, 1808–1830* (Basingstoke, 2005)

Hayes, P. M., *The Nineteenth Century, 1814–80* (London, 1975)

Heffer, S., *High Minds: the Victorians and the Birth of Modern Britain* (London, 2013)

Hewitt, M., *An Age of Equipoise?: Reassessing Mid-Victorian Britain* (Aldershot, 2000)

Heyck, T. W., *The Transformation of Intellectual Life in Victorian England* (London, 1982)

Hibbert, C., *George IV* (London, 1976)

——, *The Great Indian Mutiny 1857* (London, 1978)

——, *Victoria* (London, 1979)

Hill, R., *Toryism and the People, 1832–1846* (London, 1929)

Hilton, B., *Corn, Cash, Commerce: the Economic Policies of the Tory Governments 1815–1830* (Oxford, 1977)

——, *The Age of Atonement: the Influence of Evangelicalism on Social and Economic Thought, 1795–1865* (Oxford, 1988)

Himmelfarb, G., *Poverty and Compassion: the Moral Imagination of the Late Victorians* (New York, 1991)

——, *The Spirit of the Age: Victorian Essays* (New Haven, 2007)

Hinde, W., *George Canning* (London, 1973)

——, *Castlereagh* (London, 1981)

Hobsbawm, E. J., *The Age of Revolution, 1789–1848* (New York, 1962)

——, *Industry and Empire: an Economic History of Britain since 1750* (London, 1968)

——, *The Age of Capital, 1848–1875* (London, 1975)

Hollis, P., *Pressure from Without in Early Victorian England* (London, 1974)

Hone, J. A., *For the Cause of Truth: Radicalism in London 1796–1821* (Oxford, 1982)

Hoppen, K. T., *The Mid-Victorian Generation, 1846–1886* (Oxford, 1998)

Houghton, W. E., *The Victorian Frame of Mind, 1830–1870* (New Haven, 1957)

Hurd, D., & Young, E., *Disraeli, or the Two Lives* (London, 2013)

Iremonger, L., *Lord Aberdeen: a Biography of the Fourth Earl of Aberdeen, K.G., K.T., Prime Minister 1852–1855* (London, 1978)

James, R. R., *Rosebery: a Biography of Archibald Philip, Fifth Earl of Rosebery* (London, 1963)

Jay, R., *Joseph Chamberlain: a Political Study* (Oxford, 1981)

Jenkins, R., *Gladstone* (London, 1995)

Jenkins, T. A., *The Liberal Ascendancy, 1830–1886* (Basingstoke, 1994)

——, *Parliament, Party and Politics in Victorian Britain* (Manchester, 1996)

Jenkins, T. A., *Disraeli and Victorian Conservatism* (Basingstoke, 1996)

Jones, W. D., *Lord Derby and Victorian Conservatism* (Oxford, 1956)

Jupp, P., *Lord Grenville, 1759–1834* (Oxford, 1985)

Kitson Clark, G. S. R., *Peel and the Conservative Party: a Study in Party Politics 1832–1841* (London, 1964)

——, *The Making of Victorian England* (London, 1965)

——, *An Expanding Society: Britain 1830–1900* (Cambridge, 1967)

Klingender, F. D., *Art and the Industrial Revolution* (London, 1947)

Landes, D. S., *The Unbound Prometheus: Technological Change and Industrial Development in Western Europe from 1750 to the Present* (Cambridge, 1969)

Leonard, R. L., *The Great Rivalry: Disraeli and Gladstone* (London, 2013)

Longford, E., *Victoria R.I.* (London, 1964)

——, *Wellington* (London, 1992)

Lynd, H. M., *England in the Eighteen-Eighties: Toward a Social Basis for Freedom* (London, 1945)

MacDonagh, O., *Early Victorian Government, 1830–1870* (London, 1977)

Mackay, R. F., *Balfour, Intellectual Statesman* (Oxford, 1985)

MacLeod, C., *Heroes of Invention: Technology, Liberalism and British Identity, 1750–1914* (Cambridge, 2007)

Magnus, P., *Gladstone: a Biography* (London, 1954)

Mandler, P., *Aristocratic Government in the Age of Reform: Whigs and Liberals 1830–1852* (Oxford, 1990)

Marriott, J. A. R., *England since Waterloo* (London, 1913)

Marsden, G., *Victorian Values: Personalities and Perspectives in Nineteenth-Century Society* (London, 1990)

Martin, K., *The Triumph of Lord Palmerston: a Study of Public Opinion in England before the Crimean War* (London, 1963)

McWilliam, R., *The Tichborne Claimant* (London, 2006)

Mitchell, L. G., *Lord Melbourne, 1779–1848* (Oxford, 1997)

Moneypenny, W. F., & Buckle, G. E., *The Life of Benjamin Disraeli, Earl of Beaconsfield* (6 vols) (London, 1910–1920)

Murphy, P. T., *Shooting Victoria: Madness, Mayhem, and the Rebirth of the British Monarchy* (London, 2012)

Newsome, D., *The Victorian World Picture: Perceptions and Introspections in an Age of Change* (London, 1997)

O'Brien, C. C., *Parnell and His Party, 1880–90* (Oxford, 1957)

O'Gorman, F., *The Emergence of the British Two-Party System 1760–1832* (London, 1982)

O'Kell, R., *Disraeli: the Romance of Politics* (Toronto, 2013)

Pakenham, T., *The Boer War* (London, 1979)

Palliser, D. M., Clark, P., & Daunton, M. J., *The Cambridge Urban History of Britain* (3 vols) (Cambridge, 2000)

Parry, J. P., *Democracy and Religion: Gladstone and the Liberal Party, 1867–1875* (Cambridge, 1986)

——, *The Rise and Fall of Liberal Government in Victorian Britain* (New Haven, 1993)

Parsons, G., Moore, J. R., & Wolffe, J. (eds), *Religion in Victorian Britain* (5 vols) (Manchester, 1988–1997)

Paterson, M., *A Brief History of Life in Victorian Britain: a Social History of Queen Victoria's Reign* (London, 2008)

Pearce, E., *Reform! The Fight for the 1832 Reform Act* (London, 2003)

Pelling, H., *The Origins of the Labour Party, 1880–1900* (Oxford, 1966)

——, *Popular Politics and Society in Late Victorian Britain: Essays* (London, 1968)

Perkin, H. J., *Origins of Modern English Society* (London, 1985)

Plumb, J. H., *The First Four Georges* (London, 1966)

Pollard, A., *The Victorians* (London, 1970)

Porter, A. N., & Louis, W. R., *The Oxford History of the British Empire.* Volume 3: *The Nineteenth Century* (Oxford, 1999)

Prest, J. M., *Lord John Russell* (London, 1972)

Ramsay, A. A. W., *Sir Robert Peel* (London, 1928)

Read, D., *Cobden and Bright: a Victorian Political Partnership* (London, 1967)

——, *Peel and the Victorians* (Oxford, 1987)

Reay, B., *The Last Rising of the Agricultural Labourers: Rural Life and Protest in Nineteenth-Century England* (Oxford, 1990)

Robbins, K., *John Bright* (London, 1979)

Roberts, A., *Salisbury: Victorian Titan* (London, 1999)

Robson, R. (ed.), *Ideas and Institutions of Victorian Britain: Essays in Honour of George Kitson Clark* (London, 1967)

Royle, E., *Chartism* (London, 1980)

Royle, T., *The Kitchener Enigma* (London, 1985)

——, *Crimea: the Great Crimean War 1854–1856* (London, 1999)

Russell, C. A., *Science and Social Change: 1700–1900* (Basingstoke, 1983)

Saintsbury, G. E. B., *The Earl of Derby* (London, 1892)

Schivelbusch, W., *The Railway Journey: Trains and Travel in the 19th Century* (Oxford, 1980)

Searle, G. R., *Entrepreneurial Politics in Mid-Victorian Britain* (Oxford, 1993)

Shannon, R., *Gladstone* (2 vols) (London, 1982–99)

——, *The Age of Disraeli, 1868–1881: the Rise of Tory Democracy* (London, 1992)

——, *The Age of Salisbury, 1881–1902: Unionism and Empire* (London, 1996)

Shenton, C., *The Day Parliament Burned Down* (Oxford, 2012)

Slater, G., *The Growth of Modern England* (London, 1932)

Smelser, N. J., *Social Change in the Industrial Revolution: an Application of Theory to the Lancashire Cotton Industry, 1770–1840* (London, 1959)

Smith, E. A., *Lord Grey, 1764–1845* (Oxford, 1990)

——, *George IV* (New Haven, 1999)

Smith, F. B., *The Making of the Second Reform Bill* (Cambridge, 1966)

Somerset, A., *The Life and Times of William IV* (London, 1980)

Southgate, D., *The Passing of the Whigs, 1832–1886* (London, 1962)

Stansky, P., *Ambitions and Strategies: the Struggle for the Leadership of the Liberal Party in the 1890s* (Oxford, 1964)

——, *Gladstone: a Progress in Politics* (New York, 1979)

Stewart, R., *The Foundation of the Conservative Party, 1830–1867* (London, 1978)

Swartz, M., *The Politics of British Foreign Policy in the Era of Disraeli and Gladstone* (London, 1985)

Sweet, M., *Inventing the Victorians* (London, 2001)

Taylor, A. J. P., *The Struggle for Mastery in Europe, 1848–1918* (Oxford, 1954)

Temperley, H. W. V., *The Foreign Policy of Canning, 1822–1827* (London, 1966)

Temperley, H. W. V., & Penson, L. M., *Foundations of British Foreign Policy from Pitt (1792) to Salisbury (1902); or, Documents, Old and New* (Cambridge, 1938)

Tholfsen, T. R., *Working Class Radicalism in Mid-Victorian England* (London, 1976)

Thompson, D., *The Chartists* (London, 1984)

Thompson, E. P., *The Making of the English Working Class* (London, 1980)

Thompson, F. M. L., *English Landed Society in the Nineteenth Century* (London, 1963)

——, *The Rise of Respectable Society: a Social History of Victorian Britain, 1830–1900* (London, 1988)

Thornton, A .P., *The Imperial Idea and Its Enemies: a Study in British Power* (London, 1959)

Trevelyan, G. M., *British History in the Nineteenth Century (1782–1901)* (London, 1922)

——, *History of England* (London, 1926)

——, *Lord Grey of the Reform Bill: the Life of Charles, Second Earl Grey* (London, 1952)

Turner, M. J., *The Age of Unease: Government and Reform in Britain, 1782–1832* (Stroud, 2000)

Vernon, J., *Politics and the People: a Study in English Political Culture, c. 1815–1867* (Cambridge, 1993)

——, *Re-reading the Constitution: New Narratives in the Political History of England's Long Nineteenth Century* (Cambridge, 1996)

Vincent, J., *The Formation of the Liberal Party, 1857–1868* (London, 1966)

——, *Disraeli* (Oxford, 1990)

Walpole, S., *A History of England: from the Conclusion of the Great War in 1815* (6 vols) (London, 1900–1912)

——, & Lyall, A. C., *The History of Twenty-Five Years: 1876–1800* (London, 1904–1908)

Webb, R. K., *Modern England: from the Eighteenth Century to the Present* (London, 1969)

Webster, C. K., *The Foreign Policy of Castlereagh, 1812–1815: Britain and the Reconstruction of Europe* (London, 1931)

——, *The Foreign Policy of Palmerston, 1830–1841: Britain, the Liberal Movement and the Eastern Question* (London, 1951)

Weintraub, S., *Victoria* (London, 1996)

Williams, W. E., *The Rise of Gladstone to the Leadership of the Liberal Party, 1859 to 1868* (Cambridge, 1934)

Williamson, J. A., *The Evolution of England: a Commentary on the Facts* (Oxford, 1931)

Wilson, A. N., *Victoria: a Life* (London, 2014)

Wilson, B., *Decency and Disorder: the Age of Cant 1789–1837* (London, 2007)

——, *The Making of Victorian Values: Decency and Dissent in Britain, 1789–1837* (New York, 2007)

Winstanley, M. J., *Gladstone and the Liberal Party* (London, 1990)

Wise, S., *Inconvenient People: Lunacy, Liberty and the Mad-doctors in Victorian England* (London, 2012)

Woodham Smith, C., *Queen Victoria: Her Life and Times 1819–1861* (London, 1995)

Young, G. M., *Early Victorian England, 1830–1865* (London, 1934)

——, *Victorian England: Portrait of an Age* (London, 1936)

Young, G. M., & Handcock, W. D., *Victorian Essays* (London, 1962)

Ziegler, P., *Addington: a Life of Henry Addington, First Viscount Sidmouth* (London, 1965)

——, *King William IV* (London, 1971)

——, *Melbourne: a Biography of William Lamb, 2nd Viscount Melbourne* (London, 1976)

Index